$2⁻

9/23

CALVINUS SACRAE SCRIPTURAE PROFESSOR

D1565558

Calvinus Sacrae Scripturae Professor

Calvin as Confessor of Holy Scripture

Die Referate des
Congrès International des Recherches Calviniennes
International Congress on Calvin Research
Internationalen Kongresses für Calvinforschung
Vom 20. bis 23. August 1990 in Grand Rapids

Herausgegeben von

Wilhelm H. Neuser

WILLIAM B. EERDMANS PUBLISHING COMPANY
GRAND RAPIDS, MICHIGAN

Copyright © 1994 by Wm. B. Eerdmans Publishing Co.
255 Jefferson Ave. S.E., Grand Rapids, Michigan 49503
All rights reserved

Printed in the United States of America

Library of Congress Cataloging-in-Publication Data

International Congress on Calvin Research (4th: 1990: Grand Rapids, Mich.)
Calvinus sacrae scripturae professor: Calvin as confessor of Holy Scripture: die
Referate des Congrès international des recherches calviniennes, International
Congress on Calvin Research, Internationalen Kongresses für Calvinforschung,
vom 20. bis 23. August 1990 in Grand Rapids / herausgegeben von
Wilhelm H. Neuser.
p.   cm.
English, French, and German.
Includes bibliographical references.
ISBN 0-8028-0716-X (pbk.)
1. Calvin, Jean, 1509-1564 — Congresses. 2. Reformed Church — Doctrines —
History — 16th century — Congresses. 3. Theology, Doctrinal — History —
16th century — Congresses. I. Neuser, Wilhelm H.   II. Title.
BX9418.I67   1990
230'.42'092 — dc20   93-41123
CIP

Das Umschlagbild "Calvin Refusing the Lord's Supper to the Libertines,
in St. Peter's Cathedral, Geneva" entstammt dem Werk von J. A. Wylie,
The History of Protestantism 2 (London, 1899).

Das Motto des Kongresses 1990, Calvinus sacrae theologiae professor,
findet sich als Adresse in Calvins Briefwechsel (CO 17,562).

Inhalt

Seminare

Business Meeting

Vorwort

W. H. Neuser

Der Vierte Internationale Kongreß für Calvinforschung folgte der Einladung des Präsidenten Dr. James A. De Jong, im Calvin Theological Seminary in Grand Rapids (Michigan) zu tagen. Der Name des Seminars weist die Bedeutung auf, die man dem Genfer Reformator zumißt. Dem Seminar und College angeschlossen ist das H. Henry Meeter Center for Calvin Studies, das in der internationalen Calvinforschung einen festen Platz hat und großes Ansehen genießt. Das im einem Park gelegene Seminar war ein idealer Tagungsort, die 1989 erbaute Chapel eine moderne, alle Anforderungen erfüllende Tagungstätte und die Großzügigkeit des Gastgebers dem Kongreß gegenüber war überwältigend. Präsident De Jong, dem Calvin Congress Steering Committee und besonders Peter De Klerk, dem Coordinator, sei auch an dieser Stelle gedankt. Der Dank gilt weiter den im Programm genannten Geldgebern:

> "Anonymus Friend of Western Michigan
> Fieldstead & Company
> The Jay and Betty Van Andel Foundation"

Der Kongreß tagte zum ersten Mal außerhalb Europas und wurde damit seinem Namen auch in dieser Hinsicht gerecht. Auch dies wäre ohne die Hilfe der Ebengenannten nicht möglich gewesen. Der Druck dieses Buches wurde von ihnen ebenfalls ermöglicht.

Die weiteren Kosten wurden von den folgenden Institutionen getragen, denen unser herzlicher Dank gilt:

- Bremische Evangelische Kirche
- Deputaten Hulpverlening Christelijke Gereformeerde Kerken
- Evangelische Kirche der Pfalz
- Evangelische Kirche im Rheinland
- Gereformeerde Bond in de Nederlandse Hervormde (Geref.) Kerk
- Schweizerischer Evangelischer Kirchenbund, insbesondere dem bzw. der Reformierten Kirchenrat des Kantons Aargau
- Eglise Nationale Protestante de Genève
- Evangelisch-Reformierten Kirche im Kanton Solothurn
- Kirchenrat der evangelisch-reformierten Landeskirche des Kantons Zürich
- Stichting Het Nederlands Protestants Convent
- Stichting Zonneweelde
- Synode der evangelisch altreformierten Kirchen in Niedersachsen

In den neueren Büchern und Aufsätzen zu Calvins Leben und Werk werden die bisher vorliegenden vier CALVINUS-Bände oft zitiert. Die Aufsätze und Seminarberichte gehören inzwischen zum festen Bestand der Calvinforschung. In diese Reihe tritt nun der Band CALVINUS SACRAE SCRIPTURAE PROFESSOR. Herr Professor D. Dr. Heiko A. Oberman hat freundlicherweise sein Referat "Initia Calvini: The Matrix of Calvin's Reformation" in der erweiterten Form zur Verfügung gestellt, wie sie in den Mededelingen van de Afdeling Letterkunde, Nieuwe Reeks, Deel 54 no. 4, der Koninklijke Nederlandse Akademie van Wetenschappen 1991 erschienen ist. Adriaan D. Pont veröffentlichte den Aufsatz "Confession of Faith in Calvin's Geneva" (W. van 't Spijker, Hrsg., *Calvin: Erbe und Auftrag. Festschrift für Wilhelm Heinrich Neuser zum 65. Geburtstag,* Kampen 1991, 106-16). Andere werden sicherlich gleichfalls ihre Seminarthemen weiterverfolgen.

Begrüßung

W. H. Neuser

Sehr geehrte Teilnehmer am 4. Internationalen Kongreß für Calvinforschung, verehrter Herr Präsident De Jong und verehrte Kollegen des Calvin Theological Seminary,
meine Damen und Herrn!

Sie alle begrüße ich im Namen des Präsidiums des Kongresses. Es ist uns jedoch ein Anliegen, nicht nur die Gastgeber besonders zu begrüßen, sondern auch die Teilnehmer aus den Ländern 'hinter dem Eisernen Vorhang'. Wir alle freuen uns mit ihnen, daß der Begriff 'Eiserner Vorhang' nun der Vergangenheit angehört. Ihr persönliches Leben hat sich grundlegend geändert und der wissenschaftliche Austausch beginnt sich zu bessern. Ich muß aber auch anmerken, daß ein Wissenschaftler aus Rumänien trotz der Einladung nicht gekommen ist.

Viele sind von weither angereist, aus Südkorea, Japan, Südafrika und Professor Linder hat sogar einen Australienaufenthalt unterbrochen, um hier ein Seminar zu leiten. Sie alle begrüße ich herzlich und ebenso die übrigen Teilnehmer aus Europa, den Vereinigten Staaten und Kanada. Der Gedanke, den Kongreß nicht mehr in Europa abzuhalten, hat uns eigentlich wenig Mühe bereitet. Der Name 'Internationaler Kongreß' machte den Wechsel zu etwas Selbstverständlichem.

Als ich vor vier Jahren hier war, um mit Präsident De Jong die technischen Vorbereitung des Kongresses zu besprechen, fanden wir unter den Hörsäälen keinen völlig geeigneten Raum, um in einer großen Runde die Vorträge zu hören und zu diskutieren. Wir waren nicht wenig überrascht, als Präsident De Jong uns in Wien 1988 eröffnete, es werde ein Gebäude erbaut, in dem auch Kongresse abgehalten werden könnten. Ein solcher Aufwand für unseren Kongreß — ich sage nicht; alleine für unseren Kongreß — ist uns noch nicht begegnet, auch nicht in den gastfreien früheren Tagungsorten, der Freien Universität in Amsterdam, der Universität Genf und der Akademie Debrecen.

Das Calvin Theological Seminary hat keine Kosten und Mühen gescheut, um uns einen angenehmen Aufenthalt und einen erfolgreichen Kongreß zu bieten. Dafür danken wit jetzt schon. Als Sekretär hatte ich diesmal weniger Arbeit bei der Vorbereitung als früher. Daraus schließe ich, daß Präsident De Jong und sein Team sehr viel Arbeit hatte und in diesen Tagen noch haben wird.

Mit dem heutigen Abend beginnt unsere Arbeit im Kongreß. Die Calvinforscher in der weiten Welt erwarten nicht nur neue Ergebnisse, sondern vor allem neue Impulse für die Weiterarbeit. Dem sollen die Vorträge und Aussprachen im Plenum, die 13 Seminare und nicht zuletzt die persönlichen Gespräche dienen. Uns verbindet miteinander die Gewißheit, daß es sich lohnt, das Leben und die Verkündigung Calvins zu studieren. Dieses Studium bringt nicht nur Wissen, sondern auch Wegweisung für Theologie und Kirche. In diesem Sinne wollen wir an die Arbeit gehen.

"An Anatomy of All Parts of the Soul": Insights into Calvin's Spirituality from His Psalms Commentary[1]

James A. De Jong

John Calvin's commentary on the Psalms was published in Geneva in 1557, three years after he had finished lecturing on the material. The existence of Martin Bucer's highly regarded and widely circulated commentary on this book of the Bible caused Calvin to hesitate, but the unrelenting urging of his colleagues and his own apprehension that someone might produce an un-authorized version of the lectures, drawn from the copious transcripts of them, made him relent. As he prepared the material for the press, his own benefit from this important biblical material assured him that he could help others profit from it as well.

This commentary is significant for several reasons. It is the largest of his biblical expositions, amounting in sheer volume to almost twice the length of the 1559 edition of *The Institutes*. The work was composed and refined through the early and mid-1550s, a time of his own spiritual valleys and peaks when the reformer grappled with some of his most formidable opponents (Bolsec, Castellio, Servetus, Westphal, and the Libertines) and consolidated his position in Geneva. The Psalms were, furthermore, liturgically prominent; they were the only Old Testament material that he preached on Sundays — at the afternoon service — as part of his *lectio continua* regimen, and they formed the substance of congregational singing.

1. My indebtedness to research assistant Mr. Ronald Kool is gratefully acknowledged. He read through the bulk of the commentary with me and served me with insight and reaction as this address was prepared.

I. The Mirror of the Soul

But by his own testimony in the preface of the commentary, the Psalms were important to Calvin as a mirror of his soul.[2] They reflected his spirituality and that of the church, particularly concerning the practice and content of prayer, like no other material in Scripture. He says,

> I have been accustomed to call this book, I think not inappropriately, 'An Anatomy of all the Parts of the Soul'; for there is not an emotion of which any one can be conscious that is not here represented as in a mirror. Or rather, the Holy Spirit has here drawn to the life all the griefs, sorrows, fears, doubts, hopes, cares, perplexities, in short, all the distracting emotions with which the minds of men are wont to be agitated. The other parts of Scripture contain the commandments which God enjoined his servants to announce to us. But here the prophets themselves, seeing they are exhibited to us as speaking to God, and laying open all their inmost thoughts and affections, call, or rather draw, each of us to the examination of himself in particular, in order that none of the many infirmities to which we are subject, and of the many vices with which we abound, may remain concealed.[3]

The book is a primer on prayer, then, encouraging us to approach God and assuring us that One who is girded intercedes for us. It reveals the privilege of approaching God and reinforces our permission "to lay open before him our infirmities, which we would be ashamed to confess before men." There exists "no other book in which we are more perfectly taught the right manner of praising God" or how to be "stirred up to the performance of this religious exercise."[4] The Psalms motivate us to bear our cross and to submit entirely to God's providence and governance. They teach us to look to God for all things. In a special way Calvin identifies with David, the principal author, for he also endured the "internal afflictions" of the church caused by those who "gave themselves out to be her members."

2. James Luther Mays, "Calvin's Commentary on the Psalms: The Preface as Introduction," in *John Calvin and the Church: A Prism of Reform* (Louisville: Westminster/John Knox, 1990), 195-204, especially the last four pages, deals with material used in this address. It approaches the material from the perspective of Calvin's hermeneutics, however, rather than from the perspective of his spirituality.

3. John Calvin, *Commentary on the Book of Psalms,* 5 vols., trans. James Anderson (Grand Rapids: Eerdmans, 1949), 1.xxxvii. This edition has been used in preparing this paper, and in later notes references to it are abbreviated as "Com. Ps.," followed by the volume number and page reference. Helpful background is found in T. H. L. Parker's translation of Calvin's commentary of the first 33 Psalms (London: James Clarke & Co., 1965), "Editor's Preface."

4. *Ibid.,* xxxviii-xxxix.

I have no hesitation in comparing myself with him. In reading the instances of his faith, patience, fervour, zeal, and integrity, it has, as it ought, drawn from me unnumbered groans and sighs, that I am so far from approaching them; but it has, notwithstanding, been of very great advantage to me to behold in him as in a mirror, both the commencement of my calling, and the continued course of my function; so that I know the more assuredly, that whatever that most illustrious king and prophet suffered, was exhibited to me by God as an example for imitation.[5]

Having identified with David, Calvin devotes the remainder of the preface — two-thirds of its entire content — to his spiritual autobiography. The mirror metaphor, which he has twice employed, is the key to his purpose for including here, in uncharacteristically Calvinian fashion, a review of his own life. The Psalms are the anatomy of *his* soul. They vividly reflect the swirling, wide-ranging, sometimes conflicting and competing religious dispositions of this complex and sensitive man of Geneva as he strove to live faithfully before the face of God. He shares the struggles and the triumphs — mostly the struggles — of his life in the light of the Psalms in order that his readers may know that he, like David, "did not wander . . . in an unknown region." His commentary endeavors "to open up this treasure for the use of all the people of God," so that the church may be edified by seeing its experience in the light of God's Word.[6]

Calvin's preface, then, does not belong to the biographical genre. It is a confession, a testimony, a *pro vita mea* designed to serve the exposition by acknowledging how a believing commentator cannot engage this material without becoming totally and personally absorbed into it. His candor is refreshingly honest. And it gives his exposition poignancy, integrity, and power. Alexandre Ganoczy in his superb study *The Young Calvin* concludes that the dominant theme of the preface "is not Calvin's conversion but his vocation." Calvin does not write "as a historian or an autobiographer, but as a theologian concerned to prove the infallible predestination of God and the supernatural origin of his calling."[7] Yet, this interpretation is slightly skewed. *Vocatio* as a

5. *Ibid.,* xl.
6. *Ibid.,* xlviii-xlix.
7. Alexandre Ganoczy, *The Young Calvin,* trans. David Foxgrover and Wade Provo (Philadelphia: Westminster, 1987), 306. Ganoczy summarizes and analyzes the preface on pp. 302-7. T. H. L. Parker is in accord with the recent writers who resist lifting Calvin's passing reference to his "sudden" or "unexpected conversion" *(subita conversione)* out of its context in the preface, "rather than with those whose aim is primarily to fix a date." *John Calvin: A Biography* (Philadelphia: Westminster, 1975), 62. Also see W. H. Neuser, "Calvin's Conversion to Teachableness," *Nederlands Gereformeerd Teologisch Tijdskrif,* 26 (1985), 14-27. William J. Bouwsma judges that by his conversion reference Calvin "meant only a

child of God, in this instance one who by providential leading became a pastor and theological doctor, is Calvin's point of purpose. As a theologian, using his own spiritual life as illustrative, he writes his preface to help all believers who read his commentary see the anatomy of *their* souls in this remarkable mirror.

II. Possibilities of Research

To my knowledge no historian has undertaken a careful, systematic analysis of John Calvin's commentary on the Psalms as an exercise in learning more about the reformer's piety as it reflects his attitudes and Christian experience.[8] Yet his preface suggests that such an investigation might yield valid insight into his faith-life. It could, perhaps, complement his material on faith and regeneration, the "Golden Book of the Christian Life," Christian freedom, and prayer as found in the 1559 *Institutes*.[9] It might help to dispel the stubborn perception of Calvin as cold, rationalistic, vindictive, and aloof. Without turning him into a North American evangelical, we could possibly expose an experiential believer of considerable depth and warmth. Any number of other more focused reasons could be suggested for the endeavor. All these possibilities beckon us to the task.

III. The Soul

If Calvin sees the Psalms as "an anatomy of all parts of the soul," it is important to ask what he understands by "the soul." Key passages in the commentary itself show that for him the soul is the living core of the believer's subjective feelings, attitudes, responses, and convictions. His term of preference is "affections." Calvin rejects the understanding of "soul" as merely referring to "life," since this meaning is "very cold and unsatisfactory." The word is closer

---

shift and quickening of his interests" since there was no "Protestantism," in the subsequent sense of that word, to which to "convert." Bouwsma also argues that Calvin "always emphasized the gradualness rather than the suddenness of conversion and the difficulty of making progress in the Christian life." *John Calvin: A Sixteenth Century Portrait* (New York: Oxford University Press, 1987), 10 and 11). The gradualness, or, better, the continuousness of the believer's turning to God is an emphasis prominent in Calvin's Psalms commentary.

   8. In his comprehensive recent study John H. Leith examines Calvin's teachings on the Christian life rather than the subjective or experiential dimensions of his spirituality as reflected in the Psalms commentary. *John Calvin's Doctrine of the Christian Life* (Louisville: Westminster/John Knox, 1989).

   9. Cf. *The Institutes* 3.2-3, 3.6-10, 3.19, and 3.20.

to what is meant by the heart.[10] As he says of Psalm 34:2, "the term *soul* . . . signifies not the vital spirit, but the seat of the affections."[11] This "seat of the understanding and affections" the Psalmist arouses from its natural sluggishness to bless God, and he appeals to "his inward parts" or heart and mind to echo the praise of the soul.[12]

Calvin's theory of the soul includes the idea that it can also be weakened or dissipated. This occurs when the soul is "poured out," an expression that appears with some frequency in the book of Psalms. When the soul is poured out, "the affections lose their vigour, and begin to flow out."[13] This release happens when religious emotions are expressed to an extreme degree. Either spiritual joy or a deep religious misery can cause this phenomenon. The believer is counseled to regulate the affections to avoid this debilitation of the soul, therefore. The most effective regulation in Calvin's estimation is to relate our joy to God's fatherly love and favor and our grief to his possible anger with us.[14] In another context Calvin notes the importance of dislodging "those morbid affections which belong to the corruption of our nature."[15]

For Calvin, then, the soul is that seat of affections which includes our sentiments, emotions, feelings, and insights. The soul for the believer must remain steadily focused on God by directing all its affections to him alone. The closeness of the soul and the heart in his thinking allows us to cite his heart-in-hand motto, "Cor meum tibi offere Domine, prompte et sincere," as closely paralleling his advice for keeping our souls.

His understanding of the soul and its movements clearly suggests that Calvin was most comfortable with a spirituality that included a wide variety of emotions expressed in moderation.

IV. Trust in the Promises

The most prevalent disposition of the soul identified and discussed in the Psalms commentary is the believer's unrelenting trust in God. The theme recurs with such consistency and with such a wide range of nuances and applications

10. Com. Ps. 69:1; 3.46.

11. Com. Ps. 34:2; 1.558.

12. Com. Ps. 103:1; 4.125-26. Keeping God's testimonies with his soul means that the Psalmist "had the doctrine of the law enclosed within the deepest recesses of his heart," according to Com. Ps. 119:167; 5.43.

13. Com. Ps. 42:4; 2.133-34. He says, "As the soul of man sustains him, so long as it keeps its energies collected, so also it sinks within him, and as it were, vanishes away, when any of the affections, by excessive indulgence, gains the ascendency."

14. Com. Ps. 42:4; 2.134.

15. Com. Ps. 44:24; 2.172.

that it is impossible to summarize it adequately. But, to begin — in Psalm 5 David, afflicted by his enemies, testifies "that he was not turned hither and thither, nor drawn different ways by the temptations to which he was exposed, but that to betake himself to God was the settled order of his life." This shows the "contrast between the rambling and uncertain movements of those who look around them for worldly helps, or depend on their own counsels, and the direct leading of faith, by which all the godly are withdrawn from the vain allurements of the world, and have recourse to God alone."[16]

This trust is expressed most often under duress. It is seen in a willingness to suffer just punishment for wrongs done.[17] To trust is simply to endure oppression by the unrighteous in the certainty that their evil will, under God's direction, turn on them.[18] It is to face calamities that weigh believers down so heavily that they see no sign of help from him and begin to think that God has forgotten them.[19] Or, when they face their enemies, trust is to recall past mercies that inspire hope of future deliverance.[20] Frequently believers experience the pressure of God's delay in sending aid. This apparent abandonment by God is simply intended "to succour them at a more convenient season." Even though his people might be reduced to proverty, sorrow, and weeping, God's delay teaches them the trust that will help them to understand his reasons more clearly.[21]

The last two verses of Psalm 106, which Calvin dates from Jewish captivity after the time of Haggai and Malachi, summarize themes to which he returns frequently. In adversity, he says, "scarcely one in a hundred . . . draws near to God." "Scarcely one in a hundred" is a favorite expression by which the reformer indicates that few are able to trust wholeheartedly. This pitifully small percentage indicates how prevalent are a proud heart, praying in a "careless and insipid manner," and "pouring out complaints" about one's problems. Calvin concludes,

> But the only way in which we can expect God to lend a favourable ear to the voice of our supplications is, in the spirit of meekness to submit to his corrections, and patiently to bear the cross which he is pleased to lay upon us. It is with great propriety, then, that the prophet exhorts the afflicted captives to bless God, even when he was chastising them with considerable severity. It is to the same purpose that it is added, 'let the people say, "Amen" '; as if he were commanding them all to consent to the praises of

16. Com. Ps. 5:3; 1.54.
17. Com. Ps. 7:5; 1.80.
18. Com. Ps. 9:12; 1.123. Cf. Com. Ps. 9:14; 1.126-27.
19. Com. Ps. 13:1; 1.182.
20. Com. Ps. 9:3; 1.110. Cf. also Com. Ps. 102:16; 4.114.
21. Com. Ps. 9:9; 1.119.

God, though both privately and publicly they were overwhelmed in a sea of troubles.[22]

Calvin's unshakable trust is in the sovereign God of heaven and earth who achieves his purposes. Unfortunately, this doctrine of "great importance" has been the subject of idle speculation and "frantic reveries."[23] But believers, even though they "find themselves cut off from all means of subsistence and safety," should "take courage from the fact, that God is not only superior to all impediments, but that he can render them subservient to the advancement of his own designs."[24]

In the Psalms commentary the believer's trust is determined, resolute, vigilant. So long as she remembers the promises of God, her trust is also confident and hopeful. While God is kind, merciful, and provident, even during the believer's considerable struggles and afflictions, the love and affection of God for his people and of believers for him do not receive the same prominence as an enduring, relentless trust. Occasionally Calvin speaks of being "ravished" by God's love or of the consideration of God that can "ravish us with love to him."[25] But the affection of trust is most often expressed as a persistent dependence on God and his promises. Like Jacob at the Jabbok, the believer will not let go until the Lord blesses her!

V. Confident Prayer

Confident prayer is a frequent action of the soul in Calvin's Psalms commentary. It is the clearest, most direct manifestation of trust in God.

Prayer is learned in the school of adversity. "The time of sad adversity is most proper for abounding in prayer," says Calvin. Depending on him for deliverance, we discover in prayer at such times "an antidote for all our ills."[26] We learn by being laid low by God's hand that he uses adversity "to prove our allegiance, to arouse us from our torpidity, to crucify our old man, to purge us from our filthiness, to bring us into submission and subjection to God, and to excite us to meditate on the heavenly life."[27] Thus, rather than causing us to vacillate between doubt and uncertainty, our difficulties compel us to call on God all the more earnestly.[28]

22. Com. Ps. 106:48; 4.244-45.
23. Com. Ps. 107:19; 4.254.
24. Com. Ps. 115:3; 4.344.
25. Com. Ps. 5:11; 1.63.
26. Com. Ps. 118:5; 4.379.
27. Com. Ps. 118:18; 4.386.
28. Com. Ps. 116:11; 4.368.

Confidence is essential for effective prayer. Confident prayer appeals to God's promises, yet is patient in waiting for their fulfillment. That we do not immediately receive the same benefits as our fathers should not shake our confidence, for God is unchanging.[29] Confident prayer requires a clean and clear conscience, for nothing undermines the confidence that God hears and answers as much as the knowledge that we are not living in his will.[30] Confidence as we pray will be proportional to the degree of our integrity.[31] Likewise, communal or corporate prayer enhances confidence.[32] So does the knowledge that he gives us the freedom to approach him stammering like little children.[33] God's kindness and goodness to us instill great confidence in approaching him.[34] God's governance of the world as a just Judge inspires confidence in prayer.[35] But the assurance that God hears us in prayer rests most basically on the knowledge that we can approach him through the Mediator he has provided.[36] Summarizing the matter of confidence, Calvin says, "In prayer, too, nothing is more needful for us than sure confidence in God, and therefore he not only invites us to come to him, but also by an oath hath appointed an advocate for the purpose of obtaining acceptance for us in his sight."[37]

Calvin is aware that confidence can be distorted. So he maintains,

the Prophet, who, having exhorted all the faithful to cherish confidence, teaches them at the same time, that instead of sitting in listless inactivity, they should betake themselves to God, earnestly beseeching him by prayer, for what he has bidden them hope for by his word.[38]

Calvin is continuously aware of the God to whom we pray. God's person conditions the soul as well as the prayer it offers. This exercise of the soul makes God "the witness of all our affections," which also greatly enhances our confidence.[39] Furthermore, we must pray according to the will of God, learning to ask what he desires of us.[40] And prayer ought to begin "by affirming that God is the great source and object of [our] joy," for this also fortifies

29. Com. Ps. 44:2; 2.151.
30. Com. Ps. 109:21-22; 4.288.
31. Com. Ps. 59:1; 2.381.
32. Com. Ps. 102:14; 4.111.
33. Com. Ps. 102:2; 4.98.
34. Com. Ps. 42:9; 2.141.
35. Com. Ps. 7:11; 1.87.
36. Com. Ps. 20:1; 1.335.
37. Com. Ps. 110:4; 4.306.
38. Com. Ps. 125:4; 5.94.
39. Com. Ps. 10:13; 1.150.
40. Com. Ps. 7:6; 1.81.

confidence in making our appeals to him.[41] Our ardor or fervency in prayer comes from our confiding in God.[42] Prayer becomes "clamouring and complaining against him" unless it mingles praise to God and petition that he meet our needs.[43] We pray in the name of God, which represents his essence, for from his name "proceeds confidence in calling upon him."[44]

The unifying, underlying affection of the soul reflected in Calvin's frequent comments on prayer is confidence. The term finds its way into almost every reference to the subject. Confident prayer is the shape that trust takes in the believer's direct address to God.

VI. Surprising Imprecations

The imprecatory passages in the Psalms are a species of prayer that warrants a close, if short, look in presenting the anatomy of Calvin's soul.

The enemies of the Lord are found inside the church as well as outside it. The Psalmist's prayers include both. Concerning those who falsely boast that they belong to God's people, we should "beseech God quickly to purge his house, and not leave his holy temple exposed to the desecration of swine and dogs, as if it were a dunghill."[45]

When David says, "I will pursue my enemies, and will overtake them; nor will I return till I have consumed them" (Ps. 18:37), Calvin offers an interesting interpretation. While we might think that the writer speaks too much like a soldier and has forgotten "the gentleness and meekness which ought to shine in all true believers," David is simply obeying God's commands. Here "his affections were governed and regulated by the Holy Spirit." "These are not the words of a man who was cruel, and who took pleasure in shedding blood," says Calvin. David was a gentle man. But he was also under divine orders. He represented Christ in "gently alluring all men to repentance" and in breaking in pieces "those who obstinately resist him to the last." Calvin urges his readers, however, to remember what kind of enemy they face and what weapons they have received. He counsels them to be satisfied with having "the devil, the flesh, and sin overthrown and placed under our feet by his spiritual power." However, those with the power of the sword have other responsibilities that Christ will bless if they rule under him as their Head.[46] A

41. Com. Ps. 9:2; 1.112.
42. Com. Ps. 25:19; 1.434.
43. Com. Ps. 18:3; 1.263.
44. Com. Ps. 20:1; 1.334.
45. Com. Ps. 10:16; 1.155.
46. Com. Ps. 18:37-40; 1.294-96.

few verses later Calvin explains that the church militant must conquer its enemies "by doing them good"; it is enjoined "to pray for their salvation." Vengeance must be left to the Lord.[47] In discussing prayers for vengeance in connection with Psalm 28, Calvin reminds his readers that it is "unquestionable that if the flesh move us to seek revenge, the desire is wicked in the sight of God." God forbids us from praying for evil upon our enemies as much as he forbids us from hating them. We must also restrain ourselves from "intemperate zeal" against evil. Rather, "we must observe this general rule, that we cordially desire and labour for the welfare of the whole human race."[48]

Calvin abhorred evil, including vengeance. His affections of the soul concerning the wicked were toward their conversion by the spiritual weapons at the church's disposal. These were his heart's expressed desires in the years when he confronted Bolsec, Castellio, and Servetus. To regard him simply and categorically as mean and vindictive for his part in handling dissent and heresy, as was done in Geneva, is to ignore the anatomy of his soul as expressed in the Psalms commentary, and to assess him only in terms of his actions, his polemical statements, or by imposing the standards of a later age upon his heart. Responsible historical judgment will take into account all the evidence. And if our verdict on his complicity in outcomes remains primarily negative, our appreciation of his spirituality might well be quite positive.

VII. Contrary Affections

The spirituality of Calvin embraces a definite tension between those who live by resolute trust and those who do not. This dynamic includes the tension between true Israel and the hypocrites or "heathen" within the church. This opposition between belief and unbelief gives rise to one set of differing affections. But Calvin's spirituality also encompasses contrary affections within the soul of the believer. These dispositions of the soul concerning himself or herself must be brought under the rule of Christ through trust and prayer. On a theological level Calvin handles them well, using his well-studied categories of mortification and vivification, crucifying the flesh and being raised to new life in the Spirit. On the level of the struggles of the soul, he wrestles with them existentially. These personal struggles Calvin sees more clearly reflected in the mirror of the Psalms than anywhere else in Scripture.

His exposition of Psalm 22:1 is instructive in this regard. "My God! My

47. Com. Ps. 18:47; 1.305.
48. Com. Ps. 28:4; 1.469. Another extended passage making many of the same points is found in connection with Psalm 79:6. Cf. Com. Ps. 79:6; 3.287.

God! Why hast thou forsaken me?" "The first verse contains two remarkable sentences, which, although apparently contrary to each other, are yet ever entering into the minds of the godly together."[49] The Psalmist speaks on the one hand of being forsaken by God, which appears to be "the complaint of a man in despair." On the other hand, he shows that "the spark of faith" remains, for he twice addresses God as "my God." This is "an inward conflict" experienced by the godly whenever God withdraws his favors and they see only darkness. In wrestling with themselves about this, believers both "discover the weakness of the flesh" and "give evidence of their faith." David's words indicate that he was able to cope with this tension. Calvin then summarizes,

> There is not one of the godly who does not daily experience in himself the same thing. According to the judgment of the flesh, he thinks he is cast off and forsaken by God, while yet he apprehends by faith the grace of God, which is hidden from the eye of sense and reason; and thus it comes to pass, that contrary affections are mingled and interwoven in the prayers of the faithful.[50]

Calvin goes on to expand and embellish these competing affections. The temptation to unbelief, when we no longer look for or expect a remedy, is strong. Looking into the mirror of divine promises, however, brings faith to our rescue. Living "between these two contrary affections" unsettles us. Because "the affections of the flesh, when once they break forth, are not easily restrained," we are advised to repress them as immediately as they appear. Therefore, David wisely begins the Psalm by affirming twice over that God is still his God. Only then does he acknowledge his soul's struggles.[51]

Either side of the tension that he has described at such length can occasion an entire range of derived responses or affections. The temptation to unbelief can quickly produce despair, embitteredness, uncertainty, spiritual listlessness, and so on. Then one becomes vulnerable to sins of the flesh, such as avarice, greed, immorality, and selfishness. Calvin realizes that these are sinful affections that can quickly lead to sinful behavior. These responses are no longer those of the believing heart and life. They have passed into the arena of unbelief.

On the other hand, when faith prevails, the affections of joy, hope, praise, thanks, meekness, gentleness, self-control, moderation, and ultimately peace prevail. Here as well there is the danger of passing into pride, ambition, selfishness, hypocrisy, and other carnal affections. The entire range of human

49. Com. Ps. 22:1; 1.357.
50. *Ibid.,* 357-58.
51. *Ibid.,* 359-61.

emotional, spiritual responses can, therefore, be fitted into Calvin's framework of "contrary affections."

This framework helps us to understand his sustained counsel to moderation, self-control, self-denial, cross-bearing, and discipleship. It is Calvin's conceptual model for understanding the assaults of Satan and the warfare between light and darkness that goes on within the believer's heart and soul. Obedience to God's revealed will is essential for maintaining our spiritual health and equilibrium. God provides the means of grace and the fellowship of his people to fortify us in the struggle. Most profoundly, he instills in us a fear and reverence of his name.

Calvin's anatomy of the soul recognizes and organizes the entire range of possible spiritual responses in a person's life.

VIII. The Fear of the Lord

Despite its role in Israel's corporate as well as individual worship, the book of Psalms received little liturgical comment by Calvin in his commentary. Calvin frequently dismisses the musical instructions in the Psalm prefaces with some conjecture on what these obscure references might intend, then waves them off by stating that their meaning is not very important. Not surprisingly, H. Hasper in his massive, two-volume study of Calvin's contributions to congregational singing bypasses the Psalms commentary quickly.[52] Calvin's *Ecclesiastical Ordinances,* Psalm versifications, letters, and other sources provide his liturgical contributions.

The reason for this absence of liturgical interest in the commentary is consistent with Calvin's emphasis on the "affections of the soul." The Psalms are about "the fear of the Lord," not the technicalities of the worship service. While hypocrites profane God's name by their simulated worship, we ought

---

52. H. Hasper, *Calvijns Beginsel voor den Zang in den Eredienst,* 2 vols. ('s-Graven-hage: Martinus Nijhof, 1955 and 1976). Hasper discusses Calvin's identity with the Psalmist in the preface of the commentary, 1.477-79. He correctly emphasizes that for Calvin the book of Psalms was "meer dan een bundel Joodse zangen"; it is the expression of the believer's varied religious responses that spoke the faith of the church of all ages.

> Door het persoonlijk geloof, dat God in de harten werkte, te herkennen als het geloof van de gemeenschap, was het oude Israel ervan overtuigd, dat het in de Psalmen maar niet to doen had met een herderslied of een liturgische bijdrage voor een koor, doch met zangen die door God zelf waren ingegeven aan door Hem verkoren en begenadigde personen, opdat heel de wereld zou weten, wie God voor zijn volk is. 2.18.

In other words, Hasper recognizes that Calvin regarded the Psalms as the anatomy of the church's soul.

"to come in the fear of God, in order to worship him with a sincere and upright heart."[53] "The fear of God is the root or origin of all righteousness," says Calvin concerning Psalm 119:63, "and by dedicating our life to His service, we manifest that His fear dwells in our hearts."[54] Repeatedly in the commentary he emphasizes that true religion is a matter of the heart, not of external or "carnal" formalities. In an especially ample yet pointed comment on Psalm 22:23, "You who fear the Lord," Calvin says,

> By engaging in this exercise [of corporate worship], every man in his own place invites and stirs up the church by his example to praise God. . . . Impure and wicked men may sing the praises of God with open mouth, but assuredly, they do nothing else than pollute and profane his holy name. It were, indeed, an object much to be desired, that men of all conditions in the world would, with one accord, join in holy melody to the Lord. But as the chief and most essential part of this harmony proceeds from a sincere and pure affection of heart, none will ever, in a right manner, celebrate the glory of God, except the man who worships him under the influence of holy fear.[55]

If he had little to say concerning the liturgical aspects of congregational singing, on the same premises Calvin was clearly opposed to musical instruments in worship services and skeptical of their private use.

> If believers choose to cheer themselves with musical instruments, they should, I think, make it their object not to dissever their cheerfulness from the praises of God. But when they frequent their sacred assemblies, musical instruments in celebrating the praises of God would be no more suitable than the burning of incense, the lighting up of lamps, and the restoration of the other shadows of the law.[56]

Of praising God Calvin says, "there is no better exercise in which they [believers] can be . . . employed."[57] Praise should be corporate, not simply because it is believers' "duty to stir up one another to this religious exercise," but because the substance of worship is "worthy of being publicly and solemnly celebrated," indeed, of filling the entire earth.[58] And our praise ought always to follow the Word in obedience to the commands of God.[59] The

---

53. Com. Ps. 5:7; 2.58.
54. Com. Ps. 119:64; 4.448.
55. Com. Ps. 22:23; 1.380.
56. Com. Ps. 33:2; 1.539.
57. Com. Ps. 33:1; 1.538.
58. Com. Ps. 9:11; 1.120.
59. Com. Ps. 9:12; 1.123-24.

commanded forms of worship in the old dispensation differ from those in the New Testament, which is marked by maturity and simplicity. But in every essential respect the praise of the heart is identical in in both.[60] Empty-handedness is never permitted in worship, in which we always ought to present ourselves in service to God.[61] In Psalm 33 the writer directly instructs believers to praise God, "because they alone are capable of proclaiming the glory of God. Unbelievers, who have never tasted his goodness, cannot praise him from the heart, and God has no pleasure in his name being pronounced by their unholy tongues."[62] It is because God has delivered his people that "it is our duty . . . to sing his praises with our tongues."[63] If praising God is a duty, it occurs in the eschatological perspective held by the writer of Psalm 150. The time was approaching when these songs once sung only in Judea "would resound in every quarter of the globe." Concluding his commentary on this triumphant note, Calvin states that the New Testament worshiper has been united in the same "symphony with the Jews, that we may worship God with constant sacrifices of praise, until being gathered into the kingdom of heaven, we sing with elect angels an eternal hallelujah."[64]

IX. Conclusion

To conclude on the note of perfect, corporate praise reverberating forever through the New Jerusalem is entirely Calvinian. It is the ultimate affection of the soul. Moving through the troubles and pains of this sinful life, burdened by afflictions imposed from without and temptations and weaknesses from within, the believer has clung with tenacious trust and by confident prayer to the promises of the Word. Life is throughout a series of contrary affections that are to be controlled and channeled under the rule of God's Word.

The Psalms commentary is primarily the anatomy of Calvin's soul. It is a rich source on the subjective spirituality of one who identified intimately with David. While limited by Calvin's own biases and predispositions, it is also a perceptive anatomy of the soul of the Psalmist, of Israel, and of the church in all ages. Always it is the anatomy of the soul that crucifies self and comes to new life in Christ. Ultimately, it is the anatomy of the soul that comes to perfect peace and rest in the purposes of the sovereign God.

60. Com. Ps. 50:14-15; 2.271.
61. Com. Ps. 96:8; 4.54.
62. Com. Ps. 33:1; 1.537.
63. Com. Ps. 30:1; 1.486.
64. Com. Ps. 150:6; 5.321.

The Concept of Federal Theology —
Was Calvin a Federal Theologian?

James B. Torrance

One of the most significant words in the Bible is the word "covenant." We read about God making a covenant with Abraham and renewing that covenant "430 years later" in the giving of the law at Sinai, about David making a covenant with Jonathan and again with the elders at Hebron when he became king. Jeremiah speaks of the day when God will make a new covenant with the house of Israel and write his law on their hearts, and in the New Testament Jesus is presented to us as the Mediator of the New Covenant. "This cup is the new covenant in my blood."

On the one hand, God binds himself unconditionally to men like Abraham and David with solemn promises. On the other hand, he binds Israel to himself under solemn unconditional obligations — proleptic of the day when he will bind himself to humanity and humanity to himself in Jesus Christ in covenant love. Again we read about men like Joshua, Hezekiah and Josiah binding themselves and the nation in loyalty to in covenant God to keep his law.

It is therefore very understandable that the twin concepts of covenant and law caught the imagination of Reformed theologians both theologically and politically in the period after the Reformation, as they spoke of the covenant of grace as the heart of the gospel and as they struggled for justice and liberty to proclaim this gospel. In the upheavals of the late sixteenth and seventeenth centuries, with the breakup of feudalism and the emergence of the late post-Renaissance doctrine of absolute sovereignty and the divine right of kings, and the resultant struggles for liberty to preach the gospel, we read about people making "bands," "pacts," "covenants," "contracts," and "political leagues" to defend their rights and freedom, binding the nation, or church, or groups of individuals in loyalty to God and one another. Between 1556 and 1683 we read about 31 public bands or covenants of this kind in Scotland alone, 24 of which were between 1556 and 1599.[1] It is precisely this period, the late sixteenth and seventeenth centuries, which marks the rise of the so-called "federal theology" or covenant theology, which was to become the criterion of orthodoxy in the Calvinist, Puritan world on both sides of the Atlantic. The Westminster Confession of Faith (1646), with the Larger and Shorter Catechisms, was the first Reformed Confession to enshrine the scheme of federal theology, though in a mild way. Theologians, politicians, and jurists looked to the Bible for justification of their views.

Federal theology is that form of Calvinism which gave central place to the concept of covenant *(foedus, pactum, testamentum),*[2] and which distinguished different covenants *(foedera)* in God's relation to the world, in particular a "covenant of works" *(foedus operum* or *foedus naturale* — the covenant of law) and a "covenant of grace" *(foedus gratiae).* This provided the schema in terms of which Reformed theology, and in particular Calvin's theology, was interpreted and reinterpreted in the context of the ecclesiastical, social, and political issues of the day, about the relations between church and state, divine and human sovereignty, justification and justice. How do we understand the relationship between law and gospel in the Bible as well as in the interests not only of politics but also of preaching and evangelism — questions about the *ordo salutis?* The legacy of these debates and the resulting theology is enormous, not only in laying the basis of modern democracy but also in the development of experiential Puritanism and the rise of modern evangelicalism.

The concern of this paper is to look at the rise of federal theology, to offer a critique of its content, and to ask how far Calvin can be called "a federal theologian." Although the seeds of federal theology may be seen in his writings, the federal scheme constitutes at several decisive points such a shift in theology that the latter question must be answered in the negative. Although the concept of "the covenant of grace" or "covenant of life" appears frequently in his writings, particularly in his discussion of the relation between the Old and New Testaments and of baptism and the Lord's Supper, it is in no way a key concept in his theology. We shall be particularly concerned with

1. John Lumsden, *The Covenants of Scotland* (Paisley, 1914); J. B. Torrance, "Covenant or Contract? A Study of the Theological Background of Worship in 17th-Century Scotland," *Scottish Journal of Theology,* 23 (1970), 51-76; see also J. B. Torrance, "The Covenant Concept in Scottish Theology and Politics and its Legacy," *Scottish Journal of Theology,* 34 (1981), 225-43 (repr. Philadelphia Center for the Study of Federalism, Temple University, 1980).

2. See David A. Weir's chapter on the use of these words: "The Lexical and Biblical Evidence," in *The Origins of the Federal Theology in 16th-Century Reformation Thought* (Oxford, 1990), 51-61.

the interpretation of grace and the relationship between law and grace in Calvin and in the later federal theology.

I. The Meaning of Grace in Calvin

A central concern of the Reformation, and certainly of the theology of John Calvin, was the recovery of the meaning of grace. Justification by grace alone *(sola gratia)* lies at the heart of all Reformed theology. Calvin contended for this in different ways.

1. Grace in Trinitarian Terms

One way in which Calvin argued for justification by grace alone was in his assertion that our salvation is from beginning to end the one work of the one God, Father, Son, and Holy Spirit. In his exposition of John 3:16 and Ephesians 1:5, as in his discussion of justification and baptism in the *Institutes,* he makes use of the distinction between the four causes[3] to counter medieval misuses of this Aristotelian distinction, to assert that the love of the Father "before the foundation of the world" is the *efficient cause* of our salvation, Jesus Christ with his obedience on our behalf (not our faith and repentance or *merita poenitentiae*) is the *material cause,* the Holy Spirit, preaching, and faith the *formal* or *instrumental cause,* and his own glory the *final cause.* Grace and glory are the two poles of Calvin's theology. Everything flows from grace and leads to glory.[4] By grace the eternal Father accepts us for what we are in Christ the Son, clothed with his righteousness through faith, the fruit of the Spirit by whom we are united to Christ and submit to his rule in the *regnum Christi.* Grace is expounded in trinitarian terms.

2. Salvation Complete in Christ

Sola gratia for Calvin therefore embraces the *twin doctrines,* expounded respectively in Books Two and Three of the 1559 *Institutes,* that, first, "all parts of our salvation are complete in Christ" — the Father has done everything for us in the

---

3. On John 3:16, CO 47.63-65; on Ephesians 1:5, CO 51.148.

4. So he quotes with approval St. Bernard's words, "the mercy of the Lord is from everlasting to everlasting upon them that fear him, from everlasting to everlasting through predestination, to everlasting through glorification: the one knows no beginning, the other no end." *Institutes* 3.22.10 (OS 4.392).

person of the Son — and, second, "participation in Christ through the Holy Spirit." His doctrine that our salvation is achieved not simply *per Christum* but *in Christo* finds beautiful expression in the passage at the end of chapter 16 of Book Two, where he sums up his exposition of Christ's work of redemption: "We see that our whole salvation and all its parts are comprehended in Christ (Acts 4:12). We should take care therefore not to derive the least portion of it from anywhere else . . . ."[5] But the fact that "Christ has not left any part of our salvation incomplete" does not mean that "We are now in possession of all the blessings purchased by him." So he argues against Servetus, who taught a form of "realised eschatology" in which we are called to participate through the Spirit in Christ and his blessings — to become in ourselves what we are in him but not yet in ourselves.[6] This, as we shall see, is the heart of Calvin's understanding of the covenant of grace, or covenant of life, made for fallen humanity in Christ and expounded in terms of promise and fulfillment, and in which we participate in this through the Spirit, through Word and sacraments.

3. Election

Another prime way in which Calvin contended for *sola gratia* was to say that this is the meaning of *election,* that salvation is grounded in the free, unmerited grace of God, without any prior consideration of works or merit, not on any foreknowl- edge by God of our fulfilling any prior conditions. In keeping with his under- standing of grace, Calvin modeled the 1559 edition of the *Institutes* with its four books on the trinitarian pattern of the Apostles' Creed — Father, Son, Holy Spirit, and the church and her sacraments — throughout making it clear that our salvation is from beginning to end the work of grace, from the triune God. It is therefore highly significant that he now deals with election, not in Book One, at the beginning of his theology and under any doctrine of the eternal decrees of God, but at the end of Book Three, chapters 21–24, after he has said everything about the love of God the Father in creation, after he has expounded all he has to say about Incarnation and Atonement — that "all parts of our salvation are complete in Christ," — and after he has expounded the doctrine of the Holy

---

5. *Institutes* 2.16.19 (OS 3.507-08, also 3.12). The gospel "refers to the proclamation of the grace manifested in Christ . . . by which God fulfilled what he had promised, *these promises being realised in the person of the Son.* For 'all the promises of God find their yea and amen in Christ' . . . because he has in his flesh completely accomplished all the parts of our salvation." *Institutes* 2.9.2 (OS 3.399-400).

6. *Institutes* 2.9.3 (OS 3.400). See J. B. Torrance, "The Vicarious Humanity and Priesthood of Christ in the Theology of John Calvin," in *Calvinus Ecclesiae Doctor,* ed. W. H. Neuser (1978), 69-84.

Spirit, that Christ unites us with himself in faith. Only after he has expounded the twin doctrines of the vicarious humanity of Christ (who is himself the "bright mirror of election") and union with Christ does he then expound the doctrine of election in and through Christ, as another way of saying that it is all of grace, that God's grace is free and unconditioned, and that election is therefore not, as the semi-Pelagians thought, grounded on God's foreknowledge of merit and repentance. Unconditional election is another way of saying unconditional grace.[7] Here he has in mind the views of some of his opponents like Pighius, Bolsec, and Castellio, whose views of election were grounded on their notions both of free will and of "legal repentance," that God's grace and forgiveness are conditioned by human repentance and merit. Calvin's line of argument was developed and heightened in the doctrine of "the double decree" which was to play such an important part in the rise of federal theology. In Calvin's hands the doctrine asserted that God in his sovereignty is the ultimate source of all, in providence and election. If in reprobation God is the remote cause, as sovereign over all that happens, nevertheless the human agent is the proximate cause, being responsible for his own sin. In his often repeated phrase, reprobation is "accidental to the gospel," as the sun is the "cause" of the shadows it casts. All sin is against grace — "denying the Lord who bought us." In election, on the other hand, God is both the ultimate and proximate cause of salvation.

The doctrine of "the double decree" was not the major premise of Calvin's system of theology, but this is precisely what it was to become at the hands of Calvin's successor in Geneva, Theodore Beza, who in 1555 published his *Summa totius Christianismi,* in which[8] he subsumed the whole of doctrine

7. This is important in the light of the later post sixteenth-century debates between Calvinists and Arminians, the one making election prior to grace, the other making grace and the possibility of salvation for all prior to election. Calvin is doubtless himself ambiguous here both in his controversial phrase *"si gratiam praecedit electio"* (3.22.1) and in his appearance of arguing back from experience to election that *experientia docet.* See the discussion of this in J. K. S. Reid's translation and in his Introduction to Calvin's *Concerning the Eternal Predestination of God* (London, 1961).

8. *Summa totius Christianismi, sive descriptio et distributio causarum salutis electorum et exitii reproborum, ex sacris literis, collecti.* See his diagram in the Appendix (p. 39) and David Weir, *Origins of Federal Theology,* ch. 2, "The Background to the Prelapsarian Covenant," 72ff. See also Richard A. Muller, "Perkins' *A Golden Chaine: Predestinarian system or Schematised Ordo Salutis,"* *Sixteenth Century Journal,* 9.1 (1978), 69-81; *Christ and the Decree, Christology and Predestination in Reformed Theology from Calvin to Perkins* (Grand Rapids: Baker, 1986). (See the diagram on p. 40.) Beza's high supralapsarian doctrine of predestination, however, does not appear to feature in his commentaries or pastoral work, nor does it, in Perkins, militate against his deep pastoral concern, as Muller shows. Nevertheless it was by this diagram and his interpretation of the double decree that Beza was known in Puritan England, where his diagram was expanded by William Perkins and John Bunyan in the interest of calling people to "examine themselves" for evidences of grace, to make their calling and election sure.

under the concept of the double decree and expounded each doctrine in terms
of predestination. In this work he produced his famous chart or Table *(Tabula)*
to show how God decrees all that happens, electing some and reprobating
others, all for his own glory, loving the elect and hating the reprobate, and
then in grace sending Christ to be the Mediator, not for all humanity but only
for the elect. It is as though he takes Calvin's doctrine of election away from
where Calvin was to deal with it in the 1559 *Institutes,* at the end of Book
Three, and begins with it. By making the double decree prior to grace, he then
finds himself teaching what Calvin had not taught, the doctrine of "a limited
atonement" — the doctrine that was to become cardinal in federal theology.
This at once indicates a shift away from Calvin in the place given to election
but also from Calvin's view that "reprobation is accidental to the gospel."

II. The New Debate: *Foedus Naturale*

The result of this was, as David Weir has shown so clearly, that in the period
between 1550 and 1560, already in Calvin's lifetime, lively debates broke out,
associated with the views of Pighius, Bolsec, and Castellio on the one hand
and those of Theodore Beza on the other.[9] If God is sovereign over all
humanity, not just over the elect, how is God related to the whole human race
if Christ is only the mediatorial Head of the elect? If God decrees all for his
own glory (as in the supralapsarianism of Beza), what is the relation between
the sovereign will of God and our human will? Is God responsible for evil?

---

9. See the excellent summary of these debates in David Weir, *The Origins of Federal
Theology,* ch. 2. Albert Pighius, a Roman Catholic theologian, attacked Calvin's views on
the bondage of the will, predestination, and providence in his earlier editions of the *Institutes,*
those of 1536, 1539, and 1541. In 1542 Pighius published his *De libero hominis arbitrio et
divina gratia, libri decem,* to which Calvin wrote a reply in 1543. Jerome Bolsec, a member
of the Geneva community, in 1551 attacked Calvin's doctrine of the sovereignty of God,
arguing that God looked upon people as elect or reprobate by foreseeing belief or unbelief.
He felt Calvin's views made God the author of sin and that he willed the Fall. This drew
forth Calvin's famous response of 1552 in his *De aeterna Dei Praedestinatione,* where Calvin
expounded with great care and clarity his distinction between remote and proximate causes,
and argued that if God is the ultimate cause of all, the proximate cause of human sin and
ruin in Adam and in us is in ourselves. Similar issues were taken up by Sebastian Castellio,
a Protestant theologian in Basel who translated the New Testament and who argued against
Calvin in 1554 that God has a permissive will but not an ordaining will, that God created
all for salvation, and that man has not totally lost the image of God. He likewise felt that
Calvin's doctrine of the secret will of God made the Fall part of the plan of God and thereby
made God the author of evil. As David Weir shows, these debates are important to our
understanding of the rise of federal theology and the notion of a prelapsarian covenant with
Adam.

Is the Fall a *felix culpa?* Again, the elect, the saints who are justified by faith and live by grace, must live responsibly in the world at large, in the state as well as in the church. How then do they interpret their existence and the will of God in the world at large, in culture, in the state, in the struggles for liberty, in the spheres of public morality? We can understand the resultant search for a basis for a social ethic. In other words, the question was emerging powerfully about the relation between justification and justice, *Rechtfertigung und Recht.* The believer is justified by the grace of God and accepted in Christ as a member of the body of Christ, but he must also do justly and seek justice in the world. God has a sovereign concern, indeed a passion, for righteousness, in both the church and the world.

With these questions doubtless very much in his mind, Zacharias Ursinus of the University of Heidelberg and the Collegium Sapientiae, and one of the authors of the Heidelberg Catechism — a Lutheran who became a Calvinist — in 1562, in his *Major Catechism,* first put forward the concept of a *foedus naturale,* as a prelapsarian covenant, as a way of interpreting Genesis 1–3, creation, and the story of man prior to the Fall. Calvin, Zwingli, Bullinger, and the other magisterial reformers had seen the covenant of grace *(foedus gratiae)* as a postlapsarian covenant made for sinners after the Fall — the promise of salvation fulfilled in Christ. Now here, for the first time in the Reformed tradition, the word *foedus* was being used to interpret *creation and human existence prior to the Fall.*[10]

Q. 10 What does the divine Law teach?

A. What sort of covenant in creation God had entered into with man; by which pact man would have conducted himself in that service, and what God would require of him after beginning with him a new covenant of grace. . . .

Q. 36 What is the difference between the Law and the Gospel?

A. The Law contains the covenant of nature initiated in creation by God with man, that is, it is known to man by nature *(lex continet foedus naturale in creatione a deo cum hominibus initium, hoc est, natura hominibus nota est)* and it requires from us perfect obedience to God, and it promises eternal life for those who keep it, and threatens eternal punishments for those who do not fulfill it. But the Gospel contains the

---

10. David Weir, *The Origins of Federal Theology,* pp. 104ff. In this paper I am deeply indebted to David Weir's historical researches into the origin of the concept of a *foedus naturale* in Ursinus and its influence on the early Puritans. My concern is to expand his thesis theologically and show its political significance in the rise of federal theology.

covenant of grace, that is, existing but not known naturally: it shows to us the fulfillment in Christ of his justice, which the law requires, and its restoration in us through the Spirit of Christ: and it promises eternal life by grace because of Christ to those who believe in him.

In other words — and this is federal theology in embryo — when God created man (Adam), he created him the child of nature who could discern the laws of nature (the Decalogue) by the light of reason, and then made a mutual covenant or contract with him *(foedus, mutua pactio)* that if he obeyed, God would give him eternal life, but if he disobeyed, he would be eternally punished. But Adam transgressed, broke the contract, and brought down divine judgment on himself and on his posterity — all for whom he contracted.

Clearly, then, human beings are responsible for evil and the Fall, not God. Man has abused his God-given freedom. Here is a way in which by the concept of *foedus* the harsher elements of a high doctrine of the decrees are mitigated, in a way that does justice to the absolute sovereignty of God (Ursinus is a high Calvinist) and to human dignity; a way of relating the sovereignty of God and human responsibility. Here is a way of answering the debates of the preceding ten or twelve years.

By drawing this distinction between a "covenant of nature" and "a covenant of grace," Reformed theology is clearly adopting a Western nature-grace model. The concept of a *foedus naturale* embraces *the twin concepts of natural law and of covenant (contract),* familiar in Western thought from the Middle Ages. God the Creator is the (Stoic) Lawgiver, related to all by natural law but only to some by grace. The concept of *foedus* (covenant or contract) is that of a "mutual pact" based on mutual conditions, be it between God and man or man and man.[11] We can notice at once two things about it, significant for our question whether Calvin was a federal theologian. First, this is a way of inter-

---

11. In his *Catechesis religionis Christianae,* Ursinus gives his definition of a covenant.

Q. 18 What the covenant of God is *(quod sit foedus Dei).*

A. A covenant in general is a mutual pact between two parties, where one obligates the other to certain conditions for doing, giving, or receiving something, employing signs and external symbols for solemn testimony, as a confirmation that the promise may be inviolable. From here certainly the definition of the covenant of God is deduced. For it is a mutual pact between God and man. . . . *(Foedus in genere est mutua pactio duarum partium, qua altera alteri certis conditionibus obligat. . . . Hinc facile colligitur definitio foederis Dei. Est enim mutua pactio inter Deum et hominibus.* See D. Weir, *The Origins of Federal Theology,* pp. 109, 114.

Such definitions of a covenant as a contract between two parties based on mutual conditions abound among the later federal theologians, Fenner, Perkins, Rollock, Witsius, etc. It is this prior definition of *foedus* which is then read into the biblical material, as we shall see below.

preting God's relation to man in creation (Gen. 1–3) prior to the Fall, distinct from the covenant of grace made for sinners after the Fall. We do not find this in Calvin. Again, in terms of the definition of *foedus* as a covenant or contract, we have to ask the question whether the God of the Bible is a covenant God (as certainly in Calvin) or a "contract God" who needs to be (or wills to be) conditioned into being gracious by human obedience.[12] Second, the distinction between the *foedus naturale* and the *foedus gratiae* is based on the distinction between the law (decalogue) and the gospel, contrasting them sharply and clearly giving primacy to law over grace. Is it appropriate to interpret creation in terms of (natural) law and restrict grace to redemption? Can we so readily equate the decalogue (the light of revelation) with natural law (the light of nature), as for example later sabbatarians did, in seeking justification for sabbatarian laws in the civil code, enshrining the contract of nature?

It is important to recognize at once, however, as David Weir has so carefully demonstrated, that for Ursinus and Olevianus and the theologians of the Palatinate, the concept of a *foedus naturale* was the answer to genuine questions about the relation between God and humanity, but *it was not for them a coordinating principle* in their theology. There is no reference to it in the Heidelberg Catechism, nor is there any reference to it in Pareus's commentary on Ursinus's Catechism. But that is precisely what it became before the end of the sixteenth century, first in English Puritanism and then in Scottish covenanting Calvinism. This is the identifying feature of "federal Calvinism" — a system built on the twin notions of natural law and *foedus,* the adaptation of Reformed theology to a nature-grace model. To this let me turn very briefly.

III. The Concept of *Foedus Naturale*

Let us now consider the concept of *foedus naturale* as a coordinating principle, first in theology and then in politics.

1. In Theology

Among the many students who flocked to Heidelberg to study under Ursinus and Olevianus was an English scholar, Thomas Cartwright (1535-1603), an early Puritan and a friend of Beza, who had been Lady Margaret Professor of Divinity in Cambridge but who was deprived of his chair after a controversy with a Dr. Whitgift over vestments in 1569 and went to Geneva to be with Beza. He studied

12. Cf. J. B. Torrance, "Covenant or Contract?" 51-76.

in Heidelberg between 1573 and 1574, going on to Antwerp, where he was joined in 1574 by another Puritan, Dudley Fenner. In 1585 Dudley Fenner published his *Sacra Theologia,* with a preface by Thomas Cartwright. This was the first work, so far as we know, to use the phrase "a covenant of works" *(foedus operum),* or "the covenant of law," and lay the basis for what we now call *federal theology,* with its clear distinction between "the covenant of works," made by God for all humanity in Adam, the federal (contracting) head of the race, and "the covenant of grace," the unilateral covenant made by God for the elect in Christ. Fenner's method is to offer a definition of the meaning of the word "covenant" *(foedus)* and then in Ramist fashion to subdivide it into two species. *Foedus duplex est; operum foedus, gratuitae promissionis foedus.* In any covenant there are two parties and mutual conditions and stipulations. *Foederis membra sunt, actio Dei stipulantis, actio hominis stipulationem recipientis.* The parties in the covenant of works are God and man, and the condition is obedience *(operum foedus est foedus, ubi conditio annexa est perfecta obedientia).* The parties in the covenant of grace are God and the elect in Christ and the condition that we receive Christ *(foedus gratuitae promissionis est foedus (a) de Christo . . . (b) ubi conditio est, si recipiatur Christus).* The initial definition of a covenant as a contract between two parties based on mutual stipulations and conditions controls all that follows. This method, as I see it, is the true beginning of Calvinist scholasticism.

The two covenants (law and grace) are the two stages by which God executes the eternal decrees. This is clearly seen in William Perkins's *A Golden Chaine or the Description of Theology, containing the Order and Causes of Salvation and Damnation according to God's Word* (1591). Here he produces his famous diagram, based on Beza's *Tabula,* and follows Dudley Fenner's method of defining a covenant in contractual terms, and then, again in Ramist fashion, distinguishing two species of it, the covenant of works and the covenant of grace. Throughout he uses the twin notions of natural law (decalogue) and covenant, defining both in highly contractual terms. God will be gracious IF law is satisfied. William Perkins was the most widely read Puritan in the first half of the seventeenth century, doubtless read by all the Westminster divines. His most famous pupil was William Ames, whose pupil in turn was Johannes Cocceius, through whom federal theology was so extensively expounded in Holland.[13]

---

13. In *The Golden Chaine,* Perkins expounds the two covenants of works and of grace as the stages in which God executes the decree of election, identifying the two stages as those of first law and then gospel. The law is the schoolmaster by which God brings the elect to salvation. The Bezan predestination system and the Western *ordo salutis* are being brought together in the practical mind of the Puritan, pastorally concerned about "law work" and the salvation of the elect. So in ch. 19, "Concerning the outward means of executing the decree of election, and of the Decalogue," he says, "The means are God's covenant and the seal thereof. *God's covenant is his contract with man, concerning life eternal, upon*

In 1596 Robert Rollock, in his *Treatise of God's Effectual Calling,* introduced the distinction between the "covenant of works" and the "covenant of grace" into Scotland, where the concept of covenant was historically highly congenial and where the nature-grace model of federal Calvinism soon became absolute orthodoxy. (See the nature-grace diagram on p. 38.)

Clearly by the end of the sixteenth century, the concept of a *foedus naturale* was not only the coordinating principle of the widely accepted interpretation of Reformed theology as federal theology, but, with the doctrine of a double decree and a limited atonement, became the major premise of the whole federal schema. The covenant of grace is the covenant provided for us by God whereby "the conditions" of the covenant of works (law) are met by Christ on behalf of the elect. Not only is law prior to grace, but grace is in danger of being subordinated to law, the God-given means whereby law is satisfied. Covenant is the means whereby the ends of the law are secured. Is this not an inversion of the biblical order? One can also understand later lively debates in Scotland worried about the legalism in much Calvinist preaching and questioning the doctrine of the "conditionality of the covenant of grace." But even those federal divines[14] who rejected this doctrine were still to argue that grace is "unconditionally free for the elect," because Christ has fulfilled

---

certain conditions. The covenant consisteth of two parts: God's promise to man, man's promise to God. God's promise to man is that whereby he bindeth himself to man to be his God, if he break not the condition. Man's promise to God is that whereby he voweth his allegiance unto his Lord, and to perform the conditions between them. *Again there are two kinds of this covenant. The covenant of works and the covenant of grace* (Jer. 31.31, 42.43). The covenant of works is God's covenant made with condition of perfect obedience and is expressed in the moral law." Then in ch. 31, "Of the covenant of grace," he says, "Hitherto concerning the covenant of works, and the law, now followeth the covenant of grace. The covenant of grace, is that whereby God, freely promising Christ and his benefits, exacteth again of man that he would by faith receive Christ and repent of his sins" (Hos. 2:18; Ezek. 36:25; Mal. 3:1).

Here, as in Fenner's *Theologia Sacra,* the covenant of grace is interpreted as a subspecies of covenant defined as a contract with conditions. Such a doctrine of the conditionality of the covenant of grace paves the way for a concept of repentance as a condition of grace — "legal repentance," which Calvin so vigorously attacked in the *Institutes* 3.3 in his distinction between "legal" and "evangelical repentance," and his rejection of the medieval sacrament of penance — the Western *ordo salutis* that made repentance (*contritio, confessio, satisfactio* — the *merita poenitentiae*) the condition of forgiveness. The *ordo* is: man — law — sin — repentance — grace. Was Calvin's concern not to reverse this order? Does grace come only at the end? See Dudley Fenner, *Theologia Sacra, sive Veritas est secundam Pietatem, Amstelodami,* (1632) *liber quarta, de Foedere Dei et Christo, cap. 1,* 48-50. Notice that the "covenant of works" is "the covenant of God" and "the covenant of grace" is "the covenant of Christ."

14. For example, Thomas Boston, Ralph and Ebenezer Erskine, and others, the so-called "Marrow men" in the controversies about *The Marrow of Modern Divinity;* cf. J. B. Torrance, "Covenant or Contract?" *Scottish Journal of Theology,* 23 (1970), 51-76.

for them the conditions of the covenant of works! We must ask the question, Is the God of Calvin the God who needs to be conditioned into being gracious, even by the obedience of the Son? Certainly at times Calvin's use of the language of propitiation appears to be saying as much, but in an eloquent passage in the *Institutes* 2.6.4 he quotes Augustine with great approval to reject any such thought.[15] Propitiation, like the fulfilling of the law, is the work of grace, not the condition of grace — not the satisfying of the terms of a contract.

2. In Politics

The Reformed Church found herself from the very beginning under persecution and having to defend her liberties and rights to preach the gospel as she understood it from the Bible and the teaching of the reformers. She was inevitably plunged into political controversy. We see this among the Huguenots in France, the Puritans in England, and the covenanters in Scotland in their struggles against the doctrine of the divine right of kings. Here, as in their theology, the twin notions of law, and covenant — the nature-grace model — becomes enormously important. Two events deeply disturbed Western Europe in the sixteenth century after the Reformation. The first was the deposition of Mary Queen of Scots in 1567 (and her beheading in England in 1587), raising the question: What are the rights of a sovereign vis-à-vis his or her people? Have the people a right to depose their sovereign? The second event was the massacre of the Huguenots on the Eve of St. Bartholomew in 1572, raising the complementary question: What are the rights of a people vis-à-vis the sovereign? Has the sovereign the right to massacre his people? How do you safeguard the rights of both king and people? The answer given was: "By covenant *(foedus)*" — by "contract of government."

---

15. "I will quote a passage of Augustine — 'Incomprehensible and immutable is the love of God. For it was not after we were reconciled to him by the blood of his Son that he began to love us, but he loved us before the foundation of the world, that with his only begotten Son, we too might be sons of God before we were anything at all. Our being reconciled by the death of Christ must not be understood as if the Son reconciled us, in order that the Father, then hating, might begin to love us, but that we were reconciled to him already loving, though at enmity with us because of sin. . . . In a manner wondrous and divine, he loved us even when he hated us . . .' " (Tract. in Jo. 110). *Institutes* 2.16.4 (OS 3.485). We see here again the trinitarian nature of God set against any notion of a contract God who needs to be conditioned into being gracious. Calvin returns to the same theme of the trinitarian nature of grace in ch. 17 in his discussion of how it can be rightly and not improperly said that Christ has "merited" God's grace, in the sense that his obedience is the material cause of our salvation, flowing from the love of the Father. *Institutes* 2.17.1ff (OS 3.508ff.).

At the time of his coronation, a king makes a solemn covenant or contract with his people whereby they bind themselves together under law to guarantee each other's rights under specific conditions. This raised a very important set of questions. What is the nature and source of human rights? What constitutes lawful government? What is the seat of sovereignty in law? Is it in the monarchy, in the people, or above both in God. Is the king above the law? Is violence very justified in the defense of liberty? John Calvin argued that we must never resort to violence in the defense of religious liberty. But situations emerged in France, England, and Scotland, where Reformed churchmen were prepared to use violence — but only lawfully where a legal contract had been broken. Again the twin concepts of covenant and law, of *foedus* and natural law, were seen as foundations for civil law. *There was a passionate concern to maintain the universal reign of law.* Scholars searched the Bible, especially the Old Testament, and examined every conceivable passage where the word "covenant" appears in order to find a basis for "lawful government," to defend their freedom against tyranny — using the Bible as a book of legal precedents. In the process, they appealed to medieval notions of natural law and social contract (contract of society and contract of government). A wealth of literature appeared that was to be enormously influential on the rise of modern democracy. The argument was that no one is above the law, neither king nor people. Civil law enshrines natural law *(foedus naturale),* the law of equity, discerned by reason. Justification for these views was found in the Old Testament covenant passages, in medieval contractarian writers, and in historical precedents in European history, not least in France and Scotland.

An anonymously published work, *De Iure Magistratuum in Subditos,*[16] almost certainly the work of Beza, argued from natural and historical examples that rulers have a duty to their people as well as a right to expect obedience from them, that there is a reciprocal relationship of mutual obligation between rulers and subjects, *mutuo consensu ac publice contracta obligatio,* or again an *obligatio solemni et publico consensu contracta.* Beza then defends this by appealing to historical examples of covenants in the Old Testament as well as in European history. This work is thought to have been first published in 1550; a French version appeared in 1574, two years after the massacre of the Eve of St. Bartholomew, *Du Droit des Magistrats sur leur Sujets* and one year after François Hotman's similar *Franco-Gallia* in 1573. Already in 1571, there had appeared in Scotland George Buchanan's *De Jure Regni Apud Scotos,* appeal-

---

16. *De Iure Magistratuum in Subditos et Officia Subditorum erga Magistratus* — concerning the mutual rights of rulers over their subjects and the duties of subjects towards their rulers, under the law of equity. See the edition of this by A. H. Murray, H.A.U.M., Capetown, 1956. See J. W. Gough, *The Social Contract* (Oxford, 2nd ed. 1963), 52ff.

ing to the twin notions of law and contract (covenant) in justification of the deposition of Mary Queen of Scots, who had broken her contract with the people.

This was followed in the same decade (1579) by the influential Huguenot work *Vindiciae contra Tyrannos* by Junius Brutus (almost certainly the French Huguenot Duplessis Mornay), said by the late Professor Harold Laski to be the most influential book in the sixteenth century in the rise of modern democracy.[17] The fascinating thing is that this defense of liberty is based entirely on exposition of the Old Testament, with the theme that Israel was a covenanted nation under God, whose kings were therefore the servants of God and whose people were under the law and the testimonies of a covenanted nation. Throughout, numerous relevant covenant passages are interpreted in terms of the twin concepts of law and contract, which were seen as the biblical warrant for maintaining under God the universal reign of law, safeguarded by covenant. Four questions are asked:

1. Whether subjects are bound to obey princes if they command that which is against the *law* — the question of civil disobedience.
2. Whether it be *lawful* to resist a prince who doth infringe the law of God or ruin the church. Is it right to resist a state that interferes in the life of a church — the question of religious liberty?
3. Whether it be *lawful* to resist a prince who doth oppress or ruin a public state. Is resistance to a state justified in the defense of justice and freedom?
4. Whether neighboring princes or states may be, or are, bound by *law* to give succor to the subjects of other princes (states) afflicted for the cause of true religion, or oppressed by tyranny.

This work was extremely relevant in England and Scotland, not least when the Scots sent a presbyterian army to fight shoulder to shoulder with their English puritan brethren, when together they signed the Solemn League and Covenant in their common struggle against tyranny and toward a "covenanted uniformity of doctrine, worship and government" in the three kingdoms. The book was also discussed by Richard Hooker in his *The Laws of Ecclesiastical Polity* (1594), which more than any other work at the time introduced contractarian natural law theory into England and later influenced John Locke's theory of a social contract. In Scotland, the arguments of the *Vindiciae* (together with those of George Buchanan) were developed in Samuel

---

17. See Harold Laski's Introduction to his 1924 English edition of this under the title *The Defence of Liberty against Tyrants* (New York, 1972).

Rutherford's *Lex Rex, the Law and the Prince,* which was the political manifesto of the Covenanters. The book is full of quotations from medieval contractarian writers, the Spanish Jesuit Juan Mariana, and the Jesuit philosopher Francisco Suarez, as well as from the Old Testament. No one is above the law, neither king nor people. Civil law is based on natural law, discerned by the light of reason. Scotland, like old Israel, is a covenanted nation under God, and therefore the king, like kings in old Israel, is under the law and testimonies of a covenanted nation — The National Covenant, The Solemn League and Covenant, and The Westminster Confession of Faith.

Out of all this literature emerged two principles in the struggles against tyranny and the doctrine of "the divine right of kings." (1) The passionate belief in *Justice* — the doctrine that "right and not might" is the basis of all political society and of every political order in a true democracy (the reign of law); and (2) the passionate belief in *Liberty* — the conviction that will — human consent — and not force is the basis of true government (secured by covenant).

It is abundantly clear that the concept of a *foedus naturale* was not only the coordinating principle of federal theology but fundamental for the political thinking of our Puritan, covenanting forefathers. Here was a conceptual matrix (with its notions of natural law, contract, *ius naturale, ius civile, ius gentium,* sovereignty, etc. so familiar in Western Europe) within which Calvin's theology was readily reinterpreted as federal theology and went to the grassroots of nations and churches struggling for justice and liberty, seeking always biblical justification and precedent for their theology and practice. How do we understand the relation not only between divine sovereignty and human will, but also between the will of the human sovereign and the will of his people under God? This was the question discussed by Beza, Duplessis Mornay, and Rutherford. To both there is given the same answer, by natural law and covenant. The Western nature-grace model provided for Reformed churchmen the basis for a "Calvinistic synthesis" not only between "the light of nature" (natural law) and "the light of revelation," but also between federal theology and their political views — seen later in the powerful influence of Puritan thinking on the American federal Constitution. As in the Bible, so in England, Scotland, and New England, historical content is given to the will of God by the notion of covenant. Federal theology, it has been argued, as in Cocceius was an early form of *heilsgeschichtliche Theologie.*[18] The nature-grace, or law-grace

18. This was argued long ago by T. M. Lindsay in his influential article "Covenant Theology," in the *British and Foreign Evangelical Review,* 28 (1879), 521-38. Cf. G. Schrenk, *Gottesreich und Bund im älteren Protestantismus* (Gütersloh, 1923). It is seen in Cocceius's notion of the progressive promulgation of the covenant of grace and the progressive abrogation of the covenant of works.

model, together with the concept of covenant, was to prove a powerful instrument for social renewal in the rise of democracy, but also to be used tragically
in certain contexts for biblical justification for slavery in the Deep South, or
for *apartheid* in South Africa, by a misuse of the concepts of "natural law,"
"orders of creation," "ethnicity," "pluriformity," and so on. Federal theology
was to be used as the theology of politics in widely differing historical contexts.[19] It was by the covenant concept that the ends of natural law (however
interpreted), as well as civil law, were secured.

IV. Theological Comments on the Nature-Grace Model in Federal Theology

For all that the nature-grace model was so influential on the rise of modern
democracy and the concern for justice, liberty, and human rights, theologically,
it has great weaknesses which highlight the importance of our understanding
of the relation between grace and law. Here again we ask the question, Was
Calvin a federal theologian?

1. Law and Grace

In his discussion of Jeremiah 31:31, Calvin is quite explicit. "God has never
made any other covenant than that which he made formerly with Abraham and
at length confirmed by the hand of Moses" in the giving of the law. This is
the covenant of grace, promised to Abraham and fulfilled in Christ. Therefore
"old" and "new" do not mean two different covenants, but within the one
covenant of grace we distinguish two different forms, related as shadow and
substance, promise and fulfillment. They are different in dispensation *(administratio)* but one in substance *(substantia),* which is grace. This is spelled out
in great detail in Book Two of the *Institutes,* in chapters 10 and 11. Within
this one covenant, law is given as the gift of grace, to spell out the obligations
of grace, to make us aware of our need of grace — "added because of trans-

---

19. See J. B. Torrance, "The Covenant Concept in Scottish Theology and Politics
and its Legacy," *Scottish Journal of Theology,* 34 (1981), 225-43. See also Torrance, "Cal-
vinism and Puritanism in England and Scotland: Some Basic Concepts in the Development
of Federal Theology," South African Congress for Calvin Research, *Calvinus Reformator:
His Contribution to Theology, Church and Society* (Potchefstroom, 1982), 264-86. Also,
"Interpreting the Word by the Light of Christ or the Light of Nature? Calvin, Calvinism and
Barth," in Robert V. Schnucker (ed.), *Calviniana: Ideas and Influence of Jean Calvin (16th-
Century Essays and Studies),* 10 (1988), 255-67.

gressions" — to lead to Christ. Both promise and law must be interpreted christologically and soteriologically in the light of Christ, in the light of his *purposes* of redemption. So the discussion of law and gospel is set in the context of Book Two of the 1559 *Institutes,* our knowledge of God as Redeemer. Here Calvin follows Paul's exposition of the relation between grace and law in Galatians 3, which he cites at the beginning of his discussion in chapter 7. God in grace gave his promises to Abraham; 430 years later came the law, not to impose conditions for grace (as the Judaizers taught) but to spell out the unconditional obligations of grace. In the 1536 first edition of the *Institutes,* Calvin had followed the pattern of Luther's *Short Catechism,* treating first law and then gospel (also followed, as we have seen, in Ursinus's *Major Catechism* in 1562). But in the light of Galatians 3, Calvin abandons that order and argues for the priority of grace over law — the whole Old Testament in the larger sense of the word is "Gospel" (2.9.2) — the good news of grace.[20] For Calvin, as for Paul, law is given to secure the ends of covenant. So he speaks of the law as "law clothed *(vestita)* with the gospel," given to keep Israel in "suspense" *(suspensio)* until Christ should come. For Calvin, law has a double meaning. (a) In the wider sense of "the whole law *(tota lex)"* it is the whole Mosaic system, law "clothed with the covenant of free adoption." (b) In the narrower sense of "naked law" *(nuda lex),* it is law abstracted from grace, shorn of the promise, "dead letter." This is its accusatory, condemnatory function, "the curse of the law." This is the "accidental" function of the law, not God's primary purpose, which is to realize the ends of grace, the fulfillment of the promise, to lead to Christ, the Mediator of the New Covenant.

Calvin never appears to have used the word *foedus* to interpret creation prior to the Fall, but restricts the word to the covenant of grace made for sinners — a postlapsarian covenant. He never taught the concept of a *foedus naturale,* or a covenant of works *(foedus operum).*[21] As we have seen, this came later in

20. See I. John Hesselink, "Law and Gospel or Gospel and Law? Calvin's understanding of the Relationship," in Robert V. Schnucker (ed.), *Calviniana: Ideas and Influence of Jean Calvin (16th-Century Essays and Studies),* 10 (1988), 13-32. Also his "Luther and Calvin on Law and Gospel in their Galatian Commentaries," *Reformed Review,* 37.2 (1984), 69-82.

21. Calvin occasionally refers to "natural law" discerned by conscience, as in his discussion of Romans 1:19-22 and 2:14-15. See his *Commentary on Romans* (1539) (CO 49.23ff., 37ff.) and the *Institutes* 4.20.14-16 (CO 2.1164-67). Different estimates have been made of its significance by A. Lang, E. Doumergue, G. Gloede, and Emil Brunner. Calvin has no systematic discussion of the subject, and it is not integral to his theology nor ever wedded to the notion of *foedus.* See John T. McNeill, "Natural Law in the Teaching of the Reformers," *Journal of Religion,* 26 (1946), 3. The question is fundamental for determining the meaning of the *duplex cognitio* of God as Creator and Redeemer. Have we two separate

the sixteenth century with Ursinus, Cartwright, and Fenner. Nor, do I believe, would Calvin have taught it! The distinction between the covenant of works (law) and the covenant of grace not only implies the priority of law over grace, but implies the subordination of grace to law! On this schema, the *foedus naturale,* the covenant of law, embodies God's primary purpose for humanity in creation. Therefore when Adam falls and breaks the contract, the covenant of law, there is need for a second covenant, the covenant of grace, to secure the ends of law! The covenant of grace is in fact subordinated to the covenant of works. So the federalists said that God made the covenant of works (law) three times — first with Adam, who broke it; second with Israel at Sinai, who also broke it; third with Christ, who kept it on behalf of the elect! This, as I see it, is a form of the medieval principle that *gratia non tollit sed perficit naturam.*

Once again, as with the covenant of works, so with the covenant of grace, covenant secures the ends of law, which, as we have seen, is the inversion of the Pauline order. It is a serious shift away from Calvin and the first reformers on different accounts. First, there is a shift from the Old Testament / New Testament (old covenant / new covenant) scheme, where Calvin sets law in the framework of grace, to a covenant of works / covenant of grace scheme with the absolute priority of law over grace. Second, it is surely false, in the light of Paul's argument in Galatians 3, to see the covenant at Sinai as the republication of the covenant of works — that God was imposing obedience to the law as a "condition" of grace (the error of the Judaizers). Calvin attacks any such notion, seeing "the error of those who, in comparing the law with the gospel, represent it merely as a comparison between the merit of works and the gratuitous imputation of righteousness. . . . The gospel has not succeeded the whole law in such a sense as to introduce a different method of salvation. It rather confirms the law, and proves that everything which it promised is fulfilled" (2.9.4). Third, we see here the dangerous confusion between a "covenant" and a "contract." (The Latin word *foedus* means both.) The covenant of grace is the unilateral covenant whereby God binds himself in unconditional promises to man, binds man to himself under unconditional obligations, and undertakes to fulfill those promises and obligations for man in Christ. The notion of the covenant as a mutual bilateral contract, where the responsibility of fulfilling the covenant rests on man, was built into later federal theology, as we have seen, but was foreshadowed by Zwingli and Bullinger.[22]

---

avenues to knowledge of God or are both given to us in Christ? Calvin prefers to speak of the *ordo, rectitudo,* and *integritas* of creation in which we see the paternal favor of God displayed.

22. See D. Weir, *The Origins of Federal Theology,* 26, where he contrasts Calvin and the Genevan theologians, with their emphasis on the covenant as unilateral, with Zwingli,

2. *Sovereignty of God and Mediatorship of Christ*

The federal scheme sees all under the sovereignty of God, but not under the mediatorial Headship of Christ as Man. It does not do justice to the Pauline teaching of Ephesians and Colossians, taken up by Irenaeus and the great Greek Fathers, that God's concern is to reconcile and sum up all things in Christ. By operating with an abstract concept of sovereignty and the decrees of God it subordinates grace in Christ to the task of executing these (logically) prior decrees — teaching, as Calvin had not done, the doctrine of a limited atonement.[23] Is this not an illustration of the weakness of much Western theology — of coming to the Bible and to theology with a prior concept or definition of God and then seeking to graft the Trinity onto it — of dealing with the *De Deo Uno* before the *De Deo Trino* — in ways that failed to do justice to the doctrine of the Trinity and the trinitarian nature of grace for which Calvin was contending? As Geerhardus Vos said long ago here at

---

Bullinger, and the Rhineland theologians, for whom the covenant is bilateral. See J. Wayne Baker, *Heinrich Bullinger and the Covenant: The Other Reformed Tradition* (Athens, OH: Ohio University Press, 1980); also his "Covenant and Community in the Thought of Heinrich Bullinger," where he asserts that "Bullinger was the first clearly to articulate a bilateral or conditional covenant" and "was the first to utilise the covenant as the framework for the Christian community," and again "Bullinger's covenant was conditional. He first expressed the notion of a conditional covenant in an unpublished treatise on baptism in 1525." In 1534, Bullinger published his *De Testamento seu Foedere Dei Unico et Aeterno.* There is only one covenant. See also "Covenant and Baptism in the Theology of Huldreich Zwingli," unpublished Th.D. thesis (Princeton, 1971), cited by Wayne Baker. Zwingli used the covenant concept in the defense of infant baptism against the Anabaptists' sharp distinction between the covenant of circumcision and the covenant of grace. Against this, Zwingli wrote, in 1526, *De Peccato Originali,* and in 1527, *In Catabaptistarum Strophas Elenchus,* arguing for the one covenant of grace for all nations. If children in old Israel, before they believed were members of this covenant, why should not the same be true of Christian children? See G. Schrenk, *Gottesreich und Bund im älteren Protestantismus* (Gütersloh, 1923), in Zweiter Teil, "Der Bund," 37ff. J. Wayne Baker sees Bullinger as the first "covenant theologian" in the Reformed tradition for three reasons. He was also the first to expound covenant in conditional terms with mutual obligations. He was the first to speak of God making a covenant with Adam *after the Fall* in the protevangelium in Genesis 3:15. Then, too, he was the first to use covenant as a framework for the Christian community, ruled by magistrates. For Bullinger, law spells out the conditions of the covenant for the community. I think it is right to describe Bullinger as "a covenant theologian," but he is not a "federal theologian" as we have defined it. He knows no prelapsarian *foedus naturale.* Bullinger's *Decades* were widely read in England and doubtless paved the way for the rise of federal theology, not least in stressing the social and political dimensions of the covenant concept as a mutual conditional covenant.

23. See J. B. Torrance, "The Incarnation and 'Limited Atonement,' " *Evangelical Quarterly,* 55 (1983), 83-94; R. T. Kendall, *Calvin and English Calvinism to 1649* (Oxford, 1979); J. B. Torrance, "Strengths and Weaknesses of the Westminster Theology," in A. I. C. Heron (ed.), *The Westminster Confession in the Church Today* (Edinburgh, 1982), 40-54.

Calvin Theological Seminary in his 1888 inaugural lecture on "The Covenant in Reformed Theology," "Calvin's theology was built on the basis of the Trinity, and therefore the covenant concept could not rise as a dominant principle in his case. He is a forerunner for such Reformed theologians who allocated it to a subordinate place as a separate locus."[24] Father, Son, and Holy Spirit are *one in being* in their relation to the world in creation and redemption, in love. The Son is not simply executor of a divine decree, fulfilling the terms of a contract.

3. Creation and Redemption

In dualistic fashion, the federal scheme separates creation and redemption. It fails to interpret creation christologically. In the New Testament, Christ is presented as both Creator and Redeemer. In limiting grace and the mediatorial Headship of Christ to the "elect," to the church as the *numerus electorum,* federal Calvinism falls back on the concepts of "orders of creation" and "natural law" to interpret the state, race relations, social justice, and anthropology.

Robert Rollock in his 1596 *Treatise on God's Effectual Calling,* which first introduced the federal scheme to Scotland, could write: "The covenant of works, which may also be called a legal or natural covenant, was founded in nature and in the law of God which in the first creation was engraven in man's heart. . . . Therefore the ground of the covenant of works was not Christ, nor the grace of God in Christ, but the nature of man . . . endued with the knowledge of God." This exclusion of Christ from creation reveals vividly the nontrinitarian nature of the nature-grace model, and works itself out in later doctrines of the radical separation of church and state, or the failure to interpret the relation between church and state christologically — as called for in the 1934 Barmen Declaration. Perhaps here we see also a weakness in Calvin himself, who, as Karl Barth has commented, did not interpret christologically

24. Geerhardus Vos, *De verbondsleer in de gereformeerde theologie.* Rede bijhet overdragen van het rectoraat aan de Theologische School te Grand Rapids, Michigan (Grand Rapids: "Democrat" Drukpers, 1891; repr. Rotterdam: Mazijk's Uitgeversbureau, 1939). It seems to me quite legitimate to use the concept of covenant to interpret God's (prelapsarian) purpose in creation, provided, first of all, that it is seen as an inference from the New Covenant in which God's primary purposes for humanity are fulfilled (although the word is not used in Gen. 1–3), and, second, that we are speaking of "covenant" as a bond of unconditional love with unconditional obligations, *not* of "contract." The purposes of the triune God in creation, redemption, and the kingdom of God are enshrined in the promise, "I will be your God, and you shall be my people," that we might participate by grace in the triune life of God.

his views on the state and civil government in the *Institutes* 4.20, as he did other doctrines so consistently.[25]

4. Legal and Filial

The federal scheme has substituted a *legal* understanding of man for a *filial*. That is, God's prime purpose for man is legal, not filial, but this yields an impersonal view of man as the object of justice, rather than as primarily the object of love. We can give people their "legal rights" but not see them as our brothers. In the New Testament, and on a trinitarian understanding, God's prime purpose in Creation, Incarnation, Atonement, and the giving of the Spirit at Pentecost is filial, not just legal — "to bring sons to glory." What our doctrine of God is, that is our anthropology. The counterpart of the contract God of the covenant of works is the individual with his / her legal rights — and a work ethic! The counterpart of the triune God of grace is the human person created for communion.

5. God and God as Triune

We have to ask ourselves, therefore, the question: In the movement from Calvin to federal Calvinism, do we not see a basic shift in the doctrine of God, from a prime emphasis on God as triune to a Stoic concept of God as primarily the Lawgiver, the contract God, or to an Aristotelian concept of God in whom there are no unrealized potentialities? The triune God has his being-in-loving, in the mutual indwelling *(perichoresis)* of the Father and the Son in the Spirit, who has in grace created us to find our true being-in-loving in his image. The God of Stoicism is the God of legal justice who has created men and women for legal obedience. The significance of this is seen in the writings of two outstanding federal Calvinists, John Owen in seventeenth-century England and Jonathan Edwards in eighteenth-century New England, who both taught that justice is the essential attribute of God by which he is related to all people, but the love of God is arbitrary, the attribute by which he is related (not by nature, but by will) to the elect. This may be the logic of the law-grace model of their high federal Calvinism, but it is not true to the New Testament, nor is it the theology of Calvin. On a trinitarian understanding, God is Love — he is Father, Son, and Holy Spirit in his innermost being — and what he is in his innermost being, he is in all his works and ways. Classical high Calvinism has

---

25. See J. B. Torrance, "Interpreting the Word by the Light of Christ or the Light of Nature? Calvin, Calvinism and Barth," *op. cit.*, 256ff.

been dogged by a latent Sabellianism that has created problems of assurance, as we see in the endless debates on the subject in the seventeenth and eighteenth centuries. God is loving toward the elect, but is he love in his innermost being? Does he love me? Or is there some secret will or hidden "horrible decree" that God might be in himself other than what he reveals himself to be in Jesus Christ? What then is the ground of joyful assurance? This is a question we must put to Calvin himself, although he certainly taught the doctrine of assurance — that faith is a direct act *(cognitio)* by which we see, through the Spirit, the love of the Father in the face of the Son and know that God is gracious. But it is an even more burning question when put to the later federalists, whose concept of God so often undermined assurance.[26]

6. Holy Scripture

This shift in the doctrine of God and in anthropology is reflected in the shift in attitude to Holy Scripture — from Scripture seen as the revelation of grace to Scripture as a book telling us our duty. Where the first Helvetic Confession of 1536 interprets the *scopus scripturae* as to show forth the grace of God in Christ, the Westminster Confession and Catechisms of 1646 say that Scripture principally teaches "what man is to believe concerning God and what duty God requires of man." The Bible is increasingly seen as a book of legal precedents. This use of Scripture is too readily justified in terms of a synthesis between the "self-evident light of nature" and the "evident light of revelation."

7. Ordo Salutis

As we have seen in Puritans like Fenner and Perkins, the distinction between the covenant of law made with humankind in Adam and the subsequent covenant of grace made for the elect in Christ was wedded to their understanding of the medieval *ordo salutis* — an *ordo* that grew out of the medieval period, indeed out of the sacrament of penance, with its roots in Tertullian.

Man — Law — Sin — Repentance — Grace

26. See the doctrine of God in John Owen, *The Death of Death in the Death of Christ* (London: Banner of Truth, 1956). See also the discussion of Owen and Edwards in John McLeod Campbell, *The Nature of the Atonement* (London, 4th ed., 1956), ch. 3; J. B. Torrance, "The Incarnation and 'Limited Atonement,'" *op. cit.,* and "The Contribution of McLeod Campbell to Scottish Theology," *Scottish Journal of Theology,* 26 (1973), 295-311.

God uses the covenant of law as the *paidagogos* to bring fallen sinners to Christ. So the old preachers, with a genuine pastoral concern, preached the law to give their hearers a sense of sin in order to exhort them to repent and receive grace and forgiveness, the benefits of the work of Christ — what the Puritans called "law work." This order, too, often failed to see the significance of Calvin's distinction between "legal repentance," where repentance is a condition of forgiveness, and "evangelical repentance," where repentance is a response to grace and the Word of the Cross. In true "evangelical repentance" forgiveness (the Word of the Cross) is logically prior to repentance (*Institutes* 3.3).

In each of these seven comments on the nature-grace model in federal theology, we have seen such a significant shift from the basic emphasis of Calvin that we must answer in the negative the question, Was Calvin a federal theologian? What is at stake is both the doctrine of God and our understanding of grace.

For all the influence the nature-grace model had in the rise of democracy and in the struggles for justice and liberty, today we need to recover a more trinitarian incarnational model, with a greater awareness that there is no area of life that does not belong to Jesus Christ, to transcend the dualisms of our culture and the legalism of so much religion, and to see the organic connection between justification and justice, evangelism and social concern. For too long we have used simply the language of "rights" — human rights, civil rights, women's rights — the language of natural law. Is it not better to use the language of "humanity" — the Irenaean model of the Greek Fathers — that what was lost in Adam (our sonship, our humanity) is restored in Christ — in his vicarious humanity? Here perhaps Calvin is a better guide than much federal Calvinism to Holy Scripture, with his vision of Christ as the *scopus* not only of the Scriptures but of all God's purposes for humanity. But perhaps we need therefore to interpret Calvin more in terms of his roots in the trinitarian, incarnational theology of the great Greek Fathers, Athanasius and the Cappadocian divines, and less in terms of the Latin Western Fathers — of Augustine and the Westminster divines. The God of the Bible is a covenant God, not a contract God. His grace is unconditionally free, and unconditional in the costly claims it lays upon us as he fulfills his filial purposes of covenant love. Perhaps Calvin has a better understanding of the covenant of grace than do many of his successors in federal Calvinism.

Nature/Grace Model
of Federal Theology (Puritan Calvinism)
(e.g., Westminster Confession)

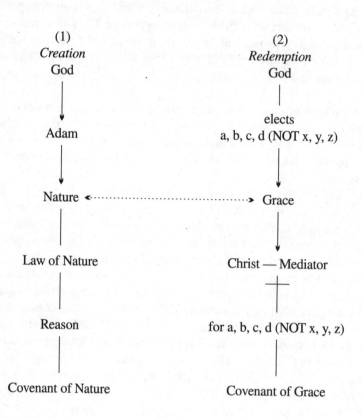

(1)
Creation
God

↓

Adam

↓

Nature ←·····················→ Grace

Law of Nature

Reason

Covenant of Nature

(2)
Redemption
God

elects
a, b, c, d (NOT x, y, z)

↓

Grace

↓

Christ — Mediator

for a, b, c, d (NOT x, y, z)

Covenant of Grace

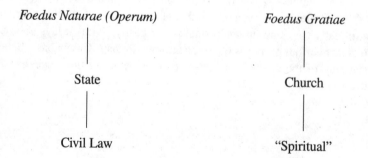

Foedus Naturae (Operum)

State

Civil Law

Foedus Gratiae

Church

"Spiritual"

The *TABULA* from Beza's *Summa totius Christianismi* (1555)

A description and distribution of the causes of election and reprobation

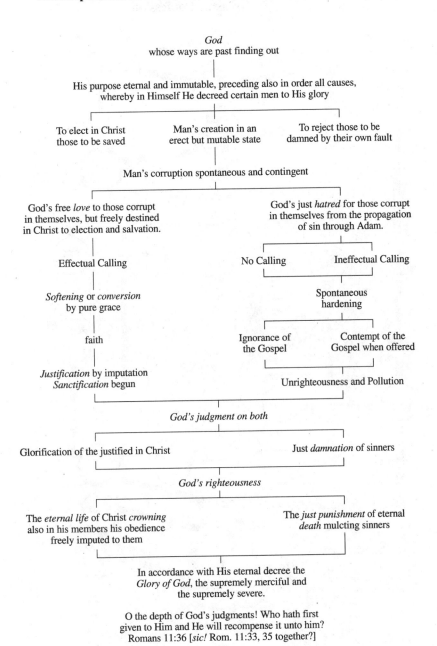

God
whose ways are past finding out

His purpose eternal and immutable, preceding also in order all causes,
whereby in Himself He decreed certain men to His glory

To elect in Christ   Man's creation in an   To reject those to be
those to be saved   erect but mutable state   damned by their own fault

Man's corruption spontaneous and contingent

God's free *love* to those corrupt   God's just *hatred* for those corrupt
in themselves, but freely destined   in themselves from the propagation
in Christ to election and salvation.   of sin through Adam.

Effectual Calling   No Calling   Ineffectual Calling

Softening or *conversion*   Spontaneous
by pure grace   hardening

faith   Ignorance of   Contempt of the
the Gospel   Gospel when offered

Justification by imputation
Sanctification begun   Unrighteousness and Pollution

God's judgment on both

Glorification of the justified in Christ   Just *damnation* of sinners

God's righteousness

The *eternal life* of Christ *crowning*   The *just punishment* of eternal
also in his members his obedience   *death* mulcting sinners
freely imputed to them

In accordance with His eternal decree the
Glory of God, the supremely merciful and
the supremely severe.

O the depth of God's judgments! Who hath first
given to Him and He will recompense it unto him?
Romans 11:36 [*sic!* Rom. 11:33, 35 together?]

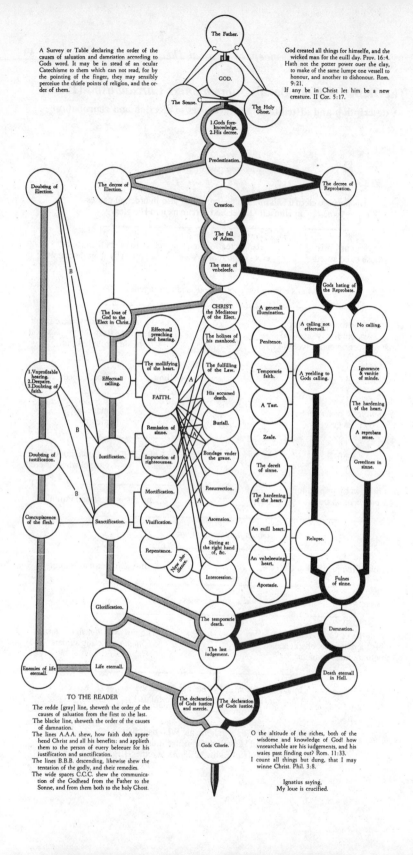

A Survey or Table declaring the order of the causes of saluation and damnation according to Gods word. It may be in stead of an ocular Catechisme to them which can not read, for by the pointing of the finger, they may sensibly perceiue the chiefe points of religion, and the order of them.

God created all things for himselfe, and the wicked man for the euill day. Prov. 16:4.
Hath not the potter power ouer the clay, to make of the same lumpe one vessell to honour, and another to dishonour. Rom. 9:21.
If any be in Christ let him be a new creature. II Cor. 5:17.

The Father.

GOD.

The Sonne.

The Holy Ghost.

1.Gods fore-knowledge. 2.His decree.

Predestination.

Doubting of Election.

The decree of Election.

The decree of Reprobation.

Creation.

The fall of Adam.

The state of vnbeleefe.

Gods hating of the Reprobate.

B

The loue of God to the Elect in Christ.

CHRIST the Mediatour of the Elect.

A generall illumination.

A calling not effectuall.

No calling.

Effectuall preaching and hearing.

The holines of his manhood.

Penitence.

1.Vnprofitable hearing. 2.Despaire. 3.Doubting of faith.

Effectuall calling.

The mollifying of the heart.

The fulfilling of the Law.

Temporarie faith.

A yeelding to Gods calling.

Ignorance & vanitie of minde.

FAITH.

His accursed death.

A Tast.

The hardening of the heart.

B

Remission of sinne.

Buriall.

Zeale.

A reprobate sense.

Doubting of iustification.

Iustification.

Imputation of righteousnes.

Bondage vnder the graue.

The deceit of sinne.

Greedines in sinne.

A

B

Mortification.

Resurrection.

The hardening of the heart.

Concupiscence of the flesh.

Sanctification.

Viuification.

Ascension.

An euill heart.

Relapse.

Repentance.

New obedience

Sitting at the right hand of, &c.

An vnbeleeuing heart.

Intercession.

Apostasie.

Fulnes of sinne.

Glorification.

The temporarie death.

Damnation.

The last iudgement.

Enemies of life eternall.

Life eternall.

Death eternall in Hell.

TO THE READER

The redde [gray] line, sheweth the order of the causes of saluation from the first to the last.
The blacke line, sheweth the order of the causes of damnation.
The lines A.A.A. shew, how faith doth apprehend Christ and all his benefits: and applieth them to the person of euery beleeuer for his iustification and sanctification.
The lines B.B.B. descending, likewise shew the tentation of the godly, and their remedies.
The wide spaces C.C.C. shew the communication of the Godhead from the Father to the Sonne, and from them both to the holy Ghost.

The declaration of Gods iustice and mercie.

The declaration of Gods iustice.

Gods Glorie.

O the altitude of the riches, both of the wisdome and knowledge of God! how vnsearchable are his iudgements, and his waies past finding out? Rom. 11:33.
I count all things but dung, that I may winne Christ. Phil. 3:8.

Ignatius saying,
My loue is crucified.

Calvins Verständnis der Heiligen Schrift

Wilhelm H. Neuser

Die Aufgabe

Das Thema unterscheidet sich auf den ersten Blick nicht von denen, die auf diesem und früheren Kongressen abgehandelt werden bzw. behandelt worden sind. Calvins Verständnis der Heiligen Schrift soll erneut untersucht werden. Es soll — wenn es möglich ist — besser verstanden werden als zuvor, das heißt, die wissenschaftliche Erkenntnis soll vertieft und die kirchliche Praxis bereichert werden. Der Behandlung des Themas müssen jedoch zwei Vorbemerkungen vorangestellt werden.

Erstens enthält Calvins berühmte Hauptschrift Institutio Christianae Religionis keine Lehre von der Heiligen Schrift. Es muß klargestellt werden, daß er dort nur Teilaspekte behandelt, nicht aber die ganze Lehre vorträgt. Allerdings ist es wichtig festzustellen, welche Einzelaspekte er behandelt und also bevorzugt. Im Buch I,6-9 entwicklt er die Lehre vom inneren Zeugnis des Heiligen Geistes (testimonium spiritus sancti internum). Sie besagt, daß es keinen Beweis für die göttliche Autorität der Bibel gibt außer dem Glaubensbeweis, der Vernunft entzogen ist. Nur der Heilige Geist kann dem Herzen (innerlich) bezeugen, daß die Schrift göttliche Autorität hat. Es ist ein Irrtum, anzunehmen, daß aus diesen Kapiteln auch eine Lehre von der Inspiration der Schrift abgeleitet werden kann.

Zu diesem Thema äußert er sich in Inst. IV,8,1-9. Doch lautet die Kapitelüberschrift "Die Macht der Kirche in Bezug auf Glaubenssätze". Calvin stellt der Lehrautorität der römischen Kirche die der Propheten und Apostel gegenüber und legt dar, wie sie begründet ist. Zur Inspiration werden Aussagen gemacht, jedoch nur ganz knapp. Calvins Inspirationslehre muß, wie auch seine anderen Lehren, aus seinen Kommentaren ergänzt werden.

Das gilt, wie wir sehen werden, auch für die Erörterungen über das Verhältnis von Altem und Neuem Testament, Inst. II,9-11.

Schließlich macht er Inst. IV,1-10 Aussagen über die "Predigt des Evangeliums". Doch wird das Verhältnis von Schrift und Verkündigung dort auch nur teilweise erörtert.

Es ergibt sich, daß unter den Werken Calvins die Institutio zwar am genausten erforscht und am meisten beachtet ist. Aber sie wird in der Forschung oft überbewertet. Sie enthält nicht alle Lehren bzw. diese nicht vollständig. Die Konzentrierung auf die Hauptschrift Calvins kann daher sogar ein Hindernis für die Erforschung seiner Theologie werden. Dies gilt in der bisherigen Forschung für unser Thema.

Als Aufgabe ergibt sich aus dieser Vorüberlegung — da der Lehre vom testimonium spiritus sancti internum nicht weiter nachgegangen werden muß — die Behandlung der folgenden Themen:

    I. Die Einheit der Bibel und die Verschiedenartigkeit ihrer Teile
    II. Heilige Schrift und Verkündigung
    III. Die Inspiration der Heiligen Schrift

Die Grundzüge der Hermeneutik Calvins sind in diesen Themen enthalten; die ganze Hermeneutik kann aber in diesem Rahmen nicht dargestellt werden.[1]

Zweitens, in der Literatur ist Calvins Verständnis der Heiligen Schrift umstritten. Ein klassisches Beispiel ist die Kontroverse zwischen J. A. Cramer und D. J. de Groot. Cramer versucht in seinem Buch "De Heilige Schrift bij Calvijn" (Utrecht 1926), Calvin geradezu zum "Vater der wissenschaftlichen Bibelkritik"[2] zu machen, während de Groot, "Calvijns opvatting over de inspiratie der Heilige Schrift" (Zutphen 1931), bei Calvin eine Verbalinspiration nachzuweisen versucht, die aber keine "mechanische Inspiration" sei. In beiden Fällen ist eine fremde Fragestellung an Calvin herangetragen worden, nämlich die des 19. und 20. Jahrhunderts. Cramer will nachweisen, daß bei Calvin nur die Heilsaussagen der Bibel inspiriert sind.[3] Für De Groot muß dagegen die ganze Bibel von Gott inspiriert sein. Beide suchen ihre Meinung aus Calvins Schriften zu belegen.

Doch Calvin hat nicht im 20. Jahrhundert gelebt, sondern im 16. Jahrhundert. Er kannte wohl das Grundproblem, nämlich die Tatsache, daß sich in der Bibel Gotteswort und Menschenwort findet, und er versuchte — das von Cramer

---

1. Vgl. die Themen bei A. Ganoczy, *St. Scheld, Die Hermeneutik Calvins.* Wiesbaden 1983.

2. Vgl. O. Weber, *Grundlagen der Dogmatik,* Bd. 1, Neukirchen 1955. S. 269, Anm. 1.

3. S. 51ff. u.ö. Vgl. auch J. A. Cramer, *Calvijn en de Heilige Schrift.* Wageningen 1932.

und de Groot richtig gesehen — dafür eine befriedigende Erklärung zu geben. Aber Calvin gibt sie nicht angesichts der neuzeitlichen "historisch-kritischen" Bibelauslegung, und zwar weder zustimmend noch ablehnend. Vielmehr gibt er die Antwort von der reformatorischen Entdeckung der Predigt als Heilsmittel her. Das Verhältnis von Schrift und Verkündigung bestimmt sein Schriftverständnis. Er weist damit auf die damals wie heute zu wenig beachtete Verkündigung in der Bibel hin, die auch das Verständnis der Heiligen Schrift bestimmt.

I. Die Einheit der Bibel und die Verschiedenartigkeit ihrer Teile

Die Überschrift zeigt bereits an, daß die Einheit der Bibel nicht schon mit dem Kanonentscheid gegeben ist. Inhaltlich, und das heißt theologisch, ist die Einheit der Bibel problematisch, wie jede sorgfältige Exegese beweist. Viele Fakten sprechen gegen eine solche Einheitlichkeit: "Bund" und "neuer Bund", "Gesetz" und "Gesetzes Ende", "auserwähltes Volk" der Juden und "erwählte Heiden", Opfergesetze der Mosebücher und das prophetische Wort "Gehorsam ist besser als Opfer" usw. Calvin kennt als sorgfältiger Exeget diese und andere Widersprüche in der Bibel genau. Er weiß: Die Gegensätze beschränken sich nicht auf die beiden Teile der Bibel, Altes und Neues Testament; sie betreffen auch die drei Teile des Alten Testament, Patriarchen, Gesetz und Propheten.

1. Alter und Neuer Bund

Das Thema wird in der Institutio breit abgehandelt; es ist dementsprechend bekannt und muß hier nur kurz zusammengefaßt werden.[4] Das Verhältnis von Altem und Neuem Testament ist das der Steigerung vom Positiv zum Komparativ. Calvin gebraucht auch durchgehend diese Begriffe der Grammatik, um das Verhältnis des Alten zum Neuen Testament auszudrücken: Erwartung Christi einst und "weit mehr Licht" durch die Ankunft Christi,[5] "maßvoll" Gnade einst und "reichlicheren Genuß" der Gnade jetzt,[6] Erwartung Christi einst und Erscheinen "in vollem Glanz" Jetzt.[7] Aus dieser durchgehend

---

4. Vgl. W. H. Neuser, "Theologie des Wortes — Schrift, Verheißung und Evangelium bei Calvin," in *Calvinus Theologus,* Neukirchen 1974, S. 17-37.

5. longe plus lucis; Inst II,9,1, OS III,398,20. Die größere Klarheit des Glaubens im neuen Bund nennt Calvin: comparative, non simpliciter; CO 50,219.

6. modice . . . uberior; Inst II,9,1, OS III,398,29.

7. nunc pleno fulgore; Inst II,9,1, OS III,398,14.

festzuzstedlenden Ausdrucksweise wird auch deutlich, daß Calvin das Heil im Alten Testament nicht als Defizit versteht, sondern als von Gott dort gegeben und also schon vorhanden. Im Neuen Testament ist es klarer und voller offenbart. Die endgültige Herrlichkeit erscheint am Jüngsten Tage; sie ist nur mit dem Superlativ ausdrückbar. Nochmals: Calvin denkt Altes und Neues Testament in der Steigerung vom Positiv zum Komparativ.

Calvin versieht Gottes Offenbarung im alten Bund also nie mit einem "nur", sondern höchstens mit einem "noch nicht". Es gehört daher zu den Grundirrtümern in der Darstellung des Denkens Calvins, wenn bei ihm von "Verheißung" im Alten und "Erfüllung" im Neuen Testament gesprochen wird.

Denn erstens ist bei ihm Verheißung (promissio) (entgegen dem heutigen deutschen Sprachgebrauch) Zusage des vollen gegenwärtigen Heils.[8] Die Zukunft wird die Vervollkommung oder Vollendung (complementum promissionis)[9] dieser Zusage bringen. Die Formel Calvins heißt also nicht "Verheißung und Erfüllung" (promissio et implementum), sondern "Zusage" des Heils damals und "Vervollkommung der Zusage" heute (promissio et complementum promissionis). Sein Grundsatz ist, "daß die Verheißungen des Alten und die des Neuen Bundes dieselben bleiben".[10]

Zweitens werden die Verheißungen des Alten Testaments im Neuen bei Calvin nicht erfüllt, sondern öffentlich bekanntgemacht (promulgare), deutlich gemacht (praestare), sichtbar herausgestellt (exstare).[11] Es wiederholen sich hier — wie nicht anders zu erwarten — die Stufen des Positivs und Komparativs.

Drittens heißt die prophetische Weissagung ('Verheissung') bei Calvin nicht promissio, sondern oraculum oder vaticinium. Ausdrücklich wird hinzugesetzt, daß sie "Weissagung über zukünftige Dinge" ist.[12] Lassen wir Calvin selbst über den Unterschied zwischen Neuem und Altem Testament zu Worte kommen. In Institutio II,11 nennt er bekanntlich fünf Unterschiede: 1. Das Heil wird unter der Gestalt von irdischen Gütern dargestellt; das neue Testament zeigt die geistlichen Güter klarer. 2. Die Verordnungen im alten und neuen Bund verhalten sich wie Schatten und Wirklichkeit einer Sache, Kindheit

8. Ebenso bei Luther, der darum promissio mit Verheißung oder Zusage übersetzt; der Heidelberger Katechismus verwendet auch beide Begriffe.
9. Inst II,9,3, OS III,400,27; Inst II,10,9, OS III,410,13; Inst II,11,4, OS III,427,8. Bei Calvin hat auch implere den Sinn von vollenden. Vgl. W. H. Neuser, *Theologie des Wortes*, S. 24.
10 . . . eadem maneant veteris et novi Testamenti promissiones; Inst II,11,1, OS III,423,14.
11. Inst II,9,2, OS III,399,35, 400,11, 400,12.
12. vaticinia de rebus futuris; Inst IV,8,6, OS V,138,6.

und Erwachsensein. 3. Und die Bünde verhalten sich wie Buchstaben und Geist. 4. Gesetz und Evangelium werden als Knechtschaft und Freiheit bezeichnet. 5. Israel und die Heiden kennzeichnen die beiden Bünde. Alle diese fünf Unterschiede geben wohlbekannte biblisache Begriffe und Sachverhalte wieder. Auch sie versteht Calvin nach dem Grundmuster von Positiv und Komparativ.

Ungeachtet der Redeweise — er kann von Altem und Neuen Testament auch als kleiner und größer (minoris et maioris) oder weniger und mehr (minus et plus) reden[13] — ist die grundsätzliche Frage zu stellen, ob Calvin dieses Verhältnis von altem und neuem Bund statisch oder dynamisch, oder mit anderen Worten ausgedrückt, unveränderlich-ontisch oder geschichtlich-dynamisch versteht. Oder theologisch gefragt: Ist die Heilsgeschichte, die Geschichte vom Anfang des Alten Bundes an bis zur Kirche des Neuen Bundes, eine Geschichte des von Anfang an unveränderlichen Heils, oder ist sie die Geschichte einer fortschreitenden Entwicklung und neuer Offenbarungen Gottes. Nach der Unveränderlichkeit Gottes und seines Handelns ist gefragt.

Die Redeweise eines Fortschrittes vom Positiv zum Komparativ gibt noch keine Antwort auf diese Frage. Denn im Alten Bund kann schon die ganze Gottesoffenbarung vorhanden sein; der Neue Bund wäre dann nur die weitere Ausgestaltung. Auch ein Fortschritt im Alten Bund, also auf den Neuen Bund hin, könnte von Calvin festgestellt und gelehrt werden, das heißt, eine eigenständige Weiterentwicklung wäre im Alten Testament vorhanden. Oder ist im Alten Testament von Anfang an Gottes ganzer Heils-bzw. Gerichtswille schon vorhanden und ausgesagt? Für welche unter diesen Möglichkeiten entscheidet sich Calvin?

Eine Vorentscheidung kann darin liegen, daß er wohl vom "ewigen Gott", aber nicht vom unveränderlichen Gott spricht. Im Zusammenhang der Heilsgeschichte redete er vielmehr von "dem Gott, der sich immer ähnlich ist" (similis).[14] Die überschrift "Von der Ähnlichkeit (similitudo) des Alten und Neuen Testaments" (Inst. II,8,2) ist auf den Gottesbegriff übertragen. Diese Aussage ist in der Forschung übersehen worden.

2. Der ewige Bund Gottes und die Bundesschlüsse[15]

Calvin stehen mehrere Begriffe zur Verfügung, um die Einheit der Bibel auszudrücken. Der meistgebrauchte ist "Bund". Calvin lehrt, es gebe nur einen

13. Komm. zu Joh 1,18, CO 47,19; Komm. zu 1. Kor 10,3, CO 49,454.
14 Inst I,4,3; OS III,42,30. Vgl. Komm. zu Hebr 1,1 und Jer 31,31.
15. Das Material findet sich bei W. de Greef, *Calvijn en het Oude Testament,* Groningen 1984, 172-91.

einzigen Bund zwischen Gott und den Menschen.[16] Er selbst zählt aber als
Exeget viele Bünde auf: der "erste" ist mit Abraham,[17] der "zweite" mit
Mose,[18] der "dritte" mit David,[19] dann der Bund geschlossen in Christus.
Den einen Bund gewinnt Calvin, indem er den Bund mit Abraham einen
"ewigen" Bund nennt, der in Mose und David "erneuert"[20] und in Christus
"wieder zum Vorschein kommt".[21] Ewig ist er, weil der Abrahamsbund sich
laut Genesis 15,3 auf Abraham und seine Nachkommen, also letztlich auf
Christus und die Kirche bezieht. Calvin argumentiert statisch, wie die Begriffe
bekräftigen (confirmare), bestätigen (sancire), besiegeln (consignare),
befestigen (stabilire), erneuern (renovare) u.a.m.[22] beweisen, die Identität des
ewigen Bundes Gottes mit Abraham mit den nachfolgenden Bundesschlüssen
aussagen. Die Begriffe beziehen sich ebenso auf den Mosebund wie auf denjenigen mit David und dem in Christus geschlossenen. Der "ewige Bund"
besteht in den nachfolgenden Bundesschlüssen fort, aber nicht unverändert.

Calvin gebraucht zur Beschreibung des Verhältnisses zwischen diesen
Bünden einen philosophischen Begriff: Der Bund mit den alttestamentlichen
Vätern war "in der Substanz" (substantia, in re) identisch mit dem Bund in
Christus, nur die Ausführung (administratio) war verschieden.[23] Eine Ver-
änderung der Heilsgeschichte durch die Bundesschlüsse will Calvin deutlich
nicht lehren; er greift darum auf den Begriff der unveränderlichen Substanz
zurück, welchem Aristoteles den Begriff der veränderlichen "Form" zuordnet.
Doch will Calvin nicht philosophisch argumentieren, sondern theologisch.
Zum "neuen Bund" (Jer 31,31) erklärt er: "Die [neue] Form besteht nicht nur
in Worten, sondern zuerst in Christus, dann in der Gnade des Heiligen Geistes
und in der ganzen äußeren Weise der Verkündigung. Die Substanz aber, das
Wesen, bleibt dasselbe. Unter Substanz verstehe ich die Lehre, weil Gott im
Evangelium nichts vorträgt, was das Gesetz nicht auch enthält."[24] Diese

---

16. Inst II,10,2; OS III,404,5.
17. Komm. zu Deut 32,101, CO 25,363; Komm. zu Jer 31,31, CO 38,688; Komm.
zu Ps 105,8, CO 32,101.
18. Komm. zu Gal 3,17, CO 50,214.
19. Komm. zu Jes 55,3, CO 37,285.
20. renovare: Komm. zu Exod 19,1, CO 24,192; Komm. zu Deut 33,1, CO 25,383;
Komm. zu Ezech 16,8, CO 40,342.
21. reperire; Komm. zu Ps 89,4, CO 31,813.
22. Komm. zu Exod 19,1, CO 24,192; Komm. zu Deut 33,1, CO 25,383; Komm. zu
Ps 111,9, CO 32,170; Komm. zu Jes 55,3, CO 37,285; Komm. zu Jer 31,31-32, CO 38,688;
Komm. zu Ezech 16,8, CO 40,342.
23 Inst II,10,2; OS III,404,7.
24. Forma autem haec non tantum posita est in verbis, sed primum in Christo, deinde
in gratia spiritus sancti, et tota docendi ratione externa: substantia autem eadem manet.
Komm. zu Jer 31,31, CO 38,688. Vgl. Komm. zu Jes 2,3, CO 36,64.

Definition ist konkreter als das Bild vom Hausbau und Fundament oder die Erklärung der veränderlichen "Form" durch den Begriff Ausführung (administratio), die in den Bundesschlüssen unterschiedlich ist. Calvin würde übrigens einwenden, die Rede von der veränderlichen Form sei biblisch; sie werde Hebr. 1.1 ("multifariam multisque modis") gebraucht.[25]

Wenn aber die veränderliche Form des Bundes "Christus, die Gnade des Heiligen Geistes und die äußere Art der Verkündigung" im Neuen Testament ist, enthält dann der Bundesbegriff Calvins nicht doch einen Fortschritt in der Offenbarung Gottes und hat dieser dann nicht doch den Karakter einer fortschreitenden, sich verändernden Heilsgeschichte? Diese Frage betrifft nicht nur den gerade erwähnten Übergang vom alten Bund zum neuen. Auch zum Abrahambund kommt im Mosebund etwas Neues hinzu, nämlich das Gesetz.

3. Abraham und Mose

Gemäß der Aussage Calvins ist die Gesetzgebung nicht mehr als eine besondere Ausführung (administratio) des Bundeswillens Gottes. Nach Calvins Meinung ist auch das Gesetz nichts anderes als eine Bekräftigung (confirmatio) des ewigen Bundes Gottes mit Abraham.[26] Zur Ausführung (administratio) des Bundes gehören aber nicht etwa die äußeren Umstände des Bundesschlußes am Horeb. Calvin verwendet, den Ausdruck administratio offensichtlich, weil 2. Kor. 3,7 das Gesetz eine "Hilfeleistung zum Tode" (mortis administratio) genannt, wird.[27] Das Gesetz ist, also eine neue Weise, wie Gott die Menschen zum Heil führt. Calvin ist der Gedanke eines Fortschritts nicht fremd: der Abrahambund ist "durch die lange Zeit und die Nachlässigkeit der Menschen abgenutzt worden" und mußte durch Mose "erneuert werden".[28] Es überwiegt aber bei Calvin die heilsgeschichtliche Kontinuität.

4. Mose und Christus

Wenn er auf das Verhältnis des Mosebundes zum Christusbund zu sprechen kommt, wird die Diskontinuität nicht verschwiegen: "Gewiß, da derselbe Bund uns und dem alten Volk gemeinsam ist, besteht kein Zweifel, daß diejenigen

25. Komm. zu Hebr 1,1, CO 55,9.
26. Komm. zu Jes 25,3, CO 37,285.
27. Vgl. Inst II,7,7, OS III,333; II,7,13, OS III,338. Im Komm. zu 2. Kor 3,7 übersetzt er: ministerium mortis; CO 50,42.
28. sed quia longo tempore et incuria hominum obsoleverat, iterum renovari necesse erat; Komm. zu Exod 19,1, CO 24,192.

das Leben erwählt haben, die einst die Lehre des Mose angenommem haben. Indessen, insofern dessen Sendung gesondert ist vom Evangelium, besteht sie mehr in dem ihm besonders auferlegten Amt, sodaß der Unterschied zwischen ihm und Christus klar hervortritt."[29] Sofort macht Calvin aber geltend: Mose ist zugleich ein Verkündiger der Barmherzigkeit Gottes, weil er nach Gal. 3,24 ein Zuchtmeister auf Christus hin ist und er durch das Gesetz die Sünde aufdeckt.[30] Das Gesetz enthält beides, Drohungen und Zusagen Gottes.[31] Es fällt auf, daß Calvin Gesetz und Christus darum aufeinander bezieht, weil er die Kritik der Propheten am Gesetz im Blick hat, die geistliche Bedeutung des Gesetzes hervorheben (Jer 31,31; Ps 19,8f.; 119,105).[32] Hinzu kommt, daß Christus nach Röm 10,4 finis legis ist. Calvin versteht "finis", anders als Luther, zuerst als Ziel und Absicht und dann erst als Ende. In diesem Punkt besteht ein grundlegender theologischer Unterschied zwischen den beiden Reformatoren.[33]

5. "Mose und die Propheten"

Das bereits erwähnte Thema hat für Calvin große Bedeutung; es bestimmt in erheblichem Maße sein Schriftverständnis. Calvin bezieht sich auf die biblischen Begriff "Gesetz und Propheten" oder "Mose und die Propheten".

a. Mose- und Davidbund

Der heilsgeschichtliche Fortschritt zwischen dem Mose- und Davidbund ist besonders zu beachten. Zwar ist der Davidbund geschichtlich nicht festzumachen; nur Psalm 89,4 (vgl. 132,12; Jes. 55,3) erwähnt ihn. Wenn ich recht sehe, lehrt Calvin als erster einen Davidbund,[34] ein Umstand, der in der Forschung nicht beachtet ist. Für Calvin ist der Davidbund nicht nur von besonderer

---

29. Et certe quum idem foedus nobis et veteri populo sit commune, dubium non est quin vitam elegerint quicunque olim amplexi sunt Mosis doctrinam. Interim, quatenus separata fuit eius legatio ab evangelio, magis in munere sibi peculiariter iniuncto insistit, ut inter ipsum et Christum clarius appareat discrimen. Komm zu Deut 30,19, CO 25,57f.

30. Praef. zu Mosis libri V., CO 24,7-8.

31. Minae et promissiones; Prael. Hos 1,2, CO 42,198; u Komm. zu Jes, Arg., CO 36,9.

32. Komm. zu Deut 30,6, CO 25,54; Inst II,7,12, OS III,338,9-17.

33. S. H. A. Oberman S. p. 126; vgl. Praef. zu Mosis libri V., CO 24,7-8, Finis et usus legis, CO 24,725-28.

34. Bullinger kennt in seinem Hausbuch nur einen Bund Gottes mit Adam, Noah, Abraham, Mose und durch Jesus Christus; vgl. G. Schrenk, Gottesreich und Bund im älteren Protestantismus, Gütersloh 1923, 41.

Bedeutung, weil dieser Bund auch mit allen nachfolgenden Königen geschlossen ist und in Christus gipfelt.[35] In David erreicht der Bund im Alten Testament seinen Höhepunkt: "Zwar hatte ihn der Herr mit Abraham geschlossen, durch Mose dann bestätigt und zuletzt endgültig besiegelt in Davids Hand, daß er dann auf ewig bleibe."[36] Nur die Ankündigung des neuen Bundes Jer. 31,31 kommt dem Davidbund gleich.

David und Jeremia sind nach Calvins Meinung beide Propheten. Im Psalmenkommentar erhält David durchgehend den Titel "Prophet", obwohl das Alte Testament ihn nicht für David gebraucht. Doch zitiert Matthäus zweimal Psalmworte eines "Propheten".[37] Da David der Verfasser der Psalmen ist, kommt ihm dieser Titel nach Calvins Ansicht zu. Calvin liegt viel daran, den prophetischen Karakter der Psalmen herauszustellen. Denn sie enthalten viele messianische Weissagungen und David ist Prototyp des Königtums Christi.[38]

b. Die Propheten und das Gesetz

Die Propheten stehen auf einer höheren Erkenntnisstufe als die Patriarchen und Mose bzw. das Gesetz. Im Vorwort zum Jesajakommentar geht Calvin breit auf das Verhältnis der Propheten zum Gesetz ein. "Die Propheten bringen das vollere und überschwenglichere Zeugnis des Gnadenbundes", heißt es dort.[39] Calvin führt dies weiter aus:

> Was aber nun den Gnadenbund betrifft, den Gott einst mit den Patriarchen geschlossen, so sind die Propheten hier viel deutlicher und befestigen das Volk darin. Immer wieder rufen sie ihn den Frommen ins Gedächtnis, wenn sie trösten wollen. Sie künden das Erscheinen Christi, der nicht minder die Grundlage dieses Bundes war wie auch das Bindeglied des wechselseitigen Bandes zwischen Gott und Volk, weshalb die ganze Summe der Verheißungen auf ihn zurückzuführen ist.[40]

35. Komm. Ps zu 89,4, CO 31,813; vgl. W. de Greef, a.a.O. 176f., 182ff.

36. Pepigit quidem Dominus cum Abrahamo, inde per Mosen confirmavit, postremo in manu Davidis sanxit hoc idem foedus, ut aeternum esset. Komm. zu Jes 55,3, CO 37,285.

37. Matth 13,35 (= Ps 78,2) und 27,35 (= Ps 22,19); vgl. die Kommentare zu diesen Stellen.

38. Vgl. W. de Greef, a.a.O., 67ff., 176f. "Die Psalmen rechne ich zu den Propheten, weil das, was wir den Propheten zuschreiben, auch ihnen gemeinsam ist." Inst IV,8,6; OS V,138,13-14.

39. (Prophetae) plenioraque gratuiti foederis et uberiora testimonia afferunt. Komm. zu Jes, Argum.; CO 36,19.

40. Quod autem ad gratuitum foedus attinet olim cum patriarchis a Deo percussum, prophetae sunt multo clariores, atque in eo populum magis confirmant. Semper enim illuc pios revocant dum volunt eos consolari, et Christi adventum proponunt, qui et foederis erat

Auffallend ist, daß dieselben Begriffe für den Unterschied zwischen Patriarchen bzw. Gesetz und Propheten angewandt werden, die Calvin für den Unterschied zwischen Altem und Neuem Testament verwendet. Calvin kennt also zwischen Gesetz und Propheten einen Offenbarungsfortschritt. Im Vorwort zum Hoseakommentar nennt er die Propheten Ausleger des Gesetzes (legis interpretes). Er belegt es so:

> Dies ist aber die Summe des Gesetzes, daß Gott sein Volk, das er an Sohnes Statt angenommen hat, durch seine Macht regieren will. . . . Die Propheten schärfen außerdem die Gebote über den wahren und reinen Gottesdienst ein, (nämlich) über die Nächstenliebe. Sie unterweisen schließlich das Volk in einem heiligen und frommen Leben. Dann legen sie die Gnade Gottes dar. Und weil es keine Hoffnung auf eine Versöhnung mit Gott gibt, es sei denn durch einen Mittler, stellen sie deshalb immer jenen Messias in den Mittelpunkt, den der Herr schon vorher verheißen hatte.[41]

Die Propheten haben also eine Botschaft, die weit mehr als das Gesetz auf die Botschaft des Neuen Testamentes ausgerichtet ist. Wie nun fast schon zu erwarten, macht Calvin auch hier geltend, Gesetz und Propheten seien nicht voneinander zu trennen; die Propheten seien nur der "Anhang" zum Gesetz und dessen "reichere Auslegung".[42] Sie haben aber doch die reichhaltigere Botschaft[43] und sind "Ausleger des Gesetzes".

Es ist deutlich geworden, daß Calvin einen Fortschritt in der Heilsgeschichte kennt. Er unterscheidet mehrere Perioden: Die Patriarchen (insbesondere Abraham), das Gesetz, die Propheten (zu denen Mose, die Geschichtsbücher und David gehören), der Täufer und schließlich die Vollendung in Christus.[44] Die nachfolgende Periode hat einen höheren Erkenntnisstand als die vorausgehende. Darum sind ihre Vertreter deren "Ausleger".[45] Eine wichtige Struktur des Schriftverständnisses Calvins ist damit aufgedeckt und zugleich ein wichtiger Grundsatz seiner Bibelauslegung.

---

fundamentum et vinculum mutuae inter Deum et populum coniunctionis: quapropter omnis summa promissionum ad eum referenda. Komm. zu Jes, Argum.; CO 36,22.

41. Haec autem summa legis est, quod Deus populum, quem sibi adoptavit, vult regere suo imperio. . . . Iam prophetae inculcant praecepta legis de vero et puro Dei cultu, de caritate: instituunt denique populum in sancta et pia vita: deinde proponunt gratiam Domini. Et quia nulla est spes reconciliationis cum Deo nisi per mediatorem, ideo semper afferunt in medium illum Messiam quem Dominus iam ante pollicitus erat. Komm. zu Hosea, Argum., CO 42,198.

42. Komm. zu Matth 3,11, CO 45,108; ebenso Komm. zu Luk 24,27, CO 45,807.

43. Inst IV,8,6; OS V,138,8-9: illustrior doctrina et amplior.

44. Vgl. Inst IV,8,6, OS V, 137f.

45. Belege bei W. de Greef, a.a.O., 57. Auch die Propheten und David waren Ausleger des Gesetzes; Inst IV,8,6, OS V,138,2-4.17.

6. Biblische Theologie

Calvin versteht die Bibel noch als eine Einheit, das heißt, er entwickelt eine biblische Theologie. In der heutigen Zeit, in der diese weitgehend verloren gegangen ist, verdient diese Tatsache Aufmerksamkeit. Die heutige kritische Theologie vermag die Kluft zwischen Altem und Neuem Testament nicht mehr zu schließen. Calvin vermag es, indem er das von Gott im alten Bund geschenkte Heil nicht darum abwertet, weil es im neuen Bund übertroffen wird. Auch kennt er einen Forschritt in der Heilsgeschichte, und zwar schon im Alten Testament. Er nimmt damit die Unterschiede in der alttestamentlichen Botschaft nicht nur ernst, er versucht sie auch dogmatisch zu fassen.

Das Problem ist aus heutiger Sicht die Einheit der biblischen Lehre. Calvin sieht sie darin, daß die Testamente von demselben Gott, von demselben Christus und demselben Heil sprechen.[46] Dabei ist Christus nicht etwa im Alten Testament nur verborgen vorhanden. Selbst Eph. 3,4f. sagt vom "Geheimnis Christi", daß es den Propheten offenbar war; und im Alten Testament gibt es Anzeichen des Königtums Christi und Hinweise auf das Kommen des Messias.[47] Sicherlich kann Calvin noch andere Lehren anführen, die in der Bibel durchgehend vorhanden sind. Man könnte sie das statische Element seiner biblischen Theologie nennen. Doch trifft dies auf keine der drei genannten Lehren zu, weder auf den Gottesnamen, noch auf Christus, noch auf das Heil. Diese Lehren sind geschichtlich-dynamisch verstanden, das heißt, als heilsgeschichtlich sich entwickelnde Lehren. Auf sie treffen die Deutungen durch Schatten / Licht, Substanz / Form, leiblich / geistlich, Zusage / Vervollkommnung usw. zu.

Der radikalste hermeneutische Schlüssel ist sicherlich der, daß die Vertreter der späteren heilsgeschichtlichen Periode "Ausleger" der früheren sind. Ausleger sind die Propheten, Paulus, Petrus und vor allem Christus.[48] Doch will Calvin durch diese "Ausleger" keine Auslegung des Alten Testaments vom Neuen her lehren. Er bleibt bei seiner Zuordnung der Bünde nach dem Schema Positiv / Komparativ, und bei seiner heilsgeschichtlichen Periodisierung (Patriarchen, Gesetz, Propheten, Johannes der Täufer, Christus). Die Apostel bilden keine neue Periode, weil sie keinen anderen Auftrag haben als die Propheten, "nämlich daß sie die alte Schrift auslegen und nachweisen, in Christus sei vollendet, was dort überliefert wird".[49]

Calvin postuliert nicht einfach die Einheit. Exegetisch gesehen hält er

---

46. Vgl. W. de Greef, a.a.O., 210.
47. Komm. zu Eph 3,4; CO 51,179f. Vgl. W. de Greef, a.a.O., 211.
48. Stellenangaben bei W. de Greef, a.a.O., 57, Anm. 178-80.
49. Inst IV,8,8; OS V,140,3-4.

die 'messianischen Texte' Gen. 3,15 und 49,8-12 nicht für Hinweise auf Christus.[50] Auch weist er z.B. nach, daß die Stellen Psalm 40,7-9 in Hebr. 10,5, Jesaja 9,1-2 in Matth. 4,15-16 und Jesaja 52,7 in Röm. 10,15, Jesaia 64,4 in 1. Kor. 2,9 "verdreht" wiedergegeben sind.[51] Er versucht nicht zu harmonisieren.

Stellt man abschließend die Frage, wie er die Aussage versteht, Gott sei "ewig" und doch "sich selbst immer ähnlich", so schließt diese Aussage die Deutung des einen Bundes als eines unveränderlichen Bundes aus. Der Fortschritt in der Offenbarung Gottes ist ein solcher, in dem Gott sich immer ähnlich bleibt. Auch hinter diesem Gottesbegriff steht Calvins Beschreibung des Bundes durch Aussagen im Positiv und Komparativ. Theologisch gesehen hilft der Begriff der Ähnlichkeit (similitudo) allerdings nicht weiter.

Aufs ganze gesehen, halten sich bei Calvin Kontinuität und Diskontinuität in der Heilsgeschichte die Waage. In dem oftgebrauchten Begriffspaar Substanz und Form dominiert die Unveränderlichkeit, in dem Begriff Ausleger (interpres) der vorangehenden Periode die Veränderlichkeit. Die mehrmalige Aussage, "die Gnade war gewissermaßen ungewiß bis zur Ankunft Christi",[52] drückt am stärksten den Bruch aus, den die Christusoffenbarung gebrachte hat.

II. Schrift und Verkündigung

Calvin unterscheidet selbstverständlich zwischen beiden. In der Institutio erwähnt Calvin oft die Schrift als Ganze (scriptura), wie auch die Verkündigung (annunciatio, praedicatio). Doch hat er, wie sich zeigen wird, die Verkündigung immer im Blick, wenn er über die Heilige Schrift redet. Unsere These ist, daß Calvin an keinen Lehraussagen über die Bibel interessiert ist, die nicht zugleich die Verkündigung mitbetreffen. Er betrachtet die Schrift nicht aus heutigem Blickwinkel heraus, das heißt, heilige Schrift und Predigt werden nicht zuerst einmal getrennt und jede für sich betrachtet, um dann einander zugeordnet zu werden. Calvin geht von ihrer Zusammengehörigkeit aus; er setzt diese voraus. Wer ihm also Fragen zum Verständnis der Heiligen Schrift stellt, die ohne Bezug auf die Verkündigung und Anwendung der Schrift sind, der stellt diese Fragen nicht im Sinne Calvins. Er würde aus ihm einen Theologen der pro-

50. Gen 3,15 besagt nach Calvin, daß das "Menschengeschlecht" den Satan überwältigen wird. Vgl. W. de Greef, a.a.O., 62f.

51. CO 31,412; 36,189; 37,248; 37,408 / 9.

52. Gratia quoddammodo suspensa erat usque ad Christi adventum; Komm. zu Kol 2,14, CO 52,108. Ähnlich Komm. zu Apg 13,32, CO 48,299, und zu Gen 49,10, CO 23,958. Vgl. I. J. Hesselink, "Calvin und Heilsgeschichte," in *Oeconomia. Heilsgeschichte als Thema der Theologie, Festschrift zum 65. Geb. O. Cullmanns,* Hamburg 1967, S. 168f.

testantischen Scholastik machen oder mit einer modernen "Sach"lichkeit an ihn herantreten, statt bei ihm reformatorische Worttheologie zu suchen.

1. Wort Gottes (verbum Dei)

Befragt werden soll der Sprachgebrauch in der Institutio und in ihr besonders der Abschnitt I,6-9, weil dort die Heilige Schrift direkt das Thema ist und über sie dogmatisch ausgewogen gesprochen wird. Der Sprachgebrauch ist dort also kein zufälliger; andere Texte wären dem Einwand ausgesetzt, für Calvin untypisch zu sein.

Es erscheinen nur zwei Definitionen, welche die "Schrift" — Calvin verwendet das Wort Bibel nicht — als Ganzes beschreiben:

1. "Die Schrift ist von Gott her herabgeflossen".[53]
2. "Die Schrift ist Wort Gottes".[54]

Calvin läßt aber solche Ist-Aussagen nicht stehen, sondern löst sie sofort auf und erklärt ihren Sinn.

1. "Die Schrift enthält Offenbarungsworte (Gottes) ... , die vom Himmel herabgeflossen sind."[55] Oder: "Das Gesetz, die Prophezeiungen und das Evangelium sind von Gott ausgegangen".[56] Oracula Dei und scriptura werden im erstgenannten Zitat unterschieden. Die oracula sind *in* der Schrift enthalten. Ebenso sind lex, prophetia und evangelium von Gott ausgeströmt. Auch sie sind nicht einfach mit der Schrift identisch. Das Problem der Inspiration der Schrift ist angesprochen.

2. Die Schrift ist gemäß der zweiten Definition Rede (sermo) oder Wort Gottes (verbum Dei). Aber dieses verbum Dei, so heißt es im selben Zusammenhang, muß man "hören".[57] Das Wort Gottes ist also geschriebenes und verkündigtes Wort.

Calvin gebraucht den Begriff Schrift (scriptura) in der Institutio oft.[58] Doch der von ihm bei weitem meistgebrauchte Ausdruck ist Wort Gottes (verbum

---

53. scriptura a Deo fluxisse; Inst I,7,2, OS III,67,3.

54. scripturam esse verbum Dei; Inst I,8,13, OS III,81,29, scripturam sermonem Dei esse; Inst I,7,1, OS III,65,8.

55. scripturae extant oracula ... e caelo fluxisse; Inst I,7,1, OS III,65,12 u.15.

56. Legem, Prophetas et Evangelium ab eo manasse; Inst I,7,4, OS III,69,14.

57. aures tamen praecipue arrigere convenit ad verbum; Inst I,6,2, OS III,63,1, ad verbum audientiam; Inst I,9,3, OS III,85,2. Qui loquitur loquatur tamquam sermones Dei [1. Petr 4,11], Inst IV,8,9, OS V,140,21.

58. F. L. Battles, *A computerized concordance to Institutio christianae religionis 1559* (usw.), Pittsburgh 1972, führt 548 Stellen an.

Dei).[59] Es ist nicht nur der Oberbegriff, sondern es faßt auch Schrift (scriptura) und Verkündigung (annuntiatio) oder Predigt (praedicatio) in einem Begriff zusammen. Die moderne Gegenüberstellung von Schrift und Verkündigung kennt er also nicht. In unserer Zeit ist die Bibel Gegenstand der wissenschaftlichen Erforschung. Die Predigt hingegen gehört in den Bereich der subjektiven Erkenntnis; sie ist bestenfalls Übertragung biblischer Sachverhalte auf das gegenwärtige Leben. Daß die Bibel selbst auf Verkündigung angelegt ist, wird heute zwar registriert, bestimmt jedoch in der Regel nicht das Schriftverständnis. Nur die kerygmatische Theologie[60] nimmt den Verkündigungskarakter des Neuen Testaments ernst. Sie definiert aber das Kerygma der Schrift so, wie es heute nach ihrer Meinung verkündigt werden muß und wird so dem Wortlaut der Bibel nicht gerecht. Calvin will beides gewahrt wissen, den Inhalt der Heiligen Schrift und ihre Ausrichtung auf die Verkündigung.

Er verwendet noch weitere Allgemeinbegriffe, die andere übergreifen: doctrina, evangelium, testimonium.

2. *Lehre (doctrina)*

Der Begriff Lehre (doctrina) wird von ihm in der Institutio sehrt häufig verwendet.[61] Die Lehre wird meistens himmlische Lehre (doctrina coelestis) genannt. Damit wird klargestellt, daß sie aus der Schrift und also von Gott stammt. Der doctrina coelestis entspricht das verbum dei. Doctrina ist wie verbum Dei ein Allgemeinbegriff, dessen Bezug zur heiligen Schrift und zur Verkündigung der Erklärung bedarf.

Das Verhältnis der doctrina zur scriptura sacra drückt Calvin in Inst. I,6 und 7 folgendermaßen aus: "Niemand kann auch nur den geringsten Vorgeschmack richtiger und heilsamer Lehre bekommen, der nicht ein Schüler der Schrift gewesen ist".[62] Die Schrift ist eine "Beglaubigung der himmlischen Lehre".[63] Die "Glaubwürdigkeit der Lehre" ist mit der Glaubwürdigkeit der Schrift gegeben.[64] Oder: "In der Schrift sind deutliche Zeichen des redenden Gottes zu sehen, aus denen hervorgeht, daß ihre Lehre himmlisch ist."[65]

---

59. F. L. Battles, *Concordance,* führt 1240 Stellen an; hinzu kommen sermo und die Verben, die das Sprechen Gottes ausdrücken.

60. Vgl. Artikel "Kerygma." *EKL* 2,592ff.

61. F. L. Battles, *Concordance,* führt 438 Stellen an; hinzu kommt docere.

62. nec quenquam posse vel minimum gustum rectae sanaeque doctrinae percipere, nisi qui Scripturae fuerit discipulus; Inst I,6,3, OS III,63,7-9.

63. caelestis doctrinae consignatio; Inst I,6,3, OS III,63,19.

64. Inst I,7,4; OS III,68,28ssq.: fidem doctrinae.

65. manifesta signa loquentis Dei conspici in Scriptura, ex quibus pateat caelestem esse eius doctrinam; Inst I,7,4, OS III,69,18-20.

Doctrina coelestis bezeichnet den göttlichen Inhalt der Schrift. Scriptura und doctrina scripturae[66] sind aber nicht identisch. Die Schrift ist "Beglaubigung der himmischen Lehre".[67] Es gibt — offensichtlich in der Schrift — "die prophetische und apostolische Lehre"[68] oder Christi "Lehre von Glaube und Buße".[69] Die doctrina faßt also den Inhalt der Schrift nach Verfasser — oder Sachaussagen zusammen. Andererseits ist die himmische Lehre von der Schrift nicht zu trennen. Wir Menschen kommen nur durch die Schrift zu dieser himmlischen Lehre.

Die "Lehre der Schrift" ist jedoch immer "heilsame Lehre". Calvin will "Lehre" im Sinne der Pastoralbriefe verstanden wissen. Nicht das Lehrgebäude und Lehrgefüge steht bei ihm im Vordergrund, sondern ihre Bezogenheit auf das Heil der Menschen.

Es verwundert nicht, daß Lehre deshalb mit der Predigt engverbunden ist. In Institutio IV,1 bis 3, wo nicht die Schrift, sondern die Verkündigung das Thema ist, bezeichnet doctrina entweder die Predigt der biblischen Botschaft oder Inhalt und Zusammenfassung der Bibel. So ist den "Pastoren" die "Predigt der himmlischen Lehre" aufgetragen.[70] Im Alten Testament wird die Lehre "durch den Mund der Priester bekanntgemacht", die das Amt der himmlischen Lehre" versehen.[71] Im Neuen Testament "unterweisen" die Pastoren "mit der Lehre von Christus das Volk zur wahren Frömmigkeit".[72]

Die Formel des Artikels 7 der Augsburger Konfession, "Predigt des Evangeliums und Verwaltung der Sakramente", kann Calvin auch mit den Worten "Verwaltung der Lehre und der Sakramente" wiedergeben.[73] Er wechselt mit dieser Formel von der Funktion der Lehre, nämlich der Predigt, zum Inhalt der Lehre über. Er unterscheidet anschließend die "Lehren, die zu wissen notwendig sind," von denjenigen, "über die zwischen den Kirchen Meinungsverschiedenheiten herrschen, die aber die Einheit im Glauben nicht zerreißen". Er zählt die betreffenden Lehren auf.[74] Da Calvin den Predigtkarakter der Lehre und die Begrenzung der Lehre auf die 'heilsame Lehre' festhält, kann er den Vertretern der späteren Lehrorthodoxie nicht zugerechnet werden.

---

66. Inst I,9,1; OS III,82,5-6.
67. obsignatio caelestis doctrinae; Inst I,6,3, OS III,63,18-19.
68. Inst 1,7,2; OS 111,66,19.
69. Inst I,6,2; OS III,62,16-17.
70. caelestie doctrinae praedicatio; Inst IV,1,5, OS V,8,8-9.
71. Inst IV,1,5; OS V,8,23. Zeile 27: colestis doctrinae ministerium.
72. Inst IV,3,6; OS V,48,26-27.
73. Inst IV,1,12; OS V,16,4-5.
74. Inst IV,1,12; OS V,16,7-12. Vgl. Inst IV,2,1-2.

3. Zeugnis (testimonium) und Evangelium

Ebenso wie "Wort Gottes" und "Lehre" sind auch Zeugnis (testimonium) und Evangelium (evangelium) sowohl Begriffe, die den Inhalt der Bibel angeben, wie auch Termini der Verkündigung. Calvin kennt noch die biblische Bedeutung von 'euangelion' als verkündigte frohe Botschaft.[75] Das Evangelium gibt es jedoch nur im Neuen Testament. Calvin hält streng an dem Wort Luk. 16,16 fest: "Das Gesetz und die Propheten galten bis auf Johannes; von da an wird das Evangelium vom Reich Gottes verkündigt."[76] Das "Zeugnis" ist allerdings immer an eine menschliche Person gebunden, den Zeugen (testis). Er gibt Zeugnis von einem Wort oder einer Tat Gottes. Die Verfasser der biblischen Bücher oder von ihnen genannte Personen kommen damit in den Blick. Das Problem der göttlichen Inspiration ihrer Schriften gestellt.

III. Die Inspiration der Heiligen Schrift

Es gehört zu den Grundaussagen Calvins über die Heilige Schrift, daß den Verfassern der biblischen Bücher vom Heiligen Geist eingegeben sei (surgere), was sie sagen und schreiben sollen. Die Schrift ist also "göttlich inspiriert". Der Hauptbeleg ist der locus classicus 2. Tim. 3,16, in dem die Schrift "vom Geist Gottes eingegeben" genannt wird. Mehrmals heißt es an anderer Stelle im Neuen Testament, der Heilige Geist habe im Psalm 69,26 und 109,8 (Apg. 1,16) "durch den Mund Davids vorausgesagt", oder "David spricht durch den Heiligen Geist" im Psalm 110,1 (Mk 12,36; Mt 22,43) oder der Geist spricht "durch den Propheten", gemeint ist Jesaja 6,9 (Apg. 28,25).

Calvin notiert diese biblischen Aussagen über das Geistwirken genau und überträgt sie auf andere Bibelstellen, wenn er deren Autorität und Bedeutung als Gottes Wort an den Leser unterstreichen will. Im Blick auf Röm. 5,10 und an anderen Stellen über das Werk Christi heißt es: "Der Geist spricht in der Schrift".[77] Oder zu 2. Thess. 2,3: "Der Geist hat genau durch den Mund des Paulus geweissagt".[78] Oder zu Phil. 1,6: "Der Geist pflegt so über die letzte Ankunft Christi zu sprechen".[79] Viele weitere Beispiele könnten angeführt werden.[80]

---

75. Inst IV,1,6, OS V,11,18 u.22-23; IV,1,13, OS V,17,10; IV,1,14, OS V,18,31-32 u.ö.
76. Inst II,7,16; II,9,4.
77. Inst II,16,2; OS III,483,20.
78. Inst IV,9,6; OS V,155,34.
79. Komm. zu Phil 1,6; CO 52,9.
80. Komm. zu Kol 1,20; CO 52,59: spiritus pronuntiat. Komm. zu Gen 49,10; CO 23,958.

Schriftwort und Geistzeugnis gehören für Calvin zusammen. Doch identifiziert er beide keineswegs. Er verbindet Schrift und Geist nur in bestimmten Fällen, das heißt, er spricht differenziert über sie, wennimmer er beide aufeinander bezieht. Erst wenn seine Aussageweise zum Thema Schriftwort und Geistzeugnis genau analysiert sind, tritt die Eigenart seiner Inspirationslehre zu Tage. Seine Auslegung des locus classicus deckt sie bereits auf.

1. 2. *Timotheus 3,16*

Die einzige Stelle, die die Schrift geistgewirkt nennt, 2. Tim 3,16, verstehet er im Kommentar zur Stelle nicht als eine Aussage über das Wesen und die Beschaffenheit des Schriftwortes, sondern als eine solche über ihre Autorität: "Um die Autorität der Schrift sicherzustellen, lehrt Paulus, diese Autorität sei göttlich inspiriert."[81] Die Autorität der Schrift stellt Calvin darum heraus, weil er sicherstellen will, daß die Verfasser nicht aus eigener Autorität reden. "Wir wissen, Gott spricht zu uns, und wir haben uns gewiß überzeugt, daß die Propheten nicht aus eigener Meinung geredet haben, sondern Werkzeuge des Heiligen Geistes waren und nur vortrugen, was ihnen göttlich aufgetragen (mandare) war."[82] Die Aussage 2. Tim 3,16 über die Inspiration ist für Calvin daher nicht eine solche über das Buch des Alten Testaments, sondern über seine Verfasser. Er weiß als Exeget, daß das Alte Testament Gesetz (Mose) und Propheten umfaßt; deren Verkündigung (doctrina) wird 2. Tim 3,16 behandelt. "Wer also in den Schriften sich bewegen will, bei dem soll das vor allem feststehen, daß Gesetz und Prophetien keine Lehre sind, die dem Belieben der Menschen entsprungen ist, sondern die vom Heiligen Geist diktiert ist."[83] Calvin geht also noch einen Schritt weiter: Nicht die einzelnen Schriften, sondern ihre "Lehre" sind inspiriert. In dieser Weise setzt Calvin im Kommentar zu 1. Timotheus seine Auslegung fort. Er betont sodann vor allem den Nutzen (usus) im zweiten Teil des Verses 2. Tim 3,16: "Alle Schrift . . . ist nützlich zur Lehre, zur Überführung, zur Besserung, zur Erziehung in der Gerechtigkeit."

Calvin versteht also die Inspiration in 2. Tim 3,16 nicht ontologisch als

---

81. Ut scripturae autoritatem asserat, divinitus esse inspiratam docet. Komm. zu 2. Tim 3,16; CO 52,383.

82. quod scimus Deum nobis loquutum esse, certoque persuasi simus, non ex suo sensu loquutos esse prophetas, sed erant spiritus sancti organa, tantum protulisse quae coelitus mandata fuerant; ibidem.

83. Quisquis ergo vult in scripturis proficere, hoc secum inprimis constituat, legem et prophetias non esse doctrinam hominum arbitrio proditam: sed a spiritu sancto dictatam. Ibidem.

Aussage über die Heilige Schrift als Buch, sondern funktional als Aussage über ihre Verfasser und deren Lehre. Ihr zweiter Teil bezieht den heutigen Leser in die Aussage über die Inspiration ein. Nur unter Berücksichtigung dieser Denkweise und also nur begrenzt, kann von einer Inspiration der Heiligen Schrift bei Calvin die Rede sein. Diese Lehrweise ist für alle seine Aussagen zur Inspiration der Schrift karakteristisch. Die Stelle 2. Tim 3,16 nimmt dementsprechend in seinen Schriften keine außerordentliche Stellung ein. In der Institutio erwähnt er sie nur dreimal.[84]

Im Kommentar zur Stelle 2. Tim 3,16 fallen alle für Calvins Inspirationslehre wichtigen Begriffe: die Schrift, ihre Verfasser, deren Lehre, die Werkzeuge des Heiligen Geistes, das Diktat des Geistes. Calvins Inspirationslehre kann an Hand dieser Begriffe zusammengefaßt werden.

2. Personalinspiration

Der anfängliche Satz, nach Calvin Lehre sei "die Schrift göttlich inspiriert" muß präzisiert werden. Calvin macht diese Aussage direkt nie, weil das Geistwirken die Verfasser der biblischen Schiften betrifft und bei ihnen wiederum ihre Lehre, das heißt, er betont die Inspiration der Verfasser und ganz bestimmter Aussagen in ihren Schriften. Das Geistwirken wird daher von ihm nicht auf die ganze Schrift bezogen. Calvin redet vom Geist "in der Schrift".[85] Wer bei Calvin die Inspirationslehre der reformierten Orthodoxie sucht, findet sie nicht. Die Reformatoren fragen — wie 2. Tim 3,16 — nach der Auslegung und Verkündigung der Schrift, nach dem "Nutzen" und also nach dem Leser und Hörer der Schrift. Sie verstehen die Schriftinspiration funktional und personal.

Fast immer [!] werden von Calvin das Geistwirken und der biblische Schriftsteller zusammengenannt. Es ist nun so oft in der Literatur mit vielen Zitaten nachgewiesen worden, daß Calvin nur eine "Personalinspiration" der biblischen Schriftsteller kennt,[86] daß eine weitere Beweisführung nicht mehr nötig sein sollte. Man beachte nur die auffällige Redeweise, Gott oder der

---

84. Inst I,9,1; II,7,1; III,16,3.
85. Inst I,9,3; OS III,84,10.
86. Vgl. R. Bach, "Unsere Bibelnot und Calvins Schlüssel zur Schrift: das innere Geistzeugnis," *Reformierte Kirchenzeitung* Jg. 72, 1922, 236; W. Krusche, *Das Wirken des Heiligen Geistes nach Calvin,* Göttingen 1957, 172; D. Schellong, *Calvins Auslegung der synoptischen Evangelien,* München 1969, 89; vgl. F. Wendel, *Calvin. Ursprung und Entwicklung seiner Theologie,* Neukirchen 1968, 135f.; H. J. Forstman, *Word and Spirit. Calvin's Doctrine of Biblical Authority,* Stanford 1962, 65, zieht diesen naheliegenden Schluß nicht, obwohl das von ihm vorgelegte Material genau in diese Richtung weist.

Heilige Geist rede "durch den Mund des Mose" (Davids, Salomons. Jesaias, des Petrus, des Paulus), wenn Calvin einen Bibelvers zitiert.[87]

Die Personalinspiration schließt eine Verbalinspiration des Wortlauts der Bibel aus. Die Schriftsteller haben ihre Botschaft individuell formuliert. "Calvin spricht nirgends von einem wortwörtlichen Weitergeben des empfangegen Gotteswortes, sondern von einem *gewissenhaften, zuverlässigen* bzw. *gehorsamen* Weitergeben des Empfangenen (fideliter, bona fide, resp. obedienter tradere)" (W. Krusche).[88] Das beste Beispiel für sein Verständnis der Inspiration ist das Vorwort zur Evangelienauslegung: Jene (drei) heiligen Zeugen hatten einen "Plan für ihr Schreiben", nämlich den, das Evangelium von Jesus Christus zu überliefern.[89] Calvin geht dann auf ihre Eigenarten ein und urteilt: "Die Verschiedenheit, die bei den Dreien auftritt, meine ich, sei nicht vorsätzlich beabsichtigt gewesen. Vielmehr war es der Vorsatz jedes einzelnen, nach bestem Wisse den Buchstaben anzuvertrauen, was sie gewiß und zuverlässig erfahren hatten. Als Anordnung erwählte jeder diejenige, die ihm die beste zu sein schien. Wie dies aber nicht zufällig geschah, sondern unter der sie leitenden Vorsehung, so hat der Heilige Geist ihnen bei der verschiedenen Form des Schreibens einen wunderbaren Konsens eingegeben (suggerere)" usw.[90]

Es fällt auf, daß Calvin eine Selbständigkeit der Verfasser voraussetzt, die aber unbeabsichtigt war. Er führt sie nicht auf das Wirken des Geistes zurück, sondern allgemein auf Gottes Vorsehung. Auf den Heiligen Geist führt er den Konsens zurück, der trotz der individuellen Verschiedenheit besteht. Diese Einigkeit besteht in dem Bestreben, das Evangelium zu überliefern. Die Vorrede zur Evangelienharmonie und zum Johanneskommentar zeigen klar, wie sich Calvin das Verhältnis zwischen Individualität der Verfasser und Geistwirken denkt.

87. Allein in der Institutio: I,7,5 (OS III,71,23); I,9,1 (OS III,82,13); I,13,23 (OS III,141,5); I,17,12 (OS III,217,4); I,18,3 (OS III,223,33); II,12,1 (OS III,438,9); II,15,5 (OS III,479,18); III,14,8 (OS IV,228,2); III,17,11 (OS IV,263,13); IV,9,7 (OS V,155,34); IV,20,4 (OS V,475,2).
88. A.a.O. 172; weitere Stellen 162, Anm. 199.
89. Harm. Evang., Argum.; CO 45,1: consilium scribendi.
90. Harm. Evang., Argum.; CO 45,3: nam quae in tribus ipsis apparet diversitas, eam non dicemus data opera fuisse affectatam, sed quum singulis propositum esset bona fide mandare litteris, quod certum compertumque habebant, rationem quisque tenuit, quam optimam fore censebat. Quemadmodum autem id non fortuito contigit, sed moderate Dei providentia, ita spiritus sanctus in diversa scribendi forma mirabilem illis consensum suggessit.

3. Das "Diktieren" des Geistes

Die Stellen, an denen Calvin den Begriff dictare verwendet, zeigen Calvins eigentliches Anliegen. Die Eingebung des Geistes wird "massiv" durch diesen Begriff betont. Die 40 Belege für dictare (siehe Anlage) beweisen, daß er jedoch "diktieren" nicht wörtlich, sondern uneigentlich versteht.

- In vier Stellen bedeutet dictare ein Befehl des Geistes zum Handeln (Jer 15,17; Matth 9,20; Apg 1,23; 19,21). Dictare ist der Befehl des "Diktators". Die Übersetzug "befehlen" bietet sich auch an anderen Stellen (z.B. Apg. 15,28) an.
- An vier Stellen "diktiert" der Geist, was die Propheten oder Jünger sagen oder wissen (Ezech 2,6; Matth 10,19; Luk 1,43; Inst. IV 8,5 [intus]), aber nicht niederschreiben sollen.
- An den meisten Stellen "diktiert" der Heilige Geist einen Wortlaut oder Inhalt, den die biblischen Schriftsteller sagen und niederschreiben sollen. Der Auftrag zur Verkündigung wird besonder herausgestellt Jer 18,21, 23,21, 36,8, Ezech 13,2, Dan, Argum, Inst IV,8,8 (franz.); er klingt auch an anderen Stellen an.
- Ausschließlich zur Niederschrift bestimmt ist, was der Heilige Geist durch den Mund (os) des Mose (Exod 3,1ff.) und des Schreibers des Psalms 77, und was er dem Semajah (Jer 29,25), dem Hesekiel (Ezech 2,8), dem Jeremia (Jer 36,4ff.), den vier Evangelisten (Joh, Argum), und was Gott den Propheten (2. Tim 3,16) und Petrus dem Markus (Harm. Ev., Argum) "diktiert" hat.

Von diesen auf das Niederschreiben hinzielende dictare-Stellen entfällt die über Semajah. Zwar gebraucht Calvin den Begriff "literae dictatae a spiritu sancto", doch ist des Semajah Behauptung eine unzutreffende Anmaßung. Hesekiel muß die Schriftrolle essen (Ezech 2,8f.); sie ist das später verfaßte Buch des Propheten. Aber das Diktieren des Geistes erklärt Calvin mit der Gottesrede: "Mein Geist spricht bald in diesem Buch". Ein wörtliches Diktat scheint nicht gemeint zu sein. Eindeutig ist jedoch, wie Jeremia dem Baruch (Jer 36,4ff.) seine Predigt erneut diktiert und Gott ihm, weil Jeremia den alten Text vergessen hat, die Predigt "aufs neue diktiert". Dies wird so erklärt: "Gott leitet des Propheten Gedanken und Zunge" und "er rezitiert, mit dem Geist als Führer und Lehrer, was Gott geboten hat". Wieder ist dictare hier eher göttliche Eingebung und individuelles Weitergeben an Baruch als Diktat des Geistes und wörtliche Rezitation des Jeremia. Hingegen bezeichnet dictare in Exod 3,1ff. wohl einen Inhalt, nicht einen Wortlaut. Das Synoptikerproblem und 2. Tim 3,16 wurden bereits behandelt.

- Daß dictare nicht wörtlich, sondern uneigentlich von Calvin gemeint ist, zeigen die folgenden Beobachtungen:

   An sechs Stellen wird das dictare von Calvin selbst als bildhafter Ausdruck bezeichnet: dictavit et quasi suggessit (Exod 2,10, 3,1ff.), quasi dictat (Jer 23,21), quasi dictatas literas (Jer 29,25), Deo intus dictante (Inst IV,8,5). quodam modo dictante (Inst IV,8,8).

   An sechs Stellen werden dictare und suggerere synonym gebraucht (Exod 2,10, 3,1ff., Ezech 11,5) oder dictare durch suggerere erklärt Ps 80,6, Jes 40,2) oder "diktieren" meint "eingeben" (Matth 27,40). Eingeben, (suggerere) ist ein Geistwirken, das nicht den Wortlaut umfassen muß, während diktieren ein wortwörtliches Weitergeben ist. Meistens verwendet Calvin den Begriff des "Eingebens durch den Geist".

- Da Calvin oft selbst seine lateinischen Schriften ins Französische übersetzt hat, ist nachprüfbar, ob er das Diktieren des Geistes wörtlich gemeint hat. Im französischen Text des Psalmenkommentars und der Institutio verwendet er statt dicter auch mise en la bouche, baille,[91] donner, avoir tesmoinage de Dieu en coer, inspirer. Nichts beweist besser, daß Calvin an einem wörtlichen Diktieren des Geistes nichts gelegen ist.

- Wichtiger noch als der Sprachgebrauch ist die inhaltliche Beobachtung, daß durchgängig bei Calvin das "Diktieren" des Geistes mit der Aussage verbunden ist, der biblische Schriftsteller spreche an dieser Stelle nicht aus sich selbst (a se ipso non loquitur), sondern der Heilige Geist habe es ihm eingegeben. "Diese Negation ist der Herzpunkt von Calvins 'Inspirations'-Lehre, wie die reichliche Bezeugung deutlich erweist" (Krusche).[92] Ja, Calvin will mit der Verbindung der Begriffe 'Diktat des Geistes' und 'nicht nach eigener Ansicht reden' (non loqui ex proprio sensu) die biblischen Schriftsteller geradezu entlasten: Sie sind für die Strafandrohungen in den Psalmen, in Jes 40,2, Jer 18,21 usw. nicht verantwortlich. Hier befindet sich der 'Sitz im Leben' für Calvins Verwendung des Ausdrucks 'Diktieren des Heiligen Geistes'.

Zusammenfassend ist zu sagen: Calvin ist nicht an einer Erklärung der göttlichen Inspiration des Wortlauts der Bibel interessiert, wie es der Begriff dictare nahelegt. Dieser Begriff ist bildhaft gemeint und soll ausdrücken, daß das (an der behandelten Stelle) vom Verfasser Gesagte nicht von ihm erdacht, sondern ihm vom Heiligen Geist "eingegeben" ist. Dictare ist bei ihm ein nachdrücklich unterstrichenes suggerere. Nicht um des Wortlauts der Bibel willen verwendet er das Wort dictare, sondern um den Leser

91. Bedeutung: to give; F. M. Higman, *Three French Treatises,* London 1970, 169.
92. A.a.O., 168.

seelsorgerlich auf die Wichtigkeit des Gesagten hinzuweisen und den Schreiber zu entlasten.

Wahrscheinlich sind so auch jene auffälligen Bemerkungen Calvins zu verstehen: Der Heilige Geist hat gewollt, daß der Psalm 119 nach den Buchstaben des Abc aufgebaut ist. Begründung: Er soll wie das Herrengegebet ein Gemeingut werden — daß der Gekreuzigte Psalm 22,2 "syrisch" betet. Begründung: Dies prägt sich besser dem menschlichen Gedächtnis ein — daß Phil 3,2 sich ein Wortspiel findet. Begründung: Der Geist meidet in seinen Organen nicht immer Witz und Spott.[93] Diese und andere Aussagen belegen nicht eine Verbalinspiration der Schrift, sondern wollen wahrscheinlich nebensächlich erscheinende Aussagen den Lesern wichtig und sinnvoll erscheinen lassen.

4. Schriftzeugnis und Geistinspiration

Die Inspiration der Schrift ist für Calvin eine Eingebung des Geistes an die Verfasser. In Calvins Lehre vom Wort Gottes handelt der Heilige Geist personal, das heißt, durch und an Menschen. Eine Sachinspiration, die direkt in das Schriftwort eingeht, kennt er nicht. Zwar nennt er die Verfasser oft "Werkzeuge des Geistes", doch sind sie "gleichsam .Werkzeuge";[94] auch diese Bezeichnung ist bildlich gemeint. Das eigentliche Werkzeug des Geistes ist die Predigt.[95] Die Eingebung des Gotteswortes durch den Geist schließt vielmehr die Individualität des Verfassers ein. Dieses individuelle Niederschreiben erlaubt es Calvin, wenn auch in begrenztem Maße, Bibelkritik zu üben. So hatten die Evangelisten sich nicht die Aufgabe gestellt, die Abfolge der Geschehnisse wiederzugeben, sondern die Hauptsache der Ereignisse zusammenzufassen.[96] Ebenso argumentiert er über die Bergpredigt bei Matthaus und Lukas.[97] Auf das unterschiedliche Zitieren alttestamentlicher Stellen im Neuen Testament wurde schon hingewiesen. Zu 1. Kor 10,8 oder Num 25,9 heißt es, in re oder de summa rei bestehe kein Widerspruch.[98]

Zieht sich Calvin damit auf eine Inspiration des Heilsinhaltes der Heiligen Schrift zurück? Wenn er im Kommentar zu 2. Tim 3,16, wie erwähnt,

93. Vgl. W. Krusche, a.a.O., 163f.

94. tanquam organum (Komm. zu Jer 28,21; CO 38,314); comme d'instrumens de son Esprit, et a parlé par leur bouche (Serm. Lc 1,1-4; CO 46,9). Weitere Stellen W. Krusche, a.a.O., 162, Anm. 198.

95. Organum Dei ad salutem; CO 45,16.

96 Komm. zu Matth 4,5; CO 45,133. Vgl. CO 45,782.

97. Komm. zu Matth 5,1; CO 45,160.

98. Komm. zu 1. Kor 10,8, CO 49,458; Komm. zu Ps 8,6, CO 31,92.

die Gleichung aufstellt: Schrift = Prophetenschrift = Lehre der Propheten, oder wenn er als Aufgabe der Evangelisten herausstellt, das Evangelium zu überliefern, so zeigt sich bei ihm ein Wissen um die Mitte der Schrift. Auch verwendet er den "massiven" Begriff dictare deutlich nur dann, wenn es um zentrale Aussagen des Zorns oder der Barmherzigkeit Gottes geht, wie z.B. um die Landverheißung (Josua, Argum.). Doch würde sich Calvin weigern, eine Grenze zu ziehen zwischen Zentralem und Nichtzentralem in einer Prophetenschrift oder zwischen Evangelium und dem Gesamttext der Evangelien. Ebenso würde er die Schrift zwar der himmlischen Lehre, nicht aber — oder nicht wissentlich — seiner eigenen Lehrweise unterordnen.[99]

J. A. Cramer hat Calvin zum "Vater der wissenschaftlichen Bibelkritik" machen wollen und er hat die Inspiration der Schriftsteller als ein Bereitgemachtwerden verstanden, die empfangenen Worte wiederzugeben.[100] So modern dachte Calvin jedoch nicht. Calvin denkt an ein zuverlässiges Weitergeben der empfangenen Botschaft durch die biblischen Schriftsteller. Doch schließt dies eine prinzipielle Offenheit gegenüber einer Bibelkritik nicht aus.

5. Die Zuverlässigkeit der biblischen Schriftsteller

Die letzten Ausführungen könnten Calvin als "liberal" erscheinen lassen. Seine "konservative" Haltung tritt jedoch zu Tage, wenn er über die biblischen Schriftsteller als von Gott eingesetzte Amtspersonen spricht. Diese Aussagen werden in der Literatur meistens mit der Inspirationslehre zusammen behandelt. Sie sind aber getrennt zu betrachten, denn sie wollen nicht die Art und Weise der Niederschrift des Diktates des Geistes beschreiben, sondern den amtlichen Karakter der Verfasser und ihre Zuverlässigkeit festhalten. Nach der Autorität der Schrift muß nun von der Autorität ihrer Verfasser die Rede sein.

Calvin gebraucht für sie die folgenden Bezeichnung: Sie sind Sekretäre (amanuenses, secretaire),[101] Schreiber (scribae, escrivans),[102] Notare (no-

---

99. A. Ganoczy, "Calvin als paulinischer Theologe," in *Calvinus Theologus,* Neukirchen 1976, 47, meint, Calvin bewege sich in einem "hermeneutischen Zirkel". Denn einerseits sei die Institutio laut der Vorrede 1539 Leitfaden zum Bibelverständnis, andererseits soll die Richtschnur aus der Schrift gewonnen werden. Calvin erklärt aber in der französischen Vorrede, die Institutio könne (pouvoir) "wie ein Schlüssel oder eine Tür" zum rechten Verständnis der Schrift führen (OS III,8,4).

100. A.a.O., 76, 31.

101. Inst IV,8,9, OS V,141,13; Harm. Evang., Argum., CO 45,3; Serm. Deut 31,22-30, CO 28,647.

102. Harm. Evang., Argum., CO 45,3; Serm. Deut 31,22-30, CO 28,647; Komm. Jer 29,25, CO 38,606.

taires),[103] Kanzelisten (actuarii, greffiers),[104] Zeugen (testes, tesmoins),[105] Diener (ministri, ministres)[106] des Geistes oder Gottes. Am meisten verwendet er die biblischen Begriffe des Zeugen und Dieners des Wortes. Die anderen 'Berufe' haben alle die Funktion des Abfassens und Niederschreibens. Doch wollen sie nicht den Vorgang der Inspiration näher beschreiben, sondern den amtlichen, offizellen Karakter ihres Tuns hervorheben. Das gilt auch für den Zeugen und Diener am Wort. Calvin setzt, um alle Unklarheit zu beseitigen, hinzu: sichere und beglaubigte Sekretäre (certi et authentici amanuenses), beglaubigte Notare (notaires authentiques), von Heiligen Geist vereidigte Notare (notaires jurez de sainct Esprit), beglaubigte Zeugen (tesmoins autentiques). Alle diese Personen sind also Amtspersonen.

Wichtigster Schriftbeleg und Ausgangspunkt der Überlegungen ist für Calvin der Lukasprolog und in ihm die Stichworte "Augenzeugen", "Geschichten, die unter uns als gewiß erwiesen sind", "Diener des Wortes" und "Zuverlässigkeit". Im Kommentar zur Stelle[107] betont Calvin, Lukas habe das Amt (officium) gehabt, alle zum Glauben zu rufen. Dem Theophilus werde das Evangelium übergeben nach der Ordnung der Gesetzeshüter (nomophylaces) in Athen, die von Gott erwählt waren, die bei ihnen niedergelegte himmlische Lehre zuverlässig an die Nachkommen weiterzugeben. Lukas beanspruche für sich die Autorität eines zuverlässigen Zeugen (fidi testis). Er folge nicht den privaten Autoren (privati autores), sondern denen, die Diener des Wortes (ministri sermonis), das heißt, die von Gott beauftragt waren, Zeugen (testes) des Evangeliums zu sein. Damit wolle Lukas sagen, das nun schriftlich Vorliegende sei sorgfältig verbrieft (fideliter consignatum).

Die juristische Begrifflichkeit in den Ausführungen Calvins fällt auf. Der Zeuge ist nicht, wie sonst im Neuen Testament, Zeuge der Wahrheit, sondern Zeuge vor Gericht, der öffentlich die Wahrheit bezeugen muß. Ebenso ist 'Zeugnis' für Calvin ein offizielles Zeugnis. Die Diener am Wort haben ein öffentliches Amt; sie verdienen Vertrauen.[108] Daher ist Lukas als Verfasser seines Evangeliums "Amts"person. Was er geschrieben hat, ist gleichsam verbrieft und versiegelt. Calvin verwendet auch sonst oft das Wort consignare. Der Lukasprolog selbst redet von "Geschichten, die unter uns als gewiß erwiesen sind". Calvin ist sich daher sicher, Lukas habe seine Auslegung nicht frei erfunden.

---

103. Serm. Lc 1,1-4, CO 46,9; in der Sache auch Inst IV,8,9, OS V,141,15.
104. Komm. zu Josua, Argum., CO 25,421 / 22; Serm. Deut 31,22-30, CO 28,647.
105. Harm. Evang., Argum., CO 45,3; Komm. zu 1. Petr 3,11, CO 55,217; Serm. Lc 1,1-4, CO 46,9.
106. Serm. Lc 1,1-4, CO 46,6.
107. CO 45,5-8.
108. " 'Minister' ist also ähnlich wie 'testis' Amtsbezeichnung für die von Gott mit der Wortverkündigung beauftragten Personen." D. Schellong, a.a.O., 87.

Calvins Predigt über Luk 1,1-4 (1562) entfaltet das Gesagte weiter.[109] Er stellt die Gewißheit (certitude) heraus, die Glaubensgewißheit, "das jeder Verdacht auf Trug oder Wankelhaftigkeit und damit jeder Zweifel an der Zuverlässigkeit ausgeschlossen ist."[110] Die Begriffe "beglaubigte Notare", "Sekretäre", "Schreiber" sollen das Gesagte unterstreichen und veranschaulichen. In der Predigt über Deut 31,22-30 nimmt Calvin die Gelegenheit wahr, die offizielle Funktion des Mose herauszustellen, der das Gesetz und sein Lied niederschreibt.[111] In der Institutio (IV,8,9) wendet er sich gegen den Wahrheitsanspruch der römischen Kirche.

Der Begriff der Privatperson spielt bei Calvin eine große Rolle. Die Propheten sind keine Privatpersonen (personnes privées), auch nicht Zacharias, der Luk 1,68ff. den Lobgesang anstimmt.[112] Die Verfasser der Apokryphen aber sind es. Die Begriffe Privat- und Amtsperson bestimmen Calvins Erörterungen der Abgrenzung des Kanons. In der Vorrede zur Genfer Bibel 1546, die Calvin zuzuschreiben ist, werden "profane Bücher" und solche "die sicherlich vom Heiligen Geist hervorgebracht sind", unterschieden. Schon der Name Apokryphen besage, "daß man sie als Privatschriften ansehen muß und als nicht rechtsgültig, wie es öffentliche Urkunden sind." Calvin will sie, Hieronymus folgend, nicht verachtet haben. Aber die volle Versicherung des Glaubens (pleine asseurance) findet man in ihnen nicht.[113]

Die Zuverlässigkeit des Schriftwortes belegt Calvin also nicht durch eine Lehre von der Verbalinspiration, sondern in der logischen Konsequenz seiner Lehre der Personalinspiration durch die Kennzeichnung der biblischen Verfasser als von Gott eingesetzte Amtsträger. Vorbild sind ihm die Propheten, deren eindrückliche Berufungsgeschichte vorliegt, und auch Mose, Paulus und andere. Eine solche Berufung durch Gott setzt er bei allen biblischen Schriftstellern voraus. An der Identifizierung der einzelnen Verfasser ist er nicht interessiert. Er diskutiert offen die Verfasserschaft des Mose, Josuas, einiger Psalmendichter, des Markus und Lukas.[114] "Die eigentliche Pointe dieser

---

109. CO 46,87-89.

110. "Die Vokabeln, die Calvin hierbei bevorzugt, sind: acquiescere, persuasio, certitudo, securitas." D. Schellong, a.a.O., 88f.

111. CO 28,647sq.

112. Serm. 1. Tim 4,1-4, CO 53,338; Serm. Lc 1,65-68, CO 46,164.

113. CO 9,827. Vgl. W. H. Neuser, "Calvins Stellung zu den Apokryphen des Alten Testaments," in M. Brecht (Hrsg.), *Text — Wort — Glaube, K. Aland gewidmet*, Berlin, New York 1980, 298-323; ders., "Die Reformierten und die Apokryphen des Alten Testaments," in S. Meurer (Hrsg.), *Die Apokryphenfrage im ökumenischen Horizont*, Stuttgart 1989, 83-103.

114. "David, aut quisquis huius Psalmi fuit auctor"; Komm. zu Ps 33, Argum. u.ö. Auch die Verfasser des Hebräer- und des 2. Petrusbriefes diskutiert er offen, vgl. D. Schellong, a.a.O., 98.

Schriftlehre als Amtslehre ist, deutlich zu machen, daß unser Glaube nicht von zweifelhaften menschlichen Worten abhängt und damit unsicher und wankend sein müßte. . . . Amt und Gewißheit sind die zwei Angeln, in denen die Schriftslehre Calvins hängt."[115] Die Individualität und Irrtumsfähigkeit der Verfasser ist damit nicht aufgehoben. Doch ist davon auszugehen, daß das von ihnen Geschriebene wahr ist. Der Leser ist auf das Schriftwort gewiesen und kann ihm vertrauen.

IV. Ausblick

Es gibt bei Calvin, wie erwähnt, Ansätze einer *historisch-kritischen* Bibelexegese. Es ist leicht aufzuzählen, welche Methoden heutiger Exegese er nicht kennt oder nur ansatzweise erörtert. Obgleich die Gefahr droht, anachronistisch zu verfahren, sollen abschließend wenigstens einige Bemerkungen dazu gemacht werden.

Die *Verfasserfrage* nimmt er, wie erwähnt, ernst, sieht sis aber nicht mit heutiger Schärfe. Er blickt zuerst auf den Schriftinhalt (res) und seine Bedeutung für den Leser; die Wahrheit verbindet er nicht mit der Historizität des Verfassers.

Textkritische Bemerkungen finden sich bei ihm eine ganze Reihe (zu 1 Joh, 13f., Eph 2,5, Jak 4,6, 1. Tim 5,23 usw.). Doch schreibt er die Fehler meistens den Abschreibern zu.[116] Ebenso finden sich *literarkritische* Anmerkungen. Auf die alttestamentlichen Zitate im Neuen Testament und ihre freie Wiedergabe wurde bereits hingewiesen.[117]

Formgeschichte liegt nicht eigentlich in seinem Gesichtsfeld. *Religionsgeschichte* und religionsgeschichtliche Parallelen kennt er natürlich nur wenige. Das Verhältnis der Sakramente zu den Mysterienkulten etwa ist ihm kein Problem.

Das Problem des *Vorverständnisses* hingegen nimmt er ganz ernst — ernster vielleicht als viele heutigen Exegeten. Er weiß, daß die Bemerkungen zum äußeren Textverständnis noch keinen Zugang zum Textinhalt bedeuten. Der Inhalt erschließt sich nur dem Glauben und nur im Glauben wird das Schriftwort wirklich verstanden.

---

115. D. Schellong, a.a.O., 87f.
116. Vgl. W. Krusche, a.a.O., 169.
117. Beispiele bringt W. Krusche, a.a.O., 180ff.

Beilage. Calvins Gebrauch des Begriffs dictare

Kommentare

Exod 2,10 CO 24,34	quod nobis utile erat *dictavit* spiritus, et quasi in os illius suggessit
Exod 3,1ff. CO 24,34	quod nobis utile erat *dictavit* spiritus [sc. Mosi] et quasi in os illius suggessit, ut quae gessit et passus est, exemplo essent in omnes aetates.
Josua, Argum. CO 25,421 / 22	modo quod praecipuum est nobis constet, doctrinam [sc. Dei promissio quoad terram Chanaan] . . . a spiritu sancto in usum nostrum esse *dictatam*
Ps 26,9 CO 31,269	Sciamus ergo *dictari* [franz. baille] a spiritu sancto has precandi formas [sc. Gen 18,25].
Ps 35,26 CO 31,357	Iam quum a Spiritu sancto *dictata* fuerit [franz. a mis . . . en la bouche de David] haec precandi forma, superbos omnes haud dubie manet exitus qualis hic praedicitur.
Ps 44,20 CO 31,445	Sciamus autem in his verbis *dictari* [franz. baille] nobis a Spiritu sancto precandi formam.
Ps 74,3 CO 31,693	quum hanc orandi formam *dictaverit* [franz. a dicté] Spiritus, immensum erga nos Dei amorem inde colligimus, quod iniurias nobis illatas tam severe velit ulcisci.
Ps 77, Argum CO 31,711	Spiritus per os eius [sc. auctoris] communem precandi formam pro afflicta Ecclesia *dictasse* [franz. a dicté], ut in saevissimis quibusque persecutionibus vota sua nihilominus in coelum dirigent.
Ps 80,6 CO 31,756	quum formam hanc precandi fere desperatis Spiritus sanctus *dictaverit* [franz. a dicté], spes nobis et libertas suggeritur ne ab invocatione peccata nostra nos prohibeant.
Ps 94,1 CO 32,19	hanc precandi formam [sc. 'Deus ultionum Iehova'] quae a Spiritu sancto *dictatur* [franz. est dictee], non dubitemus arripere.
Ps 102,9 CO 32,64	Nam Spiritus sanctus hanc precandi formam *dictando* [franz. en dictant] testari voluit, Deum talibus contumeliis moveri ut suis succurrat.
Ps 126,4 CO 32,318	Hanc precandi formam Iudaeis qui iam patria fruebantur, *dictavit* [a donné] Spiritus sanctus, ne miseros fratres suos negligerent.
Jes 40,2 CO 37,5	Praecipit hic Deus servis suis prophetis ac *dictat* quid eos afferre velit in medium, ubi ex luctu ad gaudium revocandi erunt fideles. Neque tamen tam eos hortatur et

animat, ut alacriter et strenue incumbant hoc munus, quam fidelibus certam spem suggerit, . . .

Jer 15,17
CO 38,230

Scimus hic legem ['Non sedi in consilio derisorum'] nobis *dictari* a spiritu sancto per os Ieremiae

Jer 18,21
CO 38,314

prophetam fuisse spiritus instinctu commotum, ut ita excandesceret contra hostes suos. . . . propheta hic . . . neque etiam sibi permisit hoc vel illud optare, sed quod *dictabat* spiritus sanctus, obedienter promulgat, tanquam fidele eius organum.

Jer 23,21
CO 38,432

Deus enim priore loco eligit prophetas suas, et munus docendi illis iniungit: postea praecipit quid dicturi sint, et quasi illis verba *dictat,* ne quid a se conflictum afferant, sed tantum praecones sint, quemadmodum alibi visum fuit.

Jer 29,25
CO 38,606

crimen [sc. Semajah Nehelamitis] fuit duplicatum, quod ausus est praetendere Dei autoritatem, et iactare se esse quasi eius scribam, quasi assereret *dictatas* fuisse sibi literas a spiritu sancto.

Jer 36,4ff.
CO 39,118

Hic narrat propheta se *dictasse* servo Dei Baruch quaequnque prius docuerat. Minime autem dubium est quin suggesserit illo momento Deus quae poterant alioqui deleta esse ex memoria prophetae. Neque enim semper omnia etiam quae aliquando diximus occurrunt. Ergo ex tam multis sermonibus maior pars fugisset prophetam, nisi Deus rursum illi *dictasset.* Fuit igitur Ieremias medius inter Deum et Baruch, quia Deus spiritu suo praeivit, et gubernavit prophetae mentem ac linguam. Propheta autem duce spiritu et magistro recitavit quae Deus iubebat. . . . Videmus ergo non *dictasse* [Ieremiam] pro arbitrio quae veniret in mentem, sed Deum suggessisse quidquid voluit scribi per manum Baruch.

Jer 36,8
CO 39,121

Sic quod videri posset durius, apostoli dicuntur remittere peccata, dicuntur afferre salutem, nempe quia ministri sunt gratiae Dei, et hortantur Christi nomine, ut reconcilientur homines Deo. Sic ergo absolvunt, quia testes sunt absolutionis. Ita etiam sermones Ieremiae, vocantur, quos servo suo *dictavit* Deus, interea proprie loquendo non sunt hominis sermones, quia non profecti sunt ab homine mortali, sed ab uno Deo.

Ezech 2,6
CO 40,71

spiritus sanctus [prophetae] *dictavit* quidquid posset videri nimis durum auribus teneris et delicatis.

Ezech 2,8 CO 40,74	Minime autem dubium est quin 'volumen' illud comprehenderit quaecunque postea spiritus Dei *dictavit* prophetae. Sed perinde fuit ac si Deus ex homine mortali faceret organum spiritus sui: quasi diceret, Iam nihil proferes humanum vel terrestre, quia spiritus meus iam conscripsit in hoc libro.
Ezech 11,5 CO 40,230	Deinde clarius exprimit quod dixerat, nempe 'spiritum loquutum esse'. Significavit autem sibi *dictatum* fuisse quidquid paulo post subiiciet. Hic ergo admonet Iudaeos ne sibi impunitatem stulte promittant, ubi contempserint eius prophetias, quandoquidem a se ipso non loquitur, sed tantum refert quae spiritus suggessit ac *dictavit.*
Ezech 13,2 CO 40,274	Ergo non aliud superest, nisi ut fideliter perferant prophetas [sc. veri] quidquid illis spiritus *dictavit.*
Daniel, Argum. CO 40,530	Daniel non loquutum esse ex proprio sensu, sed *dictatum* fuisse a spiritu sancto quidquid [sc. de rebus futuris] protulit.
Harm. Ev, Argum. CO 45,3	Marcum putant fuisse familiarem Petri discipulum, atque etiam quod scripsit Evangelium a Petro fuisse ei *dictatum,* ut amensuensis modo vel scribae operum praestiterit. Qua de re non est anxie nobis laborandum, quia nostra parvi refert, modo teneamus legitimum ac divinitus ordinatum esse testem, qui nihil nisi praeeunte *dictanteque* Spiritu sancto prodiderit.
Matth 9,20 CO 45,257	(Mulierem) dubitanter et perplexo animo id tentasse. Iam vero ut demus, hoc illi [mulieri] a spiritu fuisse *dictatum,* manet tamen fixa regula, fidem nostram . . . Dei verbo penitus affixam esse oportet,
Matth 10,19 CO 45,282, u.283	Christus tamen suos esse sollicitos vetat, quia Spiritus verba illis *dictabit.* . . . Non de facultate, inquit, vestra hic agitur, sed de Spiritus sancti virtute, qui fidelium linguas ad puram fidei confessionem format ac dirigat.
Matth 27,40 CO 45,771	Nam quia Iudaei Regem imaginati sunt, quem illis suus sensus *dictabat,* Christum crucifixum respuerunt.
Luk 1,43 CO 45,35	Tenendum enim memoria est, non loqui ex proprio sensu mulierculam, sed tantum proferre quae Spiritus sanctus *dictavit.*
Joh, Argum. CO 47,VIIsq.	Sed quaecunque illi [sc. evangelistae] tunc scribendi fuerit ratio [sc. priores illi corpus (Christi) in medium proferunt, Iohannes vero animam], minime tamen dubium est quin longius ecclesiae suae Deus prospexerit. Sic ergo

quatuor evangelistae *dictavit* quod scriberent, ut distributis inter ipsos partibus corpus unum integrum absolveret.

Apg 1,23
CO 48,23

totam actionem [sc. spiritus instinctu eos ad sortem confugisse] a spiritu illis fuisse *dictatum,* non dubium est.

Apg 15,28
CO 48,363.

'Visum est nobis'. Quia si quidquam censuerint apostoli seorsum a spiritu, concidet primum illud axioma, nihil a conciliis decerni, praeter spiritus *dictata.*

Apg 19,15
CO 48,449

Nam (Deus) eo usque vult sibi habere addictos, ut clausis oculis, dum res perplexae sunt, quod per spiritum suum illis *dictavit.*

2. Tim 3,16
CO 52,383

Hoc principium est quod religionem nostram ab aliis omnibus discernit, quod scimus Deum nobis loquutum esse, certoque persuasi simus, non ex suo sensu loquutos esse prophetas, sed ut erant spiritus sancti organa, . . . hoc secum inprimis constituat, legem et prophetias non esse doctrinam hominum arbitrio proditam: sed a spiritu sancto *dictatam.*

1. Petr 1,11
CO 55,217

Interea haec eximia est doctrinae eorum laus, dum vocatur spiritus sancti testimonium. Nam quamvis homines praecones ac ministri, ille tamen autor fuit. . . . Significat enim evangelium a Deo profectum esse, et veteres prophetias a Christo *dictatas.*

1. Petr 1,12
CO 55,219

Simul autem certitudinem evangelii inde comprobat, quod nihil cintinet nisi iam a spiritu Dei testatum. Deinde admonet, eiusdem spiritus auspiciis, adeoque ipso *dictante* et praeeunte, promulgatum esse evangelium, ne quid hic humanum cogitent.

Institutio

IV,8,5 (1543)
OS V,137,19ff.

Patriarchae quod acceperant, ad posteros per manum transmiserunt; ea lege apud ipsos deposuerat Deus, ut ita propagarent. Filii vero ac nepotes, Deo intus *dictante* [franz. avoyent tesmoinage de Dieu en leur coers], sciebant e caelo esse, non ex terra, quod audiebant.

IV,8,6 (1536)
OS V,138,11ff.

His [sc. scriptis] simul accesserunt Historiae, quae et ipsae Prophetarum sunt lucubrationes, sed *dictante* Spiritu sancto compositae [franz. le saint Esprit les inspirant et dressant à cela].

IV,8,8 (1543)   Hinc etiam colligimus, non aliud permissum fuisse Apo-
OS V,140,1ff.   stolis quam quod olim habuerant Prophetae; nempe ut
veterem Scripturam exponerent, ac ostenderent in Christo
completa esse quae illic traduntur; idipsum tamen non
facerent nisi ex Domino, hoc est, praeeunte et verba quodam modo *dictante* Christi Spiritu [franz. c'est à dire,
ayant l'Esprit de Jesus Christ, leur dictant ce qu'ils avoyent à dire].

Predigten

Luk 1,1-4   que les fideles se teinssent et s'appuyastent de tout sur ce
CO 46,5   que l'Esprit de Dieu avoit *dicté* à ses serviteurs.

The *Consensus Tigurinus* (1549): Did Calvin Compromise?

Paul E. Rorem

The title first proposed by the executive committee was *Consensus Tigurinus* — Did Calvin Surrender?" Suggested next was "Did Calvin Compromise?" There are many ambiguities in and about the statement on the Lord's Supper forged in 1549 by John Calvin and Heinrich Bullinger along with other Zurich clergy, which has been called the *Consensus Tigurinus* or *Zurich Consensus* only since the nineteenth century. But none of these ambiguities is more pertinent to a Calvin Congress than the nuance of difference between the words "compromise" and "surrender." Of course, Calvin compromised, in some measure; so did Bullinger, or there would have been no agreement at all where there had been such clear and persistent disagreement. But did Calvin compromise his basic sacramental theology to the point of surrender to another theological position?

That is the question that can be posed and pursued on this occasion, although time does not permit an exhaustive answer. As a specific historical event, in late May of 1549, the signing of this text must be considered in its historical context, in some detail. We must first identify the earlier teachings on the Lord's Supper by Calvin and by Bullinger, then their direct correspondence and the two prior rounds of debate, then the text itself of the *Consensus Tigurinus* in its political-military context, and finally the aftermath and assessments both by the two principals and by others up to the present.[1]

---

1. This article isolates and abbreviates one aspect of the argument in my *Calvin and Bullinger on the Lord's Supper* (Bramcote: Grove Books Limited, 1989), first published in the *Lutheran Quarterly,* 2 (1988), 155-84 and 357-89. The negotiations between Calvin and Bullinger are also discussed by Hans Grass, *Die Abendmahlslehre bei Luther und Calvin,* 2nd ed. (Gütersloh: C. Bertelsmann, 1954), 208-12, 275-78; Otto Erich Strasser, "Der Consensus Tigurinus," *Zwingliana,* 9/1 (1949); 1-16; Ulrich Gaebler, "Das Zustandekommen

I. John Calvin

We must start with Calvin's insightful *Short Treatise on the Lord's Supper* (1541), which lamented the "unhappy business" of Marburg and attempted an irenic middle course between Luther and Zwingli.[2] Luther, he wrote, should have been clearer "that he did not intend to set up such a local presence as the Papists imagine."[3] The error of local or corporeal presence confuses the bread with Christ's body and leads to idolatry and superstition. Zwingli and Oecolampadius, on the other hand, opposed such idolatry so single-mindedly that "they laboured more to destroy the evil than to build up the good,"[4] namely, the reality that *is* conjoined to the sacrament, that through the sacrament we are granted full communion with Christ's body and blood. In a Chalcedonian balancing act, Calvin says that bread as sacramental element and the body of Christ as divine reality are neither confused nor divided. But the Swiss come in for more criticism than the Germans: "they forgot to define what is the presence of Christ in the Supper in which one ought to believe, and what communication of his body and blood one there receives."[5] In conclusion, he proposed a union formula more congenial to Lutherans than to Zwinglians, "we are truly made partakers of the real [proper] substance of the body and blood of Jesus Christ."[6]

---

des Consensus Tigurinus im Jahre 1549," *Theologische Literaturzeitung,* 104 / 5 (1979); 321-32, and "Consensus Tigurinus," *Theologische Realenzyklopädie,* 8 (1981), 189-92; and Andre Bouvier, *Henri Bullinger le successeur de Zwingli* (Paris: E. Droz, 1940), 110-49 and 471-76. I wish to thank Dr. E. A. Dowey of Princeton Theological Seminary and Dr. John Burkhart of McCormick Theological Seminary for their helpful critique of much earlier drafts of this material.

　　2. *Short Treatise on the Holy Supper of our Lord and only Saviour Jesus Christ,* in *Calvin: Theological Treatises,* trans. J. K. S. Reid (Philadelphia: The Westminster Press, 1954), 163. This treatise was also translated by H. Beveridge in *Tracts and Treatises,* 3 vols. (1844; reprint ed., Grand Rapids: Wm. B. Eerdmans, 1958), 2.194; CO 5.457. The *Short Treatise* was written in 1540 and published in 1541. On Calvin's doctrine of the Lord's Supper, see B. A. Gerrish's excellent bibliography and discussion in "Gospel and Eucharist: John Calvin on the Lord's Supper," *The Old Protestantism and the New, Essays on the Reformation Heritage* (Chicago: University of Chicago Press, 1982), 106-17.

　　3. *Short Treatise,* 165; Beveridge, 196; CO 5.459.

　　4. *Ibid.*

　　5. *Ibid.;* Beveridge, 195; CO 5.458. The general, Chalcedonian rule of "distinguish, but do not separate" pervades Calvin's thought, as discussed in Jill Raitt, "Three Inter-related Principles in Calvin's Unique Doctrine of Infant Baptism," *Sixteenth Century Journal,* 11 (1980), 51-61. I owe this reference to the kindness of Professor John Burkhart.

　　6. *Ibid.,* 166; Beveridge, 197. Nous sommes vrayment faictz participans de la propre substance du corps et du sang de Iesus Christ. CR 5.460. On Calvin's consistently positive assessment of Luther, see Brian Gerrish, "The Pathfinder: Calvin's Image of Martin Luther," *The Old Protestantism and the New* (see n. 2, above), 27-48.

The two positions of this 1541 *Short Treatise* — in favor of a full sacramental communion with Christ's body and blood and yet against their local or corporeal presence — characterized Calvin's sacramental theology throughout his works for the rest of his career. Although these positions may seem incompatible, the believer can enjoy full communion with Christ's body and blood, even though they are not locally present, because "we must, to shut out all carnal fancies, raise our hearts on high to heaven, not thinking that our Lord Jesus Christ is so abased as to be enclosed under any corruptible elements."[7]

Calvin's clear affirmation of the sacrament as an instrument for communion with Christ's body and blood dominated his writings throughout his life, whether private correspondence or his published polemical, pedagogical, and liturgical works. In this same *Short Treatise* he says that the bread and the wine are "instruments by which our Lord Jesus Christ distributes them [his body and blood] to us."[8] The word "instruments" and the idea that communion with Christ's body and blood occurs *through* the eating and drinking of bread and wine become points of major dispute in the negotiations with Bullinger. Yet, as fully as Calvin affirmed this communion with the whole Christ through the instrumentality of the Supper, he also vehemently denied a local or corporeal presence, whether the Roman Catholic doctrine of transubstantiation or the Lutheran ideas of ubiquity.[9] Although Calvin was suspected by some Zwinglians of being almost Lutheran on this point, or, to turn a phrase, of being a crypto-Philippist, he was not. There was therefore no abiding disagreement with Bullinger here. Thus we need only list and not discuss Calvin's four reasons for rejecting a corporeal or local presence: the danger of superstitious idolatry of the bread, a correct and catholic Christology of Christ's human and divine natures, the proper and essential role of the Holy Spirit, and the very definition of a sacrament: "The matter *[res]* must always be distinguished from the sign, that we may not transfer to the one what belongs to the other."[10]

To summarize, Calvin took a Chalcedonian *via media,* affirming the sacrament as a means of communion with Christ's body and blood over against

---

7. *Ibid.,* 166; Beveridge, 197f. Il nous fault, pour exclurre toutes phantasies charnelles, eslever les cueurs en hault au ciel, ne pensant pas que le Seigneur Iesus soit abaisse iusque la, de estre enclos soubs quelques elemens corruptibles; CO 5.460.

8. *Ibid.,* 171. . . . pource que ce sont comme instrumens par lesquelz le Seigneur Iesus nous les destribue. CO 5.439.

9. *Institutio Christianae Religionis 1559,* in *Opera Selecta,* ed. Petrus Barth and Guilelmus Niesel (Munich: Kaiser, 1928-36), vols. 3-5; 4.12, 17, and 19. See also the English edition by John T. McNeill and Ford Lewis Battles (Philadelphia: Westminster, 1960). Henceforth, *Institutes.*

10. *Institutes* 4.14.15. For fuller textual evidence on the other reasons why Calvin opposed a local presence, see *Calvin and Bullinger on the Lord's Supper,* 9-11.

the Zwinglian separation of sacramental sign and reality, and denying a corporeal presence of Christ over against the Lutherans' closer identification of the sign and the thing itself, Christ's body. Calvin spent the first decade after his *Short Treatise,* from 1540 to 1549, negotiating this first and affirmative point with Heinrich Bullinger in Zurich. Was the sacrament an instrument, through which we share in Christ's body? Was it, in other and later words, a means of grace? Thereafter, in the 1550s, he was embroiled in disputes with Luther's followers Joachim Westphal and others, not so much over the second and negative point, the rejection of a corporeal presence, as over Calvin's reconciliation of the two positions through the *sursum corda,* that believers are lifted up by the Holy Spirit to commune with Christ's body and blood at the right hand of the Father.

II. Heinrich Bullinger

When Calvin interacted with Zurich, he knew full well what modern scholars have only recently appreciated. He knew he was negotiating not with Zwingli's memory or a static Zwinglian legacy, but with a prodigious scholar and independent theologian of enormous accomplishments, Heinrich Bullinger (1504-75).[11] Bullinger's early conversion to the Evangelical cause in Cologne in 1521 involved a rejection of transubstantiation and a new understanding of the Lord's Supper, based on his reading, it seems, of Luther, certain Waldensians, and Wessel Gansfort.[12] He returned to Switzerland to continue his voluminous

11. On Bullinger, see especially the new edition: *Heinrich Bullinger Werke,* ed. Fritz Buesser (Zurich: Theologischer Verlag, 1972–). The first two volumes were bibliographies: Joachim Staedtke, *Beschreibendes Verzeichnis der gedruckten Werke von Heinrich Bullinger* (1972), and Erland Herkenrath, *Beschreibendes Verzeichnis der Literatur über Heinrich Bullinger* (1977). The first volumes of Bullinger's edited works are devoted to his enormous correspondence, with three volumes required to reach 1533, and to early exegetical works. For a large collection of articles, see the two volumes edited by Ulrich Gaebler and Erland Herkenrath, *Heinrich Bullinger, 1504-1575. Gesammelte Aufsätze zum 400. Todestag* (Zurich: Theologischer Verlag, 1975); *Erster Band: Leben und Werk, Zweiter Band: Beziehungen und Wirkungen (Zürcher Beiträge zur Reformationsgeschichte,* 7-8). For an indication of the current rising estimations of Bullinger's importance, see Fritz Büsser, "Bullinger, Heinrich (1504-1575)," *Theologische Realenzyklopädie,* 7 (1981), 375-87. For an example of the new work on Bullinger, see Mark S. Burrows, " 'Christus intra nos vivens.' The Peculiar Genius of Bullinger's Doctrine of Sanctification," *Zeitschrift für Kirchengeschichte,* 98 (1987), 48-69.

12. For Bullinger's early theological development, see Fritz Blanke, *Der junge Bullinger* (Zurich: Zwingli Verlag, 1942), and Joachim Staedtke, *Die Theologie des jungen Bullinger* (Zurich: Zwingli Verlag, 1962). Much of Bullinger's life and work is also reflected, although in a fragmentary way, in his own *Diarium (Annales vitae) der Jahre 1504-1574*

research, to teach, and to write substantial works of Reformation theology, all before ever meeting Ulrich Zwingli. When Bullinger and Zwingli did meet in 1524, the twenty-year-old prodigy confronted the established reformer with an independent view of the Lord's Supper, one that gave Zwingli pause. Bullinger wrote in his diary,

> On September 12th, Zwingli shared his thoughts with me, how he viewed the sacrament of the body and blood of the Lord. And I in good faith expounded to him my views, which I drew from the writings of the Waldensian brethren and the books of Augustine.[13]

Notice that Bullinger is clear that he had independent sources for his thought and that the meeting was a true exchange of views, not a young man being influenced by his elder.

With Zwingli, Bullinger denied that God is bound to the sacrament and that it confers grace. Nevertheless, beyond these common denials, Bullinger made much more pointed affirmations than Zwingli about the sacraments as God's way of testifying and confirming the Spirit's work on the heart. The primary activity in the Supper, for Bullinger, is not that of the congregation, remembering and testifying to the faith, but that of God who by a visual analogy testifies to the redemption accomplished in Christ's body and blood.[14] Grammatically and theologically, the believer is not the subject, but rather the direct or indirect object of this activity, as he summarized much later:

> The supper of the Lord is an holy action instituted unto the church from God, wherein the Lord, by the setting of bread and wine before us at the banquet, doth certify unto us his promise and communion, and sheweth unto us his gifts, and layeth them before our senses.[15]

(Basel: Basler Buch- und Antiquariatshandlung, 1904), including the appended autobiographical sketch (125ff.). The standard biographies are by Andre Bouvier, *Henri Bullinger, le successeur de Zwingli* (Paris: E. Droz, 1940), and Carl Pestalozzi, *Heinrich Bullinger, Leben und ausgewählte Schriften* (Elberfeld, 1858). A good sketch of Bullinger's life and thought is provided by Robert C. Walton, "Heinrich Bullinger 1504-1575," in *Shapers of Religious Traditions in Germany, Switzerland, and Poland 1560-1600,* ed. Jill Raitt (New Haven: Yale University Press, 1981), 69-87.

13. *Diary,* 9, 11ff.

14. For a groundbreaking study of the earliest influences on Bullinger's doctrine of the Lord's Supper, and of his difference with Zwingli, see Hans Georg vom Berg, "Spätmittelalterliche Einflüsse auf die Abendmahlslehre des jungen Bullinger," *Kerygma und Dogma,* 22 (1976), 221-33.

15. *The Decades,* trans. Thomas Harding (Cambridge: Cambridge University Press, 1849-52), 5.9.403; cf. 5.6.240, 5.7.316f., 327, and 5.9.443.

Bullinger's differences with Zwingli on this crucial point, to anticipate the discussion below, did not result from Calvin's persuasive arguments in the 1540s, as many interpreters of their correspondence imply, but date rather from the very beginnings of Bullinger's own thought, before he even met Zwingli, much less fell under his shadow.

That shadow fell on Bullinger not so much through Zwingli's life and work as through his death and near-elevation to martyrdom by the Zurichers. When Bullinger accepted the duties of head pastor ("antistes") of the Zurich congregation, which he faithfully pursued for forty-four years, he was only twenty-seven years old and yet already the author of almost one hundred theological and exegetical works, most of them never published and / or lost. Yet all of this independent scholarship faded before his first and abiding pastoral challenge: to rally the spirits of the Zurichers by defending their tradition and their martyred leader from attacks, whether immediately by Swiss Roman Catholics or later on by German Lutherans. Only gradually, and under another military necessity, did Bullinger reveal his original points of difference with Zwingli, which made dialogue with John Calvin possible and eventually fruitful.

The same event that narrowed Calvin's hopes from that of general Protestant union to only Swiss Protestantism also delayed Bullinger's active involvement with Geneva, namely, Luther's renewed attack on the Zurich position as heretical. Urged on by the city magistrates, Bullinger led the Zurich clergy in a long and detailed response, the *Warhaffte Bekanntnus* (True Confession) of 1545.[16] The purpose of the book was partly to correct the historical record concerning Zwingli and Marburg, and partly to counter-attack Luther's teaching. But primarily it was to defend the Zwinglian tradition of theology in general and of the Lord's Supper in particular.

But even as the *Warhaffte Bekanntnus* was circulating, Bullinger wrote another volume on the Lord's Supper, his *Absoluta* or *De Sacramentis,* but with several striking contrasts: it was not in German but in Latin, it was initially distributed not widely but privately, and it was not a polemical response to Luther but an irenical statement shared with Calvin. Most importantly, it contrasts Bullinger the representative defender of Zurich's Zwingli with Bullinger the independent theologian whose sacramental emphasis was not on the theme of remembrance, Zwinglian or otherwise, but on the sacrament as God's testimony or analogy. This 1545 treatise, as Bullinger recorded in his

---

16. *Warhaffte Bekanntnus der dieneren der kilchen zu Zuerych* (Zurich: Froschauer, 1545), 3. On microfilm at Union Theological Seminary, New York City. The work was also published in Latin: *Orthodoxa Tigurinae ecclesiae ministrorum confessio* (Zurich: Froschauer, 1545).

Diary, became the sixth and seventh sermons in the fifth book of the *Decades* in 1551.[17]

III. The Two Early Rounds of Deliberation

Calvin welcomed the opportunity for dialogue with Bullinger's less public and polemical side, and responded to Bullinger's private work in great detail. Bullinger insisted throughout on the distinction between the sign and the signified, opposing superstition and concluding that Christ's body is therefore not present in the sign of the bread. Calvin conceded the danger of superstition, but argued that this impoverished line of reasoning neglected God's truthfulness.

> There is a union complementary with the thing figured, lest the sign be empty, because that which the Lord represents in a sign he effects at the same time, and executes in us by the power of his Spirit.[18]

Here Calvin introduces two themes that will reappear often in his dialogue with Bullinger: that the signs are not empty, and that what God represents God also effects at the same time *(simul)*.

To Bullinger, the sacraments are not instruments but testimonies.[19] They signify in that they testify or point out by means of signs. They do not bring or give grace but resemble it.

> Now in the Lord's Supper bread and wine represent the very body and blood of Christ. The reason hereof is this. As bread nourisheth and strengtheneth man, and giveth him ability to labour; so the body of Christ, eaten by faith,

---

17. *Diary,* 32f. See the Städtke bibliography, 91, regarding this rare work, entitled *Absoluta de Christi Domini et Catholicae eius Ecclesiae Sacramentis.* Of the four known copies, the one consulted for this study is that of Union Theological Seminary, New York. The precise editing that Bullinger performed on his treatise *Absoluta* or *De Sacramentis* in order to produce *Decades* 5.6 and 7 awaits a major study — perhaps a dissertation — that would collate and explicate the differences between these two versions of the same work. At least some of the changes can be traced to Calvin's influence, but an exhaustive analysis is beyond the scope of this study.

18. Unio est rei figuratae complementum: quo fit ne signum sit inane, quia Dominus quod signo repraesentat simul efficit, impletque in nobis spiritus sui virtute; CO 2.482. This letter of 25 February 1547 (#880) is actually a small essay in critique of Bullinger's work (CO 2.480-89). It is also discussed by Ernst Bizer, *Studien zur Geschichte des Abendmahlsstreits im 16. Jahrhundert,* 2nd ed. (Darmstadt: Wissenschaftliche Buchgesellschaft, 1962), 251-56.

19. *Decades* 5.7.294, 301f., 303, 305f., 309-11, and 315.

feedeth and satisfieth the soul of man, and furnisheth the whole man to all duties of godliness. As wine is drink to the thirsty, and maketh merry the hearts of men; so the blood of our Lord Jesus, drunken by faith, doth quench the thirst of the burning conscience, and filleth the hearts of the faithful with unspeakable joy.[20]

In response to Bullinger's worries that the sacraments as instruments detract from God, Calvin said, "what indeed do we abrogate or take away from God when we teach that he acts through his instruments, indeed he alone?"[21] Calvin countered Bullinger's every scriptural argument, and repeated often that the sacraments are indeed God's own instruments or implements, as are the ministers themselves. Despite Bullinger's exertions, his sacraments end up empty, concluded Calvin.[22]

Bullinger, as Calvin feared, seemed to take offense at this critique, for he suspended correspondence for six months. Calvin was increasingly concerned, not for abstract theological reasons, but because of the concrete political and military situation. In this same letter, he wrote about the calamity in Germany, where the Emperor's Counter-Reformation armies were enjoying considerable success. Calvin pressed Bullinger to see the urgency of the situation.

> Were he to enter Strasbourg, he would, you perceive, occupy an encampment whence he could invade us. Would there then be time, my Bullinger, for you to deliberate? For by keeping silence, do you not, as it were, present your throat to be cut?[23]

In the sixteenth century a military alliance often depended upon an explicit confessional agreement. In this case, Calvin knew that the Swiss Protestant cities would never form an effective military confederation without an open doctrinal consensus, especially on the Lord's Supper.

Bullinger apparently responded by the end of that year in a letter considered by Calvin's editors and others to be lost, although the current exhaustive editing of Bullinger's works may prove otherwise. In any case, Calvin assessed Bullinger's tardy response as stubborn. At this point, in early 1548,

---

20. *Ibid.,* 329. Bullinger spoke of the analogy of baptism's water (cleansing, refreshing, and cooling) on 328f., and in *Decades* 5.8.364. He also used the analogical framework of "as . . . , so . . ." in *Decades* 5.6.244 and 280, and in 5.9.410 and 467.

21. Quid enim Deo abrogamus aut derogamus quum ipsum tradimus agere per sua instrumenta, et quidem solum?; CO 2.485. Cf. quia nihil plus tribuo sacramento, quam ut sit Dei organum; CO 2.484.

22. *Ibid.,* 485-88.

23. 13 October 1547; CO 2.590f.; Bonnet 2.143 (there dated 19 September 1547).

the outlook for agreement must have seemed bleak, although Bullinger's letter could shed different light on the situation. A genuine difference in sacramental theology had been acknowledged on both sides. Calvin considered the Lord's Supper to be an instrument of God's grace, through which believers commune in the body and blood of Christ. Bullinger explicitly rejected such "instrumentalism" and considered the Supper to be a testimony to or an analogy of God's grace, whereby God testified to the believers, through the analogy of bread and wine nourishing and invigorating our bodies, concerning the salvation and nourishment won in Christ's body and blood and received in faith. The clear contrast between the sacrament as an instrument and as a testimony meant an impasse, for the moment.

But other forces were at work to keep the theologians working toward an agreement, with a second round of negotiations. Chief among these forces, besides the Holy Spirit, was the growing sense of urgency over the military threat of the Counter-Reformation, as exemplified by the Augsburg Interim in Germany. As the provisional basis of a religious settlement between Roman Catholics and Lutherans, the text of the Augsburg Interim was privately circulated during the spring of 1548, before its formal adoption in late June of that year. Like Calvin, Bullinger had a definite reaction to it. He wrote to Calvin, renewing a more cooperative correspondence and condemning their mutual enemy:

> This Interim is nothing but papism itself. . . . I have also seen Melanchthon's counsel. Good God, what panic and dislocation! . . . The Interim article on the sacraments, principally on the eucharist, is completely papist.[24]

Calvin welcomed Bullinger's cooperative spirit and shared his concern for the overall political-confessional-military situation. His response of July 6 concludes, "But may the very fewness of our numbers incite us to an alliance!"[25] Calvin's letter seized the opportunity to propose a statement on the Lord's Supper as a second round of direct negotiations based on good faith in spite of acknowledged differences. Calvin's letter did not arrive until August, and Bullinger did not respond until October. Just at this time the Roman Catholic Imperial forces occupied Constance, a strategic point on the border near Zurich. Bullinger's October letter to Calvin expressed his penitent alarm in apocalyptic terms.[26]

---

24. CO 2.707.

25. CO 2.730; Bonnet 2.172; dating it 26 June.

26. Meremur ut nos flagello excitet Dominus. Hic tamen clemens est et propitius. . . . Si placet ei nos ex hoc eripere saeculo, innumeris liberarit malis, vita donabit eterna. 15 October 1548; CO 3.60f.

Nevertheless, in November of that year (1548), Bullinger responded carefully to Calvin's June letter and to its statement about the sacraments, which he put into a series of twenty-four propositions and critiqued one by one, not rushing into any doctrinal compromise even if the need for an alliance was dire. This detailed commentary (called "Annotations") was answered, point by point, in Calvin's "Response" in January of 1549. Then Bullinger made his final comments (entitled "Notes") in March of 1549. Thus Calvin's original letter and the three subsequent pamphlets (Bullinger's Annotations, Calvin's Response, and Bullinger's Notes, each about seven columns of text) can be treated together, point and counterpoint.[27] With their accompanying correspondence, these writings constitute the two reformers' second round of direct negotiations over the Lord's Supper and reveal their positions quite thoroughly. Here there is time only for a minimal sampling of this fascinating correspondence, namely whether the sacraments can be called "instruments," and what happens "through" *(per)* them.

In his *Response,* Calvin explicitly called the sacraments the "means" *(media)* God uses,[28] although he did not here employ the expression "means of grace." Consistent with their previous correspondence, Bullinger preferred to call the sacraments "testimonies of the grace of God."[29] As to the relationship of the sacrament to the Holy Spirit (proposition 2), for Calvin the Spirit's proper work of making us partakers of Christ is done *per sacramenta,* "through the sacraments, as through instruments. . . . the Spirit is the author, the sacrament is the instrument used."[30] Indeed, in proposition 4 Calvin clearly stated that God works *through* the sacraments, which drew a comment from Bullinger:

> For this little word "through" *(per)* seems to ascribe more to inanimate things, to the signs of water, bread, and wine, than should be ascribed. The efficacy of any blessing should be rightly ascribed to the Holy Spirit.[31]

This objection prompted Calvin as a Professor of Sacred Scripture to a biblical review of how God works through baptism, through the laying on of

---

27. *Ioannis Calvini Propositiones de Sacramentis. Annotationes breves adscripsit Henricus Bullingerus,* CO 7.693-700; *Calvini Responsio ad Annotationes Bullingeri. Scripta Mense Ianuario 1549,* CO 7.701-8; *Henrici Bullingeri Annotata ad Calvini Animadversiones,* CO 7.709-16.

28. CO 7.701 (#1).

29. CO 7.709 (#1).

30. Spiritus autor est, sacramentum vero instrumentum quo utitur; CO 7.702 (#2).

31. Nam vocabulum Per videtur rebus inanimatis, aquae, pani et vino, signis inquam, plus tribuere quam tribuendum est. Recte quidem tribuitur omnis boni efficacia spiritui sancto; CO 7.694 (#4).

hands, through the human voice, and through the ministry generally. None of this was persuasive to Bullinger, who viewed all these as external symbols and testimonies.[32] Even their agreement that the sacraments lead us to Christ (#6) uncovered the same fundamental difference. For Bullinger, the sacramental "signs testify to and signify the celestial gifts"; for Calvin, they are the Spirit's very instruments.[33]

Their disagreement came to a head regarding Calvin's proposition 7: "The sacraments are instruments of the grace of God. For what is figured in them, we say is offered to the elect."[34] Although Calvin here (and in proposition #5) seems to concede something new — that the objective grace of the sacraments is qualified by limiting their efficacy to the elect — Bullinger seems not to notice any progress here toward a Zurich "subjectivism" and in fact expresses sharp disagreement on the heart of the matter:

> This proposition contains something which afflicts and irritates the faithful. If by "instrument" you mean "sign," fine. But if it is something more than sign, you seem to ascribe too much to the sacraments. . . . It is God who saves and receives us in grace. But this you ascribe to an instrument through which it is worked, some implement or flow-sluice or canal, the very sacraments, through which grace is infused into us. . . . But we do not believe this. . . . God alone works our salvation. . . . God, and no created thing, confers and indeed confers through the Spirit and faith. . . . The sacraments neither offer nor confer, nor are they instruments of offering and conferring, but they signify, testify, and seal.[35]

Bullinger consistently insisted that all the credit go, evangelically, to God, whose Spirit works on the soul directly, without crass intermediaries like

32. CO 7.702f. and 711 (both regarding #4).

33. Bullinger: CO 7.694 (#6) and 712 (#6); Calvin: CO 7.703 (#6).

34. In Calvin's original letter: Atqui docemus, sacramenta gratiae Dei esse instrumenta. . . . Quod ergo illic figuratur dicimus electis exhiberi; CO 2.727f. In Bullinger's editing: VII. Sacramenta sunt instrumenta gratiae Dei. Nam quod illis figuratur, dicimus exhiberi electis; CO 7.695.

35. Haec propositio habet quod pios affligat et urat. Si per instrumentum intelligis signum, bene est. Si amplius quiddam quam signum, videris sacramentis nimium tribuere. . . . Deus is est qui nos salvat et recipit in gratiam. Huic vos tribuitis instrumentum per quod operetur, organum inquam, et infundibulum, ac canalem quendam, ipsa inquam sacramenta, per quae nobis infundat gratiam. . . . Caeterum nos non ita credimus, . . . Deus solus operatur salutem nostram. . . . Deus, nulla creatura, conferat, et conferat quidem per spiritum et fidem. . . . Sacramenta illa non exhibent aut conferunt, ceu exhibendi et conferendi instrumenta, sed significant, testificantur et obsignant; CO 7.695 (#7). Bullinger also says here that the signs, being inanimate, are not capable (capacia) of spiritual things, which receives Calvin's agreement: Quod obiicis, non esse donorum Dei capax signum visibile, quum res sit inanima, id ego tecum fateor; CO 7.703 (#7).

implements or canals for grace, which he viewed as a medieval superstition. Here he explicitly rejects the terminology of instrument and implement *(organum)*.

Calvin responded that of course everything is ascribed to God, but "what is your argument, that God alone acts, therefore all instruments cease?"[36] What is figured in the sacrament is also offered therein, not because the sacraments are crude channels inclosing material grace, but because they are God's instruments for conferring grace, as the human voice is an instrument of God's saving work. Calvin reminded Bullinger of their previous disagreement: "what you deny to be conferred through the sacraments, I affirm."[37] Bullinger's rebuttal conceded nothing. Even praising gifted people such as Calvin himself is actually to praise God; certainly inanimate creations should not divert us from praising the Creator. "God alone does it, and what God does, implements *(organa)* do not do." The sacramental "instruments," if Calvin insists on this term, do only what they were instituted to do, namely, "represent and seal the gifts of God," just as the preacher's voice only announces what God perfects in the soul through the Spirit.[38]

In summary, of the twenty-four propositions, only two did not receive eventual agreement within this exchange of mini-treatises, yet these two revealed the foundational difference between Calvin and Bullinger: the fourth proposition, on God acting through *(per)* the sacraments, and the seventh, on the sacraments as instruments of grace. However, when Calvin spoke of the sacraments as testimonies to grace rather than as instruments of grace, agreement flourished, for this was Bullinger's theme throughout this exchange and indeed throughout his entire corpus.[39]

At this point, Bullinger and Calvin had achieved considerable agreement and had received reassurances about each other's positions. The political need for an explicit alliance was clearly pressing, and their remaining doctrinal differences were now identified with sufficient precision to isolate their options. Either Calvin would refrain from speaking of God as working *through* the sacraments, and of the sacraments as God's *instruments* or implements of grace, or else Bullinger would change his position and openly agree that the

36. Vide tamen quale sit tuum argumentum: Deus solus agit; cessant igitur instrumenta. Quid? CO 7.703 (#7).

37. Quin potius, et iam ante tibi memini me scripsisse, inde, quod tu improbas, colligo, per sacramenta quoque conferri. CO 7.704 (#7).

38. Deus agit solus, ergo id quod Deus agit non agunt organa. . . . sacramenta dona Dei repraesentant et obsignant; CO 7.712 (#7).

39. In his original Annotations, Bullinger sounded the theme of the sacraments as testimonies regarding propositions 4-8, 11, 17, 23, and 24. In his final Notes, he repeated it regarding 1-2, 4-6, 12, and 24.

sacraments were not only testimonies, analogies, and parallels to grace, but God's very instruments for conferring grace. The next six months saw a sudden turn of events, but at least the detailed correspondence before May of 1549 clarifies the underlying issue in sacramental theology and terminology between Calvin and Bullinger and thus the context for assessing what happened during the rest of that year.

IV. *The Zurich Consensus (Consensus Tigurinus)*

It was Calvin who suggested coming to Zurich for a direct, face-to-face meeting.[40] Bullinger responded immediately, tenderly consoling Calvin in his grief over the death of his wife and discouraging him from abandoning his parish for such a costly and exhausting trip. Still favoring correspondence to direct meetings, Bullinger extolled the value of continuing their exchange of letters.[41] Nevertheless, it seems that before Calvin received this letter urging him not to come he had in fact already left Geneva for Zurich. The meeting itself was in late May, after the 25th; but many details such as the exact date remain uncertain. Some hints surfaced later in related correspondence, such as Calvin's remarks that the trip was arranged in an abrupt two days, and that the entire issue was settled in a single session lasting only two hours.[42] As to the actual progress of the meeting, the historical record has left nothing like the Marburg narratives. Hardly anything about the session can be reconstructed. Calvin later wrote Bucer that things seemed hopeless at first, but "suddenly light broke out."[43] Yet some of these comments after the fact were also meant to portray the meeting in a positive light as genuinely smooth and successful. Actually, Calvin also later revealed that some Zurichers were reluctant to agree, whereas Bullinger much later remembered that Calvin tried to promote some terminology that was suspiciously "Bucerian."[44]

It is immediately apparent that the twenty-six headings of the *Consensus*

---

40. Plurimum enim gaudeo nihil fere, aut quam minimum, restare, quin verbis etiam inter nos consentiamus; CO 3.266; Bonnet 2.225.

41. CO 3.278-80. Bullinger also held fast to the Zurich objection against any compromising alliance with France over against the emperor, even if it meant military disaster.

42. Calvin to Oswald Myconius, 6 December 1549; CO 3.456f. However, the diplomatic point of this letter was to reassure Myconius that the trip had developed so quickly and successfully that there was no time to include others, such as Myconius. Calvin here gave Farel major credit for the success of the trip; Bouvier, 140f.

43. Subita lux affulsit; CO 3.440; Bonnet 2.235f.

44. Calvin to Bucer, CO 3.439; Bonnet 2.235; Calvin to Sulzer, CO 3.458; Bullinger to Beza, Bouvier, 562.

Tigurinus are not a revision of the twenty-four propositions discussed so thoroughly over the previous year, nor even derived from them.[45] Instead they derived directly from a set of twenty paragraphs or articles that Calvin had sent to a meeting in Bern in March of 1549, with an exceedingly diplomatic cover letter.[46] This introduces a major new component into these bilateral discussions. Why the sudden shift from the twenty-four propositions they had been debating to the twenty paragraphs from the Bern synod?[47] Perhaps the time had simply and urgently come for a wider alliance, for multilateral talks including Bern instead of only bilaterals.

A thorough exegesis of the *Consensus Tigurinus* must include two specific questions: First, how does this document differ textually from its parent text, Calvin's Bern articles? Second, how does it then compare conceptually with the positions taken by Bullinger and Calvin during their previous correspondence. Specifically, is the sacrament ever called an "instrument" "through" which "we are truly offered what it signifies"?

Article eight, for example, was partly a direct quotation from Calvin's Bern article 3 on partaking of Christ as the fount of all blessings, etc., but it was also a rewriting of Calvin's first article in that earlier text. There, in Calvin's original wording, the sacramental testimonies and seals are true be-

---

45. Consensio Mutua in re Sacramentaria Ministrorum Tigurinae Ecclesiae et D. Ioannis Calvini Ministri Genevensis Ecclesiae. Details of the origins of the title "Consensus Tigurinus" are provided in the article by Gaebler, *Theologische Realenzykopädie* 8.189. The Latin text is in CO 7.733-48, and in Calvin's *Opera Selecta,* ed. P. Barth and W. Niesel (Munich: C. Kaiser, 1952), 241-58. It will be cited by paragraph number without further reference to those columns. English translations of the *Consensus Tigurinus* are provided in Calvin's *Tracts and Treatises,* vol. 2, ed. H. Beveridge (repr. Grand Rapids: Eerdmans, 1958), 212-20; and in the *Journal of Presbyterian History,* 44 (1966), 45-61, by Ian Bunting, who included this translation in his (unpublished) Th.M. thesis at Princeton Theological Seminary in 1960.

46. The Bern articles are in CO 7.717-22 and will be cited by paragraph number without further references to those columns. Calvin's cover letter of 13 March 1549 is in CO 3.216-18; Bonnet 2.214f.

47. Ulrich Gaebler theorizes that Calvin saw the opportunity to strike an agreement with the moderate Zwinglians in Zurich as leverage with the extreme Zwinglians in Bern and his own opponents in Geneva, since they would surely need to go along with Zwingli's home city. "Das Zustandekommen," 323f., and *TRE* 8.189 (see n. 1, above). Yet here too caution is required. Even though these articles were originally prepared for the Bern meeting and were sent to Haller as their head pastor, they were never presented there, much less accepted as part of some other alliance taking shape before the Geneva-Zurich meeting. Haller wrote both Bullinger and Calvin that he had decided against presenting Calvin's articles, for fear of further controversies. Haller to Bullinger, 7 March 1549, CO 3.214; Haller to Calvin, 29 April 1549, CO 3.242f. Still, the need for multilateral agreement was plain, as seen by the acceptance of this *Consensus* by other cities, even eventually Bern, after Calvin's sudden trip to Zurich in May of 1549.

cause "that which they figure is truly offered to us." This, a favorite expression of Calvin's, was not accepted into the eighth Zurich article, where these testimonies are considered true because the Lord "performs internally by his Spirit what the sacraments figure to the eyes and other senses." Article 16 also replaced Calvin's earlier (Bern) phrase "the sacraments to them [the elect] alone present what they offer" with the less instrumental phrase "the elect perceive what the sacraments offer." The wording they agreed on ("the Lord performs internally by his Spirit") may have left the early Zwingli far behind, but it permitted Bullinger's view of the sacrament as an external perceptible analogy to the internal invisible work of the Spirit.

Similarly, article 9 changed Calvin's Bern #5 quite substantially, first by omitting his insistence that what is signified and promised is in fact fulfilled and presented in the sacrament, and second by altering the remaining text. Calvin had originally written, "Whoever rightly and faithfully uses the sacraments receives Christ, since he is offered there to us, along with his spiritual gifts." The wording that came out of the Zurich meeting reads, "all who in faith embrace the promises offered there receive Christ spiritually, with his spiritual gifts." Here was the Calvin-Bullinger difference at its briefest: not that the sacrament is a means of receiving Christ, but that faith in the promise there offered and illustrated is a means of receiving Christ spiritually.

Article 10 continues the discussion of Calvin's Bern #6 on the importance of the promise over against the "bare signs," but omits the latter text's clear use of *per sacramenta* in its opening clause: "through the sacraments we become participants in Christ and his spiritual gifts." Months before, Bullinger had explicitly and sharply objected to the preposition "through" in this sense of a sacramental instrumentality for participating in Christ. He did not relent here, and the entire clause was omitted.

The title given to article 13 is "God uses the implement, but such that all the virtue is God's." Here Calvin's lifelong concern for the sacraments as *instrumenta* and his explicit use of that term in his Bern article 9 were offset by his original dialectic in the Bern text that, nevertheless, "the entire work of our salvation ought to be considered ascribed to [God] alone." Nevertheless, Bullinger and the Zurich delegation would still not accept the word "instrument" and substituted "implement." This substitution bears examination. Bullinger had often objected to both "instrument" and "implement." The former term had been the focus of more disagreement, but the latter was treated as a synonym. Yet here the Zurich delegation agreed to or even insisted upon the substitution of "implement" for "instrument." For some reason, they could accept the former but not the latter. Either these words were rough synonyms, and Bullinger here yielded to Calvin's instrumental view of the sacraments while yet avoiding the word "instrument," or else some shade of meaning was different enough to permit Bullinger to use the word "implement" without adopting "instrumentalism." Short of finding an explicit discussion of these two terms by Calvin and / or Bullinger, our view of this substitution must depend upon the document as a whole.

Article 14 seems to represent Calvin's instrumentalist view of the Supper: Christ "makes us participants of himself in the Supper" (*in coena,* which Calvin later identified as Augustinian language). This expression is repeated in article 19: "Christ communicates himself to us in the Supper." Although the principal point of the latter article is that Christ also does this before and apart from the Supper, it could be that in these two cases Bullinger accepted Calvin's fuller view of the sacrament as the very means, or at least *a* means, of communicating in Christ. Yet Bullinger's subsequent writings, and other points within the text, do not suggest that he was finally convinced by Calvin on this crucial point. Like his agreement to the words "implement" and "aid," perhaps this was Bullinger's effort at compromise, here in two secondary articles, for the sake of an agreement. It is also possible, however, that Bullinger understood *in coena* not to mean "in the supper" in Calvin's sense of instrumentalism, namely "by means of the supper," but to mean simply "during the supper." Such, at least, was the meaning of the preposition "in" somewhat later in the phrase *in actu ipso,* "during the act itself" (art. 20). The flexibility of this language would permit Calvin's viewpoint, but would also permit Bullinger's view of the sacraments not as instruments but as testimonies by analogy, although here the testimony seems to be a simultaneous one, which met his objection before regarding the word *simul.*[48] Yet even here the larger point of article 20 is Bullinger's opposition to a strictly simultaneous relationship between the administration of the sacraments and the action of grace.

V. Aftermath and Conclusion

In this light, the *Consensus Tigurinus* can hardly be called a clear victory for Calvin in the sixteenth-century Reformed debate over the Lord's Supper, whether over Zwingli's lingering influence or over Bullinger's own substantial position.[49] Certain of its articles do represent a finely balanced dialectic

48. Proposition #9 of the twenty-four discussed by Calvin and Bullinger in 1548. See my *Calvin and Bullinger,* 35f.

49. Calvin is presented as the winner in W. Kolfhaus, "Der Verkehr Calvins mit Bullinger," in *Calvinstudien,* ed. A. Bohatec (Leipzig: R. Haupt, 1909), 69. Bouvier sees it as mutual, but without a penetrating theological analysis. Niesel says that Calvin's full doctrine was not in the Zurich agreement: *Calvins Lehre vom Abendmahl,* 2nd ed. (Munich: C. Kaiser, 1935), 54f., n. 1. See Grass, 211. For an example of the older view and a survey

between Calvin's concern for the sacraments as God's means or instruments for conferring grace (on the elect) and Bullinger's concern to counteract any transfer of God's saving activity to the creaturely realm. In that sense it was a true compromise on both sides. Witness, for example, the alternating emphases in article 12:

> Furthermore, if something of good is conferred upon us through the sacraments, this does not occur because of their own proper virtue, even if you comprehend the promise by which they are characterized. It is God alone who acts by his Spirit, and although he uses the ministry of the sacraments, in this he neither infuses his own power into them, nor detracts anything from the efficacy of his Spirit; but because of our ignorance he adds them as aids, but such that the entire faculty of acting remains with himself alone.

Yet even here, in this act of balancing Calvin's concerns with Bullinger's, the real resolution of their long-standing differences regarding the sacraments seems to have resulted from Calvin's willingness to omit certain phrases previously essential in his formulations and yet always objectionable to Bullinger. Completely missing from the *Consensus* were Calvin's usual references to the actual presenting ("exhibiting") of what is signified, to the sacraments as "instruments" (although they are called "implements"), and as that "through" which God confers grace.

There are several indications that Calvin himself viewed the May colloquy in Zurich as a compromise by omission on his part, namely, his proposed additions of a preface and two new paragraphs, as well as his private correspondence with Bucer and others. Calvin's original preface, perhaps composed on the spot in Zurich, had immediately claimed that the joint statement on the sacraments "does not contain everything which could usefully and aptly be said, and which otherwise perfectly fits their true understanding."[50] The Zurichers, however, had other ideas for a foreword and afterword, which eventually prevailed. After the meeting itself, Calvin proposed two new paragraphs, which were accepted and became #5, "How Christ communicates himself to us," and #23, "On the eating of Christ's flesh." Yet even they do not fully represent Calvin's instrumentalist view.

Meanwhile, Calvin's own thoughts on this entire process were shared in other private correspondence. He had sent a copy of the text and his proposed additions to Bucer, lately in exile in England. Bucer's response in August

---

of prior literature, see Alexander Barclay, *The Protestant Doctrine of the Lord's Supper* (Glasgow: Jackson, Wylie and Co., 1927), ch. 12, 158-79.

    50. Original preface, CO 7.49-50. Yet Gaebler considers the original preface and postface never published; "Das Zustandekommen," n. 51.

revealed his mixed judgment; he could see where Calvin had held firm and where he had been loose. While especially commending the two additional paragraphs, Bucer criticized at length the interpretation of heaven as a place, and had another major concern, as well summarized in Calvin's response to Bucer later that fall:

> You devoutly and prudently desire that the effect of the sacraments and what the Lord confers to us through *(per)* them be explicated more clearly and more fully than many allow. Indeed it was not my fault that these items were not fuller. Let us therefore bear with a sigh that which cannot be corrected.[51]

With this comment, Calvin reveals his own reservations about the *Consensus,* even with the two additional articles now in place. He confirms this viewpoint that the text significantly omits his concern for the sacraments as the instruments through which God confers the grace of communing with Christ's body. It seems that the absence of the terminology of "instrument," of "through the sacrament," and of "presenting / offering" *(exhibeo)* indicates Calvin's concession by omission.

Nevertheless, when the agreement became known, Calvin put the best construction on it and defended it tirelessly, especially against the Lutherans like Westphal and Heshusius.[52] For his part, Bullinger also continued to write about the Lord's Supper after these negotiations with Calvin, although his

---

51. Effectum sacramentorum, et quid per ea nobis Dominus conferat, luculentius et uberius explicari quam multi patiantur, pie et prudenter optas. Neque vero per me stetit, quin pleniora quaedam essent. Gemamus ergo ferentes ea quae corrigere non licet; CO 3.439. Bucer's letter of 14 August 1549 to Calvin is in CO 3.350.

52. For starters, see *Defensio sanae et orthodoxae doctrinae de sacramentis,* CO 9.15-36; English translation by Henry Beveridge, with the *Consensus Tigurinus* (above, n. 45), 221-44. Calvin here uses the specific expression "means of grace" or gratiae media, CO 9.20 (p. 227), media vocantur, quibus vel inseramur in corpus Christi, CO 9.17 (pp. 222f.), cf. CO 9.24 (p. 231); organa esse quibus efficaciter agit Deus in suis electis, CO 9.18 (p. 224); per sacramenta nobis confertur, CO 9.22 (p. 229), Deum per sacramenta agere volunt? Hoc docemus, CO 9.23 (p. 229). See Joseph N. Tylenda, "The Calvin-Westphal Exchange. The Genesis of Calvin's Treatises against Westphal," *Calvin Theological Journal,* 9 (1974), 182-209. Tylenda surveys Calvin's correspondence and other sources to reconstruct the chronology and circumstances of this exchange of several treatises during the 1550s. Calvin wrote *Secunda defensio* in 1556 (CO 9.41-120), *Ultima admonitio* in 1557 (CO 9.137-252), and *Delucidia explicatio* in 1561 (CO 9.457-524). Tylenda explicitly identifies this survey as a prolegomenon to an examination of the contents of the works in question. One such examination is in Heinrich Schmid, *Der Kampf der lutherischen Kirche um Luthers Lehre vom Abendmahl in Reformationzeitalter* (Leipzig, 1873). See also the new study on Calvin and Hesshusen by David Steinmetz, "Calvin and His Lutheran Critics," *Lutheran Quarterly,* 4 (1990), 179-94.

voluminous output cannot be thoroughly surveyed here. Ironically, in a perfect reversal of their earlier roles, it was Bullinger who attempted to tone down the polemics of Calvin's response to Westphal.[53]

The basic difference in sacramental theology between Calvin and Bullinger endured beyond these negotiations and their agreement on a text. Although alternative interpretations are possible, the most coherent assessment of the overall process is that they achieved a consensus statement principally because Calvin agreed to omit a crucial component of his position, to omit it for the moment but not for long. It was a big compromise, but whether it should be viewed as a surrender depends upon the reader. In my judgment, both Calvin and Bullinger compromised considerably, for the sake of securing an agreement. But neither of them surrendered.

In any case, the two views of the Lord's Supper have managed to live side by side within the Reformed tradition for centuries. Does a given Reformed statement of faith consider the Lord's Supper as a testimony, an analogy, a parallel, even a simultaneous parallel to the internal workings of God's grace in granting communion with Christ? If so, the actual ancestor may be Heinrich Bullinger, Zwingli's successor in Zurich. Or does it explicitly identify the Supper as the very instrument or means through which God offers and confers the grace of full communion with Christ's body? The lineage would then go back to John Calvin (and to Martin Bucer), despite the opposition he faced among his Reformed brethren on this very point and despite his own compromise by omission in Zurich in 1549.

---

53. Bouvier, 151; Tylenda, "Calvin-Westphal" (see preceding note), 185 and 192ff.; Bonnet 3.90. Calvin to the Zurichers, 13 November 1554. Cf. *Decades* 5.9.410, 433, and 467. Bullinger here also continued his explicit identification of heaven as a place, not a state or a condition (448). What was worrisome to the Lutherans and forewarned by Luther (*Short Confession,* Luther's Works 38.306f.) was Bullinger's designation of not only *hoc est* regarding the Lord's Supper, but also "the Word became flesh" regarding the Incarnation, as symbolic language not to be taken as literally true, since God was immutable (436). See also Bullinger's *Apologetica expositio* (Zurich, 1556), on microfilm at Yale Divinity School, and summarized in Schulze, *Heinrich Bullinger 1504-1575,* 2.292-300, who also sketches Bullinger's extended controversy with Brenz.

Current Trends in Calvin Research, 1982-90

Richard C. Gamble

The purpose of this presentation is not to scrutinize the names and titles of all the books and articles written about John Calvin in the last eight years. Appended to the written text is a list of books that is as complete as possible. Rather, this investigation will focus on only a few of the major titles, as well as on some significant articles.

This is the third time that this theme has been handled by the International Congress. The first was done by Professor Nauta in 1974 at the first European Congress on Calvin Research. His article, entitled "Stand der Calvinforschung," had five sections: Calvin bibliography; the state of critical editions of Calvin's works; presentations of Calvin's life and work; advances in our understanding of Calvin's theology; and the sources or foundations of Calvin's theology.

In Geneva in 1982, Professor Saxer presented "Hauptprobleme der Calvinforschung-Forschungsbericht 1974-1982." The structure of his research was similar to Nauta's; however, he had eight instead of five sections. These included three new ones: on ecclesiology, on collections of the works of Calvin, and on Calvin's sources and method of exegesis and preaching.

This year's presentation will be reduced to four main sections and a conclusion. The first section gives a brief summary of newer trends in Calvin research. The second examines intellectual / theological history. The third analyzes language and hermeneutic, and the fourth Calvin and theology.

I. Newer Trends in Calvin Research

As can be easily imagined, either of the two topics of this section is sufficient for a full hour's presentation. However, both of these two newer areas of research will continually impact the rest of the presentation.

1. Sociological / Political Interest

One trend in current Calvin research that was handled by neither Nauta nor Saxer concerns sociological interest in Calvin and Calvin studies. The premier leader of this movement is Robert M. Kingdon. Kingdon labored on the Registers of the Company of Pastors in the 1960s,[1] but he is also known for a series of articles on social welfare in Calvin's Geneva[2] and work in Post-Calvinian France.[3] A number of other important articles on Calvin have appeared from the vantage point of his sociological interest; for example, "The Control of Morals in Calvin's Geneva"[4] and "Calvinism and Social Welfare."[5] Kingdon has also presented reports to this international body, including most recently "Calvinus Legislator: The 1543 'Constitution' of the City State of Geneva."[6] Along with Kingdon, a number of other scholars have contributed significant articles to the field of sociological interest. One example is E. William Monter, "Crime and Punishment in Calvin's Geneva, 1562."[7] With impetus from scholars like Kingdon and Monter, in the last eight years at least two noteworthy books have been produced that underline sociological interest in Calvin's Geneva. One title is by Jeannine Olson, *Calvin and Social Welfare: Deacons and the Bourse française*[8]; another, penned by William Innes, is *Social Concern in Calvin's Geneva.*[9] This direction in Calvin research has proven to be extremely beneficial in that Calvin's labor in Geneva had not been fully analyzed prior to this groundbreaking work, which began in the 1960s and '70s. No modern Calvin scholar can ignore the advances in this field of learning, for it impinges on all the other parts of Calvin research, historical, biographical, and theological.

Church / state relations in Calvin's Geneva, on the other hand, have been a perennial topic of discussion. Much of the newer research in social history has impacted interpretation of the political situation in sixteenth-century Geneva.

---

1. Kingdon, Robert M. et J.-F. Bergier. *Registres de la compagnie des pasteurs de Genève au temps de Calvin* (Geneva: Librarie E. Droz, 1962–), 7 vols.

2. Kingdon, Robert M. "Social Welfare in Calvin's Geneva," *American Historical Review,* 76 (1971), 50-69.

3. Kingdon, Robert M. *Myths about the St. Bartholomew's Day Massacres 1572-1576* (Cambridge: Harvard University Press, 1988).

4. *The Social History of the Reformation,* ed. Laurence P. Buck and Jonathan W. Zophy (Columbus: Ohio State University Press, 1972) 3-16.

5. *Calvin Theological Journal,* 17 (1982), 212-30.

6. *Calvinus Servus Christi,* ed. W. Neuser (Budapest: Presseabteilung des Ráday Kollegiums, 1988), 225-32.

7. *Archiv für Reformationsgeschichte,* 64 (1973), 281-87.

8. (Selinsgrove, PA: Susquehanna University Press and London: Associated University Press, 1988).

9. *Social Concern in Calvin's Geneva* (Allison Park, PA: Pickwick Publications, 1983).

The question as to the nature of a Christian commonwealth, or whether Geneva had a theocracy, as well as Calvin's view of Deuteronomic law and its relationship to society, has been investigated in the past. Nevertheless, these questions will continue to spawn debate, as is observed in recent Calvin literature.[10]

2. Exegetical History

Leaving this important subject of social / political history with an all-too-brief summary, we turn our attention to exegetical history, which has also made important advances in the last eight years. There has been a renaissance of interest in exegetical history, which is easily observable in the regular meetings of scholars held most recently at the University of Geneva to discuss sixteenth-century exegesis. A number of names are associated with these advances: T. H. L. Parker,[11] David Steinmetz,[12] David Wright,[13] Susan Schreiner,[14] and Irena Backus,[15] to mention a few.

Particularly noteworthy are two recent books by T. H. L. Parker, *Calvin's Old Testament Commentaries*[16] and *Commentaries on the Epistle to the Romans 1532-1542*.[17] Parker's books have been reviewed widely and read by students and scholars alike. His *Calvin's Old Testament Commentaries* is in some sense a companion publication to his earlier *Calvin's New Testament Commentaries*.[18] These two volumes provide a considerable amount of material in comprehending the ways in which and the background from which Calvin's commentaries were written. Parker's other recent work, *Commentaries on the Epistle to the Romans,* also provides valuable information on Calvin's

---

10. Cf. Harro Höpfl, *The Christian Piety of John Calvin* (Cambridge: Cambridge University Press, 1982).

11. "Calvin the Biblical Expositor," *The Churchman,* 78 (1964), 23-31; "Calvin the Exegete: Change and Development," in *Calvinus Ecclesia Doctor,* ed. W. Neuser (Kampen: Kok, 1978).

12. "John Calvin on Isaiah 6: A Problem in the History of Exegesis," *Interpretation,* 36 (1982), 156-70; "Calvin and Abraham: The Interpretation of Romans 4 in the Sixteenth Century," *Church History,* 57 (1988), 443-55.

13. "Calvin's Pentateuchal Criticism," *Calvin Theological Journal,* 21 (1986), 33-50.

14. "Through a Mirror Dimly: Calvin's Sermons on Job," *Calvin Theological Journal,* 21 (1986), 175-93.

15. "Aristotelianism in Some of Calvin's and Beza's Expository and Exegetical Writings on the Doctrine of the Trinity with Particular Reference to the Terms *ousia* and *hypostasis,*" in *Histoire de l'exégèse au XVIe siècle,* ed. O. Fatio and P. Fraenkel (Geneva: Librarie Droz, 1978), 351-60.

16. (Edinburgh: T. & T. Clark, 1986).

17. (Edinburgh: T. & T. Clark, 1986).

18. (Grand Rapids: Eerdmans, 1971).

first full biblical commentary plus insight into Calvin's exegetical methodology, which will be presented in section three of this chapter.

Alexander Ganoczy, in conjunction with Stephan Scheld and Klaus Müller, has produced some works that have shed particular light on how Calvin performed his exegesis. In *Calvins Handschriftliche Annotationen zu Chrysostomus* the authors make a painstaking study of the actual handwriting of Calvin in the marginalia of his copy of Chrysostom, focusing especially on the commentary on *Genesis* but on other important passages of Scripture as well. They conclude, and quite convincingly, that Calvin was heavily indebted to the patristic father St. John Chrysostom.[19] Likewise, the monumental work of Ganoczy and Scheld, *Die Hermeneutik Calvins,*[20] is in my opinion one of the most significant works in exegetical history in the last decade or so. This book will be analyzed in more detail in the following sections. From their work on the hermeneutic of Calvin, Ganoczy and Scheld also produced *Herrschaft—Tugend—Vorsehung,*[21] which investigated Calvin's relationship to the Stoic philosophers Seneca and Lucian. Their thesis suggests fairly strong lines of Stoic influence on Calvin.

Elsie McKee has recently presented two titles that fall within both sociological interests and exegetical history. Her *John Calvin on the Diaconate and Liturgical Almsgiving*[22] is both a presentation of Calvin's thinking on the office of elder and an extensive exegetical history dealing with passages from Romans, Corinthians, I Timothy, and others. McKee continues that tradition in her *Elders and the Plural Ministry: The Role of Exegetical History in Illuminating John Calvin's Theology.*[23]

To summarize the results of these studies, certain streams are readily identifiable. First, in terms of the direction of Calvin studies, more work has been put into Calvin's Old Testament commentaries recently than his New Testament commentaries. Second, opinion is fairly solid that "lucid brevity" or "brevitas et facilitas" is the hallmark of Calvin's exegetical method.[24]

19. (Wiesbaden: Steiner, 1983).
20. (Wiesbaden: Steiner, 1983).
21. (Wiesbaden: Steiner, 1982).
22. (Geneva: Librarie Droz, 1984).
23. (Geneva: Librarie Droz, 1988).
24. Cf. R. Gamble "Brevitas et facilitas: Toward an Understanding of Calvin's Hermeneutic," *Westminster Theological Journal,* 47 (1985), 1-17, and "Exposition and Method in Calvin," *Westminster Theological Journal,* 49 (1987), 153-65. David Steinmetz in "John Calvin on Isaiah 6: A Problem in the History of Exegesis" says that "Calvin's 'lucid brevity' is one of his principal contributions to the intellectual heritage of the Reformation." *Interpretation,* 36 (1982), 158. Schreiner notes that Calvin rejects allegory in his search for the "plain" or "simple" sense of the text (*Calvin Theological Journal,* 191). J. L. H. Haire, "John Calvin as an Expositor," also underlines Calvin's "lucid brevity" (5). Recently, Büsser and Parker have shown that this method was first found in Bullinger.

Third, the concept of accommodation has been demonstrated as integral to Calvin's method.[25] Fourth, John Chrysostom has been proven to be a prime exegetical tutor to Calvin.[26].

The advances in exegetical history have nevertheless left a number of doors still open concerning Calvin's exegetical method. One important question that has not yet been answered concerns the continuity of Calvin's exegetical method from his Seneca commentary to his biblical commentaries. If one observes great continuity, then certain conclusions concerning the influences of his humanistic background could be made. On the other hand, if one observes more discontinuity, then rather different conclusions accrue. Although scholars have noted continuity and discontinuity between Calvin the Seneca commentator and the biblical commentator,[27] nevertheless there has been no definitive textual analysis to prove the point one way or the other.

Of course this first question could be answered by a close comparison of the commentary on *De Clementia* with Calvin's earliest biblical commentary, on *Romans*.[28] More difficult would be a comprehensive study comparing the entire corpus of Calvin's biblical commentaries with other sixteenth-century commentators, especially Erasmus and Zwingli, who are considered "humanistic" exegetes and both of whom wrote prior to Calvin.[29]

25. The groundbreaking work on Calvin's concept of accommodation was found in F. L. Battles, "God Was Accommodating Himself to Human Capacity," *Interpretation,* 31 (1977). In the last eight years, that thesis has been substantiated in the articles cited above by Gamble and by Steinmetz, who says, "all knowledge of God is accommodated knowledge" in Calvin's theology (*Interpretation,* 36 [1982], 164). Cf. also D. Wright, "Calvin's Pentateuchal Criticism" *in toto;* J. D. Douglass, "Calvin's Use of Metaphorical Language for God: God as Enemy and God as Mother," *Princeton Seminary Bulletin,* 8 (1987), 27; J. L. H. Haire, *op. cit.,* 13.

26. John R. Walchenbach, under the tutelege of F. L. Battles, did the first full-length study: "John Calvin as Biblical Commentator: An Investigation into Calvin's Use of John Chrysostom as an Exegetical Source" (Ph.D. diss., Pittsburgh, 1974). Ganoczy and Müller then went through a painstaking analysis of Calvin's actual text of Chrysostom, *Calvins Handschriftliche Annotationen zu Chrysostomus: Ein Beitrag zur Hermeneutik Calvins* (Wiesbaden: Steiner, 1981). Cf. also R. Gamble, "Brevitas et facilitas," 8-9.

27. Battles / Hugo observe continuity in *Calvin's Commentary on Seneca's De Clementia* (Leiden: Brill, 1969), 91*, while this author observes discontinuity as well. Cf. "Brevitas et facilitas," 11, 12. T. H. L. Parker contrasts the *Romans* commentary with the *De Clementia* by saying that "The new work, composed from a different motive, breathes a different spirit" (*Romans,* 71).

28. Girardin's excellent study of Calvin's *Romans* commentary, *Rhétorique et théologique* (Paris: Beauchesne, 1979), briefly compares the commentary with the 1536 edition of the *Institutes* but does not compare it to the earlier commentary on Seneca.

29. Some of this work has already been done. See Q. Breen, *John Calvin: A Study in French Humanism* (Grand Rapids: Eerdmans, 1931); J. Bohatec, *Budé und Calvin* (Graz: Hermann Böhlaus, 1950); especially the work of Ganoczy / Scheld; and more pointed research by F. Büsser, "Bullinger as Calvin's Model in Biblical Exposition," in E. Furcha

II. Intellectual / Theological History

In the first section of this presentation we examined two newer, major approaches to current Calvin scholarship. The focus of this section will be on a third direction of Calvin scholarship, which is not a new one, intellectual / theological history. Within that general area, we will focus on Calvin and his environment.

There are two main currents of influence in which Calvin navigated, Renaissance / humanism and late medieval theology. Analysis of this background will provide the foundation for an investigation of Calvin's contemporaries and their influence on his thought.

1. Calvin and Late Medieval Theology

The issue of Calvin's relationship to late medieval theology has been discussed for quite some time.[30] Certainly a complex question, this problem will be analyzed in detail by Professor Oberman later in this volume. Our purpose here is simply to indicate how scholarship has been developing in the last few years.

Late medieval theology is certainly not easy to define. Terms such as "nominalism" and "realism" are bandied about in the literature, but there are tremendous difficulties in defining the word *nominalism* and comprehending it as an intellectual movement of the late Middle Ages. Many recent scholars have doubted the usefulness of the term at all, but we will not be able to enter the depths of that discussion.

Two late medieval theological movements that have been known as nominalist are the *via moderna* and the *schola Augustiniana moderna*. Names associated with the *via moderna* would be Gabriel Biel and Pierre D'Ailly, and with the *schola Augustiniana moderna* Gregory of Rimini.

Recently Alister McGrath has asserted in two books and an article that Calvin was influenced by the *via moderna* in general and by the *schola*

(ed.), *In Honor of John Calvin, 1509-64. Papers from the 1986 International Calvin Symposium* (Montreal: McGill University, 1987); T. H. L. Parker, "Calvin the Exegete," in *Calvinus Ecclesiae Doctor,* ed. Neuser; P. Verhoef, "Luther and Calvin's Exegetical Library," *Calvin Theological Journal,* 3 (1968), 5-20; B. Roussel, "De Strasbourg a Bâle et Zurich: une 'École Rhénane' d'exégèse (ca. 1525–ca. 1540)," *Revue d'Histoire et de Philosophie Religieuses,* 68 (1988), 19-39; and T. H. L. Parker, *Commentaries on Romans 1532-1542.*

30. The earlier work of Karl Reuter, *Das Grundverständnis der Theologie Calvins* (Neukirchen-Vluyn: Neukirchener Verlag des Erziehungsvereins, 1963), in many ways began blazing the trail of this research. McGrath, Selinger, and others refer to him often.

Augustiniana moderna in particular.[31] It is also at this point that McGrath argues for the influence of this tradition upon Calvin as a tradition rather than from specific, identifiable individuals in the life and thought of Calvin.

On the other hand, T. F. Torrance speaks of similar nominalistic influences on Calvin but associates different names with those influences. Torrance contends that the *devotio moderna* and John Major are specific influences from the late medieval period on Calvin's thought.[32]

Suzanne Selinger also underlines nominalistic influence on Calvin. Her analysis is directly related to Calvin's concept of knowledge, where, in her opinion, the nominalistic conception of human limits was incorporated by Calvin.[33]

A few recent articles have also been published investigating the influence of late medieval theology in forming Calvin's theology. Perhaps the best recent article demonstrating Calvin's reaction against as well as influence by late medieval theology is David Steinmetz's "Calvin and the Absolute Power of God." Steinmetz demonstrates that Calvin attacked the distinction between the absolute and ordained power of God, here drawing upon Duns Scotus and to a lesser extent William of Occam. He confirms three different contexts in Calvin's commentaries that reject this distinction: those of miracles, providence, and predestination. In short, Calvin rejected it as a movement against any speculation, according to Steinmetz. He is convinced that Calvin refused to separate God's power from his justice, under any circumstances: "What the scholastics regard as a useful experiment in thought, Calvin regards as shocking blasphemy."[34] Steinmetz concludes that for Calvin God is always *potentia ordinata.*

On this specific topic of influence, a brief survey of the literature exhibits the continuing debate. Personally, I do not see a resolution to this subject until a comprehensive volume can be produced.

2. Calvin, the Renaissance, and Humanism

As our colleague Cornelis Augustijn said four years ago: "Eine Reihe von Calvinforschern hat in den letzten Jahrzehnten das Verhältnis Calvins zum

31. Alister E. McGrath, "John Calvin and Late Medieval Thought," *Archiv für Reformationsgeschichte,* 77 (1986), 77-78.

32. Thomas F. Torrance, *The Hermeneutics of John Calvin* (Edinburgh: Scottish Academic Press, 1988).

33. Suzanne Selinger, *Calvin against Himself: An Inquiry in Intellectual History* (Hamden, CN: Archon Books, 1984), 169.

34. *The Journal of Medieval and Renaissance Studies,* 18 (Spring 1988), 78.

Humanismus seiner Zeit studiert."[35] Interestingly, in the time that has elapsed
since Augustijn made his presentation to this Congress, another whole series
of articles and books on this theme have been penned![36]

To facilitate an analysis of the relationship between Calvin and
humanism, we must give a working definition of humanism. But that is by no
means an easy task! Scholars can only agree to disagree on this point. Nevertheless, the difficulty of the problem must be squarely faced and resolved, for
Alister McGrath is correct in stating that, ". . . any discussion of the relation
of humanism and the Reformation will be totally dependent upon the definition
of humanism employed."[37]

More specifically, it appears that how the question of Calvin's relationship to humanism is answered will depend on the definition given of humanism
itself.

The crucial question of sixteenth-century humanism, according to
Augustijn, is the connection between Christianity and antiquity, or, stated in
another way, between good literature and sacred literature.[38] This is "the
central question of the time" (that is, between 1450 and 1550); when discussing
the question of Calvin and humanism "deshalb soll sie auch bei einer
Erörterung des Verhältnisses Calvins im Mittelpunkt stehen."[39]

Augustijn's definition of humanism centers around the question of the
correlation between the work of God in the history of the people of the
covenant and his work in the world of antiquity. Precisely stated, is God so
working in the world of ancient history that one can say that the wisdom and
learning of that classical world is given by God and can be embraced as
God's wisdom and learning? A sixteenth-century humanist, according to
Augustijn, will embrace that time period fully, and acknowledge God's
sovereign control of that history, his work in that history, and his giving
wisdom and truth in that time.

Augustijn's definition of humanism has a significant advantage. He
avoids defining humanism in such a narrow way that anyone who implements
humanistic exegetical methods in producing a biblical commentary is therefore
a humanist. Using humanistic-methods does not make an author a humanist.

Very recently Alister McGrath has also struggled with defining
humanism and concludes that a humanist's primary work had to do with
eloquence. Specifically, "humanism was concerned with how ideas were ob-

35. *Calvinus Servus Christi,* ed. Neuser, 127.
36. This list would include the aforementioned works of McGrath, T. F. Torrance,
and Bouwsma's book on Calvin.
37. *Reformation Thought: An Introduction* (Oxford: Blackwell, 1988), 32.
38. *Calvinus Servus Christi,* ed. Neuser, 129.
39. *Ibid.,* 131.

tained and expressed, rather than with the actual substance of those ideas."[40] The consensus in sixteenth-century humanism was not on the unity of ideas but on how to express those ideas.

These two definitions of humanism are difficult to reconcile. If McGrath's definition is followed, most scholars would place Calvin squarely in the camp of the humanists, even Augustijn.[41] But is his definition adequate?

It would appear that McGrath's definition falls to Augustijn's criticism of being too narrow, unless McGrath is correct in asserting that there is an often overlooked facet to humanism's method. That point is that the new literary methods *themselves* could mediate from the text to the exegete an experience either of the vitality of the classical period, or in the case of the Bible, of the first Christians.[42] With that in mind, Calvin's task as a Christian humanist could be to transmit that experience of the ancient church to the church of his day.

However, following Augustijn's definition will produce a different conclusion. Since the "piety" of the ancient world had absolutely nothing to do with the God of the Bible, as Augustijn understands Calvin, and since in his view God was in no way using that time period as a preparation for Christ, Calvin does not embrace humanism. By definition, according to Augustijn, Calvin stands *opposed* to humanism.[43]

The question of Calvin's relationship to humanism is thus broken open in the middle. Is Calvin's view of human nature and of God's interaction with human nature such that it is impossible, by definition, for Calvin to embrace the piety of the ancient world? Is Calvin's view of the history of God's dealing with people, which is radically different from Zwingli's, who saw God working in the classical writings, such that Calvin cannot embrace humanism as did the humanists of his own time? If positive answers are given to these questions, Calvin is not a humanist.

Therefore, resolution of the dilemma of Calvin's relationship to humanism should involve more than analysis of his method of exegesis, namely anthropology and probably epistemology. To continue our search for answers to these questions and to shed light on the topic of current Calvin research,

---

40. *Reformation Thought,* 32.

41. For example, he says: "Calvin hat die philologische Methode der Humanisten übernommen und sie auf dem Gebiet der Theologie angewandt." Again he says: "Überall in Calvins Werken ergibt sich, dass er die Künste, die Wissenschaften und die Handwerke geschätzt hat, selbst benutzt er auch die humanistischen exegetischen Methoden in seinen Bibelarbeiten." *Calvinus Servus Christi,* ed. Neuser, 28, 139.

42. Alister E. McGrath, *Reformation Thought: An Introduction* (Oxford: Basil Blackwell, 1988), 33.

43. "Wenn man ihn dennoch einem Humanisten nennt, hat man das Wesentliche, den Kern des Humanismus, ausgeklammert." *Calvinus Servus Christi,* ed. Neuser, 140.

we should turn to a 1988 work on Calvin entitled *John Calvin's Perspectival Anthropology*.

Mary Potter Engel is convinced that Calvin's various writings must be understood from the perspective from which he is writing. Analysis of her book as a whole goes beyond the boundaries of this lecture. Her rather unique vantage point produces further insight into Calvin's understanding of humanism, and her thoughts on the subject are contained in an appendix (#2), "Calvin on Humanism."[44] Engel gives a complex answer to a complex question. She presents passages from Calvin that demonstrate that he can be classified as "an enemy of humanism."[45] Calvin rejects the new arts and sciences of his day. However, it is Engel's opinion that Calvin evades the charge of being an enemy of humanism. The reason for this is that his condemnation of these arts is a condemnation from the perspective of God as redeemer. Analyzing from that perspective, "all human arts and sciences are empty adornments of the self."[46]

However, from the perspective of humankind, Calvin acknowledges that there are different types of wisdom, all of which flow from the one source, namely God. Therefore, all legitimate arts and sciences are acceptable to Calvin. Engel goes so far as to say: "and Calvin admits, though he does not use this term, that there is such a thing as a Christian humanist"[47] and that Calvin fits this description. She is convinced that understanding Calvin's attitude toward humanism as complete rejection is inaccurate.

Her conclusion is that Calvin rejects humanism only when he is speaking from the perspective of God as redeemer and embraces human activity or humanism when speaking from the perspective of humankind. Assuming that human activity is done from the perspective of giving God glory and not praising humankind, then it is acceptable.

This third opinion brings us back to the beginning of our search. Augustijn maintains that the working definition of humanism employed by many is inadequate. He goes so far as to claim that the definition of humanism employed by those authors ignores the very heart of the movement of humanism. If we embrace Augustijn's definition of humanism and then reject that submitted by McGrath, Mary Potter Engel presents to us a further dilemma. Working with basically the same definition of humanism as does Augustijn, that is, that humanism is not only a methodology but a view of human nature

44. American Academy of Religion Series, 52 (Atlanta, GA: Scholars Press, 1988).
45. *Ibid.*, 199.
46. *Ibid.*, 200.
47. *Ibid.*, 202. T. F. Torrance agrees: ". . . science (scientia) is not to be rejected. It is *secularis scientia* that is vain and many have perished through it." *Hermeneutics*, 78.

and history, she nevertheless disagrees with the conclusion of Augustijn, that Calvin is not a humanist. Engel would provide a corrective to Augustijn's suggestion, that is, that Augustijn's definition is proper but his analysis is faulty because he does not view Calvin's statements on humanism from the perspective of humankind but rather from the perspective of God the Redeemer.

We are left, after eight years of further research and a number of articles, with no consensus. Nevertheless, a guide to further research on Calvin's relationship to humanism should follow certain rules: carefully defining terms; using the word "humanism" self-consciously rather than haphazardly; and analyzing humanism not exclusively from the vantage point of literary methodology but by implementing current research and insights into Calvin's view of both history and humankind. If these guidelines are followed, it is likely that a consensus will be reached in the near future.

3. Calvin's Indebtedness to Luther and Erasmus

In the last eight years research has continued to discern the effect of immediate predecessors upon Calvin. It appears that there has been progress in analysis of both Luther's and Erasmus's influence.

Earlier scholarship had attributed to Luther tremendous impact on Calvin. This has been noticed especially in the 1536 *Institutes*. This vast subject of Luther's effect cannot be comprehensively approached in this lecture, where we are focusing on broad influences.

More current examination of Calvin's indebtedness to Luther has, of course, verified Calvin's dependency, especially in his orientation to Scripture itself. As Protestant reformers, they shared many theological positions. Nevertheless, much that had been considered to be indebtedness to Luther may be found in other sources, sources in late medieval thought itself as well as in patristic literature. Clear differences between Calvin and Luther are also being more fully articulated. Emphasis is being placed not only on their different temperaments and early training but on their different conceptions of the connection between the two testaments and their relationship to patristic theology and exegesis as well.[48] Especially helpful at this point is the work of Ganoczy / Scheld, who in one section of their volume on Calvin's hermeneutic analyze both Luther and Erasmus. They are convinced that these three men hold different epistemological presuppositions in their approach to the relationship between word and spirit.[49] To summarize, the prevailing direction in

---

48. Torrance, *Hermeneutics,* 159.
49. Ganoczy / Scheld, *Hermeneutik,* 88.

Calvin studies is to underline the differences between Calvin and Luther, a movement that appears to me to be quite healthy.

The situation with Erasmus is just the opposite. The strongest contemporary proponent here in America of Erasmian influence on Calvin would probably be William Bouwsma, who is cognizant of the differences between Calvin and Erasmus but says that the differences are more temperamental than substantial.[50] He reminds us, for example, that the word *Institutes* as a book title had already been used by Erasmus. In many ways Ganoczy / Scheld agree with this analysis, seeing in Erasmus many foundations for later Protestant exegesis.[51]

Slightly different would be the opinion of T. F. Torrance, who also acknowledges Calvin's great indebtedness to Erasmus but maintains that Calvin has a different epistemological foundation than Erasmus. That different foundation, based on human knowledge of God, produces important implications for theology and exegesis.[52] Some of those implications will become more clear shortly.

III. Calvin, Language, and Hermeneutic

1. Introduction

It is in this third area of recent Calvin research that, in my opinion, some of the greatest advances have been made and that much more research is needed. The roots of much of this change may be observed in the renaissance of Calvin studies following the Second World War.

Karl Barth and Emil Brunner deserve much credit for reopening Calvin studies, but works such as Herman Balke's 1922 study *Die Probleme der Theologie Calvins* helped to destroy the old picture of John Calvin as the ivory tower systematic theologian and began to emphasize new aspects of his thought. Other advances in current research, especially in sociological, political, and exegetical history, as well as the new texts available for research, have also facilitated this new and improved thrust in Calvin studies.

The vision of Calvin as pastor and humanist is important for a new direction in Calvin studies. The image of Calvin as humanist has been brought out in recent times most clearly by William Bouwsma. The bottom line to his research is the destruction of the "systematic" Calvin in favor of a theologi-

---

50. Bouwsma, *John Calvin,* 14.
51. Ganoczy / Scheld, *Hermeneutik,* 43.
52. T. F. Torrance, *Hermeneutics,* 127-31.

cally humanistic Calvin.[53] In many ways Bouwsma's *John Calvin* does not deal with Calvin the theologian, which is one of the weaknesses of the book. Nevertheless, in providing the historical background to the thought world of Calvin, Bouwsma has performed a great service. The conception of Calvin as pastor rather than as systematic theologian has led to his being viewed in terms of his piety rather than in terms of such themes as the omnipotence of God. This relatively new nuancing of the image of Calvin as theologian has, in my opinion, proved to be very fruitful.

2. Calvin and Language

Research investigating Calvin and his environment has produced a reexamination of the philosophical / theological underpinnings of his thought, and this reexamination has created some new insights into the foundations of Calvin's language and epistemology. Despite the temptation to pursue these areas which are personally interesting, the purpose of this third section will be to review current literature on the subject and to trace lines of argumentation up to the present day. Having done that, I will complete my obligation to the assigned topic and then make suggestions for further research that will hopefully advance the cause of Calvin studies.

There is no question that Calvin was cognizant of contemporary discussion relative to the meaning of language and that that discourse was important to him. Bouwsma makes clear that from Calvin's earliest publication he was cognizant of how language functioned and how meaning was determined.[54] As Bouwsma analyzes Calvin's estimation of language he correctly notes that for Calvin language was conventional, that is, that usage is what distinguishes words.[55] In addition, Calvin was well aware that language has the capacity to convey feeling.

Torrance also analyzes Calvin and language and makes the point that for Calvin thought and speech were closely related and that the precise use of words was an important area of study for Calvin and the humanists.[56]

More extensive work on this topic has been done by Suzanne Selinger, who is convinced that a thorough study of Calvin's use and understanding of

---

53. "This book, then, tries to interpret Calvin as a figure of his time: as a representative French intellectual, an evangelical humanist and therefore a rhetorician, and an exile. It is not directly concerned with Calvin's theology. . . ." Bouwsma, *John Calvin,* 3.

54. *Ibid.,* 115.

55. Battles / Hugo had noted this earlier in their analysis of Calvin's Seneca commentary. *Calvin's Commentary,* 91*.

56. Torrance, *Hermeneutics,* 101.

language is necessary to penetrate his theology properly. According to Selinger, unless we grasp Calvin's implementation of language, we cannot understand his rhetoric, and comprehending his rhetoric is essential to Calvin's theological program.[57]

Furthermore, she is convinced that Calvin's perception of language is very closely associated with his study of Augustine and that Calvin took over much of Augustine's thought concerning the possibility of a Christian rhetoric.[58] Still in substantial agreement with Torrance and Bouwsma, Selinger proposes that for Calvin "Language had an independent existence so powerful that ignorance could result in deception or the prevailing of evil, while awareness of that existence could allow its enlistment in the service of the good."[59]

Analysis of Calvin's use of language can shed light on other areas of theological inquiry, such as his view of the sacraments and the nature of theology itself. Presently the work of Gilbert Vincent is the most thorough in analyzing Calvin's views of language and its impact on theology.

Vincent's book *Exigence ethique et interprétation dans l'oeuvre de Calvin* has entire sections comparing Calvin's utilization of language with that of Augustine and Thomas Aquinas.[60] With that historical background Vincent devotes quite a number of pages to developing Calvin's theory of language itself. That book has been updated in an article in 1987, "La rationalité herméneutique du discours théologique de Calvin,"[61] in which Vincent advances a number of very important ideas concerning Calvin and language. There he wrestles with how Calvin determines the meaning of a biblical text and the implications of how Calvin elicits that meaning.

3. Calvin's Hermeneutic

Calvin's theology proper, his anthropology, and his epistemology all impacted his theory of interpretation or hermeneutic. Granted that the term "hermeneutic" itself is a modern one, it is still a useful word for our own analysis.

There is a growing consensus in recent literature that Calvin was cognizant of his own culture as it related to hermeneutic and that he was influenced by and in turn influenced that culture. Ganoczy / Scheld, Parker, and T. F. Torrance analyze this topic, the fruit of which has advanced our understanding of Calvin's hermeneutic.

57. Selinger, *Calvin against Himself,* 8-9.
58. *Ibid.,* 154ff.
59. *Ibid.,* 159.
60. (Geneva: Labor et Fides, 1984), 18-33, 33-50.
61. *Archives de sciences sociales des religions,* 63 (1987), 133-54.

Mention should be made, first of all, of the fact that Calvin had a different exegetical methodology, as noted in section I.2, and a different hermeneutic from his contemporaries. Proper caution must always be exercised when claiming uniqueness for a historical person, especially at a gathering of historians! Nevertheless, my task is to report on the trends in scholarship, and there is a clearly recognizable trend in this direction. Ganoczy / Scheld assert that in contrast to his protestant colleagues Calvin is attempting "dabei eine völlig neue Schreibweise anzuwenden." They even call his method revolutionary.[62] Parker asserts: "Melanchthon, Bucer, and Calvin are all Reformers, but there is a world of difference in their expository methods and compositions."[63] Torrance claims a uniqueness for Calvin's hermeneutic as well.

Perhaps the most significant assertion of these volumes, certainly the most controversial, is that made by Professor Torrance when he says: Calvin "found himself thinking out the relation between language and the realities signified, and developed a mode of interpretation of Biblical statements in which the language employed was understood in the light of the *subjecta materia*."[64] This thesis, which appears to be correct to me, will need further verification in the future. Still, the work of Ganoczy / Scheld, Parker, and Torrance has, in the last eight years, brought our understanding of Calvin's hermeneutics to new heights.

IV. Calvin and Theology

Advances have been made on all fronts in Calvin research in the last eight years, but the most significant breakthroughs of all are found in analysis of Calvin as theologian.

1. The Structure of Calvin's Theology

Scholars of the late nineteenth and early part of this century found that one central theme was the foundation for Calvin's theology, that being the doctrine of divine sovereignty and the corresponding idea of predestination.[65]

If the doctrine of divine sovereignty or election were to be the *foundation*

---

62. Ganoczy / Scheld, *Hermeneutic,* 123f.

63. *Commentaries on the Epistle to the Romans* (Edinburgh: T. & T. Clark, 1986), ix.

64. T. F. Torrance, *Hermeneutics,* 130.

65. For further bibliographical information, cf. Gamble, "Calvin as Theologian and Exegete: Is There Anything New?" *Calvin Theological Journal,* 23 (1988), 186, n. 16.

for Calvin's theology, then his systematic thinking would take on very clear structures. The same would apply to any *loci* of his theology, for example, Christology or ecclesiology. However, this outdated view of Calvin has been rejected. As a matter of fact, most leading scholars today maintain that there is no one single key to unlock the door of Calvin's theology. There is a consensus that there is more than one centrally important theme or, to continue the key analogy, that some keys open more doors than others.

Even though many are hesitant to say that there is one basic theme of Calvin's theology, "Calvin scholarship has shown increasing unanimity that the [*duplex cognitio Dei*] must be reckoned with as either *a* controlling principle of his theology or *the* controlling principle."[66]

2. Epistemology

Much of this unanimity concerning the foundation or foundations of Calvin's theology springs from growing agreement in scholarly analysis of the foundations of Calvin's epistemology itself. In 1982 William Bouwsma's "Calvin and the Renaissance Crisis of Knowing"[67] placed proper emphasis on the epistemological questions that were raging during Calvin's time.

Bouwsma correctly said: "Evidence of Calvin's preoccupation with the problem of knowing, or with knowing as a problem, can be discerned everywhere in his work."[68] As Bouwsma analyzes the *Institutes* he is convinced that the "first nine chapters of Book I constitute, indeed, a kind of epistemological introduction to the work as a whole, as they consider the possibility and the processes of the knowledge of God before proceeding to its content."[69] Bouwsma establishes the necessity for this type of epistemological self-consciousness in light of the cultural background of the *Institutes* themselves, where the question was being addressed of the capacity of the human mind to have any certain knowledge.

Of course, this facet of Renaissance history was also faced by late medieval theology in the theological struggle between the realists and the nominalists. Our point is easy to understand, that the changes in current scholarship concerning the structure of Calvin's theology have been influenced by the increase in our knowledge of both the Renaissance and late medieval theology.

66. *Ibid.,* 180.
67. *Calvin Theological Journal,* 17 (Nov. 1982), 190-211.
68. *Ibid.,* 201.
69. *Ibid.,* 202.

We may summarize by observing two lines of analysis developed from wrestling with the epistemological foundations of Calvin's thinking. On the one hand are arguments from the side of the Renaissance. William Bouwsma was one of the first to address the question of the Renaissance crisis of knowing in Calvin's thought from the side of Renaissance history. On the other hand, is the theological side with the new analysis of late medieval theology that is basically attributable to the groundbreaking work of Professor Oberman beginning in the '60s.

Of course, antecedents to much of this thinking were produced long before the last eight years. We have mentioned Balke's work from 1922, and more recently we would think of Professor Battles's presentation in 1978 of "Calculus Fidei," a fascinating and complex analysis of the structure of Calvin's theology.

In the last two or three years, however, a few Calvin scholars have also questioned whether or not the *duplex cognitio Dei* is a foundational structure of Calvin's theology. This leads us to a discussion of the question: philosophy or theology?

3. Philosophy or Theology?

In 1987 Charles Partee pursued the question of Calvin's central dogma.[70] He argued that despite the growing consensus concerning the *duplex cognitio Dei,* another avenue should be pursued, one that is not philosophical but rather theological. He asserted that the doctrine of union with Christ serves as "a basis for surveying the Institutes from a central perspective."[71] He is convinced that his claim for union with Christ as a foundation for the structure of Calvin's theology is superior because it is a "theological rather than a philosophical basis for the description of Calvin's thought."[72] Calvin, as a theologian, would want this important theological principle to be the foundation structure.

More recently, Brian Armstrong in a chapter in the Dowey *Festschrift,* which came out the spring of 1993, continues to push for an answer to the question of whether or not the *duplex cognitio Dei* is *a* or *the* fundamental principle of Calvin's thought. Armstrong finds much to commend the argumentation for its priority. He contends that "Calvin is located precisely in the

---

70. "Calvin's Central Dogma, Again," *The Sixteenth Century Journal,* 18 (1987), 191-99.
71. *Ibid.,* 196.
72. *Ibid.,* 198.

tension and conflict which existed between the Renaissance and Reformation movements and in the conflicting ideas which these two movements represent."[73] He builds on Battles's earlier research by arguing that there will always be "two poles, two aspects, two dialectical and conflicting elements in each theological topic which he discusses" and concludes that this structure is "fundamentally based in a broad, general philosophical dialectic between the ideal and the real."[74] Armstrong also recognizes the spiritual purpose of Calvin's theology, and finds what he calls a "hypothetical" structure in Calvin's *Institutes*.

This brings us, in a sense, up to the last minute in terms of analysis of the structure of Calvin's theology. Partee is not attracted to the *duplex cognitio Dei* theme and wants to propose another, while Armstrong is attracted to the theme and wants to place it more within its historical context. These two approaches, neither of which claims to be definitive at all, reflect the tension in current Calvin scholarship between theologians and historians. Although Armstrong and Partee both wish to pose only possible answers, Partee as theologian would like to see a more pure theological foundation to the structure of Calvin's thought, and Armstrong as historian emphasizes that the historical context should be brought to the fore. Armstrong goes so far as to say that he observes an underlying philosophical structure where Partee argues that his own idea of the union with Christ is superior precisely because it is a non-philosophical foundation. This tension is also observable in various reviews of Bouwsma's work. The general impression given is that historians are delighted with it but theologians are gravely disappointed.

V. Conclusion

Calvin research continues to explode, as may be easily observed from the attached bibliography. Besides the books, hundreds of articles have been produced. But further research needs to be done, especially in the following three areas.

---

73. *Probing the Reformed Tradition: Historical Studies in Honor of Edward A. Dowey, Jr.,* ed. E. McKee and B. Armstrong (Louisville: Westminster / John Knox Press, 1989), 137.

74. *Ibid.* Interestingly, A. McGrath also observes, not a dialectical structure to Calvin's theology, but "a highly effective form of rhetorical logic which substitutes the enthymeme for the syllogism." *The Science of Theology,* ed. G. Evans (Grand Rapids: Eerdmans, 1986), 126.

1. Text-Critical Work

Professor Neuser has made a report concerning the work of a group of editors committed to seeing a new set of Calvin's *Opera* in critical edition. This work is absolutely foundational to Calvin research.

On this same line, Professor Kingdon and a host of scholars in the United States and Switzerland are producing the Minutes of the Consistory of Geneva. This labor, from my own reading of the text, has produced further insights into the workings of the Consistory and specifically Calvin's ministry during that time. In the next eight years and following, I would imagine that there will be that many different volumes coming from the resources produced by Kingdon and his company.

2. Historical and Exegetical Research

We need to continue pushing ahead in understanding the historical context of Calvin's life and writing. Books that open Calvin's background and times and exegetical works that help us to comprehend the historical context of Calvin's exegesis, as exemplified by the group that meets regularly in Geneva, must continue. Calvin as exegete especially is opening new vistas into Calvin as theologian.

3. Integration

The vast explosion of new information on the life, times, and work of Calvin must be integrated. Historians must read theologians, and theologians must read the work of historians. Only as we become cross-disciplinary and force ourselves to be immersed in sociopolitical, theological, and historical works can a better picture of Calvin as theologian be created.

Recent Books on Calvin

1982
GANOCZY, A. *Calvins Handschriftliche Annotationen zu Chrysostomus* (Wiesbaden: Steiner, 1981)
————. *Herrschaft—Tugend—Vorsehung. Hermeneutische Deutung . . . Calvins* (Wiesbaden: Franz Steiner, 1982)

GERRISH, B. *The Old Protestantism and the New* (Chicago: University of Chicago Press; Edinburgh: T. & T. Clark, 1982)

HELM, P. *Calvin and the Calvinists* (Edinburgh: T. & T. Clark; Carlisle, PA: Banner of Truth Trust, 1982)

HÖPFL, H. *The Christian Polity of John Calvin* (Cambridge: Cambridge University Press, 1982)

INNES, W. *Social Concern in Calvin's Geneva* (Allison Park: Pickwick Press, 1982)

REID, W. S. *John Calvin. His Influence in the Western World* (Grand Rapids: Zondervan, 1982)

VAN DER WALT, B. *Calvinus Reformator* (Potchefstroom, RSA: Potchefstroom University for Christian Higher Education, 1982)

1983

FILLINGHAM, P. *John Calvin* (West Orange, NJ: Warthog Press, 1983)

GANOCZY, A. *Die Hermeneutik Calvins* (Wiesbaden: Steiner, 1983)

PETERSON, R. *Calvin's Doctrine of the Atonement* (Phillipsburg, NJ: Presbyterian and Reformed Publishing Co., 1983)

POTTER, G., AND M. GREENGRASS. *John Calvin* (New York: St. Martin's Press, 1983)

SHEPHERD, V. *The Nature and Function of Saving Faith in the Theology of John Calvin* (Macon, GA: Mercer University Press, 1983)

1984

LEE, SOU-YONNG. *La notion d'experience chez Calvin d'apres son institution de la religion Chréstienne* (Thesis [doctoral] — Université des Sciences humaines de Strasbourg, 1984)

LE GAL, P. *Le droit canonique dans la pensée dialectique de Jean Calvin* (Fribourg, Suisse: Editions Universitaires, 1984)

McKEE, E. *John Calvin on the Diaconate and Liturgical Almsgiving* (Genève: Librarie Droz, 1984)

McKIM, D., ed. *Readings in Calvin* (Grand Rapids: Baker Book House, 1984)

SELINGER, S. *Calvin against Himself* (Hamden, CN: Archon Books, 1984)

VINCENT, G. *Exigence éthique et interprétation dans l'oeuvre de Calvin* (Genève: Labor et Fides, 1984)

1985

BELL, H. *Calvin and Scottish Theology* (Edinburgh: Handsel, 1985)

DOUGLASS, J. *Women, Freedom and Calvin* (Philadelphia: Westminster Press, 1985)

PRESWICH, M. *International Calvinism* (Oxford: Clarendon Press, 1985)
VAN 'T SPIJKER, W. *Luther en Calvijn* (Kampen: Kok, 1985)
VOS, A. *Aquinas, Calvin and Contemporary Protestant Thought* (Grand Rapids: Eerdmans, 1985)
WILTERDINK, G. A. *Tyrant or Father? A Study of Calvin's Doctrine of God,* 2 vols. (Bristol, IN: Wyndham Hall Press, 1985)

1986

BABEL, H. *Calvin et la Réforme* (Genève: Berger-Levrault, 1986)
BATTLES, F. L., ed. and trans. *John Calvin. Institutes of the Christian Religion. 1536* (Grand Rapids: Meeter Center / Eerdmans, 1986)
EIRE, C. *War against the Idols: The Change in Worship from Erasmus to Calvin* (Cambridge: Cambridge University Press, 1986)
FUCHS, E. *La morale selon Calvin* (Paris: Cerf, 1986)
MULLER, R. *Christ and the Decree. Christology and Predestination in Reformed Theology from Calvin to Perkins* (Durham, NC: Labyrinth Press, 1986)
PARKER, T. H. L. *Calvin's Old Testament Commentaries* (Edinburgh: T. & T. Clark, 1986)
————. *Commentaries on the Epistle to the Romans 1532-1542* (Edinburgh: T. & T. Clark, 1986)
PERROT, A. *Le visage humain de Jean Calvin* (Genève: Labor et Fides, 1986)
VAN DER WALT, B., ed. *John Calvin's Institutes: His opus magnum* (Potchefstroom: Potchefstroom University for Christian Higher Education, 1986)

1987

CALVIN, JOHN. *Sermons on Deuteronomy* (Edinburgh: Banner of Truth Trust, 1987)
FURCHA, E. *In Honor of John Calvin, 1509-1564. Papers from the 1986 International Calvin Symposium* (Montreal: McGill University, 1987)
GANOCZY, A. *The Young Calvin* (Philadelphia: Westminster Press, 1987). Eng. trans. of earlier French work

1988

BOUWSMA, W. *John Calvin. A Sixteenth-Century Portrait* (New York and Oxford: Oxford University Press, 1988)
ENGEL, H. *John Calvin's Perspectival Anthropology* (Atlanta: Scholars Press, 1988)
GEORGE, T. *The Theology of the Reformers* (Nashville, TN: Broadman Press, 1988)

McKEE, E. *Elders and the Plural Ministry. The Role of Exegetical History in Illuminating John Calvin's Theology* (Genève: Droz, 1988)

NEUSER, W. *Calvinus Servus Christi* (Budapest: Presseabteilung des Ráday-Kollegiums, 1988)

SCHNUCKER, R. *Calviniana. Ideas and Influence of Jean Calvin* (Kirksville: Sixteenth Century Journal Publishers, 1988)

SCHÜTZEICHEL, H. *Katholische Beiträge zur Calvinforschung* (Trier: Paulinus-Verlag, 1988)

TORRANCE, T. F. *The Hermeneutics of John Calvin* (Edinburgh: Scottish Academic Press, 1988)

1989

BARTON, F. W. *Calvin and the Duchess* (Louisville: KY; Westminster / John Knox Press, 1989)

HANCOCK, R. *Calvin and the Foundations of Modern Politics* (Ithaca: Cornell University Press, 1989)

LEITH, J. *John Calvin's Doctrine of the Christian Life* (Louisville: Westminster / John Knox Press, 1989)

McKEE, E., & B. ARMSTRONG, eds. *Probing the Reformed Tradition. Historical Studies in Honor of E. A. Dowey, Jr.* (Louisville: Westminster / John Knox, 1989)

MULLETT, M. *Calvin* (New York: Routledge, Chapman & Hall, 1989)

WALLACE, R. *Calvin, Geneva and the Reformation. A Study of Calvin as Social Reformer, Churchman, Pastor and Theologian* (Edinburgh: Scottish Academic Press, 1988 [actually 1989])

1990

GEORGE, T., ed. *John Calvin and the Church* (Louisville: Westminster / John Knox, 1990)

McGRATH, A. *A Life of John Calvin* (Oxford: Blackwell, 1990)

RAINBOW, J. *The Will of God and the Cross. An Historical and Theological Study of John Calvin's Doctrine of Limited Redemption* (Allison Park: Pickwick, 1990)

Initia Calvini: The Matrix of Calvin's Reformation

Heiko A. Oberman

Quand je n'aurais pour moi père ni mère,
Quand je n'aurais aucun secours humain,
Le Tout-Puissant, en qui mon âme espère,
Pour me sauver me prendrait par la main.

Conduis-moi donc, ô Dieu, qui m'as aimé!
Délivre-moi de mes persécuteurs;
Ferme la bouche à mes accusateurs,
Ne permets pas que je sois opprimé.

Clément Marot, Psaume XXVII[1]

I. "De Me Non Libenter Loquor"

Everyone who sets out to trace Calvin's "Road to Reformation" encounters not only formidable obstacles in the cultural debris separating us from the sixteenth century, but also and especially in the person of Calvin himself. The five short

1. *Clément Marot et le Psautier Huguenot, étude historique, littéraire, musicale et bibliographique,* ed. O. Douen (Paris, 1879; repr. Nieuwkoop: B. de Graaf, 1967), 2.430. In 1541 Calvin incorporated in the new Genevan liturgy psalms that Marot (†1544) had begun to "translate" from 1533 onward in what became known as the "style Marotique." Marot provided the dispersed "Churches under the Cross" both with tender hymns commensurate with their refugee experience and with battle songs preparing for mob action and survival. I open and close this essay with Marot because he has lent Calvin's piety poetic power and is to be regarded as a major cohesive factor offsetting the centrifugal forces operative in this long-dispersed underground movement.

Latin words "De me non libenter loquor"[2] raise a screen of reticence penetrable only at our own risk. Calvin's silence is especially striking when compared with the directness of Martin Luther, the reformer whom he admired as the Inceptor until his death. Whereas Luther's persona looms large on every page of his work, Calvin inclined to be so "private" that it is difficult to discern the person behind the pen and to discover the emotional heartbeat behind his intellectual drive to grasp the mysteries of God and the world. While Luther continued to be a preacher even in the most academic of disputations or exegetical lectures, Calvin remained true to his first office in Geneva as lector, so that even in his sermons he was the teacher charged with enlightening the darkness of human confusion.

Amply displayed in the biblical commentaries of Erasmus, Zwingli, Bucer, or Melanchthon, a general characteristic of this period's biblical humanism was an objective-expository thrust that anticipated the nineteenth-century ideal of descriptive scholarship. Calvin's "ego" surfaced often and explicitly, but served as a scholarly adjudicator rather than as a carrier of personal sentiments. This instructional ideal of communication colored Calvin's sermons and letters — typically the most personal literary genres — and was strengthened by his deep sense of divine immediacy, transforming the prophets and doctors from Moses and Isaiah through Paul and Augustine into instruments of the Word and notaries of the gospel.

Calvin's dislike of self-disclosure is but one of the obstacles on our path to clarify his origins and early development. The Luther scholar has many more hard data to work with thanks to three fortunate constellations, none of which apply in the case of Calvin. As the "Initiator" of the Reformation both in his own eyes and in those of Calvin — the Wittenberger continually had to confront the deeply disturbing question "are you alone wise?", "how dare you contradict the wisdom of so many centuries?" Luther responded to the challenge by relating himself to Occam, Gerson, and Staupitz in a variety of revealing ways. From the very beginning Calvin was never "alone." He provided a rare autobiographical passage in his answer to Cardinal Sadolet (1539), wherein he described his path to the "sudden conversion"[3] and ar-

---

2. *Responsio at Sadoleti Epistolam* (1539); *Opera Selecta*, 1.460.42. The *Opera Selecta* (henceforth OS), vols. 1-4, ed. P. Barth and G. Niesel (München: Chr. Kaiser Verlag, 1926, 1936), are quoted with page and line references, also where this edition omitted line numbering.

3. This is Calvin's later — and indeed late: 1557 — designation in his Commentary on the Psalms: "subita conversione ad docilitatem subegit . . ." CO 31.21 C. Since the *Calvini Opera* (henceforth CO) do not provide line numbers, I divide the columns into A, B, and C to help the reader locate the quotations in context.

This much-discussed statement deserves a fresh analysis, since it cannot be rendered with the usual — classical or patristic — dictionaries in hand. The most convincing evidence must come from Calvin's Psalms commentary itself. Fortunately, this provides an eloquent answer, and if we include the French rendering of the Preface (if not written by Calvin himself, then certainly by someone thoroughly familiar with his thought and vocabulary), even bilingual evidence. I include supportive references to the French Sermon Series of 1553, in which all the main themes of the Psalms commentary are already available, and which provides the rich extra dimension of French expressions.

Here four points suffice: (1) As in the answer to Sadolet, the wider context of the conversion passage is the argument that Calvin had not sought office on his own account — Sadolet had suggested "ambitio" and "avaritia": lust for power or riches. No, Calvin had been called directly by God — as he shows in other commentaries, David to his throne, Isaiah to his prophecy, and Paul to his apostolate. Hence, even in these two "classical" autobiographical passages, Calvin presents "official" business, speaking "ex officio" about the unexpected intersection of his own designs with God's providence.

(2) In the phrase "subita conversio," conversion means "mutatio" (this can also happen to "impii": CO 31.475 C); the suddenness of "subita," "subito" (adverb), or "repente" refers to an event "praeter spem," beyond all expectation (CO 31.78 B; 459 C; 311 B; cf. CO 48.141 C), at times also applicable to the "secure" enemy (349 B): God intervenes "in a flash." Even in the most hopeless situation, he can "restore" us (as already in the sermon of the 2nd of April, 1553, on Ps. 119) "en une minute de temps" (CO 32.614 C).

(3) Most baffling for interpreters proves to be the clause "ad docilitatem subegit." The French parallel version is more explicit: ". . . par une conversion subite il domta et rangea à docilité mon coeur . . ." (CO 31.22 C). In line with Calvin's favorite image, "dom(p)ter" and "ranger" refer to the taming of wild animals, particularly of wild horses to be placed on track by receiving a "fraenum" ("fraenare": 213 B) or bridle (CO 31.322 C; 32.639 A). Without redirection *(rectitudo legis)*, the "wild horses" get lost "in flexuosas vias" (CO 32.200 C) and do not know in or out: they are caught (perplexed) in the "labyrinth" (CO 31.368 C; 32.642 A; cf. 52.447 B), tire out and finally lose their way completely, to be drowned in the "abyss" (CO 31.368 B).

(4) Calvin describes his preconversion situation as the need to be drawn "e profundo luto," "de ce bourdier si profond" (CO 31.21 C; cf. 22 C): He is "stuck in the pits." Though "labyrinth" and "abyss" overlap in the meaning of "confusion" and "disorientation," I am inclined to believe that the labyrinth of ethical directives is intended, when he still was "under the papacy" (CO 31.204 B). In the earlier commentary on Cor. I, Calvin stated explicitly that the "beginning of salvation" is "quod ex peccati et mortis labyrintho extrahimur" (CO 49.331 C). Characteristic of the "abyssus" is the most acute stage of despair which engenders such thoroughgoing "Anfechtungen" that it leaves the believer only one refuge, namely, to call on the mercy of God and his "extended hand." Though the "abyssus" is also the place where, ultimately, the hard of heart, the "protervi" or the "méchants" *(impii)* are "exterminated," the primary function of the "abyssus" is to characterize the human condition *coram Deo:* God is committed *(foedus)* to salvage from death and the sepulchre. The *Psychopannychia* (1534) documents both how early and how seriously Calvin takes this metaphor. See further the concise definition of "docilitas" in CO 7.594 B / C (1549) and the interpretation of the confessional as a threat to the certitude of salvation *(pax conscientiae)*, with "the abyssus"as the final consequence: "Haec demum pax est conscientiae, sine qua null est salus, quum indubia est absolutionis fides . . . nihilo minus conficient, quam si aperte iugularetur . . . et tandem abyssus trahet . . . quisquis hunc laqueum sponte induet, sciens ac volens salutem suam proiicit." CO 7.604 A / B.

The Commentary on the Psalms was completed in 1552 and published in 1557. For a clarification of the three types "hidden" in what is usually referred to as "Commentaries" — commentaries proper (the books of Moses, the Psalms, and Joshua), lectures, and sermons — see the fundamental work by T. H. L. Parker, *Calvin's Old Testament Commentaries* (Edinburgh: T. & T. Clark, 1986), 9-41. See here also the helpful list of the known dates of completion and of publication; *ibid.,* 29.

ticulated his initial aversion to an ultimate approval of the spokesmen for biblical reform.[4] Confronted by two mutually exclusive claims to truth, Calvin had come to see the weight of the evangelical party's arguments. But he mentioned no specific individuals. Apart from the uncontested impact of Luther, this leaves a wide array of potential candidates as shapers of his earliest thought.

Second, for Luther we can draw on precious and extensive documentation from the periods before and after his Reformation discovery. Though we continue to debate the exact timing of Luther's Reformation breakthrough, we can document stages in his development and reconstruct a remarkably accurate list of books in his library and on his desk while he prepared his first Psalms commentary (1513-15). We possess his marginalia to the works of Augustine, Anselm, and Lombard and know that he studied the sentences commentaries of Occam, d'Ailly, and Biel. Moreover, the most recent discovery documents his early interest in Gregory of Rimini some ten years before the Leipzig disputation (1519).[5] For the preconversion Calvin we have only the Seneca commentary. Although this is indeed a rich source for our knowledge of the young Calvin, its subject matter is not yet biblical theology; hence comparisons with his later works are hazardous.

Finally, for an investigation of Calvin we have to do without what proves so illuminating for Luther research, namely structural interpretive guides that help to describe Luther's place and function as acting vicar within his order or as a professor of biblical theology within his university. Calvin's social and intellectual milieu proves more evasive precisely because the newly emerging phalanx of French biblical humanists did not easily fit into well-established medieval organizations, whether monastic orders or academic institutions. In this light it is understandable that the little we know about the young Calvin during his "student years," from 1523 to 1528 at the Collège de la Marche

---

4. "Ego vero novitate offensus, difficulter aures praebui: ac initio, fateor, strenue animoseque resistebam. Siquidem (quae hominibus ingenita est in retinendo quod semel susceperunt instituto, vel constantia, vel contumacia), aegerrime adducebar, ut me in ignoratione et errore tota vita versatum esse confiterer. Una praesertim res animum ab illis meum avertebat, ecclesiae reverentia. Verum ubi aliquando aures aperui, meque doceri passus sum, supervacuum fuisse timorem illum intellexi, ne quid ecclesiae maiestati decederet. Multum enim interesse admonebant, secessionem quis ab ecclesia faciat, an vitia corrigere studeat, quibus ecclesia ipsa contaminata est. De ecclesia praeclare loquebantur, summum unitatis colendae studium prae se ferebant." OS 1.485.17-30.

5. Jun Matsuura is presently pursuing the identification of volumes in the Erfurt library of the Augustinians, some containing Luther's marginal notes. See his report, "Restbestände aus der Bibliothek des Erfurter Augustinerklosters zu Luthers Zeit und bisher unbekannte eigenhändige Notizen Luthers. Ein Bericht," in *Lutheriana,* ed. G. Hammer and K.-H. zur Mühlen, Archiv zur Weimarer Ausgabe, 2 (Köln: Böhlau, 1984), 315-32.

and the Collège Montaigu in Paris, has had to be squeezed for more information than it could yield. This has led to a history of speculation no less fascinating than fallacious. In the next section we must therefore turn to the task of distinguishing between fact and fancy in the delicate enterprise of retracing and reconstructing the early stages in the development of John Calvin.

II. The Pitfalls of Pedigree Pursuit

Under the impact of German idealism there has been a phase in the history of ideas in which scholars looked for "systems," for so-called "unfolding principles," and in German research preferably for the right "Ansatz." In this tradition a thinker was declared to be a Platonist, an Aristotelian, or a Kantian; and those elements which did not "fit" this systematic model were declared to be inconsistencies revealing a lack of intellectual vigor. Usually the author of such a study could show himself superior to his subject by pointing to neo-Platonic deviations, to subversive pseudo-Augustinian elements, or, in rare and extremely thrilling cases, to a sniff of Averroism.

Until the middle of this century one liked to write books to show that Calvin was a thoroughgoing Augustinian, Platonist, or Scotist. A new phase in the investigation of the beginnings of Calvin can be discerned in the middle of this century when the awareness emerged that an incontestably original thinker and text-oriented exegete like Calvin is most unlikely to have been systematically derivative or, in any sense of the word, to have been a schoolman. It is to be noted that even though the tendencies of the past proved to be too stubborn to be completely exorcised, and, perhaps because the majority of interpreters were theologians, Calvin continued to be seen as a "thinker" rather than as a real historical person of flesh and blood, who in the decisive stages of his development responded not only to currents of thought, but also and especially to religious needs and political challenges, to personal encounters and social experiences.

In 1950 François Wendel made a new beginning with his study of Calvin's *Origins and Development,* published in English in 1963 and in a revised and enlarged French edition in 1983.[6] For an intellectual biography four decades is a remarkably extensive career; and its end is not yet in sight since it is still the best one-volume introduction to Calvin's theological thought. Perhaps because Wendel could draw even-handedly on French and German

---

6. *Calvin, sources et évolution de sa pensée religieuse* (Paris, 1950; revue et complétée, Geneva, 1985); Eng. trans. *Calvin. Origins and Development of His Religious Thought* (New York: Harper & Row, 1963).

scholarship, he does not look for the "master plan" but subtly points to "the echo of Scotus" or to remarkable "traces of nominalism."[7] Admittedly, while looking for the scholastic roots of Calvin's thought, Wendel fails to distinguish between Scotism and nominalism, and (as I will argue) overstates Erasmian influences at the expense of the significance of Lefèvre d'Étaples and the circle of Meaux.[8] Nevertheless, he has set a standard by which succeeding scholarship is to be measured.

Wendel's work whetted the appetite and his allusions unleashed the urge for further clarification. This has been pursued in a series of studies that have in common a search for Calvin's roots, best characterized as the pursuit of the pedigree. In 1963 Karl Reuter published *Das Grundverständnis der Theologie Calvins,*[9] in which he argued for a pervasive "scotisch-scotistische Personalismus" of Calvin after placing him at the feet of John Major (Mair, †1550) until the spring of 1528 — even though Major taught from 1518 through 1526 in Glasgow and Saint Andrews and lectured upon his return to Paris at Sainte Barbe. Calvin is said to have learned from Major "eine neue Konzeption antipelagianischer und scotistischer Theologie" as well as a "erneuerten Augustinismus."[10] Behind Calvin's doctrine of sin Reuter discerns the authority of Thomas Bradwardine (†1349), who found in Calvin "a true disciple"[11] — "bien étonné de se trouver ensemble!" — even though Calvin never "found" Bradwardine. In 1966 Hiltrud Stadtland-Neumann turned to an analysis of Calvin's understanding of the Sermon on the Mount.[12] The pursuit of the pedigree now leads to the conclusion that Thomas Aquinas, though never

7. *Calvin. Origins and Development,* 128f.

8. *Ibid.,* 130.

9. *Das Grundverständnis der Theologie Calvins unter Einbeziehung ihrer geschichtlichen Abhängigkeiten.* Beiträge zur Geschichte und Lehre der Reformierten Kirche, Band 15 (Neukirchener-Vluyn: Neukirchener-Verlag des Erziehungsvereins, 1963).

10. *Ibid.,* 20f. Major, some forty years older than Calvin, was absent from Paris — in Scotland — between 1518 and 1526, and then taught in Sainte Barbe. See James K. Farge, *Bibliographical Register* (Toronto, 1980), 304-11; with full biography and bibliography. Cf. *Orthodoxy and Reform in Early Modern France. The Faculty of Theology at Paris, 1500-1543,* Studies in Medieval and Reformation Thought, vol. 32 (Leiden: Brill, 1985), 100-104. Major went back to Paris in 1521, just long enough to oversee the printing of his vast *History of Greater Britain,* for which he wrote a dedication at the College of Montaigu, where he had taught logic and philosophy since 1499. See Alexander Brodie, *George Lokert: Late Scholastic Logician* (Edinburgh: Edinburgh University Press, 1983), 11. Here, also, the most extensive sketch of the life and works of Major: 4-31. One could only wish for an equally substantial study of Major, for over forty years the friend of Lokert (†1548).

11. *Ibid.,* 162.

12. *Evangelische Radikalismen in der Sicht Calvins. Sein Verständnis der Bergpredigt und der Aussendungsrede (Matth. 10).* Beiträge zur Geschichte und Lehre der Reformierten Kirche, Band 24 (Neukirchener-Vluyn: Neukirchener Verlag des Erziehungsvereins, 1966).

mentioned, "exerted no small influence on the thought of Calvin."[13] In the case of the permissibility of an oath, Calvin's direct dependence on Thomas is argued — without consulting the sentences of Peter Lombard, commentaries on canon law, or Duns Scotus's treatment of this burning issue.[14]

In comparison with these speculative constructions of Calvin's dependence on Thomas, Scotus, Bradwardine, or Major, Alexandre Ganoczy's *Le Jeune Calvin,* published in 1966, marked a considerable advance.[15] Ganoczy points to the fact that the young Calvin in and before the first edition of the *Institutio* (1536) does not display any knowledge of the leading scholastic theologians, whether they hail from the Thomistic, Scotistic, or Occamistic tradition.[16] Anyone who wants to argue that Calvin had been initiated in scholastic theology in Montaigu, Ganoczy points out, must prove that "Calvin between fourteen and seventeen years of age dared to go against the strict school curriculum and took instead of lectures in grammar, philosophy and science, courses in theology which were the privilege of the much senior students."[17]

Ganoczy does suggest, however, that Calvin in following lectures in scholastic philosophy was introduced to the kind of Aristotelian ethics that were "without doubt rife with scholastic casuistry," and imbibed not only dialectical reasoning but also a "metaphysics which in the nominalist fashion opposed systematically the divine and the human."[18] While this last conclusion, particularly with its loaded word "opposed!" is still the unfortunate remnant of an outdated, Thomist view of nominalism, Ganoczy achieved for

13. *Ibid.,* 64, 68f.

14. For Petrus Lombardus see *Magistri Petri Lombardi Parisiensis Episcopi Sententiae in IV Libris distinctae,* Tomus II, Liber III et IV (Grottaferrata, 1981), III d 39, 4 (153); 218-27. As Calvin's immediate background — and as explanation of any such "Thomistic" traces — Martin Bucer's 1529 Psalms commentary is most pertinent. Attached to his primarily philological interpretation of Psalm 24 is a separate "Disputatio, an Christiano liceat iurare." Thanks to the collegial help of Wim van 't Spijker (Apeldoorn), I could use the Geneva 1554 edition of Robert Stephanus, *Psalmorum libri quinque ad Hebraicam veritatem traducti et summa fide parique diligentia a Martino Bucero enarrati;* here, fol. 155f. In a number of the eighteen inserted "Disputationes" Thomas Aquinas is explicitly quoted. We know that Calvin read this Commentary at an early stage. Though he is critical of Bucer's evasiveness — he felt the first edition was inappropriately "hidden" under a pseudonym: Aretius Felinus — Calvin had high praise for this "opere alioqui praeclarissimo, si quod aliud exstat." A. L. Herminjard, *Correspondance des Réformateurs,* 4 (1536-38) (Genève-Paris, 1872), 347 (henceforth quoted as Herminjard); Letter from Geneva, 12 January 1538.

15. *Le Jeune Calvin, Genèse et évolution de sa vocation réformatrice.* Veröffentlichungen des Instituts für Europäische Geschichte, Abteilung Religionsgeschichte, Mainz, Band 40 (Wiesbaden: Franz Steiner Verlag, 1966).

16. *Ibid.,* 191.

17. *Ibid.,* 192.

18. *Ibid.,* 192.

Calvin studies what R. R. Post did for the interpretation of the Modern Devotion,[19] facilitating the return ad fontes by cutting through a thick layer of secondary literature.

Whereas it was the strength of Ganoczy that he had limited himself to the works of the young Calvin, in 1982 he revived the pedigree search in his edition — together with Stefan Scheld — of Calvin's annotations to Seneca and Lucanus, dating quite likely from the years 1545-46.[20] On this late basis Ganoczy argues for the formative influence of Stoicism on Calvin in two directions. Always suggestive rather than assertive, and with all of the usual reservations, Ganoczy relates Calvin's so-called "Weltverachtung" to the Stoics, at least as concerns its nonbiblical root, and points to "eine stoische Färbung" in Calvin's emphasis on human beings as clay in the hands of God. He further discerns "die Tendenz einer stoisch beeinflussten Schriftauslegung" in Calvin's biblical doctrine of election and reprobation.[21] Accordingly Ganoczy bases Calvin's sense of vocation not only on Christian faith but also on a Stoic view of the immutable God.[22]

19. See R. R. Post, *The Modern Devotion, Confrontation with Reformation and Humanism.* Studies in Medieval and Reformation Thought, vol. 3 (Leiden, 1968).

20. *Herrschaft — Tugend — Vorsehung, Hermeneutische Deutung und Veröffentlichung handschriftlicher Annotationen Calvins zu sieben Senecatragödien und den Pharsalia Lucans.* Veröffentlichungen des Instituts für Europäische Geschichte, Abteilung Religionsgeschichte, Mainz, Band 105 (Wiesbaden: Franz Steiner Verlag, 1982), 6f. On the popularity of Lucian, who "had a new vogue in the Renaissance," see Erica Rummel in the introduction to Erasmus's "Tyrannicida," Collected Works of Erasmus, 29 (Toronto, 1989), 72. I do not pursue here the edition of Calvin's annotations to Chrysostom, both because there is no proof that they date from the period before 1536 (Calvin used the Paris edition of 1536 but quoted this Church Father already at the Disputation of Lausanne, Oct. 5, 1536), and whereas the editors emphasize the formative influence on Calvin's hermeneutics, I find Calvin drawing on Chrysostom for support as often as criticizing him for misunderstanding the text. See *Calvins Handschriftliche Annotationen zu Chrysostomus. Ein Beitrag zur Hermeneutik Calvins,* ed. A. Ganoczy und K. Müller (Wiesbaden: Franz Steiner Verlag, 1981). Lucian is quoted in the commentary *In Isaiam,* but merely to show the agreement between biblical and Roman law concerning the legal status of the married woman. CO 36.95 A / B; Com. Is. 4:1.

21. *Ibid.,* 46, 49.

22. I quote the relevant passage in toto to illustrate the subtle, cautious, and suggestive formulation of Ganoczy, which in a summary is easily distorted: "Calvins Berufung und Selbstvertrauen wurzeln sicher wesentlich im biblisch-christlichen Glauben. Doch diesem Glauben treten stoische Vorstellungen von einer ewigen und unwandelbaren Bestimmung und Lenkung aller Dinge hilfreich zur Seite und gewinnen nicht zuletzt dort wesentlich an Gewicht, wo der Reformator, über ein christliches Verständnis der Erwählung aller Menschen hinausgehend, eine die Berufung zum Heil kontrastierende Vorherbestimmung zum Bösen und zum ewigen Tod lehrte." *Ibid.,* 52. Apart from the fact that it is improper to leave the impression that Calvin taught a "predestination to evil," there is little in Seneca — or the later Stoic tradition in general — to suggest the providential concern of the deity with the course of individual human lives. See Marcia L. Colish, *The Stoic Tradition from Antiquity to the Early Middle Ages. II: Stoicism in Christian Latin Thought through the Sixth Century,* Studies in the History of Christian Thought, vol. 35 (Leiden, 1985).

For our purposes it suffices to point out that the young Calvin, writing his *Institutio* in 1535 — and therefore well before any later elaborations — interprets the immutability of God as the reliability of his Word. As a matter of fact, for Calvin it is the cornerstone of Christian faith that God cannot undo his promise: so certain is God's truth "ut non possit non praestare, quod se facturum sancto suo verbo recepit"; God cannot but deliver what he has laid down in his Holy Word (Rom. 10,11).[23] We discern here not the Stoic but the longstanding medieval vocabulary of commitment that we encounter with Scotus and the nominalist theologians as the *pactum Dei* to which God is bound *de potentia ordinata*.[24] The Stoic notions of tranquility and moderation, which Calvin was willing to accept as biblically sound, he did find with Cicero.[25] As far as Seneca is concerned, he is for Calvin in no sense of the word a Christian. As in earlier research, Ganoczy has overlooked Calvin's uncompromising statement: "For his involvement with Christianity there is nowhere at any time even the slightest indication."[26]

The most recent publication to be considered in this context is an article by Alister E. McGrath, "John Calvin and Late Medieval Thought. A Study in Late Medieval Influences upon Calvin's Theological Development."[27] Sufficiently warned by Ganoczy's *Le Jeune Calvin,* McGrath no longer looks for proof but rather for "circumstantial evidence" to establish Calvin's dependence on late medieval theology. Defending and indeed reviving Reuter, McGrath is by no means convinced that Major could not have had a significant influence

23. *Institutio* (1536), ch. 2; OS 1.69.31. See, however, the version in the *Institutes of the Christian Religion 1536 Edition,* translated and annotated by Ford L. Battles, revised ed. (Grand Rapids: Wm. B. Eerdmans and H. H. Meeter Center for Calvin Studies, 1986 [1975]), 43. Whereas Battles's annotations are generally helpful, the translation is unclear, imprecise, occasionally incomplete, and at times so misleading that a mere revision will not suffice. One of the reasons for these insufficiencies is a lack of familiarity with the medieval matrix of Calvin's thought.

24. In Calvin's first theological treatise, the *Psychopannychia* (first printed in Strasbourg 1542, but designed probably in Orleans 1534) we find the formulation that will continue to be the shorthand for this "selfbinding of God": "Promisit hoc [i.e., life eternal] nobis qui fallere non potest," CO 5.194.23f. Cf. ed. Zimmerli (see below, n. 56), 50.15f. For the history of this covenant tradition, see Berndt Hamm, *Promissio, Pactum, Ordinatio, Freiheit und Selbstbestimmung Gottes in der scholastischen Gnadenlehre,* Beiträge zur historischen Theologie, 54 (Tübingen, 1977), esp. 345ff.

25. Quite explicit, for instance, in his Com. on Phil. 4:5; CO 52.60 B. Amid the vast international literature on "Stoic" concepts of mental health and mental growth, I have found most helpful for the interpretation of Calvin Ilsetraut Hadot, *Seneca und die Griechisch-Römische Tradition der Seelenleitung* (Berlin: de Gruyter, 1969), esp. the sections on "securitas" and "tranquillitas animi"; 126-41.

26. ". . . neque ullo unquam vel minimo indicio se Christianum esse probavit." CO 52.66 C; Com. Phil. 4:22.

27. *Archiv für Reformationsgeschichte,* 77 (1986), 58-78.

on Calvin.[28] McGrath finds the circumstantial evidence he is looking for in drawing on the early and late Calvin throughout the period 1536-60. By positing that not only in the fourteenth century, but also in the fifteenth and early sixteenth century, the theology of Gregory of Rimini (†1358) was "on the ascendency," he assumes that Gregory — and the "schola augustiniana moderna" associated with him — was so prominent in Paris that Calvin could not possibly have avoided taking note of him.

Beyond a close relationship between Calvin and Gregory of Rimini, McGrath stipulates "the essential continuity between Calvin's thought and that of the later medieval period in general and that of the via moderna in particular."[29] Throughout the footnotes he documents his conclusions with reference to secondary literature, and nowhere is the test-question raised whether or to what extent Calvin's avid reading of St. Paul and St. Augustine can sufficiently — and hence convincingly — explain convictions reemerging (in a markedly different form and context) in the *via Gregorii*. Gregory is never mentioned by Calvin and the *via Gregorii* is not incorporated into the statutes of any of the forty or so Parisian colleges. Furthermore, one of the chief characteristics of the so-called "schola augustiniana moderna" is its programmatic effort to recall the scholastic doctors to read and study the authentic writings of St. Augustine in context and not in excerpts (florilegia). Through the celebrated Basel editions of Amerbach (1503-06) and Erasmus (1520-29; Paris 1531-32), Calvin could bypass the circuitous road of scholastic reception.[30] It is uncontested that already the young Calvin of 1532-35 had an impressively broad and independent access to the *Opera Augustini*.[31]

The preceding survey, which could have been easily extended, is instructive both in alerting us to pitfalls to be avoided and in pointing to promising avenues of approach in four respects:

1. In studying the *initia Calvini* we should apply Occam's razor and

---

28. *Ibid.*, 67, 71.

29. *Ibid.*, 77f.

30. Luchesius Smits makes a strong case for Calvin's use of the Basel edition of Erasmus, *Saint Augustin dans l'oeuvre de Jean Calvin*, 1 (Assen: van Gorcum, 1957), 201-5.

31. See J. M. J. Lange van Ravenswaay, *Augustinus totus noster. Das Augustinverständnis bei Johannes Calvin* (Göttingen: Vandenhoeck & Ruprecht, 1990). Two aspects of this work deserve our particular attention: (1) the extent to which Calvin personally identified with the Bishop of Hippo; (2) the extent to which Augustine became such a "key" for doctrinal discernment that it can be argued that (after 1543) Calvin founded his own "schola augustiniana" (*ibid.*, 151f., 180). It should be noted, however, that the claim made in Calvin's "totus noster" is not to be understood as total approval. Augustine is not only incidentally "wrong" in his exegesis (CO 31.310 B; Ps. 31:19; cf. CO 48.137 B; Acts 7:14) but also belongs to those sancti (Cyprian, Ambrose, and more recently Gregory the Great and Bernard) who had the right intention, but ". . . saepe aberrarunt" (CO 49.357 A; I Cor. 3:15).

control the "plurality" of sources by limiting ourselves to the writings of Calvin prior to 1536, including therefore the first version of his *Institutio* written in 1535 in Basel. In this first edition, Calvin — according to an exceptional consensus among all Calvin scholars — speaks to us as a man who has already found both his voice and his message, and addresses the reader as a seasoned spokesman for the embattled evangelical cause. In the later editions from 1539 through 1559 (1560), this first manifest is periodically enlarged and changed; in the course of twenty years of intensive study, taking note of ever new and complex objections, the Genevan reformer had to study a large array of authorities. These additions should not be taken into consideration as the textual basis for studying the origins of the reformer.

2. A promising and already most rewarding avenue of investigation has been opened up by Francis M. Higman in studying Calvin's use of the French language. Higman set out on this path in his important *The Style of John Calvin in his French Polemical Treatises.*[32] Drawing on Higman's study of Calvin's French polemical writings from the forties and applying this to the period before 1536, we can discern the importance of Calvin's first French publication and are indeed struck by the fresh and compact power of Calvin's preface to Olivétan's French Bible. In 1535 Calvin had not only found his theological, but also his "French voice." More generally, Calvin's French writings deserve equal time, and more. My extensive list of Calvin's French expressions and proverbs not only highlights his creative use of a language *in statu nascendi,* but also the extent to which his native tongue was his primary mode of molding experience and shaping reflection.

3. Though it may sound self-evident and therefore redundant, it must be insisted upon that the terminus post quem is as important as the terminus ad quem: in our case this means that the *initia* do not start only in 1532 with his first breaking into print or in 1533 with the computed date of his conversion. We should study Calvin's "beginnings" from 1509 to 1536 and thereby take into consideration that there is far more to influence a person than the books read — including the Scriptures! — namely, political and social as well as psychological and religious experiences. Hence we should apply to the study of Calvin a rule he used with reference to understanding the mysteries of God: ". . . plus in hac inquisitione valere vivendi quam loquendi modum."[33]

---

32. Oxford, 1967. See also *Jean Calvin, Three French Treatises,* ed. Francis M. Higman (London, 1970). As concerns the period before 1536, see idem, "Dates-clé de la réforme française: le *sommaire* de Guillaume Farel et *la somme de l'escripture saincte,*" *Bibliothèque d'Humanisme et Renaissance,* 38 (1976), 237-47; idem, "Farel, Calvin et Olivétan, sources de la spiritualité gallicane," *Actes du Colloque Guillaume. Farel . . . 1980* (Genève, 1983), 45-61; idem, "Luther et la pieté de l'église gallicane: le *Livre de vraye et parfaicte oraison,*" *Revue d'histoire et de philosophie religieuses,* 63 (1983), 91-111.
33. CO 53.333 A; I Tim. 6:16.

4. There cannot be any doubt that it is essential to be committed to the close scrutiny of Calvin's late medieval *resources*. But without clear evidence these resources cannot be transformed into *sources*. They are listening devices or hermeneutical tools to uncover Calvin's own profile by highlighting — always "zur Stelle" and ad hoc — both continuity and discontinuity. In the case of his final (1562) clarification of the intimate relation between the sacramental sign *(sacramentum tantum, signum)* and the thing signified *(res sacramenti)*, we can notice Calvin's application of Scotist terminology to define his position between Zurich and Wittenberg with greater precision.[34] In every such case the interest should be not to construct a pedigree, but rather to show why and how the medieval backdrop is a pertinent and necessary tool for clarifying a particular passage or complex issue.[35] The traditional type of intellectual history is as treacherously reductionist as its twin brother "Ahnenforschung" is racist. For this reason, intellectual history is badly in need of deconstruction, this time not to eliminate but to recover the authorial intention.

Once this is clearly in place, it can be safely said that there is a whole range of themes clustered around Calvin's presentation of the *ordo salutis*,[36] which a hundred years before would have earned him the school ranking "Scotist." Each taken separately, the following seven tenets can be traced back to other traditions, but as a cluster they must have suggested a close proximity to Scotus. We in turn can most readily decode their originality with a Scotistic dictionary in hand:

34. "The 'Extra' Dimension in the Theology of Calvin," in *Dawn of the Reformation: Essays in Late Medieval and Early Reformation Thought* (Edinburgh: T. & T. Clark, 1986), 241ff.; German version, *Die Reformation von Wittenberg nach Genf* (Göttingen, 1986), 266ff. See also the cautious procedure of Jean-Claude Margolin in "Duns Scot et Erasme," *Regnum Hominis et Regnum Dei*, ed. C. Berube (Rome, 1978), 89-112. Commenting on I Tim. 4:6, Calvin points out that "fidelis Christi minister" is an infinitely higher title than to be called a thousand times over "seraphici subtilesque" — the traditional designation of Bonaventure and Scotus! (CO 52.298). The selection of these two names as the standard of comparison strongly suggests that Calvin associates scholasticism with the Franciscan tradition rather than with Thomas and the Dominican tradition.
35. A fine example of using "background" information to better grasp Calvin's intentions is E. David Willis, *Calvin's Catholic Christology. The Function of the so-called Extra-Calvinisticum in Calvin's Theology*, Studies in the History of Christian Thought 2 (Leiden: E. J. Brill, 1966).
36. In Part I of his *The Hermeneutics of John Calvin* (Edinburgh: Scottish Academic Press, 1988), Thomas F. Torrance has presented an analysis of Calvin's "Parisian background" — Scotus, Occam, Major — that takes its point of departure in epistemology. Though rich in helpful and at times precious observations in the realm of metaphysics, this abstract "grit" proves to lack the specificity that one likes to find in historical evidence. I am particularly uneasy about "developments flowing from the teaching of Duns Scotus" that are claimed to have a direct bearing on the *Devotio Moderna* (p. 12), which in turn is said to have provided "a spring-board for a leap into the Reformation" (p. 97). In the presentation of Calvin's hermeneutics, however, Torrance's study is exemplary.

1. The beginning and end of the *ordo salutis* hinge on the sovereign acts of God in predestination and acceptation;
2. there is a twofold acceptation of the Pilgrim *(Viator)* and of his works;
3. fundamental and eternal (not cancelled by "disobedience"!) is the covenant of God *(foedus, pactum)* with Israel and the church;
4. the final acceptation is unmerited "ex mera misericordia" on the basis of God's covenant commitment;[37]
5. throughout we note the retention of such terms as "ex puris naturalibus"[38] and "facere quod in se est," or (more often) "quantum in se est";[39]
6. indicative of progressive revelation and the approximation of the end (finis!) is the *felix culpa* doctrine;[40]
7. of central importance is the "formal" distinction,[41] which also underlies the favorite expression "docendi causa," once succinctly defined by Calvin as "disiungi res inter se coniunctas."[42] It allows for the distinction between the being of God *(essentia)* and his revealed power *(virtus)* which forbids on the one hand "curiosity" about the aseity of God (that is, the "being" behind the "person") and rejects on the other the late medieval expression "de potentia absoluta" as the suggestion of God's use of sheer power (tyranny for Calvin)[43] that improperly separates power and justice.[44]

---

37. CO 52.334 B / C; I Tim. 6:18. Here and in the following notes I indicate only representative passages.

38. CO 49.343 C; I Cor. 2:14.

39. CO 31.520 B; cf. 504 C; 523 B; Ps. 51:15; cf. Ps. 50:16; Ps. 51:20.

40. "In summa, hoc vult Paulus, conditionem, quam per Christum consequimur, longe potiorem esse, quam fuerit sors primi hominis; quia Adae collata fuerit suo et posterorum nomine anima vivens, Christus autem nobis attulerit spiritum qui vita est." CO 49.558 C; I Cor. 15:45.

41. The "distinctio formalis" is a distinction "ex natura rei" — in this case "ex natura Dei" — but not "inter rem et rem" *(distinctio realis)*. See the glossary in my *Harvest of Medieval Theology* (Cambridge, MA, 1963), 466. Cf. O. Muck in *Historisches Wörterbuch der Philosophie,* hrg. v. J. Ritter, 2 (Basel, Stuttgart: Schwabe Verlag, 1972), 270.

42. CO 49.522 A; I Cor. 14:14. How far this expression "docendi causa" can take over the function of "de potentia absoluta" appears from the continuation of the definition: ". . . non quia id vel possit vel soleat contingere"!

43. CO 31.387 C; 402 B; Ps. 38:4; Ps. 39:10.

44. See David C. Steinmetz, "Calvin and the Absolute Power of God," *Journal of Medieval and Renaissance Studies,* 18 (1988), 65-79. It is to be noted, however, that Calvin can use himself the expression "potentia absoluta." What he opposes is the "nuda potentia absoluta" (CO 31.402 B; cf. 387 C), that is, tyranny. It is Job who — mistakenly — regards God's punishment as "puissance excessive," which threatened to submerge him in the abyss: ". . . comme s'il me vouloit abysmer." Sermon 88 on Job; CO 34.338 A / B; cf. 336 A / B.

More important even than such single issues is to grasp the overarching view, which theologians call "eschatological" and philosophers prefer to designate as "teleological": it is characteristic of Calvin's mode of thinking that throughout the Latin "finis" or French "but" *(terme)* is given priority above the second causes or "steps" toward this goal. Hence, metaphysically, "final" causality is given precedence over "first" causality and, psychologically regarded, the human agent is not "pushed" but "reoriented," and "drawn." This perspective is operative in each of Calvin's privileged levels of discourse, which arranged here in temporal sequence has to be read backward "sub specie aeternitatis." It should be kept in mind, moreover, that in the five following paradigms we separate what Calvin would merely distinguish "docendi causa"; actually the five are closely related roles of God:

1. "Father" — family (adoption) — protection and discipline — final mercy;
2. "King" — reign (providence) — obedience — final glory;
3. "Teacher" — school — exercise — final wisdom;
4. "Lord of Hosts" — army — oath — final victory;
5. "Judge" — courtroom — scrutiny — final adjudication (acceptation / reprobation).

Two examples may serve to illustrate that what could seem an abstract analysis has far-reaching consequences for the interpretation of single aspects. (1) The German rendering of "finis legis" as "Gesetzesende" is misleading: Calvin does not — and indeed, never — mean "the end" of the Law, but its goal or "scopus." (2) "Meditatio futurae vitae" is not only a spiritual exercise, but designates the appropriate mental attitude or frame of mind with which the Christian "sees" and interprets *all* events in the world and in his own life, namely in terms of the eschaton, "the end." "Promissio" and "spes" are as future-orientated as the cosmic order itself. Yet, since faith "knows" and "grasps" the End, the present is already transformed or — more precisely — transfinalized.

Theology and metaphysics can only be distinguished "docendi causa" and only be understood in retrospect. In Calvin's case "sub specie aeternitatis" can only be rendered as "in the light of eternity," if it is understood as "in the light of the End." For Calvin's view of nature and history, the term "second causes" can only be used metaphorically: de facto they are "agents" of God-in-action; human beings come alive when they respond to the call of trekking toward the End.

In this thoroughgoing and radical finalism Calvin is "plus Scotiste que Duns Scot" — so much so that he transcends the boundaries within which such school ties make sense. Indeed, Calvin found this vision already enunciated by the prophet Isaiah: "recte docet Isaias . . . finem spectandum, eoque referenda esse omnia."[45] This is the extent to which the scotistic dictionary can assist us. From hereon in we have to start reading the book of his life itself.

III. The Historical Calvin: The Growth of a Vision

Confronted with the various claims for Calvin the Platonist,[46] the Stoic, the Thomist, the Scotist, or the nominalist — not to mention the frequent references to "humanism" and the Modern Devotion — it is not too much to conclude that Calvin is caught in a true *captivitas systematica*. What makes William J. Bouwsma's *John Calvin, A Sixteenth-Century Portrait*[47] the most significant interpretation since François Wendel is his quest for the historical Calvin, not a man of one system but a real human being exposed to a complex bundle of contradictory impulses.

Gingerly Bouwsma wades through the ocean of systematic claims, providing suggestive hints relating the reformer to Budé and Erasmus, Rabelais and Montaigne, rather than to the great medieval schoolmen. Without writing a psycho-history, Bouwsma is acutely aware of the pervasive power of Angst and hope, of terror and trust. One avenue of approach proved here to be particularly rewarding, namely Bouwsma's intent in reading Calvin's major achievement, the biblical commentaries, with a sharp eye for interpretations not required or not immediately following out of the scriptural text.

In consequence there emerge not one but two Calvins, characterized by two favorite expressions: the "labyrinth" and the "abyss." The first Calvin, "the forward-looking humanist and adventuresome discoverer," has escaped from the confusing maze of the labyrinth of medieval scholasticism. The other Calvin is the philosopher, "a rationalist and a schoolman in the high scholastic tradition represented by Thomas Aquinas, a man of fixed principles, and a conservative. . . . This Calvin was chiefly driven by terror that took shape for him in the metaphor of the abyss."[48] While some of Bouwsma's insights will

---

45. CO 36.194 C; Isa. 9:6.

46. See Charles Partee, *Calvin and Classical Philosophy,* Studies in the History of Christian Thought, vol. 14 (Leiden: Brill, 1977). Though referring to Calvin only once, James Hankins's rich reconstruction of the Platonic discourse in the (later) Renaissance documents how unsuitable Plato is as key to Calvin: *Plato in the Renaissance,* 2 vols. (Leiden: Brill, 1990).

47. New York: Oxford University Press, 1988.

48. Bouwsma, *John Calvin,* 230; cf. 233.

continue to be basic ingredients of every convincing reinterpretation, it is a mark of the significance of this book that it may take scholarship quite some time to refashion these two Calvins into the one historical person.[49]

Inclined to blend out the major theological themes in Calvin's thought, Bouwsma is both a reaction to and a correction of traditional theological Calvin research. At first sight these two approaches seem to be irreconcilable and mutually exclusive.[50] Traditional Calvin interpreters have to be convinced that Calvin's writings contain far more than this doctrina. Bouwsma on the other side has to be convinced that one cannot draw "a sixteenth-century portrait" without retracing the physiognomy of established religious language in order to capture the unique features of the Genevan reformer. And part of these features reflects his lifelong passion: the renewal of theology as the clarification of the gospel.

A case in point is Bouwsma's important discovery of Calvin's predilection for the word and concept of "labyrinth," formerly generally overlooked. Its significance can only be properly assessed, however, against the background of the fact that Erasmus had carved the expression in stone by including it among his *Adagia* (2.10, 15), of which there were twenty-eight editions between 1500 and 1536. But even before Erasmus's *Adagia* had captured the book markets in Paris and Basel, the expression "labyrinth" had already become part and parcel of the humanist arsenal against the "obscurities" of scholasticism. The correspondence in the circle around Jacques Lefèvre d'Étaples amply documents this. Charles de Bovelles — like Lefèvre and Calvin a Picardian — employs the term in defense of geometry in 1501, though not yet against a clear target.[51] Hieronymus Gebwiler (†1540), writing from Strasbourg to Sebastian Brant in March 1511, seizes upon the image of the "labyrinth" — this time with a specific attack on scholastic logic.[52] And a

49. See my review "Reforming out of Chaos," *Times Literary Supplement,* 455.4 (Aug. 19-25, 1988), col. 913f.

50. The divide is not bridged but widened by the view expressed in the extensive review of Bouwsma's *John Calvin* by William Neuser in *Historische Zeitschrift,* 250 (1990), 152-57, which I read with growing concern. Apart from the fact that it is difficult to agree with most of the propositions of Mr. Neuser — even including his rare points of praise for Bouwsma's achievement — the (for Neuser atypical) condescending tone of the magister correcting a novice in the field does not bode well for the chances of the doctrinal school to catch up *and* thus provide a hearing for its precious tradition. For such a "hearing" see the exemplary review by Edward A. Dowey in the *Journal of the American Academy of Religion,* 57 (1989), 845-48.

51. "Daedalus inextricabilem labyrinthum fabricavit, quo cuique sine glomere lini improperanti interclusus exitus negabatur." *The Prefatory Epistles of Jacques Lefèvre d'Étaples and Related Texts,* ed. Eugene F. Rice, Jr. (New York: Columbia University Press, 1972), 93.

52. ". . . praedecessorum nostrorum modorum significandi . . . inextricabiles labyrinthi, quibus totum aevum absumpsere." Rice, 244.

year later Robert Fortune (†1528), teacher of grammar, rhetoric, and philosophy at the Collège du Plessis, contrasts in the preface to his Paris edition of Cyprian (1 Nov. 1512) the clarity and revitalizing power of these writings with the confusing works of the unmentioned scholastics.[53]

Such negative use of the "labyrinth" to decry scholasticism as the prison of the mind had not always been a foregone conclusion. Hardly twenty years before, Wessel Gansfort (†1489) invoked the myth of Theseus in a strikingly positive fashion by emphasizing the "thread through the labyrinth" as the classical image for disciplined prayer and well-structured speech.[54] For Gansfort the "labyrinth" is associated with challenge rather than with doom, with the need for direction rather than with loss of orientation. For Calvin the "labyrinth" stands for confusion, and is already part of an established vocabulary that was available to express impatient disdain for scholasticism.[55] It suggests — often as synonymous with "laqueus" or the classical "nassa" — the state of perplexed moral bewilderment, typical of the troubled conscience, overtaxed in the confessional. In its most general application the "labyrinth" characterizes the human condition in terms of a natural knowledge of God that is too dim to find "the right path" but in its frustration creates "fantasies." The *docilitas* that Calvin experienced as the first gift of "conversion" is the only way out of the "labyrinth."[56]

Twice as frequent and far more revealing is Calvin's extensive use of the word "abyssus," to which again Bouwsma was the first to point. In the 1986 Kuyper lectures on "The Heritage of John Calvin" at the Free University of Amsterdam, I had already chosen the same hermeneutical path by identifying a series of favored expressions of Calvin as keys unlocking the existential strata of his thought and pointed to four such catchwords: "nonchalant," "secret" with its Latin equivalent "arcanum," and the expressions "Dei nutu"

53. ". . . opus inquam inclitum multis ante saeculis absconditum, cuius lectio dormientes excitet, calcar addat, ad Deum convertat, ad beatorum theologiam invitet et modo quodam ineffabili disponat, nec denique per scabrosa sive ambages et inextricabiles quosdam labyrinthos Gordiive nodo legentium mentes." Rice, 292-93f. For Erasmus see Jean-Claude Margolin, "Duns Scot et Erasme" (as in n. 34 above), 91; Erasmus, *Laws Stuititiae,* Leuvensche bijdragen 4.465C-466A.
54. "Scalae meditationis," in *Opera* (Groningen, 1614), fol. 269.
55. For the most immediate foil for Calvin's use of the term "labyrinth," see the concluding passage of the *Praefatio* of Bucer in his Psalms commentary (1529): "Finally, I must say something about the meaning of the word 'Selah,' which is so variously discussed in prefaces of this kind; I follow the opinion of Rabbi Kimḥi in order to escape these labyrinths": ". . . ut his me tandem labyrinthis expediam . . ." *Praefatio,* fol. iiii[v]. For Calvin's early use and respect for this commentary, see above, n. 14. For Bucer's commentary, see W. van 't Spijker, "Bucers commentaar op de psalmen: Hebraica veritas cum Christi philosophia coniungenda," *Theologia Reformata,* 30 (1987), 264-80.
56. For this "docilitas" see above, n. 3.

as well as "meditatio vitae futurae."[57] As fruitful as these four windows proved to be, I must frankly admit that Bouwsma's discovery of "abyssus" opens up even larger horizons — larger, I submit, than even his cultural interpretation admits.

With its biblical roots, "abyssus" is understandably much more prominent[58] than "labyrinth' as the classical shorthand for the intractable maze.[59] One New Testament text in particular makes Calvin reach for the term "abyssus" to describe confusion, the hell of despair, and the threat of ultimate annihilation. A second one, which in the Vulgate version reads "bestia quae ascendit de abysso (Rev. 11:7)," can be mentioned only in passing since Calvin nowhere explicitly invokes or interprets this passage. Yet, in a later version of the *Institutio* (1543), pondering why the Scriptures sometimes refer to "the devil" in the singular and sometimes to "devils" in the plural, he explains the singular as indicative of the ongoing war between the kingdom of righteousness under the one-headed leadership of Christ and the kingdom of impiety under the one devil. This adversary will finally be thrown "into the eternal fire, prepared for the devil and his angels (Matt. 25:41)" — and hence ultimately

57. *De Erfenis van Calvijn: Grootheid en Grenzen* (Kampen: J. H. Kok, 1988), 18-22. Since that time I have been pursuing other recurrent terms and phrases, such as Calvin's striking predilection for the word "porro" — his NB or the raised finger of the schoolmaster — his use of "absurd" and "absurdity" at the point were his argument slides from persuasive to coercive discourse, and the unusual frequency of "quasi" in the Commentaries and of "docendi causa" in the *Institutio*.

58. To give an impression of the relative frequency of occurrence, I Corinthians may serve as a test case for a biblical book in which the terms do not occur and for which we have both a Latin Commentary and French Sermons (CO 49). This yields the following count: In the Commentary (in toto 277 cols.) "labyrinth" 2x, "abyssus" none. In the French Sermons (in toto 249 cols.) "labyrinth" 4x, "abyssus" 5x, but "abysmer" 14x as a verb. A second test case is provided by the first part of the Book of Psalms (Ps. 1–50; CO 31), in which the word "abyssus" does occur in the biblical text (Ps. 36:7; 42:8). Here we find on 470 cols. "labyrinth" 5x, "abyssus" 12x. Throughout the Commentaries the ratio is about 1:2, climbing close to 3 when the French verb "abysmer" is added to "abyssus."

59. The one dimension of Calvin's "abyssus" that overlaps with "labyrinth" — confusion — is articulated in two sources we have reason to believe Calvin to have known. The one is Tractatus XI of Gerson's *Super Magnificat*, where the risk of penetration of the transcendent judgment of God is articulated. See *Oeuvres complètes* 8, no. 418, ed. Mgr. Glorieux (Paris: Desclee, 1968), 485f. Gerson unfolds the "abyssus" in a twofold way, namely as the immeasurable depth of the mercy *and* the immeasurable depth of the severity of God. The other foil is again Bucer's Psalms commentary (see n. 14 above), which either descriptively relates "abyssus" to water (fol. 446, Ps. 136:7; fol. 469, Ps. 148:7) or associates it — as Gerson — with the "iudicia Dei," which should not be penetrated or — according to Bucer — cannot always be grasped: "Neque enim potest animus iusti moerore oppressus, abyssum iudiciorum Dei . . . cognitive consequi" (fol. 73, Ps. 10:1). More in line with Calvin's intensification of the meaning of "abyssus" is the exegesis of Ps. 71:11, where the word indicates to Bucer that no human being can ascend from the abyss on his own power (fol. 299).

be forced to return to the abyss out of which he emerged.[60] And when Calvin argues that the sinner cannot possibly enumerate all his sins in the confessional, he invokes common sense, that is, the awareness of everybody "quanta esset peccatorum nostrorum abyssus . . . quot capita ferret et quam longam caudam traheret haec hydra."[61] This abyssmal hydra suggests the biblical "Beast" of the Book of Revelation, which threatens to emerge from the Abyss.

The key biblical text, however, and the ever present context is the story in Luke 8 about the exorcism of the legion of demons who at their own request are sent running into the abyss: "in abyssum irent" (Luke 8:32). It is this powerful image of the crazy[62] yet "voluntary" submersion and death-by-drowning that also stands behind the commentary on Jeremiah 33:44, where Calvin analyzes the unwillingness of the Jews to accept God's offer of grace and forgiveness: "they rather wanted to throw themselves in the abyss of desperation."[63] Without this sense of "existence on the brink" we would not grasp the urgency of Calvin's appeal to his old friend François Daniel, writing on 15 July 1559, "[you are] loath to climb out of the abyss of the papal church in which you have plunged. . . ."[64]

---

60. *Institutio* 1.14.14; OS 3.165.23-28. This basic discussion of the function of the devil introduces the characterization of his range of operation, which is described as the realm circumscribed "sub Dei potestate," "ipsius nutu"; OS 3.167.21f. Cf. CO 31.445 A: ". . . usque in abyssum fuisse contritos. Nam per 'locum dacronum' non intellego deserta et solitudines, sed profundissimos gurgites maris . . . [C] Meminerimus ergo, hoc verum esse pietatis examen, ubi in abyssos deiecti oculus, spes, et vota dirigimus in solum Deum." Ps. 44:20. In keeping with the psychological interpretation of "space" as Christ's descent into hell, the "abode" of the Dragon is utter despair. This characteristic form of demythologization is an aspect of another encompassing shift: in the later Middle Ages — as with Luther — Satan is the anti-type of Christ. With Calvin he is the counterforce to the Holy Spirit, assailing individual sanity and communal stability of the body of Christ, the church.

61. *Institutio* (1536), cap. V; OS 1.182.10-13.

62. See the (later) observation on the "typically biblical way" of understanding insanity: "Insanos vocat David in Ps. 5,6 more scripturae, qui caeca cupiditate ad peccandum ruunt. Nihil enim magis furiosum impiis qui abiecto Dei timore, nocendi libidine ferunter: imo nulla est amentia deterior, quam Dei contemptus, quo fit ut fas omne pervertant homines." CO 31.68 C.

63. ". . . Quum ergo porrigeret illis Deus manum, malebant sese in abysso desperationis ita demergere, ut nihil levaret eorum animos. Hanc ingratitudinem merito castigat propheta, quod adiudicent terram suam aeterno exitio cuius tamen restitutio promissa fuerat. Perinde igitur est ac si diceret, Superabit Dei misericordia et fides vestram malitiam: quantum in vobis est exstinguitis eius promissiones, aboletis eius gratiam, neque datis locum promissionibus: ipse nihilominus complebit quod pollicitus est," CO 39.48-49 (1551).

64. "[You are] tardif à sortir de l'abysme, où vous estes plongé . . ." CO 17.585 (nr. 3089). Cited by A. M. Hugo, *Calvijn en Seneca. Een inleidende studie van Calvijns Commentaar op Seneca, De Clementia, anno 1532* (Groningen, 1957), 11. It is highly desirable that this Dutch dissertation of Hugo be translated into English and / or German. Only parts of Hugo's insights could be incorporated into the critical edition, but his premature death on

The full import of the term "abyss," with both its emotional and doctrinal freight, is already accessible to us in Calvin's earliest work, the *Psychopannychia* (1534), holding treasures that still await mining. In the central and oldest part of this twice rewritten treatise, Calvin first points out that true theology cannot go beyond the boundaries of what the Holy Spirit teaches: to penetrate further and beyond these boundaries is to drown oneself in the abyss, the "abyssum mysteriorum Dei. . . ."[65] He concludes this passage with the warning that those who reach beyond their ken will invariably come to naught: ". . . eos qui supra se nituntur, semper corruere."[66] The classical myth of Icarus had already been transformed into moral advice by Erasmus in the *Adagia:* "quae supra nos nihil ad nos" (1.6.69); and used by Luther in *De Servo Arbitrio* to warn against the penetration of the hidden counsels of God.[67] For Calvin the yonder is "down under."

While Calvin's warning against reaching out for the Deus absconditus has — with the water simile of "drowning" — a flavor all its own, the report on his experience of the wrath of God permits us an unparalleled glimpse into his own psyche.[68] The wider context of this revealing passage is his argument against those who teach that the soul dies at the end of the human life. No, Calvin responds, in reality the soul dies when hit by the judgment of God, when the sinner hears the chilling challenge "Adam, where are you?" This is easier to think than to say, to ponder than to express in words; yet so terrible is the majesty of God that even thinking about it is impossible without having had the experience yourself. Those on whom his wrath falls discover the full terror before the omnipotent God; however they try to escape, they will not succeed, even though "in mille abyssos se demergere parati sunt."[69] Who does not have to admit that this is true death! But to spell this out in words is

---

24 January 1975 in Capetown prevented him from fully unfolding his life's theme. See the critical edition, *Calvin's Commentary on Seneca's 'De Clementia,' with introduction, translation, and notes by F. L. Battles and A. M. Hugo* (Leiden, 1969), 3-71. See also the use of "abimer" ("abysmer") for the final drowning — four times! — in the revealing "Sermon de dernier Advenement," perhaps so consistently overlooked while it is printed between the Latin Commentaries on II Thessalonians and I Timothy: CO 52.232f. The survivor should be grateful to God "q'il nous a retirez de tels abysmes . . ." *ibid.,* 229 A.

65. CO 5.201.13f. This same concerted effort is assailed by Calvin in the traditional way as "curiosity." See the meticulous study by E. P. Meijering, *Calvin wider die Neugierde.* Bibliotheca humanistica et reformatorica 29 (Nieuwkoop: De Graaf, 1980).

66. CO 5.201.23f.; cf. the edition of the *Psychopannychia* by Walter Zimmerli, *Quellenschriften zur Geschichte des Protestantismus* (Leipzig, 1932), 60f.

67. Cf. *Weimarer Ausgabe* 18.685.6f. For the exact parallel with Calvin, see *Institutes* 1.17.2 (ed. 1559).

68. Whereas Zimmerli already noticed this existential dimension (see his edition, p. 65, n. 1), he failed to see the function of Luke 8:31 in Calvin's formulation of his experience.

69. CO 5.204.40f.; ed. Zimmerli, 67.12f.

not necessary for those who have experienced this sharp compunction of the conscience.[70] No doubt Calvin knows what he is talking about.

In the third and final passage we draw on, the experience of conversion has solidified into a doctrine that would become typical for the teachings of Calvin and Calvinism. Often, Calvin points out, the Scriptures mean by "death" not the end of present life nor by "hell" the grave. "To die" and "to descend into hell" frequently mean "alienation" from God and "depression" caused by the judgment of God: it characterizes those who are made attrite [!] by his Hand. In this case hell does not mean physical but spiritual death: "abyssum et confusionem significet."[71]

When in the New Testament the Gospel writers refer to "Hades" they do not mean a place or location but the *condition* of utter misery, exposed to the wrath of God and assigned to exile. This is the meaning of the words in the Creed that Christ has "descended into hell." When the Bible says that "God redeems my soul from the grasp of hell," it means "He has accepted me." The *impius,* who stubbornly *(proterve)* rejects God and instead puts his

---

70. See the rhetorically powerful and personally authentic description of this heart-rending experience of the wrath of God, addressed to those who do not know this from their own experience: "Atque ut quod dictum est in universum, partibus ostendatur: si extra Deum lux non est, quae nocti nostrae luceat, ubi lux illa se subduxerit, anima certe in tenebris suis sepulta, *caeca* est. Tunc *muta* est, quae confiteri non potest ad salutem, quod crediderit ad iustitiam. *Surda* est, quae vivam illam vocem non audit. *Clauda* est, imo se sustinere non potest, ubi non habet cui dicat: Tenuisti manum dexteram meam, et in voluntate tua deduxisti me. Nullo denique vitae officio fungitur"; CO 5.204.52-205.7; ed. Zimmerli, 68.7-15. My use of italics serves to accentuate the realism and completeness of dying in the absence of God: the unforgiven sinner is all but clinically dead — all vital functions have stopped. Two conclusions are called for: (1) this is exactly what it means to be in the "abyss"; (2) once a person is awakened by saving grace, all functions of the soul are so thoroughly revitalized that clinical death can no longer induce "sleep": Conversion is the decisive "Great Awakening": ". . . mors animae alienatio est a Deo. Ergo, qui in Christum credunt, quum prius mortui essent, incipiunt vivere, quia fides spiritualis est animae resurrectio, et animam ipsam quodammodo animat ut vivat Deo . . ." CO 47.262 C; Com. John 11:25.

The briefest formulation of the "Great Awakening" is to be found in the Commentary on Isa. 19:22: "Hinc collige, conversionem esse quasi resurrectionem ab aeterna morte," CO 36.347 B.

71. "Infernus ipse non sepulcrum sed abyssum et confusionem significet." CO 5.223.43f.; ed. Zimmerli, 97.20-22. N.B.: the "confusion," characteristic of being in the "labyrinth," is here identified with the "abyss." The "labyrinth," however, has the connotation of the self-made (CO 32.551 B) contraption (and trap) of "fantasies" or "inventions"; "abyssus" designates the human condition *coram Deo,* that is, "drowning, naked, without refuge" — were it not for the extended hand of God.

It should be noted that the content of "attritus" is anything but Scotistic. As its usage in many parallel contexts shows, it means far more than "regret," namely something in the range between "beggarized" and annihilated, broken-down (in German: *zerrieben*): CO 36.202 A; 265 C; Isa. 9:10; 13:12.

hope in his own achievements, will die, descend into hell, and disappear in the abyss. But he who trusts in the Lord will be liberated from the power of hell[72] and escape the clutches of the abyss.

Let us venture now to address the implications of our findings. We started out by pointing to Calvin's extreme self-reticence. Then, following the signposts of catchwords and favorite expressions, we reached a layer of revealing primordial reactions and gut decisions that can best be described with the German word *Vorverständnis*. Three preliminary conclusions are in order.

1. By concentrating on the earliest layer in Calvin's work, we have found that a firm grasp of late medieval theology is required in order to understand a whole series of terms and assumptions, reaching from God's self-binding covenant *(pactum)*[73] to the inscrutable God *(Deus absconditus)* and the naked state of incapacitating fear *(attritio)*. All of these late medieval themes had already been integrated and transformed into a biblical theology that Calvin could have encountered in the French translations and Latin writings of Luther, including *De Servo Arbitrio* of 1525. On a much broader textbase than can be displayed here, an extensive study of Erasmus's *Adagia* must be assumed. Yet the young Calvin is theologically not an Erasmian, but — in view of his different understanding of the *iustitia Dei*[74] — to a remarkable extent in experience and at times even in expression a disciple of Luther.

2. The special characteristic of Calvin's teaching, which can therefore be designated as an extra-Calvinisticum, is to be found in his reinterpretation of hell as a condition,[75] and the descent of Christ into hell as the extreme

---

72. CO 5.224.13-46; ed. Zimmerli, 98.5-99.2. Zimmerli establishes that the reference to Hades is an addition of 1545.

73. For its far-reaching consequences in Reformed orthodoxy, see the clear analysis of Richard A. Muller, *Christ and the Decree: Christology and Predestination in Reformed Theology from Calvin to Perkins*. Studies in Historical Theology, vol. 2 (Durham, NC: Labyrinth Press, 1986).

74. This contrast calls for further investigation. Here are some preliminary observations: Luther's description of his exegetical breakthrough by interpreting the righteousness of God as "iustitia passiva" (grasped in faith), articulated in the *Praefatio* to the first edition of his Latin works (Wittenberg, 1545), may very well have been read by Calvin. More importantly, he contradicts the validity of this interpretation. Careful to interpret the expression "iustitia Dei" always in terms of the changing biblical context, Calvin in interpreting the Psalms does relate "iustitia" to "fides," yet not to the faith of the believer but to the "active" faithfulness of God as the stable foundation of salvation. See his exegesis of Ps. 7:18 (CO 31.87 B); Ps. 22:31 (*ibid.,* 237 B). When *iustitia Dei* is interpreted as the goodness of God ("pro bonitate accipitur"), it means an attribute of God: Ps. 51:16; CO 31.520 C. Though in all these contexts, *iustitia Dei* does not refer to the punishing justice of God — which Luther rejected — it does not mean the righteousness received by faith as in the case of Luther's *iustitia passiva*. See my article in the *Festschrift* for G. W. Locher (in press).

75. I owe a special debt of gratitude to my colleague Alan E. Bernstein, who, in the

experience and exposure of the Son of Man to the wrath of God. This extra-Calvinisticum is already part of the earliest stage of Calvin's thought, and with its deep sense of alienation in keeping with his own conversion experience as deliverance "from the pits" ("bourbier si profond").[76] Indeed, the interpreter — and the translator! — of Calvin needs to be as familiar with late medieval terminology as with the Latin and French of that day; yet, I repeat, this is no warrant to construe a medieval pedigree that can be as easily advanced as gainsaid. Calvin did not learn this striking psychological interpretation of the abysmal Descent into Hell in a medieval school but in the school of life.

3. Whereas William Bouwsma marked a significant advance in discovering the centrality of the terms "labyrinth" and "abyss," our analysis places us in a favorable position to start to reunite the two Calvins that Bouwsma sees in tension and even in a crippling conflict with one another. To begin with, the two metaphors are not mutually exclusive; confusion is typical of both. As we noticed, Calvin warns not to penetrate the mysteries of God; such speculation plunges us in the abyss. But this abyss is indistinguishable from the labyrinth when Calvin warns against following Augustine — as Bouwsma himself noted[77] — in speculating how the sin of Adam was transmitted: such puzzling drives you into the labyrinth.

Furthermore, Bouwsma properly points out that it is the "humanistic Calvin who chiefly dreaded . . . entrapment in a labyrinth."[78] This same concern, however, Calvin shared with the humanists of his age, particularly with the circle around Lefèvre d'Étaples in Paris. The alleged "dread" is a stereotypical humanist concern not to slide back into the labyrinth of the man-made "solutions," of scholasticism and canon law.

Finally, Bouwsma is again right in discerning that "Calvin was chiefly driven by a terror that took shape for him in the metaphor of the abyss."[79] Whereas the references to the labyrinth are standing expressions of less than central importance, with the abyss we reach the heart of the matter, and indeed into the heart of the one Calvin. Initiating his conversion is an experience of

---

process of completing an extensive history of the concept of hell ranging from early mythology through the works of Dante, helped me in tracing the importance of Calvin's formulation. See his "Esoteric Theology: William of Auvergne on the Fires of Hell and Purgatory," *Speculum,* 57 (1982), 509-31; and "The Invocation of Hell in Thirteenth-Century Paris," *Supplementum Festivum, Studies in Honor of Paul Oskar Kristeller,* ed. J. Hankins, J. Monfasani, and F. Purnell, Jr., Medieval and Renaissance Texts and Studies, 49 (Binghamton, New York, 1987), 13-54.

76. CO 31.21 C.
77. Com. Ps. 51:7; as quoted by Bouwsma on 271, n. 101.
78. Bouwsma, 231.
79. Bouwsma, 230.

drowning and annihilation that Calvin regards as generic and applies to all true Christians at all times. It is the experience of hearing God's piercing call, "Adam, where are you?" Scared to death by the majesty of God and caught in the labyrinth of a life without exit, the sinner frenetically flees and, blinded by fear, seeks "refuge" in the abyss of hell and damnation. If saved from drowning by God's outstretched hand,[80] this soul-rending experience gives way to the resuscitating power of God as pledged in his Word. This encounter with naked terror is not left behind, however, but ever present and methodically kept to mind by continuous meditation.[81]

The medieval call "de profundis" — the traditional conclusion of the funeral mass[82] — is rephrased in the language of experience: "obrutus sum,

80. The "extended hand" of God stands for his "potentia ac virtus." CO 48.260 B.

81. The young Calvin reflects on this transition and is conscious of going his own way — "meo quidem iudicio" — in defining the biblical meaning of "poenitentia." *Inst.,* cap. V; OS 1.170.1–172.38; 171.20; cf. 172.37f. In the following section, he criticizes and rejects scholastic solutions from Lombard onward (OS 1.172.39–202.30), proving to be well informed and showing his legal training by pointing to the "pugna inter canonistas et theologos scholasticos," a rift overlooked by earlier reformers (OS 1.175.22f.). His own view of "penance," however, is worked out by correcting the respected pre-Scholastic tradition ("docti quidam viri, longe etiam ante haec tempora"; OS 1.170.1f.) — which I take to reach from Augustine and Ambrose to Hugo and Richard of St. Victor — recently edited in Paris. See the ten books of Richard's *Liber Exceptionum* (c. 1160), published in Paris 1526 — under the name of Hugo — for Jean Bordier. A second part had already been published in Paris 1517 by Henri Etienne, and seen through the press by Josse Clichtove — at that time still in close touch with Lefèvre d'Étaples. See Jean-Pierre Massaut, *Critique et tradition à la veille de la Réforme en France* (Paris, 1974), 81-99. Reading Calvin's Old Testament Commentaries side by side with the *Liber Exceptionum,* one is struck by such parallels (per se inconclusive) as the frequent use of "manifestare" for the "Son of God." Cf. Calvin's favored formulation "Deus manifestatus in carne." See *Liber Exceptionum* IV, cap. 1; ed. Jean Chatillan (Paris, 1958), 267f.

The second respected tradition, which Calvin reports before choosing his own course (OS 1.171.8-10), draws on Luther and Melanchthon. The point that Calvin finds missing in the fine insights of the Fathers and the reformers is the *lasting* function of the fear of God ("verus ac sincerus timor Dei"; 171.22), first in compunction and conversion, but then in the *mortificatio.* This is not a passing stage in life — left behind in the "great awakening" — but a lasting characteristic of the Christian life: "ut morti Christi insertus poenitentiam meditetur" (172.36f.). This highly unusual formulation and spiritual directive Calvin regards as "sententia . . . simplicissima omnium"; OS 1.172.37.

82. Jean Delumeau has articulated the related question, what it meant for the first generation(s) of Reformed Christians to live without the assurance of pardon, which medieval Europe had received in the confessional; they are now directly confronted with the wrath of God. Whereas Luther reformed this key sacrament by relating it to baptism, the young Calvin placed it in the category of "false [= misleading, diabolical] sacraments"; OS 1.162.22f. For Delumeau look beyond the too impressionistic "dossier" in *L'aveu et le pardon. Les diffi-cultés de la confession XIII-XVIII siècle* (Paris: Fayard, 1990) to the more intriguing volume *La Peur en Occident (XIV-XVIII siècle)* (Paris, 1978), and — again less cohesive and con-vincing — *Le Péché et la peur, La culpabilisation en Occident XIII-XVIII siècle* (Paris, 1983).

sepultus sum, suffocatus sum" — in the abyss I am drowning, buried, chok-
ing.[83] Bouwsma is right: the *timor Dei* as awe for God has marked Calvin for
life. But at the same time, knowing about the terrifying abyss neutralizes all
other human fears. Such fears Calvin knew very well. He describes his own
all-encompassing fear of persecution in a 1562 sermon on II Samuel. Looking
back at the time before his refuge, "when tyranny reigned in France," he
remembered that he was scared to death, "j'ay esté en ces destresses là, que
i'eusse désiré voulu estre quasi mort pour oster ces angoisses . . ."[84] the same
urge to escape the anxiety that drove the "swines of the Gerasenes" into the
abyss (Luke 8:26, RSV).

Looking at all the evidence, we reach five conclusions:

1. "Labyrinth" and "abyssus" do indeed provide appropriate lenses —
together with "theater" the favorite image drawn from the vital but vitiated
world of vision — but the right focus *(scopus)* still has to be established. To
present Calvin in his campaign against the "labyrinth" as "the forward-looking
humanist and adventuresome discoverer," as does Bouwsma, is to assume a
Burckhardtian view of humanism that Calvin shared as little as we do today.
With all respect for the *studia humanitatis* as welcome tools and new resources,
Calvin does not tire of discrediting all the classical authorities for the moral
philosophy of his day: he assails the vagaries of the Platonic dialogues, as well
as the implicit or explicit "atheism" of the very best in Virgil, Horace, and
Seneca.[85] Except for glimmers ("scintillae") and disparate tidbits of truth
("poetis extortae sunt"!) nothing these unbelievers or *profani homines* can
offer alleviates the basic human disorientation, exacerbated by the confusion
of scholastic doctors and canon lawyers.

83. The images of "abyss" and "drowning" can indeed be related to the sacrament
of penance as the second plank after baptism. Yet, Calvin's cry "de profundis" is so
suggestive of the experience of death that in his case we must pay at least equal attention
to the impact of dying without extreme unction. The central theme of the *Psychopannychia*
— the "Great Awakening" is not interrupted by physical death — can be read as the elimi-
nation of the need of the "last rites."

The "pain" experience in the absence of absolution and extreme unction is the missing
link in a volume full of insight: *Conscience and Casuistry in Early Modern Europe*, ed.
Edmund Leites (Cambridge: Cambridge University Press, 1988).

84. Sermon of 1 July 1562 on 2 Samuel 5:12-17, *Predigten über das 2. Buch Samuelis*,
Supplementa Calviniana, Sermons inedits, ed. Hanns Rückert (Neukirchen: Moers, 1936-61),
122.27f.; identified by Paul Sprenger, *Das Rätsel um die Bekehrung Calvins*, Beiträge zur
Geschichte und Lehre der Reformierten Kirche, Band 11 (Neukirchen: Moers, 1960), 29, n.
5.

85. For the "blasphemy" of Virgil, CO 39.517 C; Lam. Jer. 1:8. For Horace as the
"impurus Dei contemptor," CO 31.287 C; Ps. 29:4. For Seneca see CO 52.66 C; Phil. 4:19.
The rich and creative French translations of the Latin poets, which I take to be Calvin's own
work, deserve to be overlooked no longer: "by heart" he knew the giants he was dwarfing!

2. There is no "adventurous" way out except by *docilitas* and *fraenum,* by redirection and by the bridle, so that the "wild horse" can be put back on the right track: *conversio ad docilitatem.*[86]

3. Calvin's undeniable fear for the "abyss" does not reveal him to be the "rationalist" or the "philosopher," let alone the "Thomist." The "abyss" stands for the psychological experience of hell, alienation, and ultimately annihilation when confronted before the *tribunal Dei* with the holy majesty of God the Judge. The "abyssus" is the *finis* of all mankind, except for the elect who experience exactly the same "condition" but then are moved to invoke the mercy of God and thus seize his "extended hand." To use another favorite expression, it can be said *docendi causa* that whereas faith *(revelatio)* is the map leading out of the "labyrinth," hope *(invocatio)* is the escape and life jacket for the drowning creature who has lost his footing in the "abyss." Both metaphors, "labyrinth" and "abyss," relate to confusion; yet the "abyss" does not call for enlightenment but for redemption and has the teleological connotation of the ultimate "discrimination" between life and death. In the "experienced" — and preached! — gospel, Calvin's doctrine of reprobation is sublapsarian: the reprobate are drowning in their own guilt. While the elect throw themselves at the mercy of God the Judge, the reprobate reject his "extended hand."

4. Calvin knows that on the basis of fixed credal points *(fixa stat sententia!),* theology provides a discourse of metaphors. The frequent expression "docendi causa" in the *Institutio* alerts the reader to the fact that what follows is a clarification by abstraction, transcending the cohesion of lived experience. Hitherto unnoticed, it is an important warning signal that should be especially heeded by those interpreters who make this teaching manual the mainstay of their interpretation.

In the Commentaries the same function is laid on the slight shoulders of the short word "quasi," which has not drawn the attention it deserves, though it appears some hundred times more frequently than "abyssus." Under this fascinating "quasi"-blanket of expressions, allusions, and approximations lies for Calvin the hard core of psycho-spiritual experiences and traumatic developments such as the growth and shriveling of joy and despair. The Holy Spirit, long recognized as a major and characteristic theme in Calvin's doctrine, is de facto the Divine Analyst *and* Psychotherapist. The Book of Psalms provides the manual for analysis since it offers — to use the phrase that Calvin is proud to have coined — "the anatomy of all parts of the soul."[87] In charge of God's

---

86. See above, n. 3.

87. For this view Calvin does not refer to tradition, but to his own way of speaking: "Librum hunc non abs re vocare soleo 'anatomen' omnium animae partium. Immo omnes . . . spiritus sanctus ad vivum repraesentavit"; CO 31.15 C.

Secret Service *(operatio arcana)*, the Spirit penetrates not only the thoughts, words, and deeds, as the tradition had it, but also the *affectus*, transforms external doctrine into persuasion,[88] and above all leads from inner confusion to sanity.[89]

As we shall see, this insight is already the center and heartbeat of the *Psychopannychia*. At this point it serves to underscore an aspect of Calvin's character to which Bouwsma pointed, but which he saw nipped in the bud: Calvin was indeed an "adventurer," namely an adventurer-into-the interior. He offered both a new diagnosis and a novel therapy for that part of Europe which had broken out of the protection of the confessional and, while risking to live without the benefit of absolution and without the prospect of the "last rites," henceforth found itself directly confronting the tribunal of God with a conscience still trained and sensitized by the medieval interpretation of the Seven Deadly Sins and the Ten Commandments.

The "labyrinth" marks the point of departure, namely the perplexities of the confessional, too heteronomous to assuage and redirect the conscience. The "abyssus," on the other hand, expresses the new priestless life *coram Deo*, where sins can no longer be left behind through the exercise of contrition and the sacrament of absolution. It marks at once the fierce storms outside the confessional and the fiery breath of direct, unmediated exposure to the justice of God.

5. The intensity of the quest for "sincerity" and a "good conscience," as well as the crucible of the *examen pietatis*, reveals the dimensions of the traumatic experience that those generations had to "absorb" (a verb used in connection with "abyss" almost as frequently as "drown"), who had consciously embraced the Reformation or found themselves in Reformed territories. This "exodus from the confessional" is an important dimension of the social and political exile that marked the audience of Calvin. With this exodus in mind Calvin explored the Scriptures. His Commentaries reveal best the extent to which he himself is not merely an observer but a participant who carried the full brunt of its trauma.

Calvin was at once driven by the ever present awareness *(meditatio!)* of the threat of *drowning* in the abyss of death, devil, and hell, and *drawn* by a deep-seated trust in the promise of God's saving intervention. To him applies not the expression "come hell *or* high water";[90] the diabolical abyss is hell

88. See CO 39.587 C; 586 B.

89. See CO 39.576 B; 586 C.

90 "Water" as a threat was available to Calvin in the exegetical tradition (Richard and Hugh of St. Victor!) and a commonplace in the Scriptures, as Bucer observed (Ps. 42:8; fol. 229). It is not surprising to find it to be prominent with the Dutchman Wessel Gansfort (†1489); see my contribution to the forthcoming proceedings of the 1989 Gansfort fifth centennial, edited by A. J. Vanderjagt. Yet in some respects closer to home for Calvin is the revealing "naked" poem (1547)

and high water. Yet the mercy of God subdues and swallows the power of the Beast, so forcefully formulated in his outcry: "Abyssus tuae misericordiae hanc peccati mei abyssum absorbeat" — May the abyss of my sin be drowned into the abyss of Your mercy.[91]

IV. The Decisive Decade: 1525-35

In six steps we now endeavor to place the young Calvin in his historical context, the increasing threat of persecution.

1. The chaotic structure of the *Psychopannychia* — notwithstanding or perhaps even due to the double revision in 1536 and 1542 — does not facilitate easy access. Even so, it is an amazingly rich treatise[92] for all who try to find the original thread in the labyrinth of Calvin's later thought. The unwieldy structure goes quite a way in explaining why this earliest theological work of the reformer has been given such cursory treatment during the last fifty years. When it was read at all, as in the case of George Hunston Williams, it suffered from a false contrast with Luther, who was claimed to teach the mortality of the soul.[93] This is a misreading not only of Luther,[94] but of Calvin too.

---

written by Marguerite de Navarre (†1575), to whom since 1524 all "Lutherans" in France had looked for help. See the opening two lines: "Navire loing du vray port assablée, / Feuille agitée de l'impétueux vent . . . "; edited by Robert Marichal, *La navire ou consolation du Roi François Ier à sa soeur Marguerite* (Paris: Librairie Champion, 1956), 237. Cf. the observation of the editor in the Introduction: ". . . on ne peut relire l'Institution [of Calvin] sans se rappeler en maint endroit la *Navire*"; *ibid.*, 17. For differences see p. 21.

91. *Institutio* (1536), cap. V; OS 1.183.23. This is Calvin's rendering of the public confession: "Domine, propitius esto mihi peccatori" (Luc. 18:13). For the uninitiated a bombastic statement of baroque proportions, for Calvin this sentence expresses at once the pain of the price of emancipation and the bold hymn of praise for the God who liberates from the "pit of despair." The other side is expressed in the 4th sermon on I Cor. 10:8f.: The "vileins," the enemies of the church, "sont dignes d'estre abysmez au profond des abysmes." CO 49.625 B.

92. Under the unassuming title "Quelques indications bibliographiques," B. Roussel provides essential information in "Francois Lambert, Pierre Caroli, Guillaume Farel . . . et Jean Calvin (1530-1536)," in *Calvinus Servus Christi*, ed. W. H. Neuser (Frankfurt a.M., 1984), 35-52; 43f. Throughout alert to the dangers of "reconstruction," Calvin is placed in the wider context of the opponents of the Sorbonne, "ces autres acteurs de l'agitation religieuse." *Ibid.*, 48.

93. *The Radical Reformation* (Philadelphia: Westminster Press, 1962), 104f. Even more explicitly Williams writes eighteen years later: ". . . at the University of Wittenberg Luther sustained a still more radical view, namely, that the soul dies with the body and that only at a Second Advent of Christ and as a consequence of the Last Judgement of the quick and of the dead, resurrected for that end, would salvation be experienced by the righteous." "Commentary to Lionel Rothkrug," in Lionel Rothkrug, "Religious Practices and Collective Perceptions: Hidden Homologies in the Renaissance and Reformation," *Historical Reflections,* 7 (1980), 259-64; 259.

94. From his first statement in 1522 onward, the sleeping of the souls *(dormire)* has for Luther the connotation of "quies," the "rest" so important to Calvin; *WA Br,* 2.422.4-

Calvin's point of departure is the immortality of the souls, which he believes to be a truth he can share with all reasonable humans. And indeed he himself refers to the *Psychopannychia* (which literally means "The Waking of the Soul") as his libellus "de animarum immortalitate."[95] His point is, however, that just as death strikes when the gospel is rejected, the soul receives life eternal when through justification it is resuscitated and placed on the path of the Kingdom. Calvin explicitly denies that the soul is immortal in and of itself, as if she could subsist without God's care: "sed dicimus, eius manu ac benedictione sustineri"[96] — we learn from experience that it is the might of God and not our human nature that allows us to last in eternity.[97] Not only in this central passage but throughout the *Psychopannychia,* we see how the Platonic presuppositions that swayed the minds of the leading humanists in Florence and Paris, around Ficino and Lefèvre d'Étaples, provide Calvin with a point of departure and with a vocabulary that is consciously tested and critically transformed according to the standards of biblical speech.

2. If the major thrust of the *Psychopannychia* can be so readily misunderstood, it should not surprise us that a seemingly minor aside in the preface of 1534 has not drawn the attention it deserves. Calvin argues here that "recently" a number of anabaptist authors[98] have revived the old heresy of

---

423.44; Jan. 1, 1522 to Augsburg: To sleep, Luther writes, is *not* to be dead, but to be certain of the resurrection; WA 46.470.17f. (1538).

95. See his letter of 11 September 1535 (from Basel to C. Fabri, i.e., Libertet), which does not prove a publication in print, but rather refers to the manuscript of which we still possess the preface, signed "Orleans, 1534," and first printed in 1542 under the title *Psychopannychia.* See Herminjard, *Correspondance des Reformateurs,* 3.349. Cf. CO 10.38f. Though we still have the letter in which Capito dissuades Calvin from publishing (CO 10.45f.; nr. 35; 1535), in 1538 Calvin points to Bucer as "qui editionem antea dissuaserat, nunc est mihi hortator"; CO 10.260 B.

96. CO 5.222.18-20.

97. "Nam quum dicimus spiritum hominis esse immortalem, non affirmamus contra manum Dei stare posse, aut sine eius virtute subsistere. Absint a nobis hae blasphemiae. Sed dicimus, eius manu ac benedictione sustineri . . . experimentoque discamus, quoniam ex illius magnitudine, et non ex nostra natura habemus in aeternum perseverantiam"; CO 5.222.18-22; ed. Zimmerli, 95.7-16.

98. On closer scrutiny the tracts of Karlstadt and Westerburg invoked by George Williams do not teach "mortality" in any form or fashion. See Karlstadt's *Ein Sermon vom stand der Christglaubigen Seelen von Abrahams schoß und fegfeür / der abgeschydnen Seelen* (Wittenburg, 1522). As the preface by Wolfgang Kuch forcefully highlights, this pamphlet is directed against "das arme elende unselige freß und geytzvolck / Münch und Pfaffen" (fol. a i v); cf. fol. a iiii r. Karlstadt: What Devil permitted you to declare the departed souls to be "unselig"?: "Sy haben ain ewig leben und sein nicht todt vor gott . . ." (fol. b ii v / b ii r). The same point is made by "Gerhart Westerburch" in his pamphlet *Vom fegefeuer und standt der verscheyden selen: eyn Christliche meynung* (Cologne, 1523). Before the resurrection the departed souls are "in der Schoß Abrahe zuruwen, genomen. Dan got ist nit eyn got der verstorben [the dead], sunder der lebendigenn . . ." (fol. a iiii v). Like Luther, Westerburg can use the image of "sleep" *(eyn süsser*

the mortality of the soul, which according to Eusebius was taught by Arabs and sometime later upheld by the "Bishop of Rome,"[99] Pope John XXII (†4 Dec. 1334), "whom the University of Paris forced to recant."[100] In one respect the questions raised by this passage have indeed been investigated. It is now well established that Calvin's characterization is mistaken. Pope John, though deviating from the received opinion of the immediate and full vision of the departed souls, never taught the mortality of the soul. Rather, he argued for an intermediate state in which the souls of the departed receive the beginning of their reward in seeing the humanity — though not yet the divinity — of Christ, and do therefore not yet enjoy the beatific vision.[101]

---

schlaf), not, however, as a form of death but of life "dieweyl yr leben trefflich und köstlich worden ist durch abkleydung yrer beschwerlicher leychnamen" (fol. b ii r). Since the young Calvin could have met Karlstadt in Basel, where this early ally of Luther spent the last phase of his life (1534-41) as a professor (particularly of Old Testament), it is important to note that Karlstadt also in his last publications (1535, 1538, 1540) discusses the resurrection from the perspective of the renewal (the awakening by grace) in this life. Just as Calvin did in 1534! See M. A. Schmidt, "Karlstadt als Theologe und Prediger in Basel," *Theologische Zeitschrift*, 35 (1979), 155-68; esp. 160f.

Though the Italian debate around Pomponazzi establishes indeed how "current" the problems of immortality were, they cannot explain Calvin's reference to "anabaptist authors." Since Calvin explicitly says that he had not seen these anabaptist tracts himself, he may well have relied on the information found in Zwingli's *Elenchus* of 1527. Bernard Roussel has pointed to evidence in the Orleans Preface for Calvin's use of Alphonsus de Castro, *Adversus omnes haereses*, s.v. "Anima" and "Resurrectio," published at the beginning of October 1534. Whereas this would require an exceptionally rapid transmission from Cologne to Orleans to reach Calvin, and to allow him time for reaction at the latest in December 1534, it is more likely that Alphonsus and Calvin reacted to the same common source. Most convincing, I find Roussel's suggestion that Calvin, in his attack on these as yet unknown anabaptist authors, lines up with the "politique religieuse 'allemande' du Roi" in disassociating political and heretical revolt (in Germany!) from the genuine reform intended by those falsely called "Lutherans" at the Sorbonne. See "Histoire et théologies de la Réforme," *Annuaire, École pratique des Hautes Études*, Section des sciences religieuses, 95 (1986-87), 389-97; 393.22.

99. Ganoczy properly observes that the *Psychopannychia* is still void of anti-Roman sentiment; *Le Jeune Calvin*, 77. All the more striking, however, is the designation of Pope John as "Bishop of Rome," which I am inclined to interpret as a "Gallican" statement.

100. CO 5.170-71.32-35; here I follow Walter Zimmerli's edition (see n. 66 above), 16-17: "Neque tamen nunc primum nascitur. Siquidem legimus arabicos fuisse quosdam huius dogmatis auctores, qui iactarent animam cum corpore una emori, in die iudicii utrumque resurgere. (Eus. eccl. histor. 1.6. c. 37 — Augustinus lib. de haeresibus c. 83). Et aliquanto post tempore Joannem episcopum Romanum, quem schola Parisiensis ad palinodiam adegerit (Joan. 22. de quo Gers. in serm. pasch. priore)."

101. See Marc Dykmans, ed., *Les Sermons de Jean XXII sur la Vision Béatifique, Texte précédé d'une introduction et suivi d'une Chronologie de la Controverse avec la liste des Écrits pour et contre le Pape*, Miscellanea Historiae Pontificiae, vol. 34 (Rome, 1973); Marc Dykmans, ed., *Pour et Contre Jean XXII en 1333. Deux Traités Avignonnais sur la Vision Béatifique* (Citta del Vaticano, 1975); cf. *La Vision Bienheureuse. Traité envoyé au pape Jean XXII*, Edite avec une introduction et des notes par Marc Dykmans, Miscellanea Historiae Pontificiae, vol. XXX (Rome, 1970).

The positions of Pope John and John Calvin seem quite similar when compared with the extreme alternatives of mortality and immediate full beatific vision.[102] Joseph Tylenda even concludes, "Calvin's opinion is, in fact, hardly distinguishable from that of John XXII."[103] There is one crucial difference, however, in that Pope John articulates the "not yet" dimension of the intermediate stage in relation to the resurrection, whereas Calvin places an equal emphasis on the "already." Calvin's theme is the progress of the Christian in three stages, from conversion (awakening), resting after death yet fully awake in the joyous expectation of the full beatitude, which will finally be received on the day of the resurrection. The progress of the pilgrim "in dies magis magisque" is already the mark of the earliest thought of Calvin.[104] Contrary to the impression left by Calvin scholarship, the alertness of the soul after death is not a youthful "folly": in none of the later biblical commentaries will Calvin miss an opportunity to illustrate and develop the importance of this theme.[105]

3. For our purposes even more relevant is the question what we can learn about Calvin's *initia* from his reference to the condemnation of Pope John XXII by the University of Paris. The fact itself, that is, the critical Gutachten of twenty-nine Parisian doctors concerning the eschatology of John XXII, dated 2 January 1334, is well documented.[106] The point is, however, that Calvin invokes here with great specificity, as he does again in the *Institutio*[107] and in his *Brève Instruction* of 1544,[108] the authority of Jean Gerson (†1429). Calvin does not refer to him in general terms but points accurately to the "first" Easter sermon of the famous chancellor of the University of Paris. This is Gerson's sermon "Pax

102. The best analysis to date is provided by Joseph N. Tylenda, "Calvin and the Avignon Sermons of John XXII," *Irish Theological Quarterly,* 41 (1974), 37-52. To his extensive references should be added the reliable summary in G. C. Berkouwer, *De Wederkomst van Christus,* 1 (Kok: Kampen, 1961), 55-60; 57.

103 "Calvin and the Avignon Sermons of John XXIII," 47.

104. Cf. *Institutio* (1536), cap. I; OS 1.6.3. After death the believer is no longer a pilgrim in the sense that he is no longer "in via": the *mortificatio* begun at baptism is then perfected when ". . . ex hoc vita migrabimus ad Dominum." *Institutio* (1536), cap. IV; OS 1.132.8-10.

105. See CO 31.491 C; Ps. 49:16. CO 7.28 C / 29 A; Articuli . . . cum antidoto (1544), art. 17 cum antidoto. CO 48.319 A; Acts 9:41.

106. "Litterae viginti novem magistrorum Parisiensium in theologia ad Philippum VI, regem Francorum, de statu animarum corpore exataram," *Chartularium Universitatis Parisiensis,* ed. H. Denifle (Paris, 1841), 2.429-32; 429; quoted by Tylenda, 49, n. 48 (see n. 102 above).

107. OS 5.130.23-33; *Institutio* (1543).

108. "Brieve instruction pour armer tous bons fideles contra les erreurs de la secte commune des Anabaptistes," CO 7, col. 43-142; 127. The most extensive and reliable treatment of Calvin's lifelong debate with the "Anabaptists" is presented by W. Balke, *Calvijn en de doperse radikalen* (Amsterdam: Bolland, 1977 [1973]). Here the title page of the *Instruction* and a regest of the *Psychopannychia,* 318-23.

vobis," preached on Palm Sunday 1394 (April 19) and originally delivered in French. The Latin version was not published until Jacob Wimpfeling (1450-1528) had it translated by a gifted German student in Paris and incorporated it in his *Supplementum* to the 1502 Strasbourg edition, which contains, as he says explicitly, "prius non impressa." This edition, republished in Strasburg (1514), Basel (1518), and Paris (1521), contains two further Easter Sermons and hence explains Calvin's identification of "Pax vobis" as the *first* Easter Sermon.[109] Two centuries later "Pax vobis" was incorporated by L. Ellies Du Pin in his fine edition of Gerson's *Opera Omnia;*[110] the original French version was published for the first time by Palémon Glorieux in 1968.[111]

Since the first preface to the *Psychopannychia* is written in Orléans (1534), shortly after Calvin had to flee from Paris and before settling in Basel (1535-36), he may have relied on his memory for the reference to Gerson. It certainly means, however, that if he did not work himself extensively with Gerson manuscripts, he must have used the Wimpfeling edition, that is, the *Supplementum.* In either case it shows that Calvin was early acquainted with the most eminent of late medieval French authors,[112] whose authority was

109. I am grateful to the rare book department of the Universitätsbibliothek, Tübingen, which allowed me to make this comparison by providing me with the collection of early prints of Gerson's works. For the early printing history see the article on Gerson by Chr. Burger in *Theologische Realenzyklopädie*, 12.535f. In the "Prologus" to his *Supplementum* Wimpfeling acknowledges royal support for his work, which the Court must have regarded as the presentation of high French political and religious culture to the European learned world: "Novissime vero his diebus . . . alia quaedam in intimis Parrhysiensis gymnasii penetralibus ac diversis Galliae locis quaesita et nutu summae maiestatis inventa sunt, quorum nonnulla cum Gerson gallica lingua scripsisset, aut in concionibus popularibus disseminasset operae pretium fuit ilia in latinam utcunque interpretari atque transferre." Fol. I^V. The ambivalent compliment for the German student-translator expresses respect for the French original: "Si non eleganter, tamen fideliter traducta sunt." In Wimpfeling's copy — preserved in the Haguenau Stadtbibliothek (Inc. 539) — this student is identified as Johannes Brisgoicus; see Herbert Kraume, *Die Gerson-Übersetzungen Geilers von Kaysersberg, Studien zur deutschsprachigen Gerson-Rezeption* (München: Artemis Verlag, 1980), 81.

110. L. E. Du Pin (Antwerp, 1706), 3.1204-14.

111. ". . . pour quoy en seurplus appert la fausseté de la doctrine au pape Jehan le XXIIe qui fut condempnée aux boix de Vincennes devant le roy Philippe vostre aieul, par les théologiens de Paris, de visione beata. Et en cru plus les théologiens de Paris que la court," Jean Gerson, *Oeuvres complètes* VII*, ed. Mgr. Glorieux (Paris: Desclee, 1968), 779-93; 780. I am indebted to my Leiden colleague, G. H. M. Posthumus Meyjes, who alerted me to the complex publication history of this sermon, incompletely presented by Glorieux. For the preceding assembly at Vincennes, see his volume *Jean Gerson et l'Assemblée de Vincennes (1329). Ses conceptions de la jurisdiction temporelle de l'Église, Accompagné d'une édition critique du 'De Jurisdictione Spirituali et Temporali,'* Studies in Medieval and Reformation Thought, vol. 26 (Leiden: E. J. Brill, 1978).

112. See Christoph Burger, *Edificatio, Fructus, Utilitas. Johannes Gerson als Professor der Theologie und Kanzler der Universität Paris,* Beiträge zur historischen Theologie

preeminent in Gallican circles that liked to invoke Gerson's authority for that reformation of France for which the chancellor had once delivered such an eloquent blueprint.[113]

Concluding this section on the *Psychopannychia,* it may be said that just as the text itself deserves renewed attention as documenting the method, scope, and findings of the young Calvin, the preface points to an even earlier phase when he apparently had access to the works of the great French conciliarist, or moved in circles where Gerson's memory was kept alive.[114]

4. In his plea for the reform of France, Gerson invoked the authority of Seneca. Though admitting that nothing is so poisonous as tyranny, he made quite clear that "sedicion" is rampant rebellion without rhyme or reason: "she is often worse than tyranny." But even so, also to tyranny the rule applies: "Riens violent aussi ne peust durer" — violence has no future. Hence Gerson suggests that the king submit to "reasonable" reform, since to submit to reason does not mean to bow to one's subjects. As Seneca so convincingly put it: "si vis omnia subicere tibi, subice te rationi"[115] — thus Gerson presented his king, Charles VI (†1420), with the Stoic yardstick "between severity and clemency" for that enlightened absolutism which a century later would be personified by Francis I (†1547).[116]

Calvin's Seneca commentary,[117] understandably often studied for possible hints about his conversion or nascent theological convictions, should rather be read in the context of the politically turbulent situation in France after the Concordat of 1516 and its confirmation in 1519. Initially Parliament resisted, and when it had been placated the University stepped in, blocking the printing of the text of the Concordat.[118] The new alliance between king and

---

70 (Tübingen, 1986). All three terms prove to be central to Calvin's program, in his French works gathered in the one concept "profit" — the (tenuous) basis for the later Weber thesis.

113. See Gerson's Gutachten for the King on the Reformation of the Kingdom, dated 7 November 1407; ed. Glorieux VII*, 1137-85; esp. 1183f.

114. Herbert Kraume has particularly pursued the German reception of Gerson, and in this context dedicates a special section to the circle around Wimpfeling in Strassburg. Kraume assumes that partly due to Wimpfeling's edition, Gerson was better known at the end of the fifteenth century in Germany than in France. See his *Die Gerson Übersetzungen Geilers von Kaysersberg* (as in n. 108 above), esp. 79-90; 82. But Wimpfeling apparently also found a new readership for Gerson in France.

115. *Oevres complètes,* ed. Glorieux, VII*, 1159f; 1160.7. Seneca, *Epistula* 37.

116. R. J. Knecht, *Francis I* (Cambridge, 1984 [1982]), 62f.

117. In *De Clementia,* cap. V, Seneca formulated the revealing parallel "clementia rationi accedit" amid the Stoic thesis of *misericordia* as "sickness of the soul." Understandably, this context draws Calvin's full attention — and critique! — so that we do not have his explicit response to the main clause (ed. Battles and Hugo, 360-68). His later works amply make up for this early lacuna!

118. What is best designated as Calvin's "Parisian view" of royalism and of Gallican

pope, which steadied the royal hold on the French Church, presented a challenge to which the older Gallican coalition had to provide new answers. Future interpretations of Calvin's Seneca commentary will want to draw on this challenge to politicians and legal experts as the immediate context of Calvin's earliest publication.

With the commentary on Seneca's *De Clementia* we have access to the earliest phase of Calvin's academic career.[119] At the feet of Pierre Taisan de

---

reform in the kingdom has recently been sharply criticized as "traditionalism," and once even explained as "manichaeism." So W. Fred Graham, who invokes Bouwsma's reconstruction of Calvin's fear of the "abyss." See "Calvin and the Political Order. An Analysis of the Three Explanatory Studies," in *Calviniana. Ideas and Influence of Jean Calvin,* ed. R. V. Schnucker, Sixteenth Century Essays and Studies," vol. 10 (1988), 51-61; 57ff. A further study of the Gallican-royalist tradition of jurisprudence seems to promise a stricter control of the evidence.

119. In a precious, recently discovered ear-and-eye-witness report of February 2, 1534, we have the first evidence of the academic impact of the young Calvin. The Erasmian "regens" at the Collège de Beauvais in Paris, Claude Despence, attended in the Collège de Fortet some lectures by "a certain Calvin" on Seneca, and now reports that the audience — with the exception of one small-minded colleague — was impressed: "Calvinum istum nescioquem aliquoties audivi ennarantem Senecam suis commentariis illustratum in aula Forteretica, cuius eruditionem tantum non admirabitur Simon Bouterius [unknown to the editor] vix anxie eruditus . . ." J. Dupebe, "Un document sur les persécutions de l'hiver 1533-1534 à Paris," Bibliothèque d'humanisme et renaissance 48 (1986), 405-17; 406. Since the letter reports on recent events, I am disinclined to follow the editor in dating these lectures of Calvin as early as 1531 or 1532. Since Calvin could not have publicly lectured after the address by Cop (November 1, 1533), I am rather inclined to date Calvin's Seneca course in the late summer or early fall of 1533. The rest of the letter vividly documents — with rich footnotes provided by the editor — how small and vulnerable the "network" is of the Protestant underground ("évangélisme lutheranisant"). A central pawn proved to be the poet Nicolas Bourbon (*Nugae,* 1533; perhaps also the unknown author of the Placards), who was indirectly in touch with Nicolas Cop — and hence brings us as close to Calvin as hitherto possible. This may well be the time and the situation Calvin refers to in his late Samuel sermon, in which he recounts "the time of terror" in which one blow "could have silenced us" (see n. 84 above). The editor properly calls attention to the growing distance between the "Erasmian" Despence and the "Lutheran" group (also called "Gerardini" after Gerard Roussel, like Farel a radical disciple of Lefèvre d'Étaples). The academic address of Cop — with its use of both Erasmus and Luther — may have to be seen inter alia as an effort to bridge this divide and thus to forge a coalition, which in Germany had already broken down. For the development of Calvin, the probable author, this appeal to the Rotterdammer should not be taken as proof of the direction of his own loyalties. Francis Higman kindly called my attention to the fact that Claude d'Espence dedicated in May 1547 to Marguerite de France, daughter of Francois I, a "Consolaytion en adversite" to console her on the death of her father — six years later condemned by the Sorbonne: it is a straight translation of Luther's "Tesseradecas Consolatoria" (1519). See *Index des Livres Interdits,* I, *Index de l'Université de Paris 1544, 1545, 1547, 1551, 1556,* ed. J. M. Bujanda, F. M. Higman, and J. K. Farge (Sherbrooke: Droz, 1985), nr. 528; on the remarkable career of d'Espence "between the fronts" see nr. 527, p. 433.

l'Etoile (Petrus Stella) in Orleans and of Andrea Alciato in Bourges, he was so fortunate as to be introduced to the cutting edge of the political science of his day. Different from the traditional "Fürstenspiegel" in addressing all matters of public administration, and different from a "Utopian" concern by regulating existing legal practice, this new legal prudence found its guiding principles not in canon law but in Roman law. Although Josef Bohatec has convincingly documented the overwhelming extent to which Calvin drew on Guillaume Budé in his later legal thought,[120] for the young Calvin Pierre de l'Etoile was the "prince of the jurists."[121] From Alciato (†1550; 1529-33 at the University of Bourges), Calvin occasionally distanced himself as he did in his preface to the "Antapologia" of his friend Duchemin.[122] Yet he may have encountered in Alciato the more significant and innovative legal mind, who, to quote Myron Gilmore, "became the founder of a new school of jurisprudence, based on the principle of humanist exegesis with an appreciation of the importance of the interpretation of the Roman law as a living common law. . . ."[123] This application of Roman law is what Budé tried to achieve in France and what Calvin set out to implement in Geneva. Whereas legal scholars had already been eminent carriers of Renaissance humanism in fifteenth-century Italy, in the sixteenth-century this trend reached France and Germany.[124] In this campaign for the emancipation of civil law from canon law, Alciato was an important transalpine link.

Calvin was fortunate not only in his teachers, but also in the Seneca theme, which he dared to tackle notwithstanding two earlier editions of *De*

120. Josef Bohatec, *Budé und Calvin, Studien zur Gedankenwelt des französischen Frühhumanismus* (Graz, 1950), 440.

121. CO 9.875 B. In 1530 de l'Etoile was sufficiently prominent to be drawn into the efforts of Henry VIII to find legal support on the Continent for his divorce case. See the rich dossier gathered by Guy Bedouelle and Patrick le Gal, *Le 'Divorce' de Henry VIII. Études et documents*. Travaux d'Humanisme et Renaissance, 221 (Geneva, 1987), 399.

122. "Nicolai Chemyni Aureliani antapologia adversus Aurelii Albucii defensionem pro Andrea Alciato contra D. Petrum Stellam nuper editam Paris 1531"; cf. Bohatec, *Budé und Calvin,* 439, n. 5 and n. 6. For the legal principles of the later Calvin — with only two references to Seneca — see Bohatec, *Calvin und das Recht* (Graz, 1934). Among the works of Guido Kisch, see esp. *Erasmus und die Jurisprudenz seiner Zeit. Studien zum humanistischen Rechtsdenken* (Basel, 1960); note here the important appendix with relevant legal texts and extensive bibliography, 473-538.

123. Myron P. Gilmore, *Humanists and Jurists: Six Studies in the Renaissance* (Cambridge, MA: Harvard University Press, 1963), 79.

124. After a brief stay in Orleans, some thirty years before Calvin's arrival, Erasmus started to get "Heimweh" and long for the North, since — in his opinion — "Accursus, Bartolin and Baldus," that is, the faculty of law, created a climate unfavorable for the "Musae," the true spirit of humanism. Letter from Orleans, dated 20 Nov. 1500; *Opus Epistolarum Des. Erasmi,* ed. P. S. Allen, nr. 134, I (1484-1514) (Oxonii, 1906), 312.25-27. For the resonance of Budé's critique in Germany, see Gerald Strauss, *Law, Resistance and the State. The Opposition to Roman Law in Reformation Germany* (Princeton, 1986), 42f.

Clementia by Erasmus (1515; 1529). Since 14 February 1531 documented as "Maistre Jean Cauvin, licentié es loix," he published a year later a commentary on the civic virtue of clemency that, as the personalized dimension of the issue of "peace and concord," had been the central theme in political science and reform tracts north and south of the Alps. In measuring the relationship of power and justice, and in reaching for a balance between tyranny and mob rule, "clemency" was sought after as the golden mean.[125] Whereas Calvin's Seneca commentary is too often dismissed as a youthful display of humanistic tools, or praised as the beginnings of "Calvin the exegete," and once even as his " 'pagan apprenticeship' to the christian life,"[126] the point of departure for future scholarship will be Calvin as the student of statecraft in the politically volatile situation of an emerging absolutist monarchy.

Drawing on his studies in Orleans (1528-29), Bourges (1529-31), and under the Royal Readers (1531-33), Calvin comes well prepared to design his appeal to Francis I as the preface to his *Institutio*[127] and to sketch the "humanitatis et civilitatis officia"[128] in its concluding section about power and justice in a Christian society.[129] Without the hermeneutical tool of the Seneca commentary, Calvin's early political theology could be misunderstood as a rhetorical device to win the clemency of Francis I rather than as a programmatic effort to acknowledge *and* regulate royal absolutism between the boundaries of human "aequitas" and the sovereignty of God as "rex regum."[130] Calvin defended by defining both limits and goals: "sunt certique fines!" This is not fear for the abyss, but the common sense of legal circumscription: no humanity without order,[131] no order without checks and balances, no balance without law — which itself is for Calvin the charta of all "true humanism."

125. See A. M. Hugo, *Calvijn en Seneca. Een inleidende studie van Calvijns Commentaar op Seneca, De Clementia, anno 1532,* 14 (as in n. 64 above).
126. Ford Lewis Battles, "The Sources of Calvin's Seneca Commentary," *Studies in John Calvin* (Courtenay Studies in Reformation Theology), 1 (1965), 38-60; 56f.
127. OS 1.21-36. Cf. as a parallel the dedication to Francis I by Zwingli, ten years earlier, of *De vera et falsa religione commentarius* (1525), ZW 3 (Corpus reformatorum 90), 626-37.
128. *Institutio* (1536), cap. VI; OS 1.232.34. Robert Kingdon has repeatedly called attention to Calvin's activity as an expert lawyer in Geneva. See "Calvin and the Government in Geneva," in *Calvinus ecclesiae Genevensis Custos,* ed. W. H. Neuser (Frankfurt a.M., 1984), 49-67; esp. 59f. Cf. the seminar report "Calvinus Regislator [sic!]: The 1543 'Constitution' of the City-State of Geneva," in *Calvinus Servus Christi,* ed. W. H. Neuser (Budapest, 1958), 225-32; esp. 226.
129. OS 1.270.17-280.15. Cf. Harro Höpfl, *The Christian Polity of John Calvin* (Cambridge: Cambridge University Press, 1982), 43ff.
130. OS 1.36.18 and 279.40.
131. See the conclusion of Jane Dempsey Douglass: "For Calvin a reformation requires more than preaching; it needs order." *Women, Freedom, Calvin,* The 1983 Annie Kinkead Warfield Lectures (Philadelphia: Westminster Press, 1985), 21.

Yet even more important than the use Calvin made of his legal training in defending the cause of the French loyal opposition is his vision and ability to create new institutions in the form of the Compagnie des Pasteurs and the Consistory, the General Synod and the Genevan Academy. There is a wise French saying: "Les hommes passent, les institutions subsistent." Calvin did not fade away because he incarnated his vision by designing durable legal structures. His ever growing *Institutio* would have been long dated and shelved if he had not initiated viable institutions as the underpinnings of his "textual community." No biography of Calvin can be complete without due attention to the institutional dimensions of his legacy.

5. Calvin did not publish his *Psychopannychia* in 1534 because Wolfgang Capito — among the city reformers the most sensitive to winning the radical reformers — strongly advised him against it. This is the first time we learn that the young Calvin had contacts with Strassburg and had apparently already developed such a relationship of respect and trust with Capito that he submitted his theological maidenwork[132] to the scrutiny of this Strassburg reformer.[133] The Strassburg connection cannot surprise us since, after September 1524 when the Reformation had triumphed in this imperial city, it became, to use the expression of Jean Rott, "un centre de propaganda vers les pays de l'Ouest."[134] When on 3 October 1525 the Parliament of Paris decided to take action against the Circle of Meaux, Lefèvre d'Étaples and his chief officers such as Guillaume Farel, Michel d'Arande, and (for a shorter stay) Gerard Roussel sought refuge in Strassburg and were received under the roof of Capito. From a network of secretive messages[135] we know that a stream of

132. I find the arguments advanced by Jean Rott for Calvin's authorship of "Cop's academic address" — held on 1 November 1533 in Paris — convincing. However, since we cannot exclude the possibility of at least partial authorship by Nicolas Cop and — more generally — since we cannot determine the precise interaction between ghost-writer and public speaker, I find it advisable not to draw on this document — so important for the history of the decisive "events" — for the analysis of the *initia Calvini*. See Jean Rott, "Documents strasbourgeois concernant Calvin," *Regards Contemporains sur Jean Calvin. Actes du Colloque Calvin, Strasbourg 1964* (Paris: Presses Universitaires de France, 1965), 28-73; 42. Together with a number of other precious documents, the critical edition can be found on pp. 43-49.

133. A year later Calvin and Capito cooperated again. Whereas Calvin wrote the Preface on the history of salvation (see below, n. 148), Capito contributed "le discours aux lecteurs juifs de la Bible," signed "V.F.C. . . . ," behind which we will have to discern "Wolfgang Fabritius Capito." As in the case of Bucer's Psalms commentary of 1529, the intended readership in France could not be reached if the police authorities could make out the name of one of the Strassburg preachers. For Bucer's role in the publication of the *Psychopannychia,* see also n. 95.

134. "L'Eglise des refugiés de langue francaise à Strasbourg au XVI siècle," *Bulletin de la sociéte d'histoire du protestantisme français,* 122 (1976), 525.

135. The dangers for the "reformistes," even before Oct. 3, 1525, are vividly described by Gerard Roussel in a letter dated 25.IX.1525 from Meaux to Farel: ". . . hactenus prohibuit

French refugees went to Basel and Zurich, but all of them circulated through Strassburg as the extraterritorial safeplace for the French evangelicals. For a correct understanding of the *initia Calvini,* it is important that instead of the usual opening chapter on "l'Affaire des Placards" in October 1534, the story begins to unfold on 3 October 1525, when Parliament exploited the absence of King Francis I, imprisoned in Spain after the lost battle at Pavia (24 Feb. 1525). At this point in time, Parliament decided to act on the pressure of the Sorbonne to suppress what it called "lutheranism."[136]

Apart from the horror of imprisonment, torture, and death at the stake, the ensuing wave of persecution had a clarifying and accelerating effect. The broad coalition of reform-minded Gallican Episcopalianism, which had taken institutional form in the diocese of Meaux in the years 1521-25, was now broken into three discernible parties, personified by (1) Guillaume Briçonnet, the bishop of Meaux; (2) by his learned vicar Lefèvre d'Étaples, the mastermind of the reform in the diocese; and (3) by Guillaume Farel, the radical student of Lefèvre, who would have such a decisive influence on the course of Calvin's life.

The impact of the persecutions, designed and executed through the cooperation of Parliament and University, forced each party to clarify its understanding of reform. Bishop Briçonnet, in his concern for peace and order the most Erasmian among the "reformists," purged the ranks of his clergy and reinforced traditional devotions to the Holy Sacrament and the Virgin Mary.[137]

Lefèvre d'Étaples, perhaps the most mysterious of the three and certainly the most difficult to place,[138] takes the road to Strassburg and, after his return to France, continues to be in touch with his more radical disciples such as Farel, and may well have met with Calvin two years before his death in 1536. Later Calvin would have counted him among the Nicodemites, but his best modern interpreter can answer this charge in one loaded sentence: "Lefèvre ne se cache pas, il se tait."[139]

Christi clementia." *Correspondance des Reformateurs,* ed. A.-L. Herminjard, 1 (Geneva, 1866), nr. 162, p. 391. See esp. p. 390, n. 4.

136. See James K. Farge, *Orthodoxy and Reform in Early Reformation France,* esp. 255-68. Cf. Augustin Renaudet, *Humanisme et Renaissance* (Geneva, 1958), 214ff.

137. See the well-documented and nuanced analysis of Michel Veissiere, *L'Évêque Guillaume Briçonnet (1470-1534). Contribution à la connaissance de la Réforme catholique à la veille du Concile de Trente* (Provins, 1986), esp. 386f.

138. See Guy Bedouelle, *Lefèvre D'Étaples et l'intelligence des écritures* (Geneva: Droz, 1976).

139. *Ibid.,* 131. See the conclusion, "Sans se situer nécessairement au-dessus de la melée, alors qu'il était proche des intuitions théologiques des Réformateurs et de leur interprétation de l'écriture, Lefèvre a préféré le silence qui-dit-plus que les disputes"; *ibid.,* 235. Of course Faber had been "speaking" and still "spoke" loud and clear through his *Opera* in the Dedication of his Psalms Commentary (to the eldest son of Francis I). Martin

Whereas Lefèvre responded to the use of force with the power of silence, Guillaume Farel responded by rejection: he concluded that the Antichrist raged in the Church of Rome and was stretching his greedy fingers to the kingdom of France, forcing the truly faithful to take the counteroffensive.

Reading, side by side, Lefèvre (c. 1440-1536) and Farel (c. 1489-1565) — almost half a century younger — one cannot help but notice the striking new tone of urgency expressed in the intensive and extensive use of Antichrist terminology.[140] Probably early in 1525, the handbook for the reform of instruction and preaching in the diocese of Meaux was published, which Michael Screech has properly called "un ouvrage révolutionnaire."[141] Though it was published anonymously, there can be no doubt as to the authorship of Lefèvre d'Étaples. The *Épistres et Évangiles* follow the text of his translation of the New Testament,[142] and his Paulinism, biblicism, the emphasis on the *gloria Dei,* as well as the revealing silence about the invocation of the saints, inform the preaching examples.[143] Probably inspired by Luther's "Adventspostille"

Bucer acknowledges his indebtedness and calls Faber "pietissimus ille et erudissimus senex." Psalms Com., *op. cit.* (above, n. 14), fol. iii[r].

140. *Guillaume Farel 1489-1565.* Biographie Nouvelle écrite d'après les Documents Originaux par un groupe d'Historiens, Professeurs et Pasteurs de Suisse, de France et d'Italie (Neuchâtel and Paris: Editions Delachaux & Niestle, 1930); Christoph Burger, "Farels Frömmigkeit," in *Actes du Colloque Guillaume Farel,* Cahiers de la Revue de Théologie et de Philosophie, 1, 2 (Geneva, 1983), 149-50. Not only by "swearing" Calvin into service in Geneva was Farel "direct" in his vocabulary. See Michel Peronnet, "Images de Guillaume Farel pendant la Dispute de Lausanne 1536," in *La Dispute de Lausanne 1536. La théologie réformée après Zwingli et avant Calvin* (Lausanne, 1988), 133-41; 140f. We are in the fortunate position that such reading impressions can be objectified. Henry Heller's *The Conquest of Poverty. The Calvinist Revolt in Sixteenth Century France,* Studies in Medieval and Renaissance Thought, vol. 35 (Leiden, 1986), contains an important chapter, "Popular Roots of the Reformation: The Lutherans of Meaux" (1525-46) in which the social unrest and the vulnerability of the cloth industry in Meaux are spelled out. Cf. pp. 27-69. I call particular attention to Heller's discovery of the fuller Nicolas Boivin, who was interrogated after he fled the persecutions of 1525 in Meaux; Heller, 58-60. Heller's characterization of Boivin fits exactly the case of Farel: biblicism, justification by faith, the priesthood of all believers, and religious certitude: "They supply him with the means not merely of rejecting the old faith but also give him the self-confidence of a new one." *Ibid.,* 60.

141. See his introduction to the facsimile reproduction of the edition of Simon Du Bois, *Jacques Lefèvre d'Étaples et ses disciples. Épistres & Évangiles pour les Cinquante & deux Sepmaines de l'An* (Geneva: Droz, 1964), 9-28; 13. In the following I draw on this substantial introduction with texts.

142. Cf. the edition with introduction by M. A. Screech of *Jacques Lefèvre d'Étaples: le Nouveau Testament.* Facsimilé de la première édition Simon de Colines, 1523, 2 vols. (Paris, 1970).

143. "Lefèvre 'Étaples est donc l'auteur de notre texte, dans le sens où c'est lui qui a fourni la traduction des péricopes et où c'est lui le maître qui, en toute humilité, a donné au travail de quatre de ses disciples l'empreinte de sa personnalité, de son style et de sa doctrine." Screech, introduction to *Épistres & Évangiles,* 12.

of 1522, it dares to develop a biblical theology that makes it quite understandable that the Sorbonne censured (on 6 Nov. 1525) forty-eight propositions drawn from this text as "diabolical figments" and characterized them as Manichean, Waldensian, Wyclyffite, and Lutheran.[144]

For our intent to measure the difference and, in this case, even the distance between Lefèvre and his disciples, it is important that in the later edition printed by Étienne Dolet (Lyon, 1542),[145] six new "exhortations" were added and quite a number of interpolations were made by changing words, phrases, and sometimes an entire paragraph. The changes reveal a heightened tone of critique and impatience, and are properly characterized by Screech as "plus scripturaires, plus militantes, que celles de Lefèvre lui-même."[146]

V. Conclusion: "Nous n'avons autre refuge qu'à sa providence"[147]

It is the extended line from Briçonnet via Lefèvre to Farel and his other radical disciples that brings us into the heartland of the *initia Calvini*. In this climate of persecution — and this applies to the whole decade that saw Calvin grow from puberty to adulthood, from 16 to 26 years of age — the themes developed that were to become cornerstones in Calvin's biblical theology: the glory of God,[148] the secret operation of the Holy Spirit, the growth of the Kingdom, the danger of idolatry, and the strategy of Satan.

144. See the text in Appendix B of Screech's introduction; *ibid.*, 41-51; 51.

145. On the complex task of placing Dolet (†1546) amid the reform currents in France, see B. Longeon, "Étienne Dolet: Années d'enfance et de jeunesse," in *Réforme et Humanisme. Actes du IVe Colloque* (Montpellier, 1975), 37-61. Of the same age as Calvin — born 1509 in Orléans — after studies in Padua, he describes in his *Commentarii Linguae Latinae* (Lyon, 1536), dedicated to Guillaume Budé, the wide variety of positions on the "(im)mortality of the soul": "Has de animae mortalitate, vel immortalitate sententias, simul varia de religione iudicia, sectasque hominum in deo colendo diversas discutimus iis libris, qui de opinione posteritati à nobis relinquentur, ut nos planè viros vixisse intelligat, non ineptiis cruciatos elanguisse"; quoted by Longeon, p. 55, n. 3. Cf. Judith R. Henderson, "Dolet," in *Contemporaries of Erasmus,* 1 (Toronto, 1985), 394-96.

146. See the documentation for the adaptation made in the Dolet edition in Appendix A, Screech, *ibid.*, 28-40; 28.

147. CO 53.273.

148. Suzanne Schreiner graciously allowed me to read the galleys of her illuminating *The Theatre of His Glory* (Durham, NC: The Labyrinth Press, 1990). The function of the "theater" with Calvin deserves a separate treatment under the heading of the "rhetoric of the eyes." Since Bouwsma presented "Rhetoric" and "Theater" in two separate chapters (7 and 11), Neuser could wonder what "drama" has "letzlich" to do with Calvin's understanding of the Christian life (*art. cit.* — as in n. 50 above, p. 156). In my view the answer can be brief: "letzlich" everything! But to document this view would require a separate treatment.

In Calvin's eloquent preface to the 1535 Bible of Pierre Robert Olivétan (†1538), all of these themes are integrated within the one history of the covenanting God.[149] In this brief summa of the whole history of salvation, one element is novel and deserves our special attention. After relating the liberation from Egypt and before turning to the arrival in the Promised Land, Calvin inserts the revealing sentence: "Il les a accompagnés nuit et jour en leur fuite, étant comme fugitif au milieu d'eux" — he accompanied the Children of Israel night and day on their flight, "present among them as a fugitive himself."[150]

The ten years of ever increasing persecution (1525-35) almost resulted in the annihilation of the Reformed party, but then led increasingly to the radicalization of the "rest" along stages on the line marked by the distance between Briçonnet, Lefèvre, and Farel. The political reality of persecution cried out for a religious interpretation that led to the discovery of the work of the Antichrist, a key phrase in the vocabulary of extra- and anti-hierarchical reform. The yield of this history of persecution, the refuge, made Calvin read the Scriptures anew and allowed him to discover God as the first refugee, trekking with the people of Israel through the desert.[151]

In unfolding his biblical theology and in building his institutions, Calvin used a whole range of authors from Augustine to Luther, from d'Étaples to Budé, from Erasmus to Bullinger; and he reflected currents ranging all the way from Platonism to late medieval Scotism. But at the center of the *initia* stand the never forgotten experience of the abyss as the deadly flight *from* God and the growing insight in the life-giving refuge *with* God.

149. For Olivétan and his bible, see *Olivétan: traducteur de la bible,* ed. A. Casalis and B. Roussel (Paris, 1987). For an excellent introduction and the text, see Irena Backus et Claire Chimelli, "L'Épitre à tous amateurs," *"La Vraie Piété," Divers traités de Jean Calvin et Confession de foi de Guillaume Farel,* Histoire et Société, nr. 12 (Geneva, 1986), 17-38.

150. Ed. Backus, 27.6f. Some ten years later (1546), after one of his frequent sharp asides against the philological deficiencies of Erasmus ("Erasmi cavillum") Calvin insists that Christ already in the desert was the *mediator* and *dux ecclesiae:* ". . . qui in itinere semper adfuit populo." CO 49.459 B; I Cor. 10:9.

151. This reevaluation highlights the contrast between Calvin and the so-called city reformers. With reference to Theodore Beza, Donald Kelley has pointed to the far-reaching consequences of exile in terms of the "substitution of confessional roles for familial ones": fellow exiles became brothers and sisters. *The Beginning of Ideology. Consciousness and Society in the French Reformation* (Cambridge: Cambridge University Press, 1981), 57. Beza, not only the successor of Calvin in Geneva but also following on a similar path (Bourges, Orleans, Paris, Lausanne, Geneva), found his refugee experience reflected in Abraham's sacrifice — rather than in the trek through the desert — and could perhaps therefore describe it as free choice: I went to Geneva "in exilum voluntarium." Letter to Melchior Volmar, Geneva 12, III, 1560, no. 156, in *Correspondance de Théodore de Bèze,* ed. Henri Meylan et Alain Dufour, Tome III (1559-61), (Geneva, 1963), 47, 25.

At times Calvin broke the silence of his reticence. In Genevan exile he confessed, "It is very hard to have to live far from one's fatherland."[152] This experience enabled him to understand and unfold the biblical theme: "I have been a stranger in a strange land" (Exod. 2:22). The threat of the abyss is ever present — but the fugitive God is trekking along, "manum porrexit" — his "hand is stretched out." Both this conviction and this language made Calvin the compelling spokesman for all Christians in the European diaspora. Thus Calvin initiated — after the reformation of Luther and of the cities — the resilient Reformation of the Refugees.

> Ie t'aymeray en toute obeissance,
> Tant que viuray, o mon Dieu, ma puissance:
> Dieu, c'est mon roc, mon rempar haut et seur,
> C'est ma rencon, c'est mon fort defenseur.
>
> En luy seul gist ma fiance perfaite,
> C'est mon pauoys, mes armes, ma retraitte;
> Quand ie l'exalte et prie en ferme roy,
> Soudain recoux des ennemis me voy.

Clément Marot, Psaume XVIII[153]

---

152. ". . . et scimus hoc esse durius, ubi quis longe abstrahitur a patria." CO 38.399 B; Comm. on Jer. 22:28. Cf. "Scimus enim durum esse exilium." CO 39.511 A; Lam. of Jer. 1:3 (1563).

153. O. Douen, *Clément Marot* . . . , 1.504; as above, p. 113, n. 1. The translation of Psalm 18 catches the threatened existence of the transients-in-exile in a form commensurate with what the editor calls a "véritable chef-d'oeuvre de poésie orientale." *Ibid.,* 503. See further C. A. Mayer, *La religion de Marot,* Travaux d'Humanisme et Renaissance, vol. 39 (Geneva: Droz, 1960).

John Calvin in Geneva, 1536-38 — Some Questions about Calvin's First Stay at Geneva

Richard Hörcsik

If we look at Calvin's biographies written in the last century, at first sight there seems to be nothing left to study of the reformer's first two years at Geneva.[1] A good general picture of the city herself, Farel, the activities of the City Council, Calvin's hardship, and the like has already been drawn based on well-known sources from Doumergue to Parker. *Is there anything more about which something new might be said?*

In this short chapter, I shall raise some questions that occurred to me first after the revision of the secondary sources. I would like to point out the contradictions that appear in certain authors, the general differences and biographical problems that, in my opinion, will come up if we thoroughly examine Calvin's first stay in Geneva.

Thus, I would like to contribute some new points of view and to advance future research of Calvin's biography without a full exploration of the problems of his staying in the city. I would also like to draw attention to the question of what tasks must be completed. Therefore, I would like to bring up some of the so-called historiographical questions as well as some theoretical points of view.

---

1. See the biography prior to 1900, A. Erichson, *Catalogi bibliographici,* CO 59.a517-46 (Berolini, 1900); W. Niesel, *Calvin-Bibliographie, 1901-1959* (München, 1961); J. N. Tylenda, "Calvin-Bibliography, 1960-1970," *Calvin Theological Journal* 6.2 (1971);, P. De Klerk, "Calvin Bibliography," *Calvin Theological Journal* (1972-).

I. The Problems of the Sources

Whenever anybody intends to draw up a biography, the first thing to be done is to consider the sources, as T. H. L. Parker did in his outstanding book.[2] He took into consideration such *primary sources* as the Registers, Correspondence, Chronicles, and Biographies. As for the historiographical problems of Calvin's biography between 1530 and 1536 to which Professor Roussel referred in his excellent lecture at Debrecen,[3] we must be reminded of the problems of researchers of Calvin's biography during the period 1536-38. For example, the Register of the Geneva Council[4] appeared in print only until 1528. Another important source for Calvin's ministry, *The Register of the Company of Pastors. . . . ,* begins only in 1546.[5] However, as far as the above-mentioned two years are concerned, Michel Roset's Chronicles of Geneva6 are not complete enough.

The documents for the two years at Geneva are an unfortunately small source of information compared to those of Calvin's later life. They are: the Preface to his Psalms,[7] the Register of the Geneva Council,[8] Calvin's correspondence,[9] Herminjard's work,[10] and of course the works written by Calvin himself in Geneva.[11]

The *secondary contemporary sources* must also be mentioned, namely Biographies of 1564, 1565 (Beza and Collador), and "Le levain du Calvinisme," 1565; of Jean de Jussie. The Bibliography of Calvin will show us the way to the secondary sources.[12]

2. T. H. L. Parker, *John Calvin. A Biography* (London, 1975), 175-80 ("Sources and Bibliography").

3. W. Neuser (ed.), *Calvinus Servus Christi* (Budapest, 1990), 35-52 (B. Roussel, François Lambert, Pierre Caroli, Guillaume Farel, et Jean Calvin).

4. See the H. H. Meeter Center for Calvinistic Studies handbook (Grand Rapids, 1988), 4-5. This handbook gives information about the collection of microfilms that are available in the H. H. Meeter Center in Grand Rapids.

5. P. E. Hughes (ed. and trans.), *The Register of the Company of Pastors of Geneva in the Time of Calvin* (Grand Rapids, 1966), 1-380.

6. H. Fazy (ed.), *Michel Roset, Les Chroniques de Geneve* (Geneva, 1894). See a selection of English translation, *Transition and Revolution: Problems and Issues of European Renaissance and Reformation History* (Minneapolis, 1974), 77-87.

7. CO 31.23ff.

8. Registre du Conseil. Relevant extracts printed in CO 21.

9. CO 10b-20.

10. Herminjard, *Correspondance de Reformateurs dans les pays de langue française . . .* (cesond ed.) (1878-79), 9 vols. See the English translation "Lettres de Jean Calvin," edited by Jules Bonet, vols. 1-2 (Edinburgh, 1855-75); vols. 3-4 (New York, 1858 [1972 and 1973]).

11. See n. 1, above.

12. W. Neuser (ed.), *Calvinus Servus Christi,* 35ff.

II. Tasks of the Research

From the appreciation of Calvin's two years at Geneva, as seen, for example, in B. Roussel's formulation, we can proceed without any pressure of the hagiography pointed out by Tony Lane, "There have been many myths about Calvin's position in Geneva."[13] He gave typical examples. For example, "Calvin ruled . . . with a rod of iron." Or again, "He made the civil authority subordinate to the spiritual and not the Church to the State."

In order to make advances in historiographical research we must go into certain necessary details as well as note the interconnections in this work. It would be useful, for example, to compile a chronology of Calvin's life from July 1536 to April 1538. Far be it from me to do so, if I wanted to turn my research in the direction of the positivism of the last century. But much might be cleared up in this way. We might get answers to exactly what office Calvin was holding, what and how often he was preaching, to whom he was writing letters, and the like.

Thus, it would be worth making clear the major interconnections in the activities of the first two years. Of course, Calvin's contemporaries and the researchers do not always set forth the same opinions. Our first task is to see the city herself.

III. The Environments of Calvin's Work

Modern biographies of Calvin pay fairly close attention to the description of the political relations of the city. It is well known what forces clashed within and outside the city walls. The point is well made by Ganoczy when he writes, "Geneva carried the old scars and the new Roman clergy on the one hand, and between Roman clergy and the supporters of the reform on the other."[14] Parker, too, sums up the situation excellently, "In 1536 Geneva . . . was a republic, squeezed between the Swiss cantons, the Duchy of Savoy and the Kingdom of France . . . she was situated on the frontiers of the Swiss cantons, Savoy and France.[15]

In particular, we could get an idea of the political and social situation of the city from the works of Professors Kingdon[16] and Olson.[17] We could

13. A. N. S. Lane, "The City of God: Church and State in Geneva," in *God and Caesar.* Paper given at the Study Conference organized by the British Evangelical Council . . . (London, 1973), 45.

14. A. Ganoczy, *The Young Calvin* (Philadelphia, 1987), 106.

15. Parker, *John Calvin,* 55.

16. R. Kingdon, "Was the Protestant Reformation a Revolution? The Case of Geneva," H. Fazy (ed.), in *Transition and Revolution,* 53-107.

17. J. E. Olson, *Reformation and Revolution in Calvin's Geneva* (Halcyon, 1985), 10-17.

also research the city's economy and population in the years 1536-38. Unfortunately, the lack of sources hindered E. W. Monter from finishing his unique research into the changes in the population of the city and the formation of the immigration.[18]

The first question to be raised, which concerns the denominational situation in the city, is: At what level was the Reformation when Calvin arrived there?

Fortunately, today it is an outworn conception that John Calvin transformed the city of Geneva when he arrived there.[19] At the same time it might lead one to think that the revolutionary influence is more important. "It is obvious to me," writes Kingdon, "that the changes in Geneva between 1526 and 1559 constitute a genuine revolution."[20] As he pointed out, there was a fundamental change in the political organization, in the social structure, and in the control of the property at that time. These are certainly facts. But what really is Calvin's role, particularly at the beginning of his stay at Geneva? Were Calvin's and Farel's activities due mainly to the political and economic situation? Did they really have to leave Geneva because of this in the spring of 1538?

We can still see some contradictions in the contemporary sources, too. It is a fact that the process of the Reformation was already felt and had even achieved some results in Geneva. At least, this can be understood from the Registers of the Genevan Council.[21] The expansion of new ideas was similar to that in the other Swiss cities. What were some of them? The gospel was being preached, the mass had been abolished, and the Roman Catholic priests, monks, and nuns had left the city. The city had confiscated church lands and property and used the income to provide social services. The magistrates had initiated a system of public elementary education and had organized a city hospital and a social welfare system. Through preaching, since 1532, and personal influence, a considerable number of the citizens were won.[22] We can see the same process of movement of the early Reformation in Geneva as in the other cities of Switzerland.

On the other hand, looking at the same authentic sources, such as Calvin's works and writings, we find a totally different appreciation of the events of the

18. E. W. Monter, "Historical Demography and Religious History in Sixteenth-Century Geneva," *Journal of Interdisciplinary History,* 9 (Winter 1979), 399-427.

19. Olson, *Reformation and Revolution,* 93.

20. Kingdon, in *Transition and Revolution,* 73.

21. Ganoczy gives a great number of quotations from the Registers; *The Young Calvin,* 107-8.

22. W. S. Reid, *John Calvin, Lawyer and Legal Reformer. Through Christ's Word,* ed. W. Robert Godfrey (Phillipsburg, NJ, 1985), 161.

pre-Reformation. Calvin himself wrote twenty-eight years after the events, "When I first came to this church, there was practically nothing. They preached and that's all. They searched for idols and destroyed them but, *there was not the slightest reformation*. Everything was in tumult."[23] And what is more, Calvin added in the Preface to the Commentary on the Psalms (1557), "Now a little beforehand, the papacy had been driven out by means of this good man whom I have named, i.e. Farel, and by Pierre Viret but, since *everything was not in good order,* there were terrible divisions and dangerous factions among the citizens."[24]

These words are very harsh criticisms of the pre-Reformation events at Geneva. What did Calvin mean when he said, *"there was no reformation,"* and *"everything was not in good order"?* Is this not an underestimation of Farel's work? That leads us to our next question.

IV. Who Was Calvin When He Arrived at Geneva in the Summer of 1536?

Was Calvin the well-known author of the *Institutes* or was he not?

The first fact is that Calvin had hoped to remain unnoticed at Geneva when he wanted to spend a night there. Calvin himself wrote, "I took care to conceal that I was the author of the *Institutes* and resolved to retain my privacy and obscurity."[25] But it was discovered very soon that the author of the *Institutes* was in the town: "I intended to spend only one night there . . . but, I was discovered by a man [Du Tilly] who afterwards returned to popery. And Farel . . . employed all his strength to retain me."[26]

The conversation between Calvin and Farel is well known. To read this text, we should make clear that Calvin's works and life were well known among his colleagues at Geneva. Surely, this is why Farel tried in every way to detain Calvin at Geneva. One of Farel's letters to his friend shows that Farel followed Calvin's life with attention: "I have not yet heard any certain account of the departure of our brother Calvin . . . but, *the reports abroad* and the state in which I left him afflict me greatly. . . ."[27] The majority of the authors of Calvin's

---

23. Ganoczy, *The Young Calvin,* 108. See the same quotation in several works. One of the best, which was translated by Richard Gamble, is S. Reid (ed.), *John Calvin: His Influence in the Western World* (Grand Rapids, 1982), 56.

24. CO 31.36. Preface to the Commentary on the Psalms (1557), quoted by Ganoczy, *The Young Calvin,* 336.

25. CO 31.36. Quoted by Potter and Greengrass, *John Calvin* (New York, 1983), 45.

26. H. Stebbing, *The Life and Times of John Calvin,* trans. Paul Henry, 1 (New York, 1853), 104.

27. *Ibid.,* p. 107.

biography do not forget to mention that "Farel desperately needs Calvin's help."[28] He knew exactly what kind of "support" had arrived at the Bears Inn.

No wonder the conscious result of Farel's work was "a holy triumvirate" — Farel, Viret, and Calvin. They were very complementary to each other as well as to the congregation of Geneva and greatly strengthened the church. "Calvin, a deep thinker and scholar, lived much within himself. Farel was a man who delighted to constant activity . . . lively in his speech, with a good voice. . . ."[29]

I should note that the relations between Calvin and Farel in particular call for independent research into Calvin's first two years at Geneva. Farel's significance was important to Calvin's staying at Geneva as well as for his reform activities. Indeed, the two preserved their close friendship even after leaving Geneva.[30]

Was Calvin a well-known person? One thing was certain — Farel knew him well. Second, the fact that Calvin would have liked to remain unknown during his proposed stay at Geneva gives the impression that the author of the *Institutes* was relatively known there. The notices of Roset's chronicle draw the same picture, ". . . he has become very well-known through the witness and grace by which God has built."[31]

However, a number of facts and sources bear witness to the opposite. For example:

1. The Reports of the Council

First of all, the minutes of the Council's Register point to Calvin's presence at Geneva on September 5. However, his name is not even mentioned, only "Ille Gallus."[32] Then, just five months later, the Council decided to give him a grant of six crowns.[33] On another occasion the reports only briefly note that "that Frenchman" had also received some woven clothes.[34]

William Collins is right to say that, "apparently the Council was at first not greatly impressed with Farel's new recruit."[35] From 1537 on, however, the Council appears to have been more and more concerned with him.

28. R. S. Wallace, *Calvin, Geneva and the Reformation* (Grand Rapids, 1988), 14.
29. Stebbing, *The Life and Times of John Calvin*, 108.
30. See F. M. Higman's remarkable lecture at this Conference (below, pp. 214ff.
31. *Translation and Revolution*, 87.
32. Lane, in *God and Caesar*, 46.
33. P. Pruzsinszky and Kalvin Janos, *John Calvin, A Biography* (Papa, 1909), 224.
34. *Ibid.*, 224.
35. R. W. Collins, *Calvin and the Libertines of Geneva*, ed. by F. D. Blackley (Toronto, 1968), 96.

All this tells us is that Calvin's stay at Geneva from June of 1536 until the end of the dispute at Lausanne became only gradually (or relatively) known.

2. Calvin's Official Activities

Who Calvin was when he arrived at Geneva helps to clear up what office he was holding. At the same time it is not clear what office Calvin consented to fill.[36]

Calvin gives himself the title "Reader in Holy Scripture to the Church in Geneva" at the beginning of his epistles to Duchemin and to Roussel.[37] In 1537, the Bern Council referred to him using the same title.[38] Calvin later explained that "I held the office first doctor,"[39] and he signed a letter May 12, 1537, "Sacrarum Litterarum in Ecclesia Genevensis professor."[40]

But the official notes have another title for Calvin. We can find a reference in the Geneva Register to Farel and Calvin as preachers on July 3, 1537.[41] Indeed, Calladon mentions that Calvin had been elected pastor by the 10th of November 1536, when the confession of faith submitted to the Council describes him as "being thus declared pastor and doctor in the Church."[42]

The lawyer-theologian, as Parker mentions, was a full-time pastor. But we have to mention also that at first, along with the blind Eli Courauld, he was only an assistant to Farel. Professor Olson did not forget to emphasize that Calvin was at first nothing more than a lecturer. He did not become a member of the Company of Pastors until 1537. The highest official office that he ever held was "Moderator of that Company." It is quite clear that officially he occupied a very low-profile position.[43]

Finally, it is a fact that Calvin's first job was simply to lecture on the

---

36. Parker, *John Calvin,* 57; and see V. E. d'Assonville, "Observations on Calvin's Responsio to Cardinal Sadoletus's Letter to the Genevans," in W. H. Neuser, *Calvinus Servus Christi,* 162. d'Assonville writes: "Obviously Calvin then held both offices (doctor and pastor) simultaneously. — *Dankbaar* states that we do not know when and how Calvin entered his ministerium, but that by the end of the year (1536), he attended meetings of the ministers of Geneva."

37. Ibid.

38. Ibid.

39. Ibid.

40. Pruzsinszky, *John Calvin,* 224. Calvin signed his work "Epist. duae" (the second letter of Ferrara), issued May 12, 1537.

41. Parker, *John Calvin,* 57.

42. Ibid. But W. Walker points out: "He did not become one of the preachers till nearly or quite a year later." Walker, *John Calvin* (New York, 1969), 182.

43. Olson, *Reformation and Revolution,* 11.

Scripture, as John Opiron notes in writing to Calvin from Basel on November 25, 1537: "I hear that you lecture on the Epistles of St. Paul with great acclaim and profit."[44]

In terms of his official role in the church at Geneva in October of 1536, Calvin did not have a reputation equal to that of Farel or Viret. This is evidenced by the fact that when the inhabitants of Bern organized a public dispute in Lausanne, they invited only Farel and Viret.[45] In my estimation Calvin's first public performance, the debate of 1536 at Lausanne, was the event that gave him a greater reputation not only in Geneva but also in other cities.

3. Calvin's Hardships

Finally, we must remind ourselves of another fact. "Human factors," unfortunately, do not say much about Calvin's acquaintanceship. His arrival was marred by an illness. This illness prevented him from taking part in many social activities.[46] It is also worth mentioning that Calvin experienced serious financial problems, since he did not receive any compensation until February 13, 1537.

V. Calvin's "Official Work"

In addition to formulating policies, Calvin wrote large works and letters. Two of his important functions during his first stay at Geneva were preaching and being an advisor to the Council. As far as the letters are concerned, the Council accepted his advice with pleasure.[47] What advice did he give? I believe that it is important to explore in detail the relations between the Council and Calvin. How did the Council express its opinion of the author of the *Institutes?*

There are more abundant sources regarding his other jobs. But I think we must pay more attention to Calvin's preaching, because his first "public manifestation" after he arrived in Geneva took place in the pulpit.[48] Very soon he became an eloquent preacher who clearly commanded the respect, if not always the affection, of his audience. Kingdon writes, "This was in marked contrast to many of his predecessors both in the Catholic clergy and among the earliest Protestant preachers."[49]

44. Collins, *Calvin and the Libertines,* 96.
45. Ganoczy, *The Young Calvin,* 109.
46. Pruzsinszky, *John Calvin,* 224.
47. Ibid.
48. Wallace, *Calvin, Geneva and the Reformation,* 16-19.
49. Kingdon, in *Transition and Revolution,* 70.

From where and what did Calvin preach? It would be revealing to examine what "marks" were left on his sermons by the events of the Reformation at Geneva. (His last Easter sermon of 1538 is one example.)

VI. A Nationality Problem

Calvin's nationality problem has to do with his French origin. We must take note of this because there were serious nationality conflicts in Geneva at the beginning of the sixteenth century. Did any disadvantage result from Calvin's French origin?

First of all, we must give an answer to another conspicuous question. Why did the Council refer to him only as "that Frenchman"? Why did they not mention his name? because he was an unimportant person? just an average one, who is simply Farel's recruit? Perhaps because he was a French refugee? I think that this expression says something about the nationality tensions which Calvin lived through and struggled against among the "proud Genevan citizens" — in particular, during the '20s and '30s. Robert Kingdon points out that Geneva "had become so suspicious of foreign pressures that it granted citizenship, with full rights to vote and hold office, only to certain native-born residents."[50]

We should not forget that all the pastors were immigrants — most of them, like Calvin and Farel, from France. It could be that that was one of the important reasons why Calvin couldn't be a citizen of the city and did not perhaps become a "bourgeois" of Geneva until within five years before his death.

Was nationality the reason why he occupied a very low-profile position and was never able to do anything more than advise the city council?

It only reminded them that the immigration of the greater Huguenots would not take place until 1555, when the thought of "Christian tolerance" of the Reformation set roots more deeply in the city.[51]

However, it is clear that between 1537 and 1538 Calvin's first "Ordinances" did not succeed because "they underestimated local reaction and failed to remember that *they were foreigners from France* trying to bring order within a Swiss commune."[52] The Genevans could not accept the dictates of a couple of French refugees, who were not even bourgeois.[53] In an indignant citizen's opinion, "Um sich diesen Francösischen Refugies zu unterwerfen."[54]

50. *Ibid.*
51. Monter, in *Journal of Interdisciplinary History,* 408.
52. Wallace, *Calvin, Geneva and the Reformation,* 161.
53. Reidl, 161.
54. Pruzsinszky, *John Calvin,* 243-44.

VII. The Problems in the Appreciation
of the First Two Years at Geneva

The important moment of historical research lies in the right appreciation of Calvin's first two years at Geneva. If we examine Calvin's own views, the opinion of his contemporaries, as well as the real events of the two years of the strengthening of the church, we shall get some help. Finally, if we consider the particular appreciation of the two years, what theological development shall we find in the works of Calvin?[55]

After leaving Geneva, Calvin referred many times to the past two years in his letters. Reading these lines, we can say that the scar was still fresh in the summer of 1538. There is no doubt that the main reason why Calvin became pessimistic was that he became aware of having committed considerable errors in his ministry at Geneva. Thus, he wrote to Farel, "Before God and his people let us confess that partly by our inexperience, carelessness, negligence, and errors the Church committed to us has so sadly declined."[56] Ganoczy, who quotes the above statement, emphasizes that Calvin even entertained doubts regarding his call to the ministry.[57]

His colleagues, Farel, Bucer, and the others, were aware of their young fellow worker's temporary discouragement.[58] Probably this is why Ganoczy calls this a "pastoral crisis" in Calvin's life. How deep was it? Was it really a crisis in Calvin's activity? I think it was just a temporary shortcoming. And the events of spring 1538 pressed Calvin's theology and thinking toward a practical outcome, one that pays a little more attention to building a church in the "real" Swiss environment.

What did Calvin gain at Geneva during these two years? Only bitterness? I think that we should not forget one very important fact, Calvin's opportunity to practice. When the author of the *Institutes* set off to Geneva, he also wanted to deepen his theological studies. But he did not find a quiet place to study in

---

55. For example, Hesselink compares the first and the second editions of the *Institutes*. He writes: ". . . the second edition represents a major breakthrough for Calvin where he truly comes into his own as independent theologian . . . this is an invaluable clue to the development of the young Calvin's thought. . . . In his preface to his translation of the 1538 Catechism, Ford Battles traces the development of Calvin's thought from the 1536 Institutes through the 1537-38 catechism to the 1539 Institutes." I. J. Hesselink, "An Introduction to Calvin's Theology" (Holland, MI, 1988), 5 (manuscript). On the other hand, Professor Neuser pointed out it is only the *Institutes* of 1559 that receive a new theological arrangement. W. H. Neuser, *The Development of the Institutes, 1536 to 1559. John Calvin's Institutes, His Opus Magnum* (Potchefstroom, 1986), 43-44.

56. CO, 103, 246. Quoted by Ganoczy, *The Young Calvin,* 122.

57. Ganoczy, *The Young Calvin,* 122.

58. *Ibid.*

Geneva. The "practical work" of building the church and the university brought him opportunities he had not known earlier. These first two years of trying to consolidate the Reformation met with considerable frustration. Only after he returned in 1541 was he able to help frame a church and city, writes Professor Olson.[59]

Without the demand to explore it fully, I have raised some questions and problems that I came across during the last years of my research and on which I would like to work systematically in the near future.

---

59. Olson, *Reformation and Revolution,* 94.

Calvin in Strasbourg

Cornelis Augustijn

I. The Task

It is an easy matter to list the events that took place during Calvin's stay in Strasbourg. They cover his personal life and marriage; his day-to-day occupations in Strasbourg as Professor of Theology at the University and as pastor to the congregation of French refugees; his activities at the meetings of the Schmalkaldic League and in the religious colloquies at Hagenau, Worms, and Regensburg; and his writings, of which the second edition of the *Institutio,* his *Commentary on the Epistle to the Romans,* and the *Response to Sadoleto* may be counted as the most important. The number of topics is limited.

The available source material is largely published. It comprises, first, Calvin's correspondence, his writings, and a few records relating to school and church. We should remember here that the extant letters constitute merely a fraction, and a one-sided fraction at that: out of a total of eighty letters from Calvin's pen, forty are addressed to Farel; likewise, of forty-five letters addressed to Calvin, eleven stem from Farel. Fortunately, as compensation for this one-sidedness, these very letters display on both sides a personal tone that is otherwise exceptional in Calvin and to a lesser extent in Farel. Second — and I should like to emphasize this since it is frequently ignored — there are some remarks about Calvin which are worth noting, especially some judgments made by Bucer.

There is an abundance of literature, including much from recent years. The foundation was laid in 1925 by Jacques Pannier.[1] Of the more recent studies, I would refer you to the following publications: Jean Rott on the Strasbourg material; Philippe Denis on Calvin's congregation; Wilhelm H. Neuser and Pierre Fraenkel on Calvin and the religious colloquies; Willem Nijenhuis on Calvin's relationship to Luther and the German Church; Willem van 't Spijker

---

1. J. Pannier, *Calvin à Strasbourg* (Strasbourg / Paris, 1925).

on Calvin and Bucer; and T. H. L. Parker on the *Commentary on Romans*.[2] I have heard from Dr. Rott that he is now able to determine the exact location of Calvin's house and will shortly publish an article on the subject.

Since this is the present state of affairs, I do not think it necessary to indicate the many sorts of gaps in our research. Of course there are such gaps. But the most disturbing gap cannot be closed; both the Strasbourg records and the correspondence are preserved only in very incomplete form. It is, admittedly, quite possible to convey a general impression on the basis of the material we have at our disposal. But Calvin research is thin at the heart of the matter. We have at our disposal a great number of bricks, a variety of studies, but the character of the man Calvin remains hidden. This thesis may appear to many to be too bold, yet I would wish to maintain it. The greatest threat to a true biography has always been the ineradicable tendency to view Calvin as a man who was unchangingly consistent. This idea goes back to Beza, who pointed the way for it in his biography and his publication of the correspondence, especially by the omission of many passages that might destroy the image of a Calvin who was serenely sovereign. Or should we perhaps say that this impression goes back to Calvin himself, who sketched his self-image as that of a man who, after a sudden radical conversion, remained unchanged both theologically and ecclesiastically?

I do not wish to be unfair to those biographers who have presented us with their attempts. I still consider François Wendel's book[3] to be a pioneering

---

2. I am confining myself to a few important studies that are either fundamental or related to the aspects I emphasize. J. Rott, "Documents strasbourgeois concernant Calvin," in *Regards contemporains sur Jean Calvin. Actes du Colloque Calvin Strasbourg 1964* (Cahiers de la Revue d'Histoire et de Philosophie Religieuses 39) (Paris, 1965), 28-73; P. Denis, *Les Eglises d'étrangers en pays Rhénans (1538-1564)* (Bibliothèque de la Facultée de Philosophie et Lettres de l'Université de Liège 242) (Paris, 1984); W. H. Neuser, "Calvins Beitrag zu den Religionsgesprächen von Hagenau, Worms und Regensburg (1540/41)," in L. Abramowski und J. F. G. Goeters (eds.), *Studien zur Geschichte und Theologie der Reformation. Festschrift für Ernst Bizer* (Neukirchen-Vluyn, 1969), 213-37; idem, *Die Vorbereitung der Religionsgespräche von Worms und Regensburg 1540/41* (Texte zur Geschichte der evangelischen Theologie 4) (Neukirchen-Vluyn, 1974); P. Fraenkel, "Quelques observations sur le 'Tu es Petrus' chez Calvin, au Colloque de Worms en 1540 et dans l'Institution de 1543," *Bibliothèque d'Humanisme et Renaissance*, 27 (1965), 607-28; idem, "Les protestants et le problème de la transsubstantiation au Colloque de Ratisbonne," in *Jahrbuch für ökumenische Forschung 1968* (Gütersloh, 1968), 70-115; W. Nijenhuis, *Calvinus oecumenicus. Calvijn en de eenheid der kerk in het licht van zijn briefwisseling* ('s-Gravenhage, 1958); W. van 't Spijker, "Die Lehre vom Heiligen Geist bei Bucer und Calvin," in W. H. Neuser (ed.), *Calvinus Servus Christi. Die Referate des Internationalen Kongresses für Calvinforschung 1986 Debrecen* (Budapest, 1988), 73-106; T. H. L. Parker, *Calvin's New Testament Commentaries* (London, 1971); idem, *Calvin's Old Testament Commentaries* (Edinburgh, 1986).

3. F. Wendel, *Calvin. Sources et évolution de sa pensée religieuse* (Etudes d'Histoire

work, and each of us thinks naturally today of William J. Bouwsma's biography[4] — a study that depicts the man Calvin in his inconsistency. Both these works are trail-blazing, and, as I see it, it is absolutely essential that particularly theologians should give their attention in depth to Bouwsma's "new Calvin," in willingness to learn from it. Nonetheless, it cannot be denied that Wendel primarily paints a portrait of Calvin the theologian while Bouwsma is more concerned with the mature man. The very choice of sources — the sermons — made by the latter leads us to this conclusion.

With the topic "Calvin in Strasbourg," however, we are dealing with a radical transition in the life of a man who was barely thirty. Shaken by his traumatic experiences in Geneva, he felt himself unable — and lacking any divine calling — to serve the church in the future in any way whatsoever. The ministers of Strasbourg nevertheless compelled him to do so by pointing to the admonitory example of Jonah;[5] and three years later he felt unable to resist the call to Geneva. This was another change, less radical, but he prayed just as earnestly that God would avert it.[6] I am trying in my wording to do justice to the tension to which the man was exposed. The totally different world, till then unknown to him, with which he became acquainted in the German free city, in the empire, and in German Protestant churches, the figures of Capito, Bucer, and the German theologians, especially Melanchthon: these all broadened his horizons, influenced this theology, and — even more important — sharpened his awareness that the gospel is embedded in a particular social situation and does not remain unaffected by it. This fact did not ease the tension but intensified it, or raised it to a higher level. In this sense it was a more mature man who returned to Geneva.

In what follows I touch on four aspects of Calvin's stay in Strasbourg that are still too little regarded, but which are important in this respect; and I indicate the reasons for selecting them.

---

et de Philosophie Religieuses 41) (Paris, 1950); German: *Calvin. Ursprung und Entwicklung seiner Theologie* (Neukirchen-Vluyn, 1968).

4. W. J. Bouwsma, *John Calvin. A Sixteenth-Century Portrait* (New York / Oxford, 1988).

5. CO 10.II.126:219; CO 11.284:165. I always mention first the number of the volume, then the number of the letter, and after a colon the column(s).

6. CO 11.252:104: ". . . ayant tousiours en memoire quelle (l'église de Genève) ma une fois este recommandee de Dieu et commise en charge, et que par cela iay este oblige a iamais de procurer son bien et salut"; s. also CO 11.217:36; 243:91-92; 246:95-97; 248:99-100; 254:113-14; 318:230-32; 338.258.

II. Strasbourg and Geneva

The first aspect is Strasbourg itself. When Bucer and Capito offered Calvin a position as minister to the French congregation, this was intended as a temporary measure until he could return to Geneva, and Calvin understood it as such.[7] In the whole affair Bucer was more concerned with the interests of the people and towns directly involved — Calvin, Farel, Geneva, the Swiss cities[8] — than with Strasbourg, where Calvin could be of use but where he was not really strictly needed. When the first attempts started two years later to get Calvin back to Geneva, Bucer was reluctant to allow him to leave although he was convinced that he should go.[9] In spite of Calvin's great reluctance, however, it is clear that in the following year of uncertainty the conviction prevailed in him, too, that he could not decline a call if it should come. He felt himself under obligation to Geneva, and that is not surprising: at this period pastor and town belong together; staying away is desertion.[10] This lends his sojourn in Strasbourg the character of a temporary apprenticeship in which Calvin could develop and become acquainted with the life of a church that was firmly rooted in the life of the people.

Viewed from this angle, Bucer's reaction to the first request to allow Calvin to go is instructive. He replied that Calvin could perhaps work more fruitfully in Strasbourg than in Geneva, and supported this with a characterization of Strasbourg: apart from Wittenberg only a few churches took care of other churches, not to mention future generations, in the way the church of Strasbourg did. Here Bucer referred to the University, but also to the unique position occupied by Strasbourg as an ecclesiastical-political centre in the empire.[11] When we remember the similar position taken by Geneva at a later date — albeit in a partly different geopolitical situation — as it was built up by Calvin — the conclusion is justified that Strasbourg served as a model. This holds good both for the ultimate goal and for the paths leading to it. Consider the mediating role played by Geneva between both Reformed and Lutheran churches and theology; Geneva as a center for refugees, as a center for the establishment and development of the French church (as Strasbourg was for the church in the territories of Upper Germany); the University; the diplomatic threads that met in Geneva. In almost every respect Geneva takes over the role

7. CO 10.II.126:219; 136:236.

8. CO 10.II.126:219; 149:278.

9. CO 11.222:54-56. Capito was more reserved; s. CO 11.281.163.

10. CO 11.233:74: "Neque enim minor est perfidia si quis ecclesiam relinquat, quam semel susceperat in suam fidem, quam si pater filios suos abiiciat"; cf. CO 11.243:91; 252:105; 284:165-66; 318:232.

11. CO 11.222:54-55.

previously played by Strasbourg. Of course, to explain the unique position of the city on the Rhone we must point to Calvin's genius; but this genius ripened in Strasbourg under the influence of the leading personalities and the prevailing ecclesiastical-political climate there. The significance of this for Reformed Protestantism cannot be too highly estimated: after the fall of Strasbourg a new center was a vital necessity.

III. The Empire and the German Ecclesiastical-Theological Debates

A second interesting and often neglected phenomenon of those years is the interest aroused in Calvin for the empire and the German ecclesiastical-theological debates. The shift is remarkable. Until then Calvin had lived in the French and for a brief time in the Swiss environment. It is true that he had long known Luther the theologian, but detached from the latter's own ambience. Now for the first time he became acquainted with the complexities of the actual situation.

His first encounter with German politics evoked the reaction one might expect from a young man. He wrote to Farel: "Bucer has been dragged to a new task. We are not supposed to speak about it, but I shall whisper it to you...,"[12] and the same bragging tone appears elsewhere in this passage. What he talking about is the Leipzig Disputation of January 1539. Calvin quickly adapted to his new circumstances. Two months later his report on the meeting of the Schmalkaldic League in Frankfurt is much more objective, although it is clear that he enjoyed his first meeting with the famous Melanchthon and considerably exaggerated his own part in this conversation.[13] For more than a year Calvin lived and worked more in imperial surroundings than in the confines of the city. Neuser and Fraenkel have illuminated the ecclesiastical and theological aspects of his activities in this area; but research has so far neglected Calvin's *Actes de Ratisbonne* and his comments on various items.[14] Calvin's theology and his attitude to the early church, however, were little affected by these discussions — far less than was the case with Bucer.[15]

Far more important was the fact that Calvin became acquainted from the inside with the complex structure of German religious politics, including the complicated question of church property, and quickly developed a sensitive

12. CO 10.II.158:315-16.
13. CO 10.II.162:326-28; 164:330-31; 169:340-42.
14. CO 5.509-684.
15. A comparison between Bucer's speech on May 8, 1541, and Calvin's words show this difference; s. W. H. Neuser, *Die Vorbereitung* (s.n. 2), 218-21, 224-25.

feel for it. Typical of this are his detailed reports on the deliberations of the Schmalkaldic League in the spring of 1539 when, among other things, the emperor's legate, Weese, tried to separate the Germans from the Swiss. Calvin wrote to Farel: "There is nothing in the German Alliance to offend a devout heart. I ask you, why should they not combine their God-given powers for a common defence of the Gospel?" Calvin gives a full account of the reasons for this praise: the Germans recognize the Swiss as brothers, even in the face of the emperor. "Dear Farel, consider whether we are not being unjust to such people when we accuse them at our leisure, while they do not suffer themselves to be pushed from the true way by any danger or terror," is Calvin's conclusion.[16] This signifies a swing of 180 degrees compared with his remarks a year earlier.[17] Another interesting essay is his *Explicatio consilii Pauli III,* in which he deals in depth with German history of the 1530s — a foundling among Calvin's works.[18] It is clear that he is quickly finding his way in this world.

Connected to this is his radically changing assessment of leading ecclesiastical figures. It is more or less obvious that Calvin would feel drawn to Melanchthon. They were similar not only in their theological views but also in their natures. He quickly sensed that the malleability ascribed to Melanchthon only seemed to be such, in contrast to Bucer, who "burns with such zeal to spread the Gospel that he is content when he has achieved the main point."[19] The greatest change can be seen in his opinion of Luther. In January 1538 he still considered the latter contrary, vain, craving the victor's laurels, ignorant, in conflict with the truth.[20] In November 1539, after Luther had praised Calvin's writings in a letter to Bucer, there comes the open admission: "If we were not overwhelmed by such restraint, we must truly be made of stone. I am overwhelmed."[21] Of course we find this remark, which was not only brought about by Luther's praise, in every biography of Calvin. But I should like to emphasize the significance of such a change in his assessment of Luther for Calvin's biography. For it is not primarily a theological change — be it on the side of Calvin or that of Luther — that forms its basis. It is rather that in this stage of his life Calvin had won a new perspective: as he looks at things from a new angle, his view of Luther also changes. This can be seen very clearly in a letter in which he cries on Farel's shoulder about the theologians of Zurich and the Zwinglian Zébédée who, in a poem that Calvin considered

16. CO 10.II.169:341-42.
17. CO 10.II.87:137-40.
18. CO 5.461-508.
19. CO 10.II.162:328; cf. CO 11.273:147.
20. CO 10.II.87:139.
21. CO 10.II.197:432; cf. CO 11.211:24.

fatuous, had praised Zwingli in the highest terms. What is interesting is not that Calvin considers Luther to be far superior: that is nothing new. What is new is that he counts himself among the Strasbourg party: *nos, nostri,* in an emphatic contrast to *illi,* the Zwinglians; and this also means: allied to the Lutherans.[22]

IV. Ecclesiastical Offices and Ministry in General

A third topic that I think deserves special attention concerns Calvin's emphasis on the significance of ecclesiastical office and of the ministry in general. There are a number of testimonies in these years in which Calvin moves office to a central position.

In the most important writings — in the *Institutio* of 1539 and in the *Response to Sadoleto* — this is not the case. In the former office and minister do not appear, and in the latter in only one passage. This passage, however, is interesting. It is a short paragraph on *disciplina,* and by this term Calvin means the discipline of bishops and priests, which in these days, he says, is in a pitifully bad state. Calvin considers it to be the *nervi,* the nervous system that holds the body of the church together.[23] It is worth emphasizing that in the *Institutio* of 1543 there also appears a *praecipuus nervus* by which the faithful are held in one body. Now, however, it is the office in the church, the *hominum ministerium,* to which this function is ascribed.[24] The difference is conspicuous and surely not accidental. In 1539 the church was held together by *the clergy,* whose conduct in life and of office should be irreproachable. In 1543, following Ephesians 4:11-12, it is the service of *homines* (in the plural) that holds the body of the church together.[25] This could signify that Calvin's understanding of office underwent a change between 1539 and 1543.

It is not surprising that ministry, office, and vocation were always at the center of Calvin's thought in these years. The fact that the Genevan episode had ended in a catastrophe brought Calvin to an internal crisis: Had he really followed a divine calling? His old friend, du Tillet, saw in the events at Geneva

---

22. CO 11.211:23-26.

23. CO 5.406-7 = OS 1.479-80. Cf. *Institutio,* CO 1.544 = OS 5.15: "Eius [satanae] arte factum est, ut pura verbi praedicatio aliquot saeculis evanuerit, et nunc eadem improbitate incumbit ad labefactandum ministerium: quod tamen sic in ecclesia Christus ordinavit, ut illo sublato huius aedificatio pereat."

24. CO 1.562 = OS 5.44.

25. S. E. A. McKee, *Elders and the Plural Ministry. The Role of Exegetical History in Illuminating John Calvin's Theology* (Travaux d'Humanisme et Renaissance 223) (Genève, 1988), 134.

a divine admonition: Calvin should humble himself before God, seriously consider whether he had really been called by God for that purpose, and on no account interfere again in any such matter.[26] Calvin, who had just arrived in Strasbourg, replied by referring to Bucer's exhortations and God's future judgment concerning his post at Strasbourg. But we can sense from the wording of his letter that he was in considerable doubt about the legitimacy of his Genevan office.[27] A year later he appealed to his conscience and the divine call.[28]

The events that took place in Geneva after his departure played a considerable part in compelling Calvin to become aware of his office. His supporters were unwilling to recognize the new pastors appointed by the Council. When Calvin advised them to do so and totally ruled out a schism, they accused him of being inconsistent; had not Farel and Calvin refused to celebrate the Lord's Supper and by so doing caused a break in the church? How could they now warn the Genevan congregation to be obedient? Calvin firmly rejected this conclusion, basing his argument on the fact that there is a basic difference between *minister* and *plebs:* the former is responsible for the administration of the Lord's Supper and consequently for the sacrament itself; the man in the pew, on the other hand, has simply to search his own heart.[29] The congregation is obliged to accept the minister of the Word — and that also means the newly installed pastors — as a father.[30] Calvin expresses his thought in a nutshell in the succinct sentence,[31] *"Difficultas mea in ministerio vertebatur."* In a letter to the Genevans on the matter of the renewed call to Calvin, the ministers, who were at the time in Worms, state quite unequivocally that it is the minister's duty not only to serve in word and sacrament but also to be the *curator animarum* — should care as a father or mother for the people entrusted to his care and for the individual members.[32]

Finally, the introduction of a *probatio* in Calvin's congregation at Strasbourg is worthy of note. It is known that Calvin introduced it in the spring of 1540 as an *examen,* a scrutiny, in which he gave instruction in the faith and sometimes also admonished or comforted members who wished to participate in the celebration.[33] The comparison or even equation with confession is

26. CO 10.II.139:241-44.

27. CO 10.II.147:271-72; cf. CO.10.II.187:391. Calvin's sharp reaction reveals his uncertainty.

28. CO 11.233:74; 243:91.

29. CO 10.II.156:307-10; 162:323; 175:350-55, 200:437.

30. CO 10.II.175:352.

31. CO 10.II.156:309.

32. CO 11.253:107.

33. CO 11.214:30-31, 218:41, 260:121; cf. CO 10.II.169:339-40.

obvious and was immediately noticed by an unknown person (Pierre Viret?) and an extremely outraged Bullinger.[34] Although Calvin set great store by his innovation, he never tried to introduce the like in his later period in Geneva.

Why do I mention these facts, which are, after all, well known? Because they show that Calvin attached to the office of pastor an importance that we are in danger of forgetting because we know that Calvin's historical contribution to the constitution of the Reformed Church lies particularly in the formation of the Consistory and the multifold office. This has been made very clear to us in the books written by Elsie A. McKee.[35] We should not, however, lose sight of the sober fact that during this period Calvin's thought is focused on a single spiritual office, the *ministerium* — in contrast to the later plurality of ministries — also known as *administratio* and *munus,* which was of all the *munera* "the most exalted but also the most dangerous."[36] The superlative obviously is not used in relation to other ecclesiastical offices but to the different forms of service in the *respublica christiana.* We are here dealing with an ecclesiological question, but in our context it also particularly concerns Calvin's own self-assessment and self-awareness.

V. Relationship to Bucer

A fourth aspect concerns Calvin's relationship to Bucer. Here, too, my central concern is not with theology or church constitution, important though these questions are. They have often been discussed, in recent years as well.[37] What interests me is the question of what part Bucer played in Calvin's development in this period. I put it in this way because I have the impression that Bucer is the key figure in the very significant changes that appear during these years in Calvin's attitude and outlook. How far did Calvin become another person through his contact with Bucer — but also how far did he not change? I cannot go into detail about this here, but I should like to make some observations on this complex of questions.

My starting point is Calvin's letter to Bucer in January 1538, in which the author, while still in Geneva, heaps accusations on Bucer.[38] The main concern is about two matters. First, there is the Wittenberg Concord and Bucer's attempt to persuade the Swiss to accept it. I have already mentioned

---

34. CO 11.218.41 (cf. Herminjard 6, p. 223, n. 38); 292:183.

35. E. A. McKee (s. n. 25); eadem, *John Calvin on the Diaconate and Liturgical Almsgiving* (Travaux d'Humanisme et Renaissance, 197) (Genève, 1984).

36. CO 11.284:165-66; cf. CO.11.206.11 on "sacrum ministerium."

37. S. W. van 't Spijker (s. n. 2).

38. CO 10.II.87:137-44; cf. CO.10.II.90:148, 149:278.

the completely negative assessment of Luther. Calvin is not pleased with Bucer's *Retractationes*. The latter's appearance in Bern in favor of the Lutheranizing pastors leads to "these self-important fools" crying "victory," etc. The second accusation is much more serious. Bucer is continually attempting to establish a new realm that might hold the middle ground between Christ and Pope. This can be seen particularly in his *Defensio contra episcopum Abricensum* (1534).[39] According to Calvin, this document, in which doubt is cast on the sole authority of Holy Scripture by quotations from the Church Fathers, has had a disastrous effect on the *simpliciores* in France and England, and the majority of the godly would like to correct it at a stroke — that is, to strike it out entirely. As far as I am aware, this passage has never been taken into account in any essay on the development of the young Calvin. In the present context it betrays above all Calvin's self-assessment. He warns Bucer against fabricating a "new Gospel." This can only be a reference to the "different Gospel" of Galatians 1,[40] which means that the 28-year-old is putting himself in the somewhat elevated position of Paul over against those who distort the gospel.

On this point I am inclined to say that rather less would perhaps have been more appropriate. Grynaeus of Basel at any rate was of this opinion. Two months later he wrote to Calvin, who had obviously also complained to him about the two ministers at Bern. His reply was sharp.[41] Calvin's letter is very nasty to the Bernese. Of course he is right — Kuntz *is* boorish, a lout who perhaps does speak a barbaric Latin with syntactical mistakes; but in his aims and industriousness he is a brother. Why should we not bear in mind his

39. S. R. Stupperich, "Bibliographia Bucerana," in H. Bornkamm, *Martin Bucers Bedeutung für die europäische Reformationsgeschichte* (Schriften des Vereins für Reformationsgeschichte 169) (Gütersloh, 1952), nr. 45. Characteristic is the author's blurb on the title page: "Hic videbis, christiane lector, nos nihil prorsus in doctrinam vel ritus ecclesiarum nostrarum admisisse, quod non pulchre conveniat et cum scriptis orthodoxorum patrum et cum observatione ecclesiae catholicae."

40. CO 10.II.87.142: "Ego vero pro meo more tibi respondeo, si vis omnibus facere Christum plausibilem, tibi non esse fabricandum evangelium." Herminjard 4, Nr. 677, p. 347, has the same reading, and this corresponds to the manuscript, a copy. This reading is, however, senseless. R. Schwarz, *Johannes Calvins Lebenswerk in seinen Briefen. Eine Auswahl von Briefen Calvins in deutscher übersetzung*, vol. 1 (Neukirchen, 1961), p. 62, hat: "Wenn Du einen Christus willst, der allen gefällt, so darfst Du deshalb doch kein neues Evangelium fabrizieren"; apparently he has inserted the word "novum" and has given a dubious translation. The most simple solution is to assume that the copyist had read "non" instead of "nouum." The difference is confined to a line above "non"/"nou." The allusion to Gal. ' is also found in the words "si vis omnibus facere Christum plausibilem"; cf. Gal. 1:10: "Modo enim hominibus suadeo aut Deo? aut quaero hominibus placere?"

41. CO 10.II.97.158-61; cf. CO 10.II.126.219.

education and background in the rough Alps? Calvin has been privileged to be educated in the heart of France among the most highly cultivated men of the time. There is, however, no need to compare Kuntz with himself. Grynaeus demands a different attitude from Calvin: he should be "all things to all men" (I Cor. 9:22). This reprimand shows that Grynaeus was clearly aware of Calvin's weak side: arrogance on the basis of intellectual superiority.

In this portrait Grynaeus depicts the Calvin who was to leave Geneva. It is fairly similar to Calvin's self-portrait in his letter to Bucer! The Calvin who returns to Geneva is a different person. My thesis, put briefly, is: the difference can to a large extent be traced back to Bucer. To a large extent, of course, because Melanchthon and even Luther made their contributions too. But it is only Bucer whom Calvin wants to take with him to Geneva in 1540 in order that he may help him with the first rebuilding of the church.[42] There is also no parallel to the words that Calvin addressed to Bucer after his return to Geneva. "If, in anything I do, I do not live up to your expectation, you know that I am in your power. Admonish me, beat me, do everything that a father is allowed to do to his son."[43] The contrast to his judgment in January 1538 is radical: the distorter of the gospel has become the father in Christ and Calvin's own pastor.[44]

It is not necessary to pursue the stages of this development in detail. I do, however, want to emphasize that it was not a straightforward development. As early as April 1539 Bucer had won Calvin over,[45] and in May Calvin defended the Wittenberg Concord and Bucer's *Retractationes* against the Zwinglian Zébédée: if only Zwingli had done the same![46] But in October 1539 Calvin is furious when Caroli tries to become reconciled with those in Strasbourg and meets with a certain amenability on the part of Bucer; although in Calvin's report to Farel we can see glimpses of admiration for Bucer, who amid all the agitation dominated the scene.[47]

Another thing that is interesting is the matter of the statements about the Lord's Supper in the *Institutio* of 1539 and in the *Response to Sadoleto*. In these sections Calvin had expressed himself in such a way on the relationship of the God-man Christ to the elements that the Zwinglians read it with delight and the Nurnberger, Veit Dietrich, lodged a complaint with Bucer.[48] The latter replied that it was an *"intempestiva disputatio"* — that is, untimely. Calvin

---

42. CO 11.318:232; 321:236; 339:259; 341:262.
43. CO 11.363:299.
44. Cf. dazu CO 11.253:107, where the theologians use the same terms.
45. CO 10.II.169:341.
46. CO 10.II.171:345-46; cf. CO 10.II.172:348.
47. CO 10.II.188:396-400.
48. S. J. Rott (s. n. 2), 65-67.

expresses himself in such a way out of consideration for the French Protestants; but he is prepared to produce an "antidote."[49] The affair is instructive because it shows that Calvin had obviously discussed with Bucer the differences between himself and the latter that he had earlier emphasized.

Thus it is no linear development. This would have been scarcely possible since it was, in the first place, not a matter of theological influence that only gradually becomes effective, but more the influence of Bucer as a person to whom Calvin was attracted and, at the time, repelled again. In this dialectical way Bucer became Calvin's mentor in Strasbourg.

In the above I have tried to outline some aspects of Calvin's biography in the years 1538 to 1541. Their heart lies in the simple observation that we should not construct our picture of Calvin retrospectively by beginning with his later years, but should attempt to do justice to the fact that Calvin, too, went through a process of development.

49. S. J. Rott (s. n. 2), 67, n. 12.

The *Imago Dei* Theme in John Calvin and Bernard of Clairvaux

Luke Anderson

These pages seek to unfold the meaning of the *imago Dei* as understood by John Calvin and Bernard of Clairvaux. Why the combination? Because Calvin knew Bernard's doctrine, ostensibly disagreed with it, but is basically set with the same dilemma. Admittedly both "reformers" were powerful leaders in the renaissance of their respective centuries, the twelfth and the sixteenth centuries. Admittedly both used *imago Dei* theory as an integral part of their doctrine on redemptive justification. In the text Genesis 1:26, Calvin, exegetically correct, finds no basis for Bernard's distinction based on the same text. Bernard reads *imago* as a reality distinct from *similitudo*. Moreover, Bernard, using the text II Corinthians 3:18, as does Calvin, finds a corroboration of the distinction already perceived in Genesis. The "fall" of Adam presents both authors with a fundamental question: "Whatever happened to the *imago Dei* in man's postlapsarian state?"

I. The *Glossa Ordinaria* and Our Authors

Something of an echo of the *imago Dei's* threefold distinction as found in the ninth-century *Glossa Ordinaria* is heard in Calvin's *Institutes* 1.15.40:[1] "Now God's image is the perfect excellence of human nature which shone in Adam before his defection, but was subsequently so vitiated and almost blotted out that nothing remains after the ruin except what is confused, mutilated, and disease-ridden."[2]

1. *Glossa Ordinaria (in S. Scripturam)* (PL 113.III.92A).
2. John Calvin, *Institutes of the Christian Religion*, ed. John T. McNeill, trans. Ford Lewis Battles, in The Library of Christian Classics, vols. 20 and 21 (Philadelphia: Westminster Press, 1960), 1.15.4.

The *Glossa* defines Calvin's "the perfect excellence of human nature" as the *imago creationis* and locates it in Adam's rational nature, *ratio*. Is this Calvin's understanding of *imago*? The *Glossa* predicates this *imago* of every individual.

Calvin's text continues: "Therefore . . . some part of it [i.e., *imago*] is manifested in the elect, in so far as they have been reborn in the spirit. . . ."[3]

In the *Glossa,* Calvin's "reborn in the spirit" is expressed by *imago recreationis.* Calvin says that this image "can be nowhere better recognized than from the restoration of his [man's] corrupted nature." The *Glossa* defines "re-creation" in terms of *gratia,* and limits the *imago* to the "justified," or in Calvin's term "the elect," but only insofar as they are reborn.

Calvin now concludes his enumeration: ". . . but it [i.e., *imago*] will attain its full splendor in heaven."[4]

Obviously, for Calvin the *imago Dei* is only fully realized in heaven. *Imago* in its perfection, according to the *Glossa,* is named *imago similitudinis* and pertains only to those who have come to *visio.* And the *Glossa* cites the Psalmist: "The light of your countenance, O Lord, is signed upon us" (Ps. 4:7).

Clarifying as these revered distinctions are, it remains true that the terms *imago creationis* and *imago recreationis* interface in ways that reveal intrinsic ambiguities. Both Calvin and Bernard perceived these, and in analogous ways set about to resolve them.

Bernard's *imago-similitudo* resolution of the question also reflects the *Glossa*'s threefold distinction: creation, re-creation, and similitude. In the *Cantica* we read:

> Certainly in the natural order like seeks like *(similis similem quaerit).* This is the cry of one who seeks: "Return, O Shunamite, return that we may look upon you." He [God] would not see her when she was unlike him. *(Intuebitur similem, qui dissimilem non videbat; sed et se intuendum praestabit.)* But when she is like him he will look upon her, and he will allow her to look upon him. . . . So think of the question, "Lord, who is like you?" in terms of difficulty, not of impossibility. . . . It is assuredly a most marvelous and astonishing thing, that likeness *(illa similitudo)* which accompanies the vision of God and is itself that vision.[5]

---

3. *Ibid.*
4. *Ibid.*
5. Bernard of Clairvaux, *On the Song of Songs,* 4, trans. Irene Edmonds (Kalamazoo: Cistercian Publications, 1980). Abbreviation: SC 82.7.178; 8.170. S. Bernardus, *Sermones Super Cantica Canticorum,* in *S. Bernardi Opera,* 2, J. Leclerq, C. H. Talbot, et H. M. Rochais (Romae: Editiones Cistercienses, 1958). Abbreviation: *OSB* 2.82.297.13-21.

In the natural order, the principle *similis similem quaerit* is seen as the basis for the union of man and God. Man seeks the essential likeness, man sees the essential likeness, and for this reason he can be defined as *similitudo*. He is "likened" to God as spirit, intellect, will, etc. This is the *imago creationis* of the *Glossa*.

But for Bernard, the unlikeness *(dissimilitudo)* caused by unrighteousness fractures the union of likeness. But at the moment the soul becomes like God again, the moment of *imago recreationis,* two things will happen: God will look upon his likeness, the soul; and God will allow the soul to look upon him, the essential likeness. For Bernard the refound "likeness" in man poses a process that is difficult, but the task is not impossible.

The restored image is spoken of by Bernard as the *similitudo* and a likeness that is marvelous and astonishing because of its perfection. It is effected when man **sees** God face to face; and the *Glossa* names this the *imago similitudinis*.

Bernard's text must also face the ambiguities of *imago creationis* and *redemptionis*. If the use of *similitudo* is a key to opening the mystery, we are still faced with the problem of the true meaning of *imago*.

In this study, we have rigidly held to the examination of Calvin's *Institutes* I.15, and Bernard's *Sermones super Cantica,* Sermo 80. We have from time to time used other corroborative material from both sources; but the two texts in question are rich and provocative statements of a central Christian theme.

II. Calvin's Doctrine in His *Institutes 1.15*

Calvin looks not to Genesis, but to Paul and to the Apostle's concept of **renovated** man as his primary source for the concept of man as God's image: "Now we are to see what Paul chiefly comprehends under this renewal."[6]

Calvin finds in Paul the *quid maxime* elements of the **restored** image.[7] He immediately lists these elements: *priore loco, agnitionem (ponit); altero sinceram iustiam et sanctitatem.*[8] Because the righteousness and holiness spoken of in the text are obviously matters of redemptive grace, the knowledge spoken of is also presumed to be of redemptive grace. If we then reread Genesis 1:26, and attend to Calvin's use of Colossians 3:10 and Ephesians 4:24 (Vg.),

6. Joannis Calvinus, *Opera Selecta Joannis Calvini,* ediderunt P. Barth et G. Niesel, *Institutio Christianae Religionis 1559,* libros I et II continens vol. III; librum III in vol. IV; librum IV in vol. V (München: Monachii in Aedibus Chr. Kaiser). Abbreviation: OS 2.179.22-27. Cf. *Institutes* 1.15.4.

   7. *Ibid.,* 23.

   8. *Ibid.,* 24-25.

we can conclude that the *imago Dei* is not properly founded upon creation, *qua talis,* but rather its basis is to be discovered in some **elevation** of the created nature, in some gift bestowed gratuitously on created nature. In his *Commentarius in Genesin,* when Calvin speaks of the contempt one might have for one's corrupted nature, he cautions against too absolute a condemnation. Man remains, he insists, a "pre-eminent specimen of Divine wisdom, justice and goodness."[9] But this specimen of divine attributes is not the *imago* of 1.15.4, where we read: ". . . what was primary in the renewing of God's image also held the highest place in creation itself." This appears to be something beyond the mirroring of attributes, more than effects being like their cause. The restored image must be in the same order as the original image. And for Calvin the restored image seems something beyond mere *ratio.*

In the opening lines of this fourth paragraph Calvin appears to locate the *imago* in the faculties of the soul.[10] He says that God's image was, by inference, discernible *ab initio.* He tells us of the *plena imaginis definitio,* and it is not had, he says, *"nisi clarius pateat quibus facultatibus praecellat homo."* The reference here is clearly to the intellect and the will. And the faculties are *"speculum . . . gloriae Dei."*[11] Hence this text appears to favor a facultative definition of *imago.* Yet the new restored man appears to be very different from this *ab initio* interpretation.

But it is worth noting that Calvin expands this *plena definitio* when he speaks of the *conditions* of the faculties. He enumerates these conditions: *in luce mentis, in cordis rectitudine, partiumque omnium sanitate.*[12] Light, rectitude, and integrity are the substantives in our passage; mind, heart, and all the parts are the genitives. The shift from faculties to conditions seems significant. And the inference that these conditions belonged to man's primordial state argues in favor of some kind of special integrity, if not directly supernatural at least as connected with it, as properly preternatural. The original image appears to have been, if not **above** nature, at the minimum **beyond** nature.

In paragraph 8 of this same chapter, we have some scattered and varied descriptions of the original, prelapsarian image. We shall examine three statements.

In this first text, Calvin speaks explicitly of *prima conditio hominis.*[13] This man excelled in preeminent gifts, directive and decisional.[14] The gifts of

---

9. Joannis Calvinus, *Commentarius in Genesin,* in *Corpus Reformatorum: Joannis Calvini Opera quae sunt omnia,* 23.1-622.

10. OS 2.179.3-4.

11. *Ibid.,* 5.

12. *Ibid.,* 26-27.

13. *Ibid.,* 185.31.

14. *Ibid.,* 32.

mind served not only for the directing of man's earthly life, but for his ascent to God and to eternal happiness. These endowments set new goals, beyond the earth and beyond human exigencies. The human mind is the product of creation, but the *praeclaris dotibus* are significant additions.[15] Calvin's words "... *transcenderent usque ad Deum et aeternam foelicitatem*" suggest a higher objective and subjective destiny for man than mere nature demands.[16] To the gifts of mind is added the gift of "choice," *electio*. This gift (1) directs the appetites (i.e., sensitive appetites) and (2) tempers all man's organic motions.[17] And thus it happens that the human will is rendered amenable to the guidance of reason: "... *atque ita voluntas rationis moderationi esset prorsus consentanea.*"[18] Then Calvin makes a significant addition. Like the mind, the human will reaches out to a transcendent goal, an end not connatural to it: "... *libero arbitrio pollebat homo, quo si vellet, adipisci posset aeternam vitam.*"[19]

Calvin here again speaks of "integrity" and of the orderly disposition of Adam's nature. This opinion is but an expansion of the *partiumque omnium sanitate.*[20] In man's first state, reason and will are subjected to God; the lower powers are subjected to reason; and the body subjected to the soul. The same teaching is found in Calvin's *In Genesim* (1:26), where we read of the prelapsarian Adam that "perfect intelligence flourished and reigned," and that "uprightness attended as its companion," and that "all the senses were prepared and moulded for due obedience to the reason," and that "in the body there was a suitable correspondence with the internal order." This integrity, although traditionally associated with grace, differs essentially from the *agnitionem, sinceram iustiam,* and *sanctitatem* that in the restored image are clearly things of grace.

Calvin here makes one final claim. He is not speaking in this text of some hypothesis, but of a fact of faith: "... *non agitur quid accidere potuerit necne sed qualis fuerit hominis natura.*"[21]

Hence we conclude that the *prima conditio* included supernatural and preternatural gifts above and beyond the *natura hominis.*

We come now to a second view of the *prima conditio.* This view centers on a discussion of the human will. "Therefore, Adam could have stood if he wished, seeing that he fell of his own free will."[22]

15. *Ibid.*, 31.
16. *Ibid.*, 33-34.
17. *Ibid.*, 34-36.
18. *Ibid.*, 36.
19. *Ibid.*, 186.1-2.
20. *Ibid.*, 179.20.
21. *Ibid.*, 186.4-5.
22. *Institutes* 1.15.8.

The *potuit stare* declares real and positive possibility, but as such it is contingent. The *si vellet* places the responsibility for standing strong squarely on the shoulders of the human will. Man could stand, if he willed to stand.[23] That he did not stand is attributed to the *proprie voluntate* and to it alone.[24] Calvin explains the "fall" by pointing out two conditions of the will's nature. First, the will is by its nature flexible; it can move in either of two directions: *in utrumque partem.*[25] Second, it is not fixed on the "good" or, as Calvin expresses it, it is not *"ad perseverandum constantia."*[26] And these two factors render human failure *tam facili.*[27] The "fall" is, however, culpable. Free choice supported by the gift of rectitude elected badly: *"Libera tamen fuit electio boni et mali."* In rejecting the "good," the original image, which was *". . . in mente et voluntate summa rectitudine"* and *"omnes partes organicae rite in obsequium compositae,"* is under one aspect lost, and under another corrupted.[28]

Calvin concludes that in the "fall" man lost himself *(ipsum perdendo)* and that he corrupted his blessings *(bona sua corrupit).* There seems to be some contradiction here: is the *imago* lost? or is the *imago* corrupted? Or are we dealing here with a paradox: some things are lost and some things are corrupted!

Another and third presentation of *prima conditio* is derived from Calvin's comparing the first man and his posterity. *". . . man was far different at the first creation from his whole posterity, who, deriving their origin from him in his corrupted state, have contracted from him a hereditary taint (haereditatem labem)."*[29] The obvious question comes to mind: what was the first man's uncorrupted state?

Calvin gives us the answer as he describes the original image: (1) *"Nam ad rectitudinem formatae erant singulae animae partes."*[30]

Rectitude is that toward which all the human parts are ordered. It is not altogether clear what rectitude signifies here. Can it be equated with "righteousness"? Since all the parts are spoken of as "ordered to rectitude," the final cause of this ordination may only signify "free choice."

Another aspect of the original image is mentioned: (2) *"et constabat mentis sanitas. . . ."*[31]

23. OS 2.186.5.
24. *Ibid.,* 6.
25. *Ibid.,* 6-7.
26. *Ibid.,* 7-8.
27. *Ibid.,* 8-9.
28. *Ibid.,* 9-10.
29. *Institutes* 1.15.8; OS 2.186.24-26.
30. *Ibid.,* 26-27.
31. *Ibid.,* 27.

The health of the mind in this context seems to be very different from the *lux* of faith; neither is it simply *"ratio."* It seems to indicate a *donum* inseparable from the righteousness of grace, but formally defined in terms of "integrity."

Finally, Calvin looks at the will in the original image: *". . . et voluntas ad bonum eligendi libera."*[32]

The first man was free to elect the "good," yet he did not do this. Calvin concedes that the human will was placed in an "insecure position because its power was weak." But on the other hand, he adds: *". . .* his status should have availed to remove any excuse."[33] He says nothing about the nature of this status. Is it then the *"robur"* of integrity or the gift of righteousness? It is not at all clear that we are beyond the integrity associated with grace, but distinct from it.

These three examples, therefore, indicate that the *prima conditio* means something either above or beyond human nature and that the *imago creationis* signifies something other than simple "ratio." Calvin sees no urging exegetical reason to distinguish *imago* from *similitudo.* And he correctly points out that *similitudo* in the Genesis text is simply an addition *vice expositionis.*[34]

Interpreters of such a distinction claim a *differentiam quae nulla est.*[35] Scripture here employs a literary device, *repetitio;* and this instrument does no more than explain *rem unam bis.* For Calvin this text is neither complex nor ambiguous: *". . . imago nominetur homo, quia Deo similis est."*[36]

Calvin extends his argument against any distinction. Various interpreters — and Bernard is counted among them — say that the term *imago* or the Hebrew *zelem* means *substantia animae* and that the word *similitudo* or the Hebrew *demuth* is taken to signify *qualitates animae.* But Calvin denies this interpretation and adds his own definition of *imago.* When God made man, says Calvin, he wished to represent himself *(se ipsum) in imagine.* This was accomplished by means of engraved marks of likeness, *propter insculptas notas similitudinis.*[37] The *insculptas notas* convey a clear notion of exemplarity: the creature is **like** his Creator because the Creator wished to give an expression of himself in something other than himself, but **like** him. Yet what that **likeness** consists in is not identified. In the *Commentarius in Genesin,* Calvin is more conciliatory: "The thing [i.e., the distinction] is true; but I do not think that anything of the kind entered the mind of Moses." Earlier in this

---

32. *Ibid.,* 28.
33. *Institutes* 1.15.8.
34. *Ibid.,* 1.15.3; OS 2.178.3.
35. *Ibid.*
36. *Ibid.,* 6-7.
37. *Ibid.,* 13-14.

text he sees the distinction in terms of *imago* = "forshadowing," and *similitudo* = "realization" and "perfection." But in the *Institutes,* the distinction finds no place. It is not the creation story that raises the issue of *imago-similitudo;* it is rather the "fall" and the consequent postlapsarian state that occasions the question.

Calvin states the matter succinctly: "There is no doubt that Adam when he fell from his state was by that defection alienated from God."[38]

There are subjective and objective results of this "fall": Adam's previous state is abandoned; and his union with God is lost. The defection occurred when Adam *excidit e gradu suo.* And because of the defection Adam is said to be *a Deo alienatus.* But what was the previous state? "Therefore, even though we grant that God's image was not totally annihilated and destroyed in him, yet it was so corrupted that whatever remains is frightful deformity."[39] *Imago Dei* in this text is *non prorsus exinanitam ac delectam,* but what remains is unmistakenly *corruptum.* Here Calvin views the *imago* as **not totally** *exinanita ac delecta,* but certainly *corrupta.*

In yet another text, 2.2.12, Calvin reports that a distinction he has discovered in Augustine pleases him. He recites the distinction in his own words: ". . . *naturalia dona fuisse corrupta in homine per peccatum, supernaturalibus autem exinanitum fuisse.*"[40] What is Calvin saying here? The *corrupta* in this text matches nicely with the *non prorsus exinanitam ac delectam* in paragraph four. The stance appears to favor placing *imago* in the nature of man and viewing the "fall" as corrupting this nature; destruction would be an impossibility.

On the other hand, the *exinanitum* does not match the *non prorsus exinanitam* of paragraph four at first blush. But if the *supernaturalibus* are truly destroyed and the *naturalia* are corrupted, then *imago* must be placed, not in nature, but in something above and / or beyond nature. This seems to be the movement of Calvin's argument.

Let us look first at Calvin's definition of *supernaturalibus.* He repeats here what we have already seen to be the explicit teaching about the "restored image" and the implicit teaching on the "original" image. *"Nam hoc posterior membro (supernaturalibus) intelligunt tam fidei lucem quam iustitiam, que ad caelestem vitam aeternamque foelicitatem adipiscendam sufficerent."*[41]

This key text lists the light of faith and the will's righteousness as the supernatural gifts. But equally important is Calvin's teaching that these gifts

38. *Institutes* 1.15.4; OS 2.179.7-8.
39. *Institutes* 1.15.4.
40. OS 2.254.31-32.
41. *Ibid.,* 245.34-35; *Institutes* 2.2.2.

are instruments or means to an end. The end is spoken of in terms of subjective beatitude: heavenly life and eternal happiness. Clearly the naked faculties are inadequate for attaining these *super-naturam* goals, but *fidei lux* and *iustiam* are equal to the task of objective attainment. The "fall" has devastating effects upon faith, justice, and God-given goals for man.

Calvin describes the "fall" as *"abdicans a regno Dei";* hence man is deprived of *(privatus) spiritualibus donis,* and the true goal, *ad beatam animae vita,* is lost. The act of abdication is accomplished by man's free act. But the act of banishment, *"exultare a regno Dei,"* is God's reaction to this bad free act. If *imago* is seen then as the graced possibility of everlasting light and life with God, it is correctly said to be *exinanita!*[42]

These *dona* will, however, be recovered through the "grace of regeneration."[42] "All these, since Christ restores them to us, are considered adventitious, and beyond nature: and for this reason we infer that they were taken away."[43]

Faith, love of God and love of neighbor, zeal for righteousness, and aspirations for holiness are *adventitia* and *praeter naturam.* If these *dona* are adventitious, they are neither inherent in nature nor due to nature. By consequence they are totally gratuitous, transcendent, and separable. In this sense, if we place the *imago* in the realm of the *adventitia,* we can say that as a result of the "fall" the *imago Dei* is destroyed and abolished.[44]

But what of the *naturalia?* The "fall" of man results in the corruption of natural gifts: *"naturalium donorum corruptio."*[45] These gifts are **health** of mind and **rectitude** of will, but these are said to be abolished by sin, even as the *imago* is said to be abolished by sin.[46] The text and context strongly suggest that Calvin may be speaking of the **corruption of nature**, and the **abolition** of the **preternatural** gifts of nature. Nature is said to be **integral** when (1) all of its parts are harmoniously in place and when (2) there is no defection from perfection. Health of mind and rectitude of will would be examples of these gifts, nor formally *supernaturam,* but properly *praeternaturam.* Health of mind is not faith; nor is rectitude righteousness. We have already seen that Calvin makes use of these concepts of "gifts," although he does not use the vocabulary.

Calvin follows the whole of Christian tradition when he speaks so frequently of the effects of sin in the mind, in the will, and in the sense appetites. But these disorders are very different from the loss of faith and the unrighteousness of the will.

42. OS 11.252.1.
43. *Institutes* 2.2.2.
44. OS 2.255.6.
45. *Ibid.,* 8.
46. *Ibid.,* 6-8.

Corruptio reveals itself in the condition of the mind: it is after sin weak *(debilis),* darkened *(multis tenebris immersa),* without health or integrity. *Corruptio* reveals itself also in the condition of the human will: it is after sin quite simply perverse *(pravitas).* This corruption sounds very much like the medieval concept of *vulnera peccati.* The corruption of nature does not destroy the nature. And because of this basic stability many have seen the *imago Dei* simply in terms of our created nature. We will always be God's image because we will always be his creatures. But this solution does little to explain our "regeneration" by Christ. Calvin has exact notions on nature, and is not unappreciative of this "gift" of the Creator, but neither does he locate the *imago Dei* in this context.

Calvin spoke of the faculties as the *residuum.* He insists that because *ratio* is a *naturale donum,* it cannot be destroyed. Partly debilitated and partly darkened, the rational "ruin" stands. Mental corruption is not mental destruction. In a highly unusual use of John 1:5, Calvin refines this notion in order to balance the doctrine of damaged intellect. So sparks still gleam, he says, in the degenerated nature of man. And these very *scintillae* manifest man's power of understanding and prove him to be essentially different from brute beasts. But he promptly adds that man's light is suffocated by the great density of ignorance so that it does not shine out very efficiently. *Ratio* is corrupt, but not extinct.[47]

The teaching on the damaged will needs also to be balanced. Calvin asserts that the faculty *voluntas* is *"inseparabilis . . . ab hominis natura."* Were it to perish, man's nature would likewise perish. But at the same time the captive and freely enslaved will is bound by perverse desires *(pravis cupiditatibus);* and it consistently strives after nothing that is right *(nihil rectum).*[48] Hence the *voluntas* is corrupt, but not extinct.

There is one final point: the relationship of the *imago Dei* and Christ. Calvin's remark, *"Christus perfectissima sit Dei imago,"* introduces a new series of questions.[49] So, for example, is man in any way an *imago Christi?* Is Christ the exemplar according to which we are said to be fashioned according to him? Of the Son, we read: ". . . who is the Image of the invisible God, the firstborn of creatures" (Col. 1:15).

And it is also written that the Son precisely as *Imago* is the one "who being the brightness of His glory and the figure of His substance, . . . sitteth on the right hand of the majesty on high (Heb. 1:3)." What Calvin intends is that we understand that the exemplar in the case of Christ and in the case of man is *Deus.* Christ **is** God's image; man is like God and **in** His image.

47. *Ibid.,* 13-21.
48. *Ibid.,* 21-23.
49. *Ibid.,* 180.3.

It is true that Calvin says that we are to be conformed *(formati)* to the *perfectissima imago,* and that we are to be restored *(instauramur)* to the *perfectissima imago.* But the ultimate meaning of this is that we are to bear God's image: *". . . ut . . . imaginem Dei gestemus.".* This purpose has been indicated earlier in this same paragraph: *". . . hunc regenerationem esse finem, ut nos Christus ad imaginem Dei reformet."*[50]

Thus the work of Jesus Christ, the God-man, is to restore the *imago Dei* in man; and we, through his passion, death, and resurrection, are restored to God's image. But man is not to be seen as the *imago Christi* in any proper sense of the term. Calvin quotes Paul's letter to the Colossians (3:10) to reiterate the basic truth which affirms that the "new" man is renewed *"secundum imaginem eius qui creavit illum,"* that is, God.[51] And to this Calvin adds a text from Ephesians (4:24) admonishing them to put on the new man, *"qui secundum Deum creatus est."*[52] And this *imago Dei* is a "good" within man: *". . . quum penes ipsum non extra proprie quaerenda sit: immo sit animae bonum."*[53]

The first Adam revealed this inner good; its restoration in Christ serves only to highlight its essence from the beginning; man's nature was graced from the beginning, but we know it directly only in its restored form.[54]

Conclusion

It would seem, then, that *imago Dei* for Calvin is a supernatural reality lost in the "fall," and in this sense it is destroyed by sin. Moreover, health of mind and rectitude of the will as gifts of a fortified nature are also lost in the "fall." But as these endowments look to the faculties, it can be said that corruption has set in; darkness and depravity are the legacies of sin. In a word, only nature remains intact after the "fall," but the bare nature does not fulfill the definition of *imago Dei,* as understood by Calvin.

III. Bernard's Doctrine in the *Super Cantica, Sermo 80*

There are, according to Bernard himself, two expressions of his doctrine of man as the *imago Dei. Grace and Free Choice* (1128?) is the earlier expression,

50. *Ibid.,* 179.18-19.
51. *Ibid.,* 19-21.
52. *Ibid.,* 22.
53. *Ibid.,* 181.2-3.
54. *Ibid.,* 178.26.30; *Institutes* 1.15.3.

and the final section of the *Super Cantica Canticorum,* penned in 1148, some five years before his death, is yet a different expression.[55] He says of these two works that the doctrine of the *imago Dei,* using the distinctions of *imago-similitudo,* is ". . . *disputa . . . diversa fortassis . . . sed . . . non adversa.*"[56] He also asks his audience to decide for itself which of the two expressions is better.[57]

Bernard's doctrine in the Canticle sermons seems to be deeper, but there are elements in *Grace and Free Choice* which suggest that Bernard himself had not decided in favor of the one or the other.

There is a significant substitution of terms in Bernard's eightieth sermon; he moves from the Christ-church terms combination to the Word-soul pairing. Bernard will speak of the Word *(Verbum)* as the *imago Dei;* and he will speak of the soul *(anima)* as *imago Dei.* Bernard sets about to explain this shift in language. " 'What have the Word and the soul in common?' Much, on all accounts (Rom. 3:2). In the first place, there is a natural kinship, in that the one is the Image of God *(ut hoc imago)* and the other is made in that image *(illa ad imaginem).*"[58]

The distinction is an important one: the *Verbum* is **the** image *(hoc);* and the soul is yet another image *(illud),* and best described as **according** to the image of God, **after** the image of God, or **in** the image of God: *illa (anima) ad imaginem sit.* Immediately Bernard introduces yet another distinction, but now in terms of the *anima: "For the soul is made not only in the image of God, but in his likeness. Nempe non ad imaginem tantum: et ad similitudinem facta est."*[59]

This crucial distinction between *imago* and *similitudo* will allow Bernard to maneuver dexterously through the welter of theological themes surrounding the imago-lapsus conundrum.

Setting aside the kinship of *Verbum and anima,* Bernard now speaks of the differences. Bernard, in terms reminiscent of the Nicene Creed, argues that the *Verbum* is in fact of the same specific nature as God.[60] The *hoc imago* is then the perfect image of God. Because the soul is not *justitia de justitia* or *de lumine, lumen,* or *de Deo, Deus,* but simply *ad imaginem,* it is an imperfect

55. S. Bernardus, *Liber de Gratia et Libero Arbitrio* in *Sancti Bernardi Opera,* vol. 3, ed. J. Leclercq and H. M. Rochais (Romae: Editiones Cistercienses, 1963), 165-203. *On Grace and Free Choice,* trans. Daniel O'Donovan (Kalamazoo: Cistercian Publications, 1977), 53-111.
    56. OSB 2.81.291.13-15; SC 81.11.168. ·
    57. OSB 2.81.291.15-16; SC 81.11.168.
    58. *Ibid.,* 80.2.146; OSB 2.80.277.22-23.
    59. SC 80.2.146; OSB 2.80.277.24-25.
    60. *Ibid.,* 278.1-4. Cf. also Aquinas, *Summa Theologica,* 1.q.35. a 2.r 3.

image. Yet its capacities and its yearnings are the *loci* of its *imago* and *similitudo*. *"Capax appetensque"* have very technical meanings in Bernard's theology. They match very neatly the *imago-similitudo* themes.[61] Bernard is also concerned here with the mode of predication; the *imago Dei* is not predicated of *anima* as some externally conceived metaphor. "For what is made in the image *(ad imaginem)* should conform to the image *(cum imaginem)*, and not merely share the empty name of image."[62]

Bernard will now begin to fill with **content** the name *imago Dei* as it is predicated of man. He will clearly demonstrate that this term is very far from being a mere *vacuo nomen: "Celsa creatura, in capacitate quidem maiestatis, in appetentia autem rectitudinis insigne praeferens."*[63]

"Capacity for greatness" will in Bernard's thought be equated with imago, properly so-called; but "a token of its righteousness" will come to be associated with *similitudo*. This text repeats the two expressions of Bernard's theology of *imago*. But first Bernard reasserts the nature of *imago* as applied to the *Verbum*. David sings of him: "Great is the Lord, and great is his power (Ps. 146:5)." This "greatness" in the Lord will be the basis for *capacitas maiestatis*.

In yet another place we read of him: "The Lord is upright, and in him there is no unrighteousness (Ps. 91:16)." Here again is the basis for the *similitudo* in man, and the "token of its righteousness." But the perfect image shares "greatness" and "righteousness" substantially: "For the image of God is the same substance as God, and everything which he seems to share with his image is part of the substance of both, and not accident."[64]

Moreover, the *Verbum* is "equal to God," and hence he **is greatness**; the *Verbum* is "in the form of God," and hence he **is righteousness**. But the human soul is simply **like** the *Verbum:* it is simply capable of greatness, and yearns for righteousness; in brief it is *capax* and *appetens*. "He [the Word] is the image of this upright and great God; therefore, the soul which is his image is like him *(ad imaginem)*."[65]

The Verbum looks back to God as origin of his *capax* and greatness, and in this way he is *imago Dei;* but he looks forward, so to speak, toward the soul as the mediate *locus* of the soul's *ad imaginem*. Both *Verbum* and *anima* image GOD.

Bernard makes other clarifications. To the human soul greatness and

61. OSB 2.80.278.4-5.
62. *Ibid.,* 8-10.
63. *Ibid.,* 5-6; SC 80.2.146.
64. OSB 2.80.278.27-29.
65. *Ibid.,* 2.147; OSB 2.80.278.17-19.

righteousness come because of *creatio* or *dignatio;* these belong to the Word through *generatio*. Again, the soul's *capax* and *appetens* are from God, *a Deo*. While in the *Verbum* they are *de Dei substantia*.

In a deeper synthesis we discover: "For the image *(Verbum)* greatness is not merely the same as uprightness, but existence itself is greatness and uprightness." ". . . *sed etiam id magnum rectumque esse, quod esse.*"[66]

The *ad imaginem* qualities of capacity and yearning both involve possibility. They may or may not be realized. If, for example, "the soul . . . does not desire or have a taste for heavenly things, but clings to earthly things, [it] is clearly not upright but bent (curva)."[67] In this way the possibility for righteousness goes unrealized! The *curvitas* is seen as a turning toward the earth, and a turning from *supernorum*. This state suggests that the *anima* has seriously altered its destiny; sin has entered the picture. In this way, the discussion of *similitudo* and *dissimilitudo* is introduced. But the *capacitas aeternorum* remains fully intact. So we return to our original statement: *imago* is not *similitudo, capax* refers to *imago,* and *appetens* to *similitudo; capax* is permanent and *similitudo* waxes and wanes because it is in the category of free choice. This set of distinctions will permit Bernard to move more easily in the postlapsarian world than John Calvin.

Bernard now attempts to respond to two distinct, but related questions: Is greatness to be really distinguished from righteousness? And is each of these qualities distinct from the soul itself? We can summarize his response before we look at his full argument in its favor. In the first place greatness and righteousness *diversae ab invicem sint;* and in the second place, they are *diversae ab ea (i.e., anima).*[68]

The easiest route to distinguish greatness from righteousness would have been to define the terms: the one touching upon a being's possibility, the other touching upon the free election of the good. But Bernard argues otherwise. When righteousness is lost, then, *similitude* is lost; and it is replaced by *dissimilitude*. Capacity cannot be lost. And Bernard poses a rhetorical question: "*Quid vero sperare posset, cius capax non foret?*"[69]

And his immediate response is: "*Itaque per magnitudinem, quam retentat etiam perdita rectitudine. IN IMAGINE PERTRANSIT HOMO. . . .*"[70]

If, then, righteousness can be lost and capacity cannot, then, one is not the other and they are distinct *ab invicem*. Indirectly, a similar argument proves that righteousness is distinct from the soul. And this is so simply because it is

66. SC 80.3.148; OSB 2.80.279.1-2.
67. SC 80.3.148; OSB 2.80.279.5-6.
68. *Ibid.,* 2-3.
69. *Ibid.,* 13-14.
70. *Ibid.,* 15-16.

separable from the soul. But there remains a question of the capacity's distinction from the soul. And so Bernard asks: "But how can it be proved that greatness of soul is distinct from the soul?"[71]

To adequately respond to this question we begin with a somewhat convoluted text of Bernard's, looked at first in its Latin garb which better expresses its not always obvious connotations: *Cum itaque nec **illa in omni**, nec **sitista in sola anima**, patet utramque indifferenter differe ab ea.*[72] "And since the one (righteousness) is not found in every soul, and the other (greatness) is found otherwise than in the soul, it is obvious that each without distinction is distinct from the soul."[73]

What is Bernard saying here? He is saying that righteousness is distinct and **separable** from the soul. But that greatness is distinct yet **inseparable** from the soul. Similitude is separable, image is inseparable.

Bernard's use of *in omni* and *in sola . . . anima*, although this latter in a peculiar negative form, suggests his acquaintance with Porphyry's doctrine concerning the *praedicabiles,* and more specifically with the predicable named *proprium.* Use of this predicate to explain capacity will allow Bernard to define *ad imaginem* in a uniquely sophisticated and highly technical fashion that safeguards the evangelical, postlapsarian doctrine of the *imago Dei* as applied to humankind.

In the context in which we are reading the text, Bernard can be said to be concerned with righteousness and greatness not as direct universals, that is, not in terms of their thought content and comprehension. His real interest here is in how these predicates may be applied to the human soul; he is interested in the indirect universal or in the extension of these terms.

The predicate *righteousness* is for Bernard a **separable accident,** and thus *similitudo* is a separable accident. The fall of man separates the righteousness of man from his soul.

But what does Bernard say of capacity for greatness as it relates to the soul. In the first place it is distinct from the soul; it is not the soul! In the second place, and here the problem appears in its fullness, capacity is inseparable from the soul. Let us listen to Bernard: "The soul itself does not consist of its greatness, any more than a crow consists of its blackness or snow of its whiteness, or a man of his ability to laugh or his ability to reason, but you never find a crow without blackness, or a man devoid of his ability to laugh and to reason."[74]

Bernard's examples liken *capax* to something that flows necessarily from

71. SC 80.5.150; OSB 2.80.280.10.
72. *Ibid.,* 18-19.
73. SC 80.5.151.
74. *Ibid.;* OSB 2.80.280.23-26.

the soul or perhaps more exactly with the soul, although it is not the soul itself. Hence *capax* as a predicate is properly a *proprium,* a property distinct, but necessarily inseparable from the soul.

In Chapter Four of Porphyry's *Isagogue,* we read of his fourfold division of the predicate proprium: (1) what is predicated of **ONE species**, but **not of all the individuals** of that species; (2) what is predicated of a **whole species**, but **not of it alone**; (3) what is predicated of **one species** and **all the individuals** of the species, but **not at all times**; and finally (4) that which is the most proper predication form of *proprium,* that is, what is predicated of **one species**, of **every individual** of that species, and **always,** *omni, soli, et semper.*

As an example of this *omni, soli, et semper* Porphyry suggests risibility as predicated of man.[75] Bernard sees **capacity** as an example of *omni, soli, et semper;* but he also makes some use of the second form of *proprium:* black and white as applied to crows and snow.

Bernard has already posed a significant question that reveals his response to that very question: "What hope of salvation can there be for one who has no capacity for receiving it."[76] In this text *appetens* is defined as *sperare posset,* but that hope demands the capacity of receiving salvation. The disposition to receive is another aspect of *proprium.*

This text also manifests that the proof of the distinction between *capax* and *anima* must follow different lines from that used to establish the distinction between righteousness and the soul. *Dissimilitude* is a postlapsarian fact; hence *similitude* or righteousness is separable from the soul. Capacity, too, is distinct from the soul: the *imago Dei* is not to be confused with the soul, yet is an inseparable property.

> . . . for even if the soul is never found apart from (its capacity for) greatness, yet that capacity for greatness is found outside the soul.

> *Nam etsi anima non invenitur absque magnitudine sua, ipsa tamen et extra animam reperitur.*[77]

Extra anima sets up the true distinction, and *non . . . absque* maintains the inseparability. In what at first appears to be a digression, Bernard says that the angelic natures are also distinct from their capacities for greatness, and he defines these: ". . . *ex captuvidelicet aeternitatis.*"[78] The *locus* of the *imago*

---

75. Porphyry, *Isagogue,* trans. Boetius in *Commentaria in Aristotelem Greca,* vol. IV.9, ed. A. Busse (Berlin, 1887), C IV #1 and #6.

76. SC 80.3.149; OSB 2.80.279.13-14.

77. SC 80.5.150; OSB 2.80.280.13-14.

78. *Ibid.,* 15.

Dei, therefore, is neither in human nature nor in angelic nature *qua talis.* To explain it we need to predicate it of these natures as a *proprium,* as a permanently present property of the soul. And it is predicated of the human soul *omni, soli, et semper.*[79]

Capax is then to the human soul what *rationality* and *risibility* are to the human soul, it is a *proprium* distinct but inseparable. The *capax* is an attribute derived from the connotation of the *anima,* not unlike the mode in which an effect is said to be in the cause, or a conclusion in its premises. The *capax* is seen in some kind of necessary connection with the soul, though clearly not identified with it.

By the same token, some other distinctions have to be kept in mind. Traditionally, the human soul has been described as *capax* in two ways: one is the capacity of a natural power always fulfilled by God since the reduction of power to action is **due to the nature**: *rationality* and *risibility* are really due to the nature of man. But other capacities of the human soul depend for their realization on the divine power **alone** and are reduced to act by God **alone**, but also because of an obediential potency of the human nature.[80] The *imago Dei* belongs to this category of capacity.

Capax then proves too much if it is seen as a *proprium* demanding realization due to the nature only; this is Pelagian!

But *capax* proves too little if it is seen simply as a divine action elevating an indifferent human nature; this is Pseudo-supernaturalism!

For Bernard, *capax* has a technical theological meaning: it is **not** the **self-realization** of a **potential agent**, as *risibility* and rational activity follow from the nature of the human soul. It is rather the **received realization** of a **patient**. But it is also the **ability** to receive *(. . . cuius capax non foret?)* an **extrinsically bestowed actuality**.

Bernard's *proprium* is the **obediential potency** of a later theology. It follows, therefore, that the use of the word *proprium* is analogous; that is, *imago Dei* is to the soul what risibility and rationality are to soul, but in ways that are *simpliciter* **different**, but only *secundum quid* **the same**. This strongly suggests that for Bernard the *imago creationis* is something more than merely natural. And although *proprium* in its fourth form — *omni, soli, et semper* — best meets Bernard's needs to explain *capax,* it is not without significance that he uses examples from form two as well; this perhaps indicates his awareness of analogous usage.

In Sermon 83 Bernard speaks of the soul's reaction to its own sins and

79. Porphyry, *Isagogue,* C IV #5.
80. Aquinas, *Summa Theologica,* 3.q.1. a.2.r 3.

failures. He urges the soul to "hope for mercy and pardon," and goes on to suggest that the soul surpass this and "aspire to the nuptials of the Word."[81]

What is of note here is the foundation upon which this aspiration is built; it is a confidence or perhaps an audacity flowing from the soul's *imago* state: *"Quid enim non tute audeat aput eum cuius eius insignem cernit imagine, illustrem similitudine novit?"*[82]

The honored image and the glorious similitude render the soul **like** the *Verbum*. The basis for union is a likeness in the lovers: both are *imago Dei*. There can be no fear here of majesty: "Why should it *(anima)* fear a majesty when its very origin gives ground for confidence?"[83]

The soul's *fiducia* is set upon its history, the *de origine*. This is something beyond the fact of creation; it is the creation with that addition of possibility expressed in *capax majestatis* or *magnitudinis*.

The soul's confidence is consonant with the action of God that sets the possibility, but remains totally free as regards its realization, but the *similitudo ab initio* already indicated God's decision.[84]

Yet Bernard will speak of man's possibilities: *"Grande profecto in nobis donum naturae ipsa est."*[85]

This innate natural gift is not *ex natura,* but rather a reality *cum natura.* Nevertheless, any attempt to stay the development of this *natura*'s addition will in turn be destructive of the nature itself: ". . . if it is not allowed full play [i.e., the natural gift] the rest of our nature will go to ruin, as if it were being eaten away by the rust of decay."[86]

Here the *capax* seems to take on some of the qualities of the *appetens,* bringing *imago* and *similitudo* closer to one another. We insult God when we hamper the flowering of the *imago;* for he is its author.[87] Yet to hamper its development is not to destroy it!

> . . . God, its creator desires the divine glory and nobility to be always preserved in the soul *(perpetuo voluit in anima conservari)* so that it may have within itself that by which it may always be admonished by the Word, either to stay with him, or to return to him if it has strayed.[88]

81. SC 83.1.181.
82. OSB 2.83.298.23; 299.1.
83. SC 83.1.181.
84. OSB 2.83.299.1-2.
85. *Ibid.,* 6-7.
86. OSB 2.83.6-8.
87. *Ibid.,* 9.
88. SC 83.2.189.

The *capax magnitudinis* always present to the soul, "... *haec in sese ... habeat,"* is the basic link between the *imago imperfecta* and the *Verbum, imago perfecta.* The *Verbum* is under this aspect an exemplar for the *anima.*[89] But the staying with or the returning to ultimately look to God, since *Verbum* and *anima* are each in their own way *imago Dei.*

Man's failures lead to dissimilitude: "... *cum se sibi vitae et morum pravitate dissimilem facit.*"[90] But then he repeats his famous distinction: *"quae tamen dissimilitudo, non natura abolitio, sed vitium est."*[91] Vice destroys similitude, it does not erase the image.

The soul that is converted or, more exactly, returns (anima redita) to the *Verbum,* is said to be reformed *per ipsum* and conformed *ipsi.*[92] Reformation through the Word would seem to refer to the efficient cause of salvation, namely, the salvific work and efficacy of the Word's redeeming action. But Bernard explains that the conformity of the soul to the Word weds *anima* to *Verbum.* Because the *anima* is **like** the *Verbum, similis per naturam. Imago,* in this instance, means the fulfillment of *capax.* But the *anima* is **like** the *Verbum* in yet another way: in the exercise of wills, *similem ... per voluntatem.* The reference here is to *similitudo,* and to that exercise of will which has as its term virtue.[93] Reformation through the Word brings to perfection *capax* and *appetens,* image and similitude.[94]

Conclusion

Bernard maintains that the *imago Dei* remains intact in humankind's post-lapsarian state. This is because the *imago* is defined as capability. *Capax* is, according to Bernard, a *proprium,* a property real, inseparable, but distinct from the soul. Hence Bernard does not place *imago* either in the intellectual or volitional nature of the soul, that is, the *ratio.* Vestiges of God's creative action can be found in our human attributes, but it is not these that constitute *imago.* In a word, *imago Dei* is not properly speaking a gift of nature; it is connected to the nature inseparably, but is distinct; moreover, the realization of this capacity is beyond the power of the nature. On the other hand, *imago* is not to be confused with the de facto gift of grace or with integrity of nature. If it were, then the loss of grace and / or integrity would issue in the loss of

89. OSB 2.83.299.11.
90. *Ibid.,* 14-15.
91. *Ibid.,* 15-16.
92. *Ibid.,* 18.
93. *Ibid.,* 21-22.
94. *Ibid.,* 80.277.23.

the *imago*. For Bernard **image** is never lost. What can be lost is *similitude*. In the *imago-recreationis, imago* is fulfilled because *similitudo* is restored. Bernard, then, takes a kind of middle position. The *imago Dei* in man is not essentially *a natura,* nor is it essential *a gratia.* It is a predicate of the soul, as a *proprium,* as a capacity; but it is a capacity in an analogical sense, for its actualization depends on the spontaneous, free action of God always and everywhere gratuitous.

IV. Finale

Calvin, having rejected the *imago-similitudo* distinction so central to Bernard's thinking, finds himself in something of a quandary when he comes to explain man's postlapsarian state. Bernard uses the distinction effectively and more easily explains how the *imago* survives the disaster of Adam's failure.

For Calvin the *imago* is destroyed when *lux mentis* and *iustificatio cordis* are lost; since these are what is restored by Christ, they existed in some form *ab initio.* But speaking of the *prima hominis conditio,* Calvin also views **integrity** as a gift of nature: *sanitas mentis* and *rectitudo.* He appears to include these in the *imago* concept. When these are withdrawn, the *imago* can be described as corrupted. After sin, says Calvin, only "OBSCURE LINEAMENTS" of a once perfect nature remain because that nature is "vitiated and maimed." There is, however, a sense in which these *dona naturalia* are indeed destroyed since the perfect subjection of body to soul, of sensitive appetite to reason, and *sanitas mentis* and *rectitudo* are not spoken of as restored. Yet mind and will remain, but as "ruins." The *super naturam* gifts of *agnitio* and *sanctitas* will be restored.

For Calvin *imago recreationis* best manifests the meaning of *imago Dei.* When speaking of man's *prima conditio,* he makes use of Augustine's *super naturam / natura* distinction. Adam's sin causes the loss of *super naturam* gifts; it corrupts man's **integrity**, the gifts of *natura.* But the nature as such, although debilitated, remains, but in ruins. Hence *imago creationis* would seem to include gifts of nature and grace, but not simply the term of creation, *"ratio."* Thus, *imago Dei* is never something simply of nature.

Bernard, like Calvin, is especially concerned with the *imago recreationis.* The "new" man, mirroring God even as the *Verbum* mirrors, remains an imperfect image. Yet Bernard does not see the image in terms of the re-creation. What happens in this re-creation is that *similitudo* is restored and fostered. Our personal moral history is the tale of the waxing and waning of *similitudo. Imago*'s permanence transcends the vagaries of our moral life.

According to Bernard *imago Dei,* defined as a *proprium* and specifically as a *capax maiestatis,* can never be lost. It is distinct from the human soul, but likewise inseparable from it. As the soul cannot be destroyed, neither can its *proprium, capax.* But this *proprium* must be predicated analogically of the soul, which in effect signifies that its "realization" depends on the gratuitous act of God so that God's totally free and spontaneous will is safeguarded. Again, like Calvin, Bernard's *imago creationis* is something beyond *natura* and *ratio;* it is the passive ability to transcend mere nature; it is the passive ability to receive a higher destiny and to suffer the elevation of our human faculties in order to attain that destiny.

For both authors the *imago Dei* was *ab initio* something receiving its value from grace.

Hermeneutische Schlüssel zur alttestamentlichen Prophetie in Calvins Hesekielpredigten

Erik A. de Boer

Zur Vorbereitung wurden Calvins Praelectiones zu Kapitel 1 des Hesekiel-buches und seine Predigt zu Hes 40 bis 48 in Transskription versandt. Folgende Fragen wurden gestellt. Erstens wurde der Rahmen angesprochen: Wie sieht Calvin den Wert dieses Buches im Ganzen der Bibel? Und wie sieht er die Erfüllung in Christus und in der Geschichte der Kirche? Mein zweites Interesse galt der Frage: Haben wir es im Prophetenbuch mit Apokalyptik zu tun, und wie steht Calvin dazu? Hinzu kam die Frage nach der Bedeutung der Visionen bezüglich ihrer Sprache und ihres Inhalts.[1]

I. Bibliographie zum Thema

Als Johannes Calvin im Jahre 1564 starb, hatte er in den Praelectiones noch nicht ganz die Hälfte des Hesekielbuches ausgelegt. Seine Auslegung der ersten 20 Kapitel in 65 Praelectiones liegen uns vor. Theodor Beza schreibt in der Widmung der Erstausgabe an Gaspar Coligny: "Hätte der Herr uns noch ein oder zwei Jahre den Gewinn eines so großen Lichtes gestattet, dann wüßte ich nicht, was uns zu wünschen übiggeblieben wäre zu dem vollen Verständnis der Bücher beider Testamente."[2]

---

1. Ich bin dankbar, daß ich in dem Seminar die Möglichkeit hatte, meine Disserta-tionspläne mit den Herrn Bihary, Langhoff, Márkus, Moehn, Scheld und Van 't Spijker zu diskutieren. Meine Dissertation hat das Thema: Die Prophetenauslegung Calvins auf Grund der Predigten und Praelectiones zu Hesekiel.
2. CO 40,11 / 12.

Wir verfügen allerdings nicht nur über den Torso des Hesekielkommentars, sondern auch über eine fast vollständige Auslegung des Buches Hesekiel in Predigten. In drei Manuskriptbänden der Genfer Bibliothek haben wir 55 Predigten über Hesekiel I–XV,69 Predigten über Kapitel XIII–XLVIII und (in einem Band mit Nachschriften) noch drei weitere, die einzelne Stücke aus den Kapiteln XVII–XXII behandeln. Der Totalbefund der Predigten und Praelectiones ergibt, daß uns nur die Auslegung der Kapitel XXI–XXII fehlt (aber auch zu XXII,9ff. gibt es eine Predigt). Wir können deshalb sagen, daß die Hesekielauslegung Calvins fast vollständig ist und uns für die hermeneutischen Fragen zur Verfügung steht.

II. Der Blickwinkel

Die Hesekielpredigten sind für mich eine Entdeckung. Mein besonderes Interesse gilt der Eschatologie Calvins. Ich habe mir die Frage gestellt: Wie legt Calvin die "eschatologischen" Texte der Bibel aus? Angefangen habe ich mit einem Kommentar, der nie geschrieben wurde, oder besser: mit der Johannesoffenbarung, dem eschatologischen Buch, das Calvin weder in Predigten noch in einem Kommentar oder in Praelectiones ausgelegt hat. Die Ergebnisse dieser Untersuchung brachten mich zu der Frage: Wie legt Calvin die alttestamentlichen Propheten aus und besonders — wie wir es nennen — die apokalyptischen Kapitel in ihren Schriften? Man wird verstehen, daß ich zuerst Calvins Auslegung der Schlußkapitel des Buches Hesekiel gelesen habe, nachdem ich über die Manuskripte seiner Predigten verfügen konnte.

Warum erwarte ich etwas Spezielles von Calvins Auslegung der letzten elf Kapitel, Hesekiel XXXVIII bis XLVIII, der Gog- und Magogprophetie und der Tempelvision? Weil sich hier aus unserer Sicht die "Apokalyptik" dieses Buch findet. Meine Nachforschungen zu Calvins Benutzung der Johannesoffenbarung in Zitaten hat ergeben: In den 43 Stellen, in denen er klar die Offenbarung zitiert, gibt es nur wenige Anhaltspunkte für die Auslegungsregeln der Visionen. Dann ist die Frage umso brennender: Welches ist die besondere Bedeutung dieser Visionen als spezielle Offenbarungsmittel Gottes in Calvins Sicht?

Mit Absicht habe ich die Predigt über die Schlußkapitel zur Vorbereitung vorgelegt. Es ist nur eine Predigt, die ganze neun Kapitel auslegen soll. Die historisch exakte Antwort auf die Frage muß gefunden werden: Welche hermeneutischen Schlüssel hat der Reformator bei der Auslegung dieses exilischprophetischen Buches angewandt? Die kritische Frage ist die: Warum hat Calvin überhaupt "apokalyptische" Interessen gehabt? T. H. L. Parker hat vor Jahren geschrieben: "Accepting then that Calvin did not write on Revelation we should ask the reason. The facile answer is that he did not understand or sympathize with apocalyptic." Und: "Yet I believe that a theological reason may have deterred him from attempting Revelation. For him, this Old Testament proclaimed Christ in an obscure manner, but in the New Testament Christus had appeared in complete clearness. It was like the difference between twilight and noontide. Hence, apocalyptic, involving the use of allegory, was part of this Old Testament method of teaching. . . ."[3] Deshalb ist die Frage umso wichtiger: Was lernen wir aus Calvins Auslegung der apokalyptischen Teile des Alten Testaments?

Die Grundlage meiner Untersuchung war bis jetzt schmal: 28 Predigten über Kapitel I und X, XXIII, XXXIV und XXXVII–XLVIII. Hesekiel berichtet dort hauptsächlich über Visionen.

III. Geschichte und Erfüllung

1. Erfüllung in der jüdischen Geschichte

Calvin beginnt mit der Datierung: Hesekiel wird im Exil, in Babylon, zum Prophetenamt berufen "im 30sten Jahr seit dem letzten Jubeljahr". Das heißt, er wird außerhalb Israels und Jerusalems berufen, wo Jeremia schon seit 35 Jahren als Prophet des Herrn seinen Auftrag und Wirkungsbereich hatte. Diese zwei Pole bestimmen seine Auslegung: das jüdische Volk im Exil in Babylon und der zurückgebliebene Rest des Volkes in Jerusalem und Juda. Auf diese beiden Gruppen des einen Volkes bezieht sich seine ganze Auslegung. Die Datierung gibt den Rahmen der Erfüllung an.[4] Es ist vor allem die aktuelle Lage Israels, in die Hesekiel hineinspricht.

In der Predigt 171, der ersten über die Gog- und Magogprophetie, deutet Calvin Gog als "Sohn des Japhet" (Gen 10: "une similitude"). Deshalb soll dieser Feind Isreals auch aus Europa kommen, weil die Kinder Japhets dorthin gezogen sind, während seine Brüder den Orient erfüllt haben. Calvin kennt und nennt "die Auslegung der Juden", daß es sich nämlich hier um eine Prophezeiung im Blick auf die Türken handelt.[5] Die Christen haben diese

---

3. Calvin's New Testament Commentaries, 1971, 77. Später sagt er zu Calvins Hesekielauslegung: "Here we see Calvin struggling courageously with an unfamiliar and uncongenial form" (Calvin's Old Testament Commentaries, 1986, 208).

4. Zu Hes 17,22 sagt Calvin: "Diese Prophetie sieht zweifellos auf Christus . . . , aber die Rückkehr [aus dem Exil] war der Anfang der ganzen festen Freiheit, die endlich in Christus offenbar wurde" (CO 40,417).

5. Calvin sieht die Türkengefahr (Ms. fr.22, f.24a-b). Das wilde Tier scheint noch weit weg zu sein, aber wenn Gott es frei läßt, kann es schnell kommen. Doch ist dies nur eine Möglichkeit, die Gott hat, um uns zu züchtigen.

Kapitel allerdings alle auf den Antichrist gedeutet. In ihrer Sicht spricht
Hesekiel "nur von dem, was in den letzten Zeiten kommen soll". Calvin
verweist zwar auch auf 2. Thess 2, bestreitet aber dennoch diese eschatolo-
gische Auslegung. Mahumet, "cest apostat", ist das eine und der Papst das
zweite Horn des Teufels. Aber darum geht es bei Hesekiel nicht. Denn Calvin
führt seine Auslegung so weiter: "Kommen wir nun zur Geschichte, und es
wird uns sehr leicht sein, zu beurteilen, was der Prophet hier sagt". Das ist
"le sens naturel du prophete".

Diese rein geschichtliche Deutung setzt Calvin sehr auffällig fort: "Ver-
gleichen wir es mit anderen Propheten und vor allem mit Daniel. Denn Daniel
schrieb wie er eine Geschichte der Tatsachen, die lange Zeit nach seinem Tod
kommen sollten, und zeigt klar alles, was seitdem geschehen ist, so wie es
gemacht wird in Denkschriften und Annalen. Das gibt Gottes Wort große
Majestät, so daß man nicht sagen soll, "es sind [nur] Prophetien", sondern er
spricht wie ein Historiker, der alle Sachen, so wie er sie erzählt, kennt und mit
eigenen Augen gesehen hat.[6] Daniel "erzählt" uns die Geschichte, wie das
jüdische Volk sie erleben sollte, von Alexander dem Großen an bis zu Anti-
ochus Epiphanes.[7] Das sind die Feinde, die nach der Rückkehr aus dem Exil
aufs neue Israel quälen würden. Und genau von diesen zukünftigen Feinden
spricht Hesekiel, aber nicht wie ein Historiker wie Daniel, sondern "in einem
Gleichnis" (une similitude).

Was ist nach Daniels Prophetie, die Calvin zweimal vor derjenigen
des Hesekiel auslegt, dann noch die besondere Bedeutung des Hesekiel-
buches? Calvin liest und denkt sich so sehr in die Zeit des Exils hinein, daß
er einfach neben Jeremia auch Hesekiel auf den Plan treten sieht. (Daß
zeitlich danach erst der Prophet Daniel auftritt, steht außerhalb dieser
Betrachtungsweise.) Nach seiner Meinung geht es Gott darum, das jüdische
Volk in der Bedrängnis des Exils mit Verheißungen zu stärken. Auf der
anderen Seite geht es darum, den zurückgebliebenen Rest des Volkes in Juda
und Jerusalem zu warnen. Die direkten, aktuellen Adressaten stehen für
Calvin immer im Vordergrund.

Die Juden hatten die Verheißung, daß sie ins eigene Land zurückkehren
würden. Um zu verhindern, daß sie ein irdisches Reich erwarten würden, hat
Gott dies verhindert, indem er neues Leid ankündigte. "Mais il falloit qu'ilz
attendissent ung royaulme nouveau. qu'ilz attendissent ung temple spirituel et
une sacrificature celeste".[8]

---

6. Ms. fr.33. f.540a.
7. Etwas später nennt Calvin in dieser Predigt Daniel: "qui nous sera bon expositeur
et fidele de ce passage" (f.540a).
8. f.541b.

2. Erfüllung im Kommen Christi

Daß Hesekiel im Exil Gottes Wort zur Gegenwart und über die nahe Zukunft spricht, gibt Calvin ausreichend Gelegenheit, das Gottesvolk seiner eigenen Zeit zu trösten. Die Bedrängnisse der Kirche sind vorhergesagt. Der schönste Trost wird in Christus kommen, unserem "Redempteur". Außer der Erfüllung in Christus kennt Calvin also keine weiteren Erfüllungen der besonderen Prophetien des Hesekiel. Das scheint ein negativer Befund zu sein. Doch sollten wir die Bedeutung der Erfüllung in Christus weiter befragen. Denn es gibt für Calvin die historische Erfüllung in der Zeit direkt nach dem Sprechen der Propheten. Aber die volle Erfüllung ist in unserem Herrn Jesus Christus gekommen. In diesem Zusammenhang spricht Calvin dann auch von der Kirche. Könnte man es so sagen: In der Erfüllung in Christus entfaltet sich die Prophetie erst richtig? Calvin sagt: "Le royaulme" ist Christi Herrschaft. Es gibt keine erste und zweite Erfüllung. Es gibt einen Anfang und eine Vollkommenheit der Erfüllung.

3. Die Kirche als Volk Gottes

Dadurch, daß Calvin die Prophetie auf das damalige Israel deutet, kann er durch das Stichwort "Kirche" fast alles auf seine Zeit anwenden. Die historische Deutung und Erfüllung des Prophetenwortes auf das Volk Israel hin ist der sichere Boden für die Ermahnungen an die Kirche. "Or nous sommes succedez en la place des Juifs, il fault bien que aujourdhuy nous expermentions le sembleable", sagt Calvin in der Paränese[9]; nicht gegen die Juden seiner Zeit sind die Worte gerichtet, denn der Reformator Genfs nimmt die Mahnungen wie die Verheißungen an die Kirche sehr ernst. Sogar die Gog-Prophetie hat so eine weitere, wohl unbestimmte Bedeutung,[10] ebenso wie erst die Wahrheit der Verheißungen für das derzeitige Israel später ihre volle Kraft erhält. "Or nous avons à noter, que quand le prophète a parlé aux Juifz, il nous a comprinz en leur reng, ce qu'il dict est du regne de Jesus Christus."[11]

Besondere Erwartungen kann man auch haben, wenn man die vier Predigten über Hes 37 liest: die Zukunft des Volkes Israel. Es geht hier, sagt Calvin

---

9. Ms. fr.22, f.532a.

10. Calvin spricht auch vom Antichristen: "Le temple de Dieu est occupé par son ennemy mortel, que le diable en la personne de l'Antechrist domine la" (Ms. fr.22, f.549a). Die Papisten nennt er auch "eine Synagoge des Satans". Die Sprache Calvins ist von Endzeit-Stichworten geprägt. "Nous [avoyons] aujourdhuy comme l'Antechrist domine . . ." (f.566a).

11. MS. fr.22, f.574a.

in der ersten Predigt, um Gottes Macht, die Toten aufzuerwecken. "Car nostre vie qu'est ce sinon ung umbrage de mort?"[12] Aber diese Prophetie spricht nicht von der letzten Auferstehung der Toten (letztlich endlich doch, aber sicherlich nicht in erster Linie). Die Prophetie spricht von der Erlösung aus dem Exil. Das Exil war wie ein Grab, das geöffnet werden mußte. Das wird die erste Erfüllung sein.

Aber: Das Land der Verheißung würde den Juden keine sichtbare Ruhe bringen. Denn in Daniel (und Hes 40ff.) wird mehr Trübsal angekündigt. Darum gilt auch hier wie bei allen Propheten, die "ont estandu leurs promesses jusques à la venue de Jesus Christ, comme aussi c'est une seconde naissance de l'Eglise, que ce retour là, jusques à ce que le Redempteur du monde apparust".[13] Schon früh hat Calvin in diesen Predigten gesagt: "Or c'est la figure et l'umbrage de l'Eglise".[14] Israel ist damals die Kirche. Deshalb reicht auch diese Prophetie so weit, wie die Welt ist. Die verheißene Ruhe ist: der Schatten seiner Flügel in der Mitte der Trübsale. Daher steckt mehr in der Verheißung als die Rückkehr ins Land der Väter. "Mais qu'il y avoit une fin plus haulte et plus excellente c'est asçavoir qu'ilz fussent son Eglise, et qu'il habite au milieu d'icelle pour y estre adoré."[15]

Calvin spricht auch oft über die Teilung des Reiches nach dem Tode Salomos. Die Einheit wurde zerrissen. So hat Christus die Einheit geschaffen aus uns, "qui estions payens avec les Juifz".[16] Es entsteht ein Volk mit einem König. Christus hat mit den Juden angefangen, diese Einheit zu schaffen: es ist "ung royaulme permanente". Die Einheit muß brüderliche Liebe hervorrufen, denn die Vergebung der Sünden ist die Grundlage des neuen Lebens, für Israel und in der universellen Kirche. Zur Prophetie des Magog sagt Calvin einleitend: "Car it fault que nous commancions à ce temps entre le retour de Babilone et le jour de jugement, si nous voulons avoir la verité des promesses. . . ."[17] Es ist, als ob der Wendepunkt im Kommen Christi nicht ausgesagt zu werden braucht. Die Geschichte seit der Rückkehr ist die der Kirche![18] Calvin spricht von der Rückkehr aus dem Exil wie in der Bibel von der Sintflut gesprochen wird: nie mehr. Nach dem Kommen Christi wird die Kirche Gottes nie mehr so verfolgt werden.[19]

---

12. f.506a.
13. f.518b.
14. f.514b.
15. f.522a.
16. f.524a.
17. f.554a.
18. Auch: "Car . . . il est icy parlé de l'estat de l'Eglise depuys le retour de Babilone iusques à ce que tout soit restauré au dernier jour" (Ms. fr.22, f.555a).
19. f.566a.

IV. "Apokalyptik" oder Prophetie

1. Calvins Projekt der Prophetenauslegung

Die alttestamentliche Prophetie hat für Calvin große Bedeutung. Sowohl in seinen Predigten als in den Praelectiones können wir von einem Projekt der Propheten auslegung sprechen. Nachdem er das Neue Testament als erstes Projekt in Kommentaren fast ganz ausgelegt hatte — zwischendurch erklärt er Jesaja — fängt Calvin in den Praelectiones im Jahr 1556 mit Hosea an und kommt so in den Jahren 1563 bis 1564 zu dem letzten Buch in dieser Reihe, Hesekiel. Die anderen Bücher des Alten Testaments werden in diesen Jahren nicht in den Praelectiones, sondern direkt in Kommentaren behandelt (die Harmonie zu Exodus bis Deuteronomium, Psalmen und Josua). In den Predigten der Wochengottesdienste fängt er 1546 mit Jeremia an und predigt über alle Prophetenbücher bis hin zu Hesekiel, der 1552 bis 1554 ausgelegt wird. Beide Projekte enden also mit Hesekiel, beide Male wird das Buch Daniel vorangestellt. Dies scheint mir eine wichtige Feststellung zu sein: Calvin hat sein Projekt der Auslegung der Propheten in den Predigten der Jahre 1546 bis 1554 in den Praelectiones 1556 bis 1564 wiederholt. Das heißt, der letzte Versuch läuft bis zu seinem Tode. Auch beim zweiten Male nimmt er den Propheten Hesekiel als letzten. Warum? Weil er es für ein schwieriges Buch hält. Und weil er es trotzdem verstehen möchte und meint, es auslegen zu müssen.

2. Was sind Visionen?

Für Visionen kann Calvin auch das Wort "figure" benützen. Es sind Bilder der unsichtbaren Realität Gottes. "Visio" sagt aus, wie ein Mensch solche Offenbarung erlebt. Auch das Wort "similitude" wird vielfach benützt: Etwas aus der Schöpfung, das wir kennen, kann als Bild verwendet werden, um die unsichtbare Realität Gottes auszumalen. Calvin fragt sich auch, warum Gott mehrere Bilder gibt, wenn Er doch Eins ist. Und er antwortet: ". . . il falloit que les signes eussent quelque similitude en quelque convenance à la prophetie, ou bien aux promesses qu'il donnoit, ou à choses semblables".[20] Die Prophetie wird von den Bildern vielfältig ausgesagt.

20. f.265a.

3. Vision verglichen mit dem Sakrament

Wichtig ist, daß die Visionen keine selbständige Bedeutung im Offenbarungs-
vorgang haben. Sie unterstützen nur das Wort, das die Stimme des lebendigen
Gottes ist. Aber die Sprache ist auch die lebendige Realität des nur den
Menschen unsichtbaren Wirkens Gottes. Das besondere Ziel der Visionen ist
dann auch, daß Gott uns mahnt, das Wort mit Ehrfurcht zu empfangen. Gott
hilft unserem Glauben.[21] So kommt Calvin dann im Blick auf die Verkündigung des Evangeliums in Genf zu dem Ergebnis: "Car les visions seroient
inutiles, sinon que Dieu parlast."[22] Hier gebraucht er das Beispiel der Sakramente: ". . . que sa parolle soit comme la forme qui qualifie les visions et les
sacraments".[23] Und : "les visions de Dieu ont tousjours cest marque icy que
sa voix est adjousté".[24] Die Visionen sind gegeben, um zu lernen: ". . . ex-
pressement que Dieu n'est point visible . . . , mais qu'il nous suffice d'avoir
sa voix, c'est à dire de le congnoistre tel qu'il se declare par sa bouche et par
sa parolle, et puis s'il y a des figures que ce soit seulement pour nous ravir en
admiration et estonnement".[25]

Am Ende seiner ersten Vorlesung sagt Calvin zur ersten Vision (in
Kapitel 1): "Sie ist die schwierigste von allen."[26] Und am nächstebn Tag:
"Wenn jemand fragen würde, ob die Vision klar sei, muß ich zugeben, daß sie
für mich sehr dunkel ist".[27] Aber das hat seinen Grund darin, sagt er in einer
Predigt, weil sie über die Majestät Gottes und dann die zornige Majestät
handelt. Wir sollten versuchen, dies wenigstens zum Teil zu verstehen. Zweck
der Vision ist, daß Gott seine Majestät an sein Wort geben will, und daß wir
uns Ihn nicht menschlich vorstellen. Dann gibt Calvin ein Beispiel, das den
Sinn der Visionen klarstellen soll: Es ist wie ein Sakrament, das etwas anzeigt,
so wie die Taube in der Taufe Jesu den heiligen Geist verkörperte oder wie
das Feuer im brennenden Busch das Leiden des Volkes Israel und die Rettung
Gottes anzeigte. "Maintenant donc nous voyons comme les visions, les figures
et les sacramentz ont quelque similitude avec les choses que Dieu veult mon-
strer et qu'il fault que tousjours nous regardions la circonstance du faict present,

---

21. "Dieu monstre une grande bonté aus hommes, quand il adjouste ainsi des visions
et des signes à sa parolle". "C'est pour nous aider à croire . . . afin que nous en soyons
instruictz, et ceulx qui viendront après nous jusques en la fin du monde" (MS. fr.22, f.507a-b).
    22. MS. fr.21, f.29a.
    23. f.29b.
    24. f.30a.
    25. f.255b.
    26. Visio est omnium difficillima (CO 40,29).
    27. Iam si quis interroget an visio sit dilucida, fateor [visionem] esse valde obscuram
(CO 40,29).

dont il est question."[28] Aus den historischen Umständen soll und kann man die Bedeutung der "Bilder" feststellen. Sakramente sind Zeichen der Gnade oder des Zorns.

4. Die Symbolsprache der Visionen

Wie geht Calvin mit den Symbolen, Farben und Zahlen um, die in der visionären Sprache auftauchen? Die Zahl vier ist Bild der ganzen Schöpfung: "depuys ung bout du monde et une extremité jusqu'à l'autre".[29] Gott waltet überall in seiner Welt. "Car it y a quatre regions en l'air, comme aussi le monde universel est icy figuré".[30] Die Farben werden von Calvin nicht symbolisch gedeutet. An allen Stellen versucht er, die präzise Bedeutung der hebräischen Worte festzustellen, und beläßt es dabei. Die Farben sind Illustration, z.B. bei der Majestät Gottes. Die Pracht der Schöpfung wird benutzt, um die Verkündigung des Wortes Gottes eindrucksvoll zu machen.

Einige Symbole werden von Calvin genauer untersucht. Die Augen in den Rädern bilden Gottes Vorsehung ab: Er ist gegenwärtig, um sein Ziel im Auge zu behalten. Der Geist ist seine Providenz. Er wirkt nicht nur als "don speciale" in den Gläubigen, sondern hat auch eine "operation generalle" an allen Menschen. Feuer und sogar der Regenbogen sind Zeichen der furchtbaren Majestät Gottes: "comme si nous debvions estre abysmes de pluye et d'orages".[31] So deutet Calvin später auch den Rauch. Er ist nicht mehr Symbol der Gegenwart Gottes, sondern er wird, wenn er den Tempel verläßt, Zeichen des Zorns[32], das die Gnade verdunkelt. Auch das Feuer kann nicht mehr von Sünden reinigen.[33]

5. Die Tempelvision

Auch hier ist es so, daß Calvin die Prophetie erst historisch ("le sens naturel"), dann wie immer voll christologisch deutet. Wenn diese Auslegung überzeugend ist, sucht der Exeget nicht nach weiteren möglichen Horizonten der Erfüllung in der Geschichte. Warum soll er es auch aus seiner Sicht heraus tun? In Christus ist die große Erfüllung gekommen! Der hermeneutische Ansatz führt

28. f.12b.
29. f.18b.
30. f.252b.
31. f.29a; auch f.256b-257a.
32. f.261a; ebenso zu Jes. 6:4.
33. Prael. ad Hes 10:6f. (CO 40,212f.).

Calvin in den Hebräerbrief (und zu Haggai: die Herrlichkeit des neuen Tempels). Er sagt uns, welche Details in Christus erfüllt sind. Was die erste Erfüllung betrifft: die Vision ist zum Trost gegeben. Ohne Christus muß die Verheißung eine Unterstützung erfahrenn. Die Verheißung des Neubaus des Tempels zielt auf die Nähe Gottes, die Anwesenheit seiner Majestät hin. Die Vision will diesen Glauben stärken. In Christus wird die Vision voll erfüllt. Dauernd spricht Calvin von der Einheit des Königs- und Priesterdienstes, so wie sie gemeint waren (Kapitel 44). Es sind die beiden Augen, die zwar unterschieden sind und dennoch einem Blick ergeben.[34] Zweitens, in Christus hat eien solche Vision nicht nur Bedeutung "en ung seul lieu ou en ung petit anglet de Judée, mais pour tout le monde."[35]

Ist dieser Befund enttäuschend? Wenn ja, dann könnte unsere Erwartung falsch gewesen sein. Die Auswertung im Blick auf die Bedeutung des Herrn Jesus Christus ist nicht dogmatische Exegese, sondern sie ist heilsgeschichtliche Auswertung. Im Kommen Christi, in seinem Dienst der Herrschaft und Versöhnung entfaltet sich das ganze Zeitalter des neuen Bundes.

V. Diskussion

Die Diskussion hat folgendes ergeben: 1. Die Frage nach der Bedeutung der Prophetie wurde als wichtig angesehen. Die Predigten Calvins sind eine besonders reiche Quelle. 2. Gefragt wurde: Ist Prophetie die Historie der Zukunft oder der Geschichte? Das Urtei, Calvin spiritualisiere — gemeint ist die Anwendung der prophetischen Aussage auf die geistliche Situation der Kirche — verkennt die konkrete Anwendung des Wortes Gottes. Wir können bei ihm eine bestimmte Entwicklung der Heilsgeschichte feststellen. Es gibt hier ein Wachsen von Tag zu Tag bis zur Reife des Königreiches Christi. 3. Für die Quellen der Exegese Calvins wurde auf die Pariser Katenenausgabe hingewiesen.

34. MS. fr.22, F.576a.
35. f.574b.

Reactions to Bouwsma's Portrait
of "John Calvin"

I. John Hesselink

The seminar on Bouwsma's book *John Calvin* was unique in that for the first time in the history of the International Congresses on Calvin Research a seminar was devoted to a single book rather than a theme. Apparently no one questioned the decision of the Präsidium in this regard, however, and this proved to be one of the most popular of the seminar offerings.

The reasons are not hard to find. This book evoked a response found rarely, if ever, in the secular press as well as the scholarly world, particularly in the United States. Before the theological world could get around to responding to it, a reviewer in the *New York Times* was already hailing it as a creative new study "with a 20th-century psychological scheme, giving a genuinely new insight into the man and the 16th century as a whole" (John Todd). Other reviews appeared in *The Wall Street Journal, The Christian Science Monitor,* the London *Times Literary Supplement,* and the *Neue Zürcher Zeitung,* publications that normally wouldn't be interested in a book about Calvin.

It is not altogether clear why this study was such a sensation. Bouwsma is a highly respected Renaissance specialist from a distinguished university, the University of California in Berkeley, but that alone hardly accounts for the popular and scholarly response to this volume. Apparently it was the distinctive approach and the intriguing conclusions, combined with many years of meticulous research, that made this book such a cause célèbre. It was also unusual in its attempt to portray Calvin as a representative of the sixteenth-century Renaissance, on the one hand, and as "Mr. Everyman," on the other.

Some of the popular reviews gave the impression that here for the first time we had a portrait of the true historical Calvin as over against the villain of the Calvin haters and the hero of the Calvinists. To be sure, there are insights here not found elsewhere, and there is the fascinating but questionable portrayal of "two Calvins, coexisting uncomfortably within the same historical personage," that is, the rationalistic, moralistic orthodox theologian and the creative, free rhetorician and humanist.

I. Earlier Attempts to Get "Inside" of Calvin's Personality

Overlooked in some of the reviews were earlier attempts at getting "inside" of Calvin's personality, most recently the study by Suzanne Selinger, *Calvin against Himself* (1984), and researches that sought to understand Calvin in the light of his late-medieval heritage, for example, Karl Reuter's *Das Grundverständnis der Theologie Calvins* (1963) and Alexandre Ganoczy's *Le jeune Calvin* (1966; Eng. trans. 1987). Calvin the man — particularly the husband and father, the friend, and the pastor — was briefly but sensitively depicted by Richard Stauffer in his lectures published as *L'humanité de Calvin* (1964; Eng. trans. 1971). Some reviewers were apparently unaware of such studies and accordingly tended to overestimate the originality of certain aspects of Bouwsma's study.

Nevertheless, it must be conceded that this book is a brilliant tour de force, quite unmatched in Calvin literature. This was recognized by almost all of the more scholarly reviewers (cf. appendix), even by those who were rather critical of Bouwsma's portrayal of Calvin.

II. Questions and Statements

The reviews, and the participants in the seminar, tended to divide along the following lines: Does Calvin provide us with enough data so that we can get at the inner Calvin? (Cf. Fritz Büsser's *Calvin's Urteil über sich selbst* [1950].) Moreover, is it legitimate to try to psychologize Calvin? To what extent is Calvin a child of his age, particularly the Renaissance, and to what extent does he emancipate himself from it? Is Bouwsma's use of the labyrinth and abyss metaphors appropriate? Is anxiety a fundamental clue to Calvin's faith and personality? Is sufficient attention given in this portrait to Calvin's piety / spirituality and the place of Scripture in his thinking? In short, does this portrait do justice to Calvin the theologian?

Reviewers and participants in the seminar were divided on these questions. Here Bouwsma had both his defenders and detractors. In regard to the last question cited above, it is significant that Bouwsma himself in retrospect acknowledges:

I left a central thesis of the book largely implicit — not by design — out of an excess of subtlety, so to speak — but because I had not been quite able to manage to identify it. This thesis is, that to understand Calvin and his thought in human and historical terms, one must approach him through his spirituality . . . rather than through his theology." (A response to three reviews that appeared in the *Pacific Theological Review* 22 / 1 [Fall 1988], two years after he submitted his manuscript to the publisher.)

Professor Bouwsma had planned to join us for this seminar, but unfortunately health problems prevented him from attending the Congress.

Since there was no secretary for the seminar, it is impossible to give an accurate summary of the nature of the discussion, which was very lively. While there was universal appreciation for the book, there was by no means unanimity concerning certain theses of Bouwsma's.

III. Earlier Reviews

Some of that appreciation and divergence was expressed earlier in reviews. Hence I will conclude with some representative comments.

"Bouwsma's provocative portrait has the very great virtue of providing an interpretive framework drawn out of Calvin's own writing. It takes seriously complexities, tensions, and even frankly contradictory aspects of Calvin's thought and work." (Jane Dempsey-Douglass. Later she complains that this is "a static portrait.")

"In assessing Bouwsma's complex argument, one must first of all grant that no Calvin scholar before him has uncovered so convincingly the personal fear and trembling in which Calvin wrote and lived. On the other hand, no effort is made to delineate the general anxiety of the times, both of the later Middle Ages and of the sixteenth century, so that we cannot know to what extent Calvin speaks from his own experience or to the condition of his times" (Heiko A. Oberman).

"Bouwsmas Porträt von Calvin ist ohne Zweifel ein Buch, das zu einem neuen Bild des Genfer Reformators beiträgt. Ein Buch, das auch zur Stellungnahme herausfordert. . . . Ich selber meine, dass Bouwsmas 'John Calvin' neben zahlreichen bisher kaum beachteten Informationen äusserst wertvolle Anregungen und Ergänzungen bringt" (Fritz Büsser).

"As an intellectual biography, this volume provides a wonderfully refreshing portrait of Calvin, as good as this generation is likely to see; as an interdisciplinary effort, it succeeds in camouflaging much of the psychology and theology which intersect in its pages" (William Monter).

"This is a study that Calvin scholars have been waiting for. . . . It provides a 'disclosure model' of Calvin's personality and his work that will fertilize future studies" (W. Fred Graham).

"Bouwsma's book, taken as a whole, seems to this reviewer to be historical drama, beautifully constructed and highly informative, but lacking in certain central purposes and convictions of the main character" (Edward A. Dowey).

"Bouwsma's portrait is complex and honest. . . . [However,] Bouwsma depicts Calvin as too solitary, anxious, and insecure, less in charge of himself and his environment than he actually was. Absent is that continuity of friends with whom he worked and to whom he was tied with such strong emotion as a fast friend and faithful correspondent. . . . Missing also is Calvin as a man of prayer, his piety or spirituality, and his life as a pastor engaged with others, his advocacy of the poor, and his organization of the church in Geneva" (Jeannine Olson).

> Zusammenfassend ergibt sich ein Portrait, dessen humanistischer Rahmen sehr eingehend, ja, eindrucksvoll skizziert wird. Auch die Gestalt, die das Bild darstellen soll, ist in den Umrissen erkennbar. Mehr jedoch nicht: Das Gesicht der Person fehlt. Stellt man sich vor, dass ein Leser seine Calvinkenntnisse nur diesem Buch entnimmt, der Leser würde nicht vermuten, dass Buch 2 und 3 der Institutio von Calvin stammen. Er würde die biblischen Kommentare Calvins, im Zusammenhang gelesen, nicht mit ihm in Verbindung setzen. Die Fülle der Calvinzitate in B.s Buch — gewiss eine Fundgrube für den Forscher! — sind oft aus dem Zusammenhang gerissen. Der Grundsatz Calvins, die Heilige Schrift im Kontext zu verstehen (S. 118), sollte auch für Calvins Werk beherzigt werden. Jedenfalls rangiert bei Calvin im Gegensatz zu Erasmus die Kirche vor der Gesellschaft, die Theologie vor der Bildung, der Glaube vor den Taten, Gottes Offenbarung in Christus vor den Geheimnissen Gottes usw. (Wilhelm Neuser)

After a series of questions and criticisms, Philip Holtrop writes in his review-article, "None of this eliminates my high esteem for this book. Those who see Calvin as an icon, or his theology as trans-historical, are going to be irritated. . . . They may fail to appreciate that Bouwsma's book is balanced and even sympathetic to his subject, compared to what he could have said — even if the novice does not appreciate its integrity and profundity. Indeed, this work is the most significant, creative, and helpful book I have read in the past thirty years of Calvin studies."

"If Bouwsma has discovered two Calvins, the reader also finds many Bouwsmas: The psychohistorian who believes he can get inside Calvin's mind; the iconoclast who gleefully destroys all theological images erected of Calvin; the scholar of humanism who opens new vistas for Calvin studies; the Lucien

Febvre disciple writing to characterize an age as much as an individual; and, as always, the poet whose masterful pen always delights" (Brian Armstrong).

In short, "Bouwsma makes Calvin live again as one who truly changed the course of history of the West" (Jorge Lara-Braud).

These evaluations are often in conflict with each other. Even after the dust settles, it is unlikely that there will be any consensus concerning this provocative, fascinating, and stimulating study. All can probably agree with Robert Kingdon's conclusion: "No book of this sweep can fully satisfy every specialist at every point. It remains fresh and authoritive enough, however, to deserve the attention of every student of sixteenth-century thought."

Appendix: Reviews of Wm. Bouwsma's *John Calvin*

Armstrong, Brian G., *Church History* 58.1 (March 1989).

Barker, William S., *Eternity* (April 1988).

Büsser, Fritz, *Neue Zürcher Zeitung* (29 Marz 1989), Nr. 72.

D'Evelyn, Thomas, *The Christian Science Monitor* (January 6, 1988).

Douglass, Jane Dempsey, *Theology Today* 45.3 (October 1988).

Dowey, Edward A., *Journal of American Academy of Religion* 57.4 (Winter 1989).

Gamble, Richard C., *The Banner* (October 17, 1988).

Graham, W. Fred, *Sixteenth Century Journal* 19.3 (1988).

Gross, John, *The New York Times* (December 8, 1987).

Hesselink, I. John, *Christian Century* (March 16, 1988).

Holtrop, Philip C., review-article in *The Reformed Journal* (April 1989). The response by Bouwsma in the July 1989 issue of *The Reformed Journal* is followed by a reply by Philip Holtrop.

Kaufman, Peter I., *Journal of Religion* 69.1 (January 1989).

Kingdon, Robert M., *The Catholic Historical Review* 74.4 (October 1988).

La Grand, John, *Calvin College Chimes* (September 29, 1989).

Mallon, Thomas, *The Wall Street Journal* (February 22, 1988).

Marius, Richard, *Commonweal* (May 16, 1988).

Neuser, Wilhelm, *Historische Zeitschrift,* Band 250 (1990).

Oberman, Heiko A., *Times Literary Supplement,* Religion (August 19-25, 1988).

Olson, Jeannine, *Theological Studies* 50.1 (March 1989).

Three reviews by Benjamin Reist, Jorge Lara-Brand, and Guy Fitch Lytle, and a reply by Bouwsma, *Pacific Theological Review* 22.1 (Fall 1988).

Todd, John M., *The New York Times Book Review* (January 10, 1988).

Van Hoeven, James W., *Perspectives* (editorial) (October, 1989).

Calvin and Farel

Francis M. Higman

I. Introduction

In the "Répertoire de la correspondance de Guillaume Farel" published in the *Actes du Colloque Guillaume Farel, Neuchâtel, 1980* there appears a supplement consisting of one item: "269 bis. 1540, janvier 16, Strasbourg. — Jean Calvin à Guillaume Farel. *Quid cogitare de te debeam.* — O[rigmal]a[utographe]. Genève, MHR ms Ac1." There is no mention of a printed edition. How could this be?

A brief mention of the document appears in the *Bulletin de la Société de l'Histoire du Protestantisme français (BSHPF)*, 81 (1932), 159:

> (Collection Fatio, 2e vente, 1932) — Lettre en latin à Farel *excell. pastori et fratri mihi chariss.*, de Strasbourg 15 décembre 1539 (Argentor., 16 calend. Januar. 1540): au sujet de grands et mystérieux projets de l'empereur, des persécutions à Paris, de Capiton, de Charles (Calvin), etc. Très important document, à placer entre deux autres lettres à Farel du 12 des cal. de décembre et du 19 décembre. (*Opera* 10, col. 429 et 345)

In fact, that letter of 19 Dec. 1539 is redated by Herminjard to 29 Dec. 1538. The next known letter from Calvin is dated 31 December 1539 (Herminjard 6.154-57).

So the letter was part of the "Collection Fatio," sold in Paris in 1932. How did it reach the Musée Historique de la Réformation in Geneva? The Secretary of the Society of the M.H.R., in his Annual Report to the Society on 15 May 1933, described *inter alia* "les plus importantes de nos acquisitions," including:

> un certain nombre de manuscrits achetés en l'hôtel Drouot à Paris, en janvier

214

et juin 1932, aux ventes Henry Fatio par . . . M. Paul Chaponnière et votre serviteur (i.e. Fernand Aubert). De plus, nous avons pu racheter, jeudi dernier 11 mai, un document de tout premier ordre à celui qui en avait fait primitivement l'acquisition à ces mêmes enchères . . .

Il s'agit d'abord d'une lettre autographe signée de Calvin à Farel, datée de Strasbourg du 16 des calendes de janvier 1540 . . .

Nous avons eu le privilège de confier à la Bibliothèque publique et universitaire les documents que nous avions achetés aux ventes Henry Fatio. Ces manuscrits ont donc été exposés pendant l'été dans la Salle Ami Lullin. . . .

The point about the letter being put on exhibition may explain how it has escaped attention since its discovery. A letter in a showcase is inaccessible. It seems that no one took the matter up immediately. Then it was duly filed in the Musée; but in 1968 it was again chosen for exhibit in the Library permanent exhibition. It is still there. The next scholar to look closely at the manuscript holdings of the Musée seems to have been Henri Meylan, in the preparation of an article published in 1977. And of course this document was not in its place, but under glass.

Meylan's article was about forgeries; and before jumping to conclusions about "unknown letters by Calvin" one needs to take certain precautions. (See T. Dufour, *Le Secret des textes* [Geneva, 1925]; H. Meylan, "Comment on tire le faux du vrai, ou la destinée d'une lettre de Calvin à Farel [14 juillet 1545]," *BSHPF,* 123 [1977], 400-410.) There were two known forgers of Calvin letters in the nineteenth century; one invented letters in French but was not very clever, and his French is not of the period; the other stole at least one long letter in Latin from Paris, and concocted several short letters from individual paragraphs; these were transcribed onto genuinely old paper. These are much more convincing; but there are tiny details which give them away, such as the fact that the paper was folded *before* it was written on, not after. By the tests applied by Dufour and by Meylan, our letter seems perfectly genuine.

II. An Exercise in Text Editing

There are three stages in the process of text editing: deciphering the text, understanding the text, and annotation.

1. Deciphering the Text

We start with the original manuscript, in Latin, in Calvin's ungainly but actually very regular writing, with many abbreviations. The regular writing is of course in sixteenth-century characters, with which one needs rapidly to become familiar. The standard abbreviations used by writers of Latin at the time can only be understood today with the aid of reference works such as A. Cappelli's *Dizionario di Abbreviature latine ed italiane* (I used the 6th edition, 1967; and I acknowledge gratefully the help I received from Mmes Béatrice Nicollier and Irena Backus and from Professor Augustijn).

We end up with a transcription as follows:

Guillelmo Farello Neocomensis ecclesiae pastori fidelissimo, fratri mihi charissimo

Quid cogitare de te debeam nescio. Si vales, ac omnia istic bene habent, est cur tibi merito succenseam, qui me antea suspensum expectatione ob rumorem adversae tuae valetudinis, magis etiamnum perplexum anxiumque reddis. Scripseram superiori mense valde prolixas literas per puerum quendam Germanum. Postquam redditas tibi fuisse ex temporis supputatione colligebam: ecce ab aliis multis literae, quas Basileam attulerat Barbarinus. Abs te verbum nullum. Secutae sunt aliquanto post Christophori literae, quas domo tua venisse conjicio. Abs te tuisque nihil. Si tibi ocium non erat, saltem alicui mandasses, ut verbo uno indicaret ut valeres. Sic me molestissima ista cura.

Ego vero, quo torporem istum tibi excuterem, atque aliquid vel ab invito ex[to]rquerem, in literis quas communiter ad fratres scribo, dum excusare volo nostrorum in Carolum facilitatem, quam ipsi dissolutam indulgentiam vocant, bonam culpae partem tibi imputo. Et certe erroris causam praeposteris tuis commendationibus praebuisti. Scio autem id grave tibi nequaquam fore, si expendas qua de re et apud quos te accusem. Eas literas tibi mitto quo ex tua sententia vel proferantur vel supprimantur. Carolus ipse nuper mihi scripsit se apud D. Jametium non spe aliqua profectu[m], sed hyeme detineri. Nullam enim evangelii illic propagandi viam se videre: tametsi Dominus loci optime esset animatus. Respondi, modo ipse non deesset Christo, non defuturum illi Christum.

Nostri adhuc sunt in consultatione. Ac magnum periculum est ne non redeant, nisi conflato bello. Caesar magnum aliquid molitur, quod eos non latet. Instituit aggredi Gueldrium principio: qui a Saxone non deseretur. Sic bellum ad nos perveniet. Quum igitur compertum est nostris, se oblique peti, rationem ipsi quoque obliquam ineunt. Landgravius in Brunsvicensem movebit. Deinde latius spargentur arma. Omnino, nisi Dominus e caelo occurrerit, haec hyems ingentes tumultus nobis pariet. Sed quum omnia suspitionibus variis sunt implicata: postquam aliquid certum habuerim, tibi perscribam.

Non satis fuerat vanum comperiri, quod de parisiensi persecutione ex tuis literis asserueram: nisi id ipsum contingeret etiam de Michelio. Rediit enim scholasticus, qui attulit adhuc esse in vinculis. Quanquam ei certa mors imminet, nisi Domini misericordia liberetur. Est enim abdicatus ordine sacerdotali. Ac mirum est tamdiu detineri praeter morem: nisi quod iudex quoquomodo servatum cupit.

Basiliensis ecclesiae calamitas valde nos affligit. Nec possum Grynaeum culpa liberare, qui nimis praefracta constantia rem [eam] deduxit. Nunc de abitu deliberat. Hoc scilicet erit bene ecclesiae consulere, ipsamque relinquere Carolstadio vastandam et profligandam! Nec alia causa est, quam ne libertatem suo praeiudicio imminuat si fiat Doctor. Quasi pars sit Christianae libertatis, scholastica collegia nullis legibus alligari! Deus bone, non improbamus quod in mechanicis opificiis nulli nisi iurato artifici licet tabernam vel officinam aperire: sed putamus actum esse de regno Christi, si oporteat [*verso*] scholasticum professorem publicum doctrinae suae testimonium recipere. Queso te, mi frater, ut ab eo errore abducere eum literis studeas. Nam vir ille summa alioqui et eruditione et perspicacia praeditus, hac in re valde consilio indiget.

Vale, amiciss. frater. Dominus te diu gloriae suae ac suorum edificationi salvum et incolumem conservet. Fratres te plurimum salutant. Praesertim Capito, Sturmius, et Galli nostri. Enardus anxie ambiendo impetravit, ut in collegio locum haberet neque moleste fert puerilem disciplinam, cui subjectus est. Henrichus pridie a nobis migravit, non alia causa, quam quod ingenium illius ab omni subjectione abhorret. Gaspar et Jacobus strenue student. Brito etiam, qui Tiguro huc venit, homo valde probus et pius. Faxit Dominus ut hic ecclesiae suae illos rite praeparemus. Vale iterum, frater suaviss.

Argentor. 16 Calend. Januar. Calvinus tuus.

In Farel's hand: exceptae 18 Januarii 1540.

2. *Understanding the Text*

Stage 2: what does it mean? I again acknowledge the help received from Irena Backus, and also from the members of the Grand Rapids seminar, in the translation of the text. Incidentally, as regards the date: the manuscript reads either 16 or 17 Calends Januar. (one is overwritten, it is not clear which). In either case, the dates given in previous references, 16 January 1540 and 15 December 1539, are both wrong. It is either 17 or 16 December 1539; I have (rather arbitrarily) plumped for 17 December. So we translate:

To Guillaume Farel, truly faithful pastor of the Neuchâtel church, and my very dear brother

I do not know what I should think of you. If you are well, and everything is all right with you, that is reason for me to be deservedly angry with you, since you earlier left me in suspense over the report of your ill health, and now make me even more perplexed and anxious. Last month I wrote you a very long letter, brought by a certain German youth. I then reckoned, by the time that had elapsed, that it had reached you; and now there are letters from many others, brought to Basle by Barbarinus. Not a word from you. A little later, there followed a letter from Christophe, which I conjecture came from your home. From you and yours, nothing. If you didn't have leisure, you could have told someone else to indicate by a simple word how you are. That's how grievous my worry is.

As for me, so as to shake you out of your torpor and to make you react, although you do not want to, I lay a good part of the blame onto you in a letter which I am writing to the brethren jointly, when I want to excuse the generosity of our friends towards Caroli (which they themselves call dissolute indulgence). And certainly by your absurd recommendations you allowed the mistake to arise. However, I know it will in no way be a serious matter for you if you weigh up the subject on which, and the people to whom, I may reproach you. I am sending the letter to you so that you can decide whether it should be made public or suppressed. Caroli himself recently wrote me that he had gone to M. de Jametz, not because of any hope, but because he was detained by the winter weather. He said he sees no way of promulgating the gospel there, even though the local lord is excellently disposed. I replied that, if only he did not abandon Christ, Christ would not abandon him.

Our people are still in their meeting. And there is a great danger that they will not return without an outbreak of war. The emperor is setting something big in motion, which is not concealed from them. He is resolved first to attack the Gueldrian, but the latter will not be abandoned by the Elector of Saxony. And thus the war will reach us. So when it is clear to our people that they are being attacked indirectly, they will also respond in like fashion. The Landgrave will move against [the Duke of] Brunswick. Then armed uprising will become general. In any case, unless the Lord in Heaven intervenes, this winter has huge disturbances in store for us. But since everything is tangled in all sorts of uncertainties, when I have something firm I'll write fully to you.

What I was able to gather from your letter about the persecution in Paris might not have been worth finding out, had it not also been a question of Michelius. For the student has returned, and reports that he is still in prison. Though he is threatened with certain death unless he is freed by the mercy of the Lord. For he resigned his holy orders. And it is astonishing that he has already been detained so much longer than usual, unless the judge is hoping somehow for him to be saved.

The calamity in the Basle church afflicts us sorely. And I cannot free Grynaeus from blame, for having conducted the matter with excessively harsh inflexibility. Now he is considering leaving. That really will be good for the church, to leave it to Carlstadt to ravage and overthrow! And that, for no other cause than that it reduces his freedom if he is made a Doctor. As if it were a part of Christian liberty that the academic fraternity should not be bound by any laws! Good God, we don't object that in manual occupations no one other than someone who is legally qualified has the right to open a tavern or a workshop; but we think we have done something for Christ's kingdom if [*verso*] an academic teacher has to receive public attestation of his orthodoxy! I beg you, my brother, to guide him by your letters away from that error. For the man is in other things highly endowed with learning and perspicacity, but in this matter he is seriously lacking good advice.

Farewell, dearest brother. May the Lord long preserve you safe and sound for His glory and the edification of His people. The brothers send warmest greetings, in particular Capito, Sturm and our Frenchmen. Enardus is anxiously begging to have a place in the college lest he find it difficult to put up with the academic rules to which he is subject. Henrichus left us yesterday for no other reason than that his mind revolts against any subordination. Gaspard and Jacobus are studying hard. Brito as well, who has come here from Zurich, a very honest and pious man. May the Lord grant that we can prepare them properly here for His church. Farewell again, dearest brother.

Strasbourg, 16 Calends of January [1540] Your Calvin

In Farel's hand: received 18 January 1540.

3. Annotations

The norm in a Calvin letter is found here: a series of quite brief allusions to "current affairs" and preoccupations. These fleeting references can be elucidated by reference to "contextual letters" (one must pay tribute to the immense value of Herminjard, *Correspondance des réformateurs*); other accounts of value include '*Bèze*', *Histoire ecclésiastique,* and Sleidan (I have used the 1557 French version of his *Histoire de l'estat de la religion, et republique, sous l'Empereur Charles V* [Geneva], J. Crespin). Standard reference works like encyclopedias and dictionaries of biography are obviously important. What we get from a letter like this is a slice of micro-history, a snapshot of a moment in time.

Notes

I do not know what I should think of you: Calvin's irritability with his "dearest brother" appears in several letters of this period, e.g., his letter of 8 October 1539 (Herm. 6.52-58), where he says: "Since I know you are accustomed to my harshness, I shall not apologize for treating you rudely." Cf. Doumergue, *Calvin* 2.399-405 on Calvin's anger.

If you are well: Farel had been quite seriously ill toward the end of 1539 (*Guillaume Farel* [1930], 436).

Last month I wrote you a very long letter: 20 November 1539 (Herm. 6.122-37).

a certain German youth: unidentified.

by the time that had elapsed: the length of time letters took in transit varied considerably, depending on the availability of a messenger. But, for example, Farel wrote to Calvin from Neuchâtel on 21 October 1539; it went via Basle, where Grynaeus added a letter dated 25 October; and Calvin replied to Farel from Strasbourg on 27 October. On the other hand, the present letter took a full month to reach its destination.

letters from many others: now lost.

Barbarinus: Thomas Barbarinus, pastor of Boudri and Dean of the Neuchâtel Company of Pastors. In this capacity he had presided over the meeting at La Neuveville (see next paragraph) in July 1539. See *La France protestante,* 2nd ed., vol. 1, cols. 772-74.

a letter from Christophe: now lost. Christophe Fabri (or Libertet) was pastor of Thonon, 1536-46, and one of Farel's earliest collaborators (from 1531 on). See *La France prot.,* 2nd ed., 6.358-60.

a letter that I am writing: now lost.

I lay a good part of the blame . . . the generosity of our friends towards Caroli: Pierre Caroli, Doctor of Theology of the Paris Faculty, had been a member (with Farel) of the Meaux group of reformers in the 1520s, and at Alençon under the protection of Marguerite de Navarre in 1530. He was the first named on the list of suspects published after the Affaire des placards in 1534, and fled to Geneva. His contribution to the Dispute de Rive (Geneva) placed him rather on the Catholic than on the Protestant side in the debate, and he was viewed with considerable suspicion. However, at the Dispute de Lausanne (1536) he was impeccably Reformed. He was appointed principal pastor of Lausanne (in preference to Viret), married, and had a child. But in 1537 he accused Farel and Calvin of heresy, then went to Lyons, abjured, and was pardoned in writing by the Pope. Treated with equal suspicion by the Catholics, he failed to obtain an appointment, and in 1539 appeared again in Switzerland. At a meeting at La Neuveville (July 1539) he withdrew his accusations against the Reformers, apologized for his previous conduct, and was accepted back to the reform movement. Doumergue (*Jean Calvin* 2.397 sqq.) writes of the "débonnaireté étonnante" of the Neuchâtel pastors, and in particular of Farel. This is the "dissolute indulgence" of which Calvin writes, and for which he lays the blame on Farel. In October 1539 Caroli went to Strasbourg and (in a meeting to which Calvin was not invited, since he might have spoken too sharply) was reconciled with the Strasbourg pastors (Bucer, Sturm, Zell). Cf. Calvin to Farel, 8 October 1539 (Herm. 6.52-58). On Caroli see *La France prot.,* 2nd ed., 3.770-75; J. K. Farge, *Biographical Register of Paris Doctors of Theology, 1500-1536,* 65-71.

I am sending you the letter: I understand this to refer to the "letter . . . to the brethren jointly" mentioned above. Perhaps Farel decided on suppression.

Caroli himself recently wrote me: lost.

M. de Jametz: Jean de la Marck, duc de Bouillon, a very influential protector of the Reformation movement. Caroli, frustrated at not being given a post either in Neuchâtel or in Strasbourg, became chaplain to the duke; but he did not stay long before moving to Metz (from where, two years later, he again accused the Reformers of heresy: see Farel's published replies).

Our people are still in their meeting: the Diet of Arnstedt (Thuringia) assembled the German Protestant princes to discuss defensive steps in case the emperor did not put into effect the measures of toleration established at Frankfurt in February 1539. The meeting began on 19 November 1539, and ended on 10 December. (See Sleidan.)

an outbreak of war: the threat of war was rarely distant in this period. The meeting at Aigues Mortes in 1538 between François Ier and Charles V led to a fragile peace between the two monarchs. In November 1539 Charles began a journey across France from South to North, arriving in Paris on 1 January 1540. His aim *(setting something big in motion)* was to quell an uprising in Ghent against the new ruler, William Duke of Cleves *(the Gueldrian),* a leading Protestant. His father, John of Cleves, had died in early 1539 (Sleidan, fol. 190 v.); two of his sisters were married, one to the Elector of Saxony (in 1527), the other (in January 1540) to Henry VIII. Inevitably the action by Charles V was seen as a possible overture to a religious war.

the Elector of Saxony: The Elector of Saxony (since 1532) was John Frederick (1503-54), strong supporter of Luther from 1520 on. Calvin foresaw correctly: in 1542 John Frederick did indeed come to the aid of William of Cleves when the latter was attacked. See the entry in *Neue Deutsche Biographie.*

The Landgrave: Philip of Hesse (1504-67), the most influential of all the Lutheran princes. His notorious bigamous marriage was as yet in the future (4 March 1540). The article in *Allgemeine Deutsche Biographie* forms a succinct commentary on this entire section of our letter: ". . . Heinrich VIII . . . vermählte sich eben damals mit Anna von Cleve, der Schwester des vom Kaiser bedrohten Herzogs Wilhelm von Jülich-Cleve und Geldern. So fehlte es nicht an Kräften, die dem Kaiser feindlich waren; und es wäre nur darauf angekommen, diese alle unter sich zu verbinden, zu einem grossen Schlage zu vereinigen. In diesem Gedanken aber erschient nun vor allem wiederum Landgraf Philipp thätig. Et steht in der Mitte aller dieser Wünsche und Versuche; viele gingen von ihm aus; andere gelangen an ihn, damit er ihnen Verbreitung und Ausführung verschaffe; mit allen Parteien stand er in Verbindung, mit den Schmalkaldenern und den katholischen Fürsten und Bischöfen, ebenso wie mit den auswärtigen Mächten, den Königen von Frankreich, England und Dänemark. Aber die Zerklüftung und die auseinandergehenden Interessen der einzelnen Mächte erwiesen sich als zu stark; nach den eifrigsten Verhandlungen sah sich Phillip im Frühling 1540 eben soweit wie im Herbst 1539, oder vielmehr, es hatte sich inzwischen gezeigt, dass eine Verbindung aller dieser heterogenen Elemente wider den Kaiser unmöglich sei. Furcht und Misstrauen, Kleinmuth, Selbstsucht herrschten im protestantischen wie im katholischen Lager."

[the Duke of] Brunswick: Henry of Brunswick (1489-1568), the real villain of the piece in Sleidan's narrative: "[il] fretilloit d'envie de troubler la tranquillité publique, et ne cerchoit qu'ouverture et entrée pour faire la guerre aux Protestans" (412). He was one of the most implacable opponents of the Reformation. It was against him that Luther wrote *Wider Hans Worst* (1541). See *Neue Deutsche Biographie.*

persecution in Paris: to what letter does Calvin refer, since he complains of not having received any? Farel's letter of 20 October 1539 makes no reference to persecution in

Paris. That the question of persecution was concerning Calvin is shown by his "briefing note" to Johannes Sturm of 1 November 1539 for presentation at the Arnstedt meeting, which is in essence a list of supplications *pro afflictis in Gallia* (Herm. 6.119-22).

Michelius: there are various references to "Michaelius" in letters of this period (Herm. 4.230; 5.235-36; 6.154, 207, 222); Herminjard (6.154, n. 3) identified him with Gilles Michaux, but it seems more likely that the person in question was Jean Michel, a Benedictine monk from Bourges, whose death is described (in editions from 1582 on, but with an incorrect date, c. 1547) in Crespin's *Livre des martyrs*. N. Weiss (*BSHPF* 39 [1890], 629-35) published the death sentence pronounced against Michel on 17 December 1539, the date of our letter. Michel had been condemned in Bourges on 14 October 1539.

the student: unknown.

The calamity in the Basle church: . . .

Grynaeus: Simon Grynaeus (1493-1541), pastor and professor in Basle. "Doch weigerte er sich beharrlich den theologischen Doktorgrad sich zu erwerben und geriet dadurch in Gemeinschaft mit dem ihm gleichgesinnten Mykonius in einem lang andauernden Kampf mit der Universität" *(Realenzyklopädie für protestantische Theologie und Kirche).*

Carlstadt: Andreas Bodenstein von Karlstadt, c. 1480-1541, former colleague, then thorn in the flesh, of Luther. During the later 1520s he associated with Müntzer and other radicals, before being accepted as a colleague by Zwingli. He moved to a post as preacher and professor in Basle in 1534. Calvin disliked him, and, during the preparation of the Hagenau colloquium in June 1540, suggested specifically that Basle should not include him in their delegation. Herminjard (6.235) comments: Carlstadt s'était sensiblement modéré pendant son séjour à Bâle; mais à la diète d'Hagenau on n'aurait vu en lui que l'ancien représentant du radicalisme religieux." Both Grynaeus and Carlstadt died of the plague in 1541.

Capito, Sturm: Wolfgang Capito and Johannes Sturm, frequently mentioned in greetings in these letters, were two of Calvin's closest colleagues in Strasbourg.

Enardus: Eynard Pichon, one of Calvin's lodgers in Strasbourg. Little is known of him (see Herm. 6.29, nn. 3 and 5).

the academic rules: also referred to in Calvin's next letter to Farel, 31.12.39 (Herm. 6.154-57): they were recent, having been introduced on 26 November 1539. Although they seem quite reasonable (proper student dress, no wearing of swords, registration with the Rectorate . . .), they were much resisted by the French contingent of students, including Calvin's lodgers.

Henrichus, . . . Gaspard, Jacobus, Brito: "Henri" is also mentioned in other letters (Herm. 5.167, 183, 453; 6.225), and seems to have come from Neuchâtel; but his surname is not known. Gaspard Carmel was on the list of suspects after the Affaire des placards; in Geneva he held a teaching appointment at the Collège de Rive before going to Strasbourg in 1538 in the company of Eynard. In April 1540 he became director of the Collège de Montbéliard, and went to Paris as a pastor in 1557. He married Farel's niece. Jacques Sorel became a pastor at Valangin in April 1540. "Brito" is identified by Doumergue with Jean Curie, a Breton, who left the Calvin household in February 1540. On the subject of Calvin's lodgers see Doumergue 2.458-62.

prepare them properly for His church: the concept of the Strasbourg Academy (as later that of Geneva) was firmly based on the training of a future generation of pastors. Calvin himself was firmly of this view: "ce que le Réformateur voit en [ses pensionaires], ce sont ses successeurs" (Doumergue 2.459).

III. Conclusion

The letter adds extra touches to the Caroli affair, to the rumors of war and threats of the same, and to Calvin's attitude to Caroli, Grynaeus, and Carlstadt (I rather think he is more outspoken here than usual).

More significant, it seems to me, is what we learn about Calvin's personality. At several points in the letter an intense, almost tortured, sensitivity shows through: in his anxiety about Farel's silence, in his alarm at the potential dangers of the political situation (he turned out to be right several years later; but at that particular moment things appeared more peaceful than usual), in his comments on the "calamity" in the Basle church (where historical studies today reveal scarcely a ripple). Does he overdramatize events? Perhaps his sensitivity to implications is, in the last resort, an important positive factor in his makeup: where Farel, or the Strasbourg colleagues, were willing to take a more easygoing attitude (e.g., in relation to Caroli), Calvin is searingly sensitive to the impossibility of achieving a reconciliation with him: Caroli himself is the problem ("if only he did not abandon Christ, Christ would not abandon him").

But most of all, to return to our "Calvin and Farel" theme, the letter brings out very starkly the nature of the Calvin / Farel relationship. (Herminjard 6.118, gives a brief postscript from Calvin to Farel in French, about the only French communication between them: Calvin uses the "vous" form, not "tu." There is nothing 'pally' about their relationship.) Calvin hammers Farel for not writing (but does not express sympathy for his ill health); he criticizes Farel's judgment in regard to Caroli. And yet he writes to "his dearest brother," and leaves Farel to decide whether or not to make public the letter he is enclosing. It was altogether a very curious relationship.

Calvin's Second Catechism: Its Predecessors and Its Environment

Nobuo Watanabe

Calvin wrote two catechisms for the church of Geneva, aside from several abridgements.[1]

1) In 1537, his first catechism, "Instruction de Foy," was written in French and then translated into Latin. It was not entitled "catechism" in the French edition. But it is really a catechism of the Genevan church according to the Church Order. The first Church Order of 1537 prescribed catechetical instruction for children in the third article.[2]

2) Shortly after returning to Geneva from Strasburg in 1541, Calvin replaced the former catechism with a new one, the well-known Genevan Catechism, written first in French and then translated into Latin.[3]

Not long after he wrote the first catechism he became dissatisfied with it. This is one of main reasons for the revision, as he noted in the letter to the pastors of East Friesland, dated November 27, 1545.[4] The causes of his

---

1. There are two forms of the abridged catechism in the edition of the *Corpus Reformatorum,* vol. 6. One was originally published as the appendix to the 1553 edition of the catechism and later enlarged and appended to the 1562 edition of the Genevan French New Testament (it consists of 28 Q.s & A.s). The other is the appendix to the 1562 edition of the Genevan psalmody (it consists of 107 Q.s & A.s). We may find more frequently the abridged forms, which are not included in the *Corpus Reformatorum,* for example, the appendix to the 1552 edition of the Genevan psalmody (21 Q.s & A.s).

2. *Opera Selecta,* 1.375: "Le 3e article est de linstruction des enfans. . . . Pour ceste cause anciennement on auoyt certain catechisme pour instituer ung chacun aux fondemens de la religion chrestienne, . . . les enfans estoyent enseignez de ce catechisme pour venir testiffier a leseglise pour foy dont jl nauoyent peu rendre tesmoignage a leur baptesme."

3. The reason why he translated the French catechism into Latin was to certify the unity of Christian faith beyond the difference of languages. See Calvin's letter to the pastors of East Friesland dated November 27, 1545. OS 2.72f.

4. OS 2.73.34-39. "Nam quum ante annos septem edita a me esset brevis religionis

224

dissatisfaction were not mentioned. We can only conjecture what they were by comparing two catechisms.

In several points these two catechisms differed. It is worthwhile to compare them in order to pursue the development of Calvin's theological and practical thinking. We will also try to find some influences from his environment.

There were important changes:

1) The form of the latter became Q. & A.

2) The structure of the catechism was changed. The former consists of the elements in the order of Law, Faith, Prayer, etc., but the latter in the order of Faith, Law, and Prayer.

The second point of change corresponds somewhat to the change of order of the chapters in the last edition of *Institutio,* though Calvin still reserved the former order after the second catechism was written.[5]

There remain some questions. First, were there any other reasons to rewrite the former catechism? And, second, were these two reasons important enough to revise the former catechism? We discussed these questions but could not come to a resolution.

I. The Form of Question and Answer

The form of Q. & A. seems to be an influence of preceding catechisms of the German Reformation, especially those that were used in the church of Strasburg. The form of dialogue, following the method of Socrates, has been used by many theoretical writers since Plato. Many works of Christian literature, such as Augustine's *Enchiridion* and Anselm's *Cur Deus Homo?,* used this form.

Catechisms in the form of Q. & A. were known among the German Reformers. Most of these catechisms were also written in German. Accordingly, Calvin did not know those catechisms except for the Latin translation of Luther's shorter one (*Enchiridion Piarum Precationum,* 1529). But in Strasburg Calvin encountered a French translation of a catechism.

---

summa sub catechismi nomine: verebar nisi hoc in medium prolato anteverterem, ne illa, quod nolebam, rursum excudetur. Bono igitur publico si vellem consultum, curare me opportuit, ut hic, quem ego praeferebam, locum occuparet."

5. In the first edition of the *Institutio,* the order of the contents was the same as in the first catechism, namely Law, Faith, Prayer, Sacraments, and False Sacraments, with the last chapter including Christian Freedom, Ecclesiastical Power, and Political Order of the World. In the succeeding three editions of the *Institutio,* from 1539 to 1554, the order basically followed the former. In the last edition of 1559, the order changed to the trinitarian structure.

As the editor of Calvin's *Opera Selecta,* vol. 2, showed, there was a French translation of Bucer's 1537 (shorter) catechism.[6] Calvin seems to have promoted the publishing of this catechism's French translation. He also wrote a preface for this book.[7] Needless to say, this Strasburg liturgy, including the first Reformed metrical psalmody, is akin to the Genevan liturgy[8] as well as Genevan psalmody.[9] We did not trace the vocabularies and idioms of the Genevan catechism to this Strasburg French version, but on the basis of circumstantial evidence we may conjecture that Calvin was influenced by it.

When we compare Calvin's second catechism with the Strasburg French catechism, we cannot find any similarity except for the form of Q. & A.

The form of Q. & A. among the Reformational catechisms was preceded by the Bohemian "Kinderfrage" (1521 or 1522), namely an instruction in the faith for children in the form of Q. & A. This form can be traced further to Waldensian "Interogacion" (1489) and the earlier Hussite catechism of Palacky (1420-36).[10]

Among the Lutheran reformers, Andreas Althamer (1500-1538 / 39) used the word *catechismus* first, in the preface to his catechism of 1528. He defined the elements of the catechism as Prayer, Law, and Faith.[11]

---

6. OS 2.152-57. "Institution puerile de la doctrine chrestienne faicte par maniere de dyalogue." Published as an appendix to the Strasburg liturgy: "La manyere de faire prieres aux eglises françoyses, tant devant la predication comme après, ensemble psaulmes et canticques françoys qu'on chante ausdicte eglises. Après s'ensuyt l'ordre et façon d'administrer les sacrementz de baptesme et de la saincte cene de notre seigneur Iesu Christ, de espouser et confirmer le mariage devant l'assemblée des fideles, avecques le sermon tant du baptesme que de la cene." It was published by Jean Knobloch of Strasburg in 1542, after Calvin moved from Strasburg to Geneva. The original German text is titled "Summari für die Jungern" or "Ein Kützerer underricht für die gar Jungen und einfeltigen." J. M. Reu, *Quellen zur Geschichte des kirchlichen Unterrichts in der evangelischen Kirche Deutschlands zwischen 1530 und 1600,* I / 1.55-66, and *Bucer Deutsche Schriften,* 6 / 3.195-220. The French translation is not a literal translation of the original German text.

7. OS 2.12.

8. See OS 2.11ff.

9. We can easily compare Strasburg and Genevan psalmodies in Pierre Pidoux, *Le Psautier Huguenot du XVIe siècle. Mélodies et documents,* vol. 2 (1962).

10. See Gerhard von Zezschwitz, *Die Katechismen der Waldenser und Böhemischen Brüder als Dokumente ihres wechselseitigen Lehraustausches* (1863; repr. 1967). P. Schaff, *Creeds of Christendom,* vol. 1 (1877[1]), 574f. Joseph Müller, *Die Deutschen Katechismen der Böhmischen Brüder* (Monumenta Germaniae Paedagogica Band, 4) (1887, repr. 1982). Müller's study is most thorough concerning the predecessors of "Kinderfrage."

Balthasar Hübmaier published a catechism in the form of Q. & A. in 1526 (Eng. text; Denis Janz (ed.), *Three Reformation Catechisms: Catholic, Anabaptist, Lutheran* [1982], 141-76), but this catechism did not have any influence on Calvin's catechisms nor any of the preceding catechisms.

11. Althamer defined the main elements of a catechism to be Creed, Ten Commandments, and Lord's Prayer. "Sie sollen das kind jhnen befolhen lassen sein ziehen zu Gottes

Therefore the question remains, Why was Calvin not influenced by the form of Q. & A. previous to the preparation of the first catechism? He knew the shorter catechism of Luther before he began to write his first *Institutio*. He followed the framework or the order of contents of Luther's shorter catechism written in the form of Q. & A. But we cannot find any resemblance between these two catechisms except in the framework and a few of the expressions. Calvin was influenced mainly by the structure of Luther's shorter catechism when he wrote the first *Institutio*. After the first *Institutio*, he wrote the first catechism as an abridgment of the *Institutio*. Accordingly, there are few traces of Luther's catechism in Calvin's first catechism.

II. More Effective Instruction of Children

The Greek words κατηχέω and κατήχησις do not imply an instruction in the form of question and answer. But since Andreas Althamer, many reformers, including Catholic reformers, wrote their catechisms in the form of Q. & A. Many people think that catechism means instruction in the faith in the form of Q. & A., or a form of dialogue. But as mentioned above, catechism and dialogue differ from each other.

What was Calvin's intention when he used the form of Q. & A. for his catechism?

It seems that Calvin considered this form to be more effective for the instruction of children because 1) short sentences are more conducive to a clear expression of the faith, and 2) they lend themselves more readily to confession of faith by word of mouth. The form by which the minister asks and the child answers is a sort of oral confession of faith in the young believer elicited by the minister. In Calvin, this is not a method of explanation of faith or a method of developing theological theory but rather an exemplary form of confession by young believers.[12]

---

forcht, vnd das Vater Unser, Zehn Gepot vnd Glauben leren, vnd vnterrichten. Von dannen her auch die Latini das uerbum Catechisare, id quod scripto fas non erat." Ferdinand Cohrs, *Die evangelischen Katechismusversuche vor Luthers Enchiridion,* 5 Bde (1900-1907), Bd. 1.20.26-30; Kolde: Andreas Althamer, 86.29–87.4. Althamer added in the text of his catechism other elements, namely Law and Gospel, Baptism, Sacrament of Christ's Body and Blood, and a collection of Prayers.

12. In Calvin a catechism is not an approach to the confession of faith or an understanding of faith, but a form of confession itself. In the form in which the minister asks the question and the child answers, question and answer are not equally important. The answer is the main element and the question is introductory. As a matter of course, recitation of the answer was not compelled. Confessing faith before the congregation is not merely reciting answers from the catechism. Meanwhile we may take notice that the form of Q. & A. is

We have an example of a very short catechism of the Genevan church, supposedly written by Calvin, entitled "A Form to Ask Children Who Are Going to Be Received into the Supper of Jesus Christ our Lord" ("La maniere d'interroguer les enfans qu'on recevoir a la cene de nostre Seigneur Jesus Christ."[13] This is one of the shorter catechisms of the Genevan church of the same sort. The oral confession of young participants before the congregation was not a mere recitation of the catechism in a fixed way.

Did Calvin think, when he adopted the form of Q. & A. anew, that this form is useful not only for intellectual understanding of Christian doctrine but also for confessing faith by word of mouth? We are not sure. Yet in 1537, there was a confession in addition to the catechism, and a later catechism had the function of a confession as well. Calvin said, "the agreement which our churches had in doctrine cannot be seen with clearer evidence than from catechisms."[14]

III. More Practical Experience of Catechizing

It seems that Calvin did not have practical experience of catechizing with a catechism before he came to Geneva the first time. Among the French reformers catechism had not been known in the early stage of Reformation. They stressed openly evangelical preaching even in the early period of the Genevan Reformation.

But Calvin had known the importance and usefulness of catechetical teaching in the church. He named his work *Institutio*. At this period *Institutio*

---

dialectical and dynamic. On this point Calvin's catechism differs from the following Reformed catechisms.

13. We mentioned this formula in n. 1. In this short catechism children summarize the Apostles' Creed as follows: "Que Dieu qui est le Pere de nostre Seigneur Jesus Christ, et consequemmet de nous tous, par son moyen, est le commencement et cause principale de toutes choses, lesquelles il conduit tellement que rien ne se fait sans son ordonnance et providence.

Puis apres, que Jesus Christ son Fils est descendu en ce monde, et qu'il viendra derechef du ciel en jugement, ou il est remonte, estant assis a la dextre du Pere: c'est a dire qu'il a toute puissance au ciel et en la terre.

Item le sainct Esprit est vray Dieu: car il est la vertu et puissance de Dieu, et imprime en nos coeurs les promesses qui nous sont faites en Jesus Christ. Pourtant nous confessons que nous croyons au sainct Esprit, comme au Pere et au Fils, qui est la Sapience eternelle de Dieu.

Finalment, que l'Eglise est sanctifiee et delivree de ses pechez par la grace de Dieu, et qu'ell ressuscitera en la vie eternelle" (CR 6.150-53).

It seems to have been an oral confession, and each child was required to confess it.

14. OS 2.73.22. "Sed illustriore documento, quam inter se habuerint ecclesiae nostrae doctrinae concordiam, perspici non poterit, quam ex catechismis."

was the synonym of *Catechismus*. When Andreas Althamer used the word *"catechismus"* the first time in 1528, it was needed to explain this Greek word as *"Unterricht"* in German.[15] *Unterricht* is equivalent to *Institutio,* namely teaching. The above-mentioned French translation of the Strasburg catechism was entitled "Institution puerile de la doctrine chrestienn."[16]

We believe that Calvin gained more knowledge concerning catechism after he came to Geneva. The first Church Order of Geneva in 1537 prescribed catechetical instruction in its third article.[17] We may infer that this followed the thirty-third chapter of the Synod of Bern 1532.[18] Under the political influence of Bern in Western Switzerland, the Genevan Reformation followed it. We are convinced that the pastors of Geneva were not forced to receive catechetical instruction by the political authority, but that they followed willingly, recognizing the meaning of catechism. They did not adopt Farel's "Summary" as an official text of the Genevan church, though Farel's was one of their catechisms and was reprinted repeatedly.[19]

We also think that the first article of the Genevan Confession of 1537, "The Word of God," was influenced by the first article of The These of Bern 1528.[20] The first These of Bern resembles in many points the first article of the Genevan Confession,[21] but the beginning of the first Genevan catechism does not resemble the first article of the confession.

Since 1525 various catechisms were written by the reformers, chiefly in

15. Cohrs, *Katechismusversuche,* 3.20.8; Kolde 86.8-9. "Catechismus ist ein griechisch wort, heyst auff teutsch ein vnterricht. . . ."

16. OS 2.152.1-2.

17. OS 1.375. "Le 3e article est de linstruction des enfans, lesqueulx sans doute doibuent a lesglise vne confession de leur foy. Pour cest cause anciennement on auoyt certain catechisme pour jnstituer vng chacun aux fondemens de la religion cretienne, et estoyt comme vng formulayre de tesmoignage dont vng chacun usoyt pour declaire sa cretiente, et nommeement les enfans estoyent enseignez de ce catechismepour venir testiffier a lesglise leur foy dont jl nauoyent peu rendre tesmoignage a leur baptesme. . . ."

18. Der Berner Synodus von 1532. Edition und Abhandlungen zum Jubiläumsjahr 1982. Bd. I, pp. 132-35. "Die Erziehung der Jugend und die Glaubenslehre oder: Der Katechismus."

19. G. Farel's "Summaire et briefve declaration daucuns lieux fort necessaires a vng chascun chrestien pour mettre sa confiance en Dieu et ayder son prochain" (1525[1], 1533[2], 1534[3], 1538[4], 1542[5], 1552[6], 1560[7]). It contains 42 chapters.

20. E. F. Karl Müller, *Die Bekenntnisschriften der reformierten Kirche,* 30.9-11. "Die heylig Christlich Kilch, deren eynig houpt Christus, ist uß dem wort Gotts geboren, im selben belybt sy, und hört nit die stimm eines frömbden."

21. OS 1.418. "1. La Parolle de Dieu. Premierement nous protestons que pour la reigle de nostre foy et religion nous voullons suyvre la seule Escripture, sans y mesler aucune chose qui ayt este controuvee du sens des hommes sans la Parolle de Dieu, et ne pretendons pour nostre gouvernment spirituel recevoir autre doctrine que celle qui nous est enseignee par icelle Parolle sans y adiouster ne diminuer, ainsy que nostre Seigneur le commande."

South Germany. Most of the authors were educated in humanism and had strong pedagogical concerns. They wrote their catechisms mainly as means of instruction of children with a view to their confirmation. In Calvin, however, catechism is not only a means of instruction in preparation for confession of faith. It is also the rule of faith or *summa doctrinae* of a church.

IV. The Order of Calvin's Second Catechism

The order of Calvin's second catechism is not the same as that of the Strasburg short catechism mentioned above. The order of the latter is: Faith, Prayer, Law. Hence it seems that the structure of Calvin's second catechism was not influenced exclusively by Strasburg's.

Calvin wished to change the structure of his first catechism, which explained the Ten Commandments before the Apostles' Creed. The old order seemed to stress the so-called "pedagogical use" of the Law, a use that guides people to Christ, rather than the "third use," namely a use *(usus)* or function *(officium)* in the reborn. Lutheran theological tradition stresses the "pedagogical use."

To Reformed theology, the third use of the Law is more important. Calvin says in the *Institutio* of 1559: "The third and principal use, which pertains more closely to the proper purpose of the law, finds its place among believers in whose hearts the Spirit of God already lives and reigns" (2.7.12). A person's rebirth, which is treated in the third article of Creed, must be discussed before the Law. This change of structure was necessary for the identity of Reformed theology. Calvin used it in the catechism and the *Institutio*.

Yet Calvin did keep the old structure of the *Institutio* after the order of the catechism was changed. In terms of content his theological thought was not changed, but as for form, or an order of teaching, it was changed.

V. The Numbering of the Ten Commandments

Another difference between the Strasburg short catechism and the Genevan catechism has to do with the numbering of the Ten Commandments.

The first "catechism table" in Strasburg was made c. 1525.[22] At that time the numbering of the Ten Commandments is the same as in the Catholic and Lutheran catechisms, namely: i. "Du solt kein ander Götter neben mir haben" (Halt dich recht gegen Gott mit hertzen). ii. "Du solt den Namen des

---

22. Cohrs, *Katechismusversuche,* 1.119.

Herren deines gottes nit vergebenlich füren" (Halt dich recht gegen Gott mit Mund). iii. "Gedenck des Sabbatstage das du jn heiligest" (Halt dich recht gegen Gott mit Wercken). iv. "Du solt dein Vater und Muter eren, das du lang lebst auf erden" (Halt dich recht gegen Gotsverwesern).

Strasburg's second catechism, that is, Capito's "Kinderbericht" or "De Pueris Instituendis Ecclesiae Argentinensis Isagoge" of 1527, does not contain an explanation of the Ten Commandments. Only Questions 2, 123, and 124 mention true knowledge of sin based on the foundation of the Ten Commandments.[23] In the catechisms related to the Strasburg Reformation, such as the St. Gallen Catechism of 1527 and the Esslingen Catechism of 1530, the numbering of the Ten Commandments is traditional.[24]

ii) In Bucer's 1534 catechism, the numbering of the Ten Commandments in Strasburg is the same as that of Judaism: i. "Ich bin der HERR dein Gott usw." ii. "Du sollt kein andere Götter vor mir haben usw." iii. "Du sollt den namen Gottes usw." iv. "Bis eingedenck des feyertags, jn zu heyligen."[25] It seems that the Strasburg reformers were well versed in Judaistic theology, like most of the Reformed theologians in those days.

iii) In Bucer's second catechism of 1537, the numbering of the Ten Commandments is as follows: i. "Ich der Herre, bin dein Gott, usw. . . . Du solt kein andere götter neben mir haben." ii. "Du solt dir keine bildnüs noch einige gestalt machen usw." iii. "Du solt nit falsch schweren bei dem namen des Herren, deines Gottes. usw." iv. "Gedenck des feirtags, jn zu heiligen. usw."[26] This new numbering of Bucer is the same as that of Zell's Catechism of 1537.[27] This new numbering is Reformed. Bucer's 1537 short ("für die gar Jungen") catechism and its French translation neglected the distinct treatment of the first and second commandments.[28]

When Calvin was writing his manuscript of the first *Institutio,* which

23. Cohrs, *Katechismusversuche,* 2.100-201. Q. 2. "Eo quod ex Dei praeceptis me agnosco peccatorem. . . ." Q. 123. "Quod equidem perquam commode disco ex iugi decem praeceptorum meditatione. . . ." Q. 124. "Huiusmodi tui ipsius cognitio oppido quam necessaria est. Nosse vero abs te pervelim, an ex tali meditatione sedula tranquillitatem et pacem conscientiae consequaris? A. Minime. . . ."

24. The St. Gallen Catechism is a revision of the Bohemian "Kinderfrage" and not Reformed (Cohrs, *Katechismusversuche,* 2.204). The Esslingen Catechism by Jakob Otther Reu, I / 1.360ff., "Die summ des Gsatzs," 369f.

25. Reu, I / 1.61-64. *Martin Bucer Deutsche Schriften,* 6 / 3.97.7-23.

26. Reu, I / 1.83f. *Martin Bucer Deutsche Schriften,* 6 / 3.209.17ff.

27. Reu, I / 1.127-38. In his former catechism (1535), Zell did not treat the Ten Commandments as a whole, but only the first commandment (Reu, I / 1.125).

28. Reu, I / 1.87.25-27. *Martin Bucer Deutsche Schriften,* 6 / 3.219.31-37. "Warumb verdeutet r andere götter neben jm zu haben, auch die bildnüssen, die man verehret?" . . . "Was folget?" "Du solt nit falsch schweren etc."

may have been completed in early 1535, he adopted the new numbering of the Ten Commandments earlier than Bucer. It seems that when Calvin was writing his manuscript explaining the Ten Commandments in 1534,[29] at approximately the same time Leo Jud wrote his first catechism using the new numbering of the Ten Commandments.[30] Around the year 1534, Reformed theologians were well aware of the new understanding of the numbering of the Ten Commandments. Before the issue was settled, there was a tentative numbering of the Ten Commandments following the Jewish rabbis.

Did Leo Jud's first catechism influence Calvin in his numbering of the Ten Commandments? We have no evidence regarding this possibility. Obviously Leo's catechism, with Bullinger's preface dated January 3, 1534,[31] was earlier than Calvin's work. And because it was written in German, Calvin could not use it even if he knew this book. We suppose that Leo Jud and Calvin used a common source, unknown to us, in their numbering of the Ten Commandments.

29. *Institutio 1536,* cap. I, De Lege, quod decalogi explicationem continet. Mandatum I. "Non habebis Deo alienos coram me." Mandatum II. "Non facies tibi sculptile, neque similitudinem aliquam eorum quae sunt in coelo sursum, vel in terra sunt, non adorabis ea neque coles." Mandatum III. "Non usurpabis nomen Dei tui vanum." Mandatum IV. "Recordare diei sabbati, ut sanctifices illum, etc." CO 1.32ff.

30. August Lang (Hrsg.), *Der Heidelberger Katechismus und vier verwandte Katechismen (Leo Juds und Micronius kleine Katechismen sowie die zwei Vorarbeiten Ursins) mit einer historisch-theologischen Einleitung* (1907), Leo Jud's catechism, 61ff. (though the text is from the 1541 edition). In this Einleitung Lang said, "Leo Jud hat also, soweit wir sehen, zuerst in der 'ynleitung' von 1534 die herkömmliche reformierte Form der Gebote eingeführt" (xxi-xxii).

31. August Lang, *Heidelberger Katechismus,* 21. Carl Pestalozzi, *Leo Judä* (Leben und ausgewählte Schriften der Väter und Begründer der reformirten Kirche, IX / 1) (1860), 57. Leo Jud issued his catechism three times, namely 1) Der größere Katechismus, 1534. 2) Der kürtzer Katechismus, 1541. 3) Catechismus in Latin, earlier than the former. And it is almost the same as Calvin's first catechism, which was published in Latin translation in March 1538 (Pestalozzi, *Leo Judä,* 62; Lang, *Heidelberger Katechismus,* xxxif.).

Calvin's Judgment of Eusebius of Caesarea*

Irena Backus

The aim of the seminar was to throw some light on the issue of Calvin's attitude to history in general and to church history in particular. We began by sketching out:

I. The Reception of Eusebius from the Middle Ages to Calvin's Time

The *Chronicle* (available only in Jerome's translation) and the *Ecclesiastical History (H.E.)* were both mentioned in the *Decretum Gelasianum*, which was itself incorporated into the *Decree of Gratian*. Thus "Gelasius's" opinion of Eusebius's historical works was common currency in the Middle Ages and would certainly have been known to Calvin himself. The author of the *Decretum Gelasianum* includes both the *Chronicle* and the *History* first of all among works that are to be considered orthodox. In spite of Eusebius's defense of Origen, those works are not to be rejected since they contain much remarkably significant information. Curiously, the same *Decretum* then includes a mention of "Historia Eusebii Pamphilii" among the apocryphal writings of the Church Fathers. Be that as it may, the *Chronicle* was known and used in the Middle Ages, as were Rufinus's translation of the *History* and its shortened, adapted versions by chroniclers such as Haymo of Halberstadt. Furthermore, Rufinus's translation of the *History* was printed from the fifteenth century onward. In 1523 Beatus Rhenanus published under the title *Autores historiae ecclesiasticae* Rufinus and the *Historia tripartita*. This becomes the standard edition of Eusebius's *Ecclesiastical History*.

---

*Since giving the seminar I have written a longer article on the subject. It was published in *The Sixteenth Century Journal* in 1991.

Rhenanus's preface tells us much about the way Eusebius was viewed by Calvin's contemporaries or near-contemporaries. The Sélestat humanist begins with a wholehearted eulogy of Eusebius's style. If profane histories are published, why should one neglect ecclesiastical historians, especially Eusebius of Caesarea "non modo doctissimus sed eloquentissimus [!]." The latter description can only be due to excessive desire for conventional politeness, since Rhenanus had no knowledge of Eusebius's original notoriously clumsy Greek style and Rufinus's version, as he points out further on in the preface, was anything but "eloquentissima."

Rather like Eusebius himself, Rhenanus then stresses the usefulness of Church History, which not only acquaints us with what was done in the early church after the death of Christ but also with what was written by the apostles and the "apostolici viri." Were it not for the extracts cited by Eusebius, we would remain ignorant of the work of Hegesippus, Justin, Melito of Sardis, Claudius Apollinarius, Dionysius of Corinth, Dionysius of Alexandria, and Irenaeus.

The *History* renders the further service of providing its readers with the edifying example of Christian martyrs who patiently endured tortures for their faith and with the warning example of emperors and other civil rulers who did everything in their power to stop the progress of Christianity. Finally, Rhenanus discusses the *Gelasian Decree* and the accusation of Origenism leveled at Eusebius. Rhenanus finds the accusation surprising: the Rufinus version, he claims, seems to contain no particular apology of Origen, unless of course Rufinus left it out deliberately! Rhenanus thus seems to turn a blind eye to the Apology of Origen in Book 6, which Rufinus naturally reproduces. As for the mention of the *History* among the Apocrypha, Rhenanus considers it to be a later addition "aliquo asino." He also absolves Eusebius of any suspicion of Arianism "as he says nothing about it in this book" *(cum in hoc opere nullam eius rei faciat mentionem)*. Nor is Eusebius to be censured for recounting "minutiora quaedam . . . quae indigna videri possint illis de quibus narrantur," such as the story of the correspondence between the Lord and Abgar (*Historia ecclesiastica* 1.13). Eusebius cites his sources — in this instance, "commentaria Syrorum" — and in any case, continues Rhenanus, a diligent historian should omit nothing. Those who are skeptical must bear in mind that the early Christians were so aware of Christ's importance that they attributed a great number of phenomena to his direct (or indirect) interference and were thus far more sensitive to miracles. This *pia simplicitas,* according to Rhenanus, is to be preferred to the excessive skepticism of his own times.

This apparent credulity as regards the content of *Historia ecclesiastica* does not stop the Sélestat scholar from emitting *caveats* on the reliability of the text he presents to the reader. He regrets not having a Greek manuscript against which to compare Rufinus's translation. He is also aware of the latter's shortcomings as translator and of the fact that books ten and eleven in his manuscript are a straightforward addition by Rufinus.

This textual acumen, coupled with a certain naïveté in matters of doctrine, is typical of Rhenanus and other Christian humanists of the period.

The *Historia ecclesiastica* and the *Chronicon* were by no means the only works of Eusebius that were available in Calvin's time. The *Vita Constantini* appeared in 1544. The *Praeparatio evangelica* had been available in Latin translation by George of Trebizond since 1448 and underwent numerous printings. A Greek text was published in Paris by R. Estienne in 1544. The *Demonstratio evangelica* appeared in Latin in 1539 (Köln, M. Novesianus) and then in Greek in 1545 from the presses of Robert Estienne. The *Liber contra Heraclem* was available in a Greek and Latin Venetian edition from 1501-2. In 1542 the Basel printer H. Petri published the Latin *Opera Omnia* comprising the Rufinus version of the *Historia ecclesiastica,* the *Praeparatio* (in the translation of George of Trebizond), the *Demonstratio* (translated by Donatus Veronensis), and the *Chronicon.* Although the Genevan Academy seems to have been rather poor in editions of Eusebius, his works, and particularly his historical works, were known.

II. Calvin's Attitude to Eusebius

We then examined several passages taken from the *Institutes,* from the *Commentaries,* and from some of the shorter treatises. The passages examined show that Calvin's attitude to Eusebius as historian of the early church is by no means straightforward. Admittedly, in very many cases the Genevan reformer is content simply to cite Eusebius in support of a particular doctrine. Thus the Bishop of Caesarea's account of Polycarp calling Marcion "the elder son of Satan" provides a clinching piece of evidence against Anabaptist Christology in *La brière Instruction.* The Anabaptist doctrines of Christ's flesh are to be identified with those of Marcion. Marcion was condemned, therefore so are the Anabaptists.

In other cases, however, Calvin appears to be either making gross errors, or making unfair use of Eusebius for his own doctrinal purposes. In the *Institutes* of 1536 and 1539 the *Ecclesiastical History* is cited, falsely, in support of the communion in both kinds!

Commenting on Daniel 9:25-26 Calvin is severely critical of Eusebius's identification of "the anointed one" with Aristobulus. He considers that account to be "Jewish" and says of Eusebius: "ille tamen est ex nostris verum est, sed lapsus est inscitia et errore." Needless to say, the basis of Calvin's criticism here is purely doctrinal. And yet he shows himself to be by no means insensitive to the question of history, in that he complements Eusebius's account by identifying (correctly) Aristobulus as the son of Alexander Jannaeus who was defeated by Pompey, sent to Rome, and poisoned by Pompey's friends. To do this Calvin would have had to have recourse to Josephus, and it is interesting to note that the Reformer's historical curiosity is quite independent of his doctrinal judgment.

It was also noted that Calvin, unlike, for example, Beatus Rhenanus, shows a certain cavalier disregard for what exactly constituted the Eusebian corpus. He frequently attributes to Eusebius statements that are to be found either in Jerome's additions to the *Chronicle* or in other compilations without checking them against the *Ecclesiastical History*. Eusebius is thus made responsible for historical errors that he did not in fact commit.

A casual attitude to what exactly constituted the Eusebian corpus situates Calvin at the antipodes of the linguistic and textual concerns expressed by Rhenanus. However, it would be naïve to say that Calvin plays fast and loose with the Bishop of Caesarea's account. While his concerns are predominantly doctrinal, he does show original sensitivity to historical detail.

Citizen's Oath and Formulated Confession: Confession of Faith in Calvin's Congregation

Adrianus D. Pont

I. Introduction

In the *Institutes of* 1536 Calvin states: "Consequently all who profess with us the same God and Christ by confession of faith . . . ought by some sort of judgment of love be deemed elect and members of the church" (2.4.26). The question arises: What exactly does Calvin mean by "confession of faith"?

Through an historical inquiry the following facts emerged. On Calvin's arrival in Geneva in 1536 he drew up a program for reforming the church, namely his *Articles concernant l'organisation de l'église et du culte à Genève* (CO 10 / 1.5-14). This, together with the *Institutes* of 1536, provided the basis for Calvin's actions in building up a church according to the scriptural norm.

II. The Citizen's Oath

In the *Articles* Calvin proposes that all the citizens of Geneva would have to attest the confession, which he and Farel had drawn up, with an oath. He asked the Council to set the example of what was required of all citizens. Calvin argues that this will be a "once only" act with the setting up of the church, and he regards it as necessary so that it will be clear what every citizen believes. At the same time this will establish which citizens and members of the church can be allowed to partake of the Holy Supper.

All evidence points to the conclusion that Calvin followed the example of Bern and Basle in this matter. The citizens of Geneva, however, did not

comply with the directives of the Council, and in the end only a minority of
citizens attested the confession with an oath.

In Strasbourg, where Calvin worked after his banishment from Geneva,
he also had to form a new congregation. Here he did not pursue the matter of
a citizen's oath but introduced a test of faith and knowledge to distinguish
between those who might partake of the Holy Supper and those who had to
be restrained. On his return to Geneva he continued with this test of knowledge
and faith. The test was not in the first place a test of personal faith but of
whether everyone accepted the confession of the church.

III. The Confession of Faith by Children

In the *Articles* of 1536 Calvin argued that baptized children "ought to make
a confession of their faith to the church." To enable the children to do this,
Calvin wrote his *Instruction et Confession de Foy dont on use en l'Eglise de
Genève.* Initially he required parents to instruct their children; then, at appointed times, the minister would question the children. If their knowledge
was satisfactory they made a confession of faith before the ministers and were
admitted to the Holy Supper.

During his sojourn in Strasbourg Calvin was influenced by Bucer's
catechetical practice. On his return to Geneva Calvin laid down his stipulations
for catechetical instruction in the Church Order of 1541. Once again Calvin
decrees that it is the parents' duty to instruct their children. Now, however,
Calvin introduces the catechetical sermon and instruction on Sunday afternoon
as the means by which the church also plays a part in preparing the children
for their confession of faith. At the same time he gives the school a definite
task in catechetical instruction. All this leads up to confession of faith in the
midst of the congregation by the children. This took place every quarter, before
the celebration of the Supper.

As a catechetical handbook Calvin's second catechism of 1541 was used.
R. Peter has already pointed out that the children also used a *primer,* a shortened extract from the catechism, which they more or less learned by heart.

In 1553 *La maniere d'interroguer les enfans qu'on veut recevoir a la
cene de nostre seigneur Iesus Christ* was published. This contained the questions the child had to answer when making his confession of faith in the midst
of the congregation. In this matter Calvin does not include a ceremony of
laying on of hands or promises by the children that they will remain in the
faith and subject themselves to the discipline of the church. In doing this Calvin
deviates from the tradition of Bucer and the church in Strasbourg that was
widely followed in Calvinist churches.

IV. Conclusion

With this evidence it becomes clear what Calvin meant when he demanded a confession of faith from "... all who profess with us the same God and Christ." He demanded an acceptance of and agreement with the confession of the church. This was the prerequisite for partaking of the Holy Supper.

La crise de l'Evangélisme français, 1525 ou l'Evangélisme radical

Mitsuru Shimura

I. Le mouvement de Meaux 1519 et 1520

Quand on parle de l'évangélisme français au début du XVIe siècle, on pense, sans aucun doute, au mouvement de Meaux, qui se situe 40 Km de Paris. Pour connaître ce mouvement éphémaire, il ne nous reste pas beaucoup de documents: la traduction du Nouveau Testament faite par Lefèvre d'Etaples, et *Epistres et Evangiles pour les 52 sepmaines de l'an*[1] nous sont les plus importants.

Nous essayons de mettre le texte des *Ep. et Ev.* dans le contexte historique. De là, nous allons trouver quelques aspects nouveaux de l'évangélisme français au début du XVIe siècle.

Le mouvement de Meaux commence par les deux discours synodaux de G. Briçonnet[2] en 1519 et 1520. Dans ces discours, Briçonnet insiste sur le travail d'évangélistes, "connaître, garder et nourir les brebis de mon Seigneur Jésus-Christ par la parole et par l'exemple". Ceci prévoit déjà la publication de la traducion du Nouveau Testament de Lefèvre d'Étaples et celle des *Ep. et Ev.* Dans le texte des *Ep. et Ev.* les principes de ce mouvement sont montrés: "C'est certe vraye religion de croire à sa paroll, en l'ayant tousjours presente et devant soy et ne liberte l'accomplir en foy et l'amour." (34A) "Bien heureux seront ceulx lesquelz Dieu fera ses apostres et evangelistes à porter l'evangile à toutes gens et nations, en toutes diversitez de langues, a dejecter les diables

---

1. Lefèvre d'Etaples et ses disciples, *Epistres et Evangiles pour les cinquante et deux sepmaines de l'an,* Genève, 1964 [*Travaux d'humanisme et renaissance,* 63].

Epistres et Evangiles pour les cinquante et deux dimanches de l'an, Leiden, 1976 [éd. par G. Bedouelle et F. Giacone].

2. "Un discours synodal de G. Briçonnet, Evêque de Meaux (13 oct 1519)", *Revue de l'histoire d'eglise de France* LX, 164 (1974), 65-84.

qui maintenant par infidelité et ydolatrie occupant toutes regions, à oster les gros serpens et horribles pechéz mortelz regnans par le monde. à guerir des traditions et doctrines des hommes contre à la saincte parolle de Dieu." (35B) Par contre "bien malheureux sont doncques et infideles ceulx qui ont voulu empescher de prescher l'evangile ou qui le vouldroyent empecher. Qui resiste à la parolle de Dieu, il risite à Dieu . . ." (35B).

Il n'est pas difficile de tirer quelques caractères essentiels. C'est rejeter les traditions et doctrines des hommes et retourner à la pureté de l'évangile. Pourant il faut regarder comment ces principes se réalisent dans le texte.

II. La fin véritable du group de Meaux 1525 / 26

Nous donnons un coup d'oeil rapide à ce qui se passe entre 1523 et 1525 à Meaux, en 1523, la traduction du N.T. est publiée, qui a été reçue favorable pour le peuple. Pourant, dans la préface de la deuxième partie du N.T., Lefèvre n'oublie pas de référer à la royauté en attendant le soutien.

Pour la Sorbonne, cette publication n'est pas bien acuillie, "il serait très pernicieux, vu les circonstances du temps de laisser répandre parmi les peuple des versions complètes ou partielles de la Bible et celles qui avaient été déjà parues devaient être supprimées que tolérées."[3]

Le 15 oct. 1523, Briçonnet a prononcé aux fidèles et au clergé les décrets[4] contre les doctrines et les livres de Luther, dans lesquels il réaffirme l'existence du purgatoire et le culte des saints et saintes. Ce qui nous est étrange est que Briçonnet prononce encore une fois en 1523[5] la révocation des prédicateurs luthériens. Ceci s'explique que deux prédicateurs de Meaux étaient en prison et la décision de la Sorbonne est prise au début de ce décembre.

Déjà en 1522, un prêtre séculier, attaché à la maison de la duchesse d'Alençon, Michel d'Arande était dénoncé par G. Petit que ses discours étaient loin de respirer l'orthodoxie en ce qui concerne le culte des Saints.[6] En 1523, ce sont Mazurier et Caroli qui étaient accusés. Et les deux autres plus tard.

"Un autre discours synodal de G. Briçonnet, Evêque de Meaux (oct. 1520)", *Revue des sciences philosophiques et théologiques* 60 (1976), 419-45.

3. Quiévreux, P., *La traduction du Nouveau Testament de Lefèvre d'Etaples*, Le Cateau, 1894, 23.

4. Herminjard, *Correspondance des réformateurs*, Genève-Paris, 1866-1897, t-1, 77, 79.

5. id. 81. Dans le milieu meldois, il est publé un traité de Luther en français. "Declaration d'aucuns motz, desquels use souvent saict Pol en ses epistres", *Palaestra Typographica, Aspects de la production du livre humaniste et religieux au XVIe siècle*, 1894, Aubel, 11-56.

6. Deslie, "Notice sur un registre des procès-verbaux de la Faculté de Théologie de Paris pendant les années 1505-1533", 13.

Nous n'avons pas de moyen pour connaître les discussions détaillées mais nous énumérons les sujets dont il s'agissaient alors: du culte des saints et du purgatoire, des oeuvres, de l'image, de l'utilisation de la langue vulgaire et de la messe.

Notre texte est publié en 1525, dont la date exacte n'est pas connue. La présence de la Sorbonne est manifestée le 6 nov. 1525 par la censure contre les *Ep. et Ev.* avec 48 propositions. Juste avant la condamnation du texte, Lefèvre d'Etaples, G. Roussel et d'Arande, se sentant la menace parisienne, se réfugient à Strasbourg chez Capiton.

La lettre du Roi, François Ier, prisonnier depuis le début de l'année, est en vain arrivée au Parlement de Paris le 12 novembre.[7]

Le 19 déc. 1525, Briçonnet étaient interrogé par "maistre André Verjus, Jacques Mesnagier, conseiller du roy en la-dicte cour, sur certain livre contenant les evangiles en françoys et s'il a fait les exhortations et annotations audict livre."[8] Il est question de la publication des *Ep. et Ev.* Il est évident que Briçonnet se mêlait à cette publication meldoise.

Le 5 fév. 1526, il est publié un arrêt de Parlement contre "certain livre contenant les evangiles en français et exhortations et annotations apposées." Et la cour interdisait "toute prédication de la doctrine de Luther ou d'autres doctrines réprouvées touchant les sainctz sacrements de l'Eglise, l'honneur de la très glorieuse Vierge Marie, mère de Dieu, les Sainctz et Saintes, leurs reliques et ymage, touchant aussi l'autorité des saincts conciles, du pape, des prelatz et ministres de l'Eglise, les prières et oraisons pour les tresspasséz, l'observance des jeunes et abstinence et toutes autres choses ordonnées et condamné par l'Eglise."

Ceci annonce la fin véritable du groupe de Meaux. Il faut ajouter une chose. La guerre de paysans donne un effet négatif au mouvement de Meaux, comme cette guerre est soulevée par "le party de sacrilège et hérétique de luther" ou "la secte et faulse doctrine de Luther." Et la guerre "concerne la conservation de l'Etat."[9]

III. Quelques sujets

Nous examinons quelques sujets.

Le sujet de la messe, qui va être discuté tout au long du XVIe siècle, n'a pas été traité ouvertement dans notre texte. Cela ne veut pas dire que les

---

7. Herminjard, *Correspondance des réformateurs,* t-1, 165.
8. Vessière, M., "Le procès de G. Briçonnet au Parlement de Paris", *Bulletin de la société de l'histoire du protestantisme français,* 130 (1984), 5-28.
9. cité par Vessière, "Le procès".

gens de Meaux ne n'intéressalent pas à la discussion de la Messe. La raison en est simple. Comme les prédicateurs de Meaux ont été accusés sur ce sujet-là, c'est trop délicat pour faire la discussion. Ou plutôt, il faut dire que leurs intérêts n'étaient pas là. Par la lettre de Roussel,[10] réfugié à Strasbourg, nous arrivons à une conclusion que la liturgie n'a pas été touchée ni changée.

Pourtant, il faut remarquer que l'introduction de la langue vulgaire a déjà faite et que le texte des *Ep. et Ev.* est écrit en français pour que le peuple puisse comprendre le texte biblique et les exhortations. C'est l'auteur de la deuxième édition qui disait que "l'auctorite irrevocable est donnee a ung chascun chrestiens de juger et penser, quand on ordonne ou qu'on propose aucune chose . . . et que ung simple chrestien de quelque condition qu'il soi, s'il a l'esperit de Dieu, il peult mieux juger que nul autre mondain, combien qu'il apparoisse grande clerc." (39B) Le texte de 1525 au moins l'a affirmé sans le mentionner.

En ce qui concerne le purgatoire, nous ne trouvons pas la négation nette, qui se trouve pendant le procès: "il n'y a pas de purgatoire, puisque l'évangile affirme qu'il n'y a pas de pardon de péchés en dehors de la mort et du sacrifice de Jésus et c'est l'avarice des prêtres qui invente le purgatoire." Dans l'exhortation sur l'histoire de Lazare, il est écrit qu' "en ce lieu là, il n'y a point d'aide, il faut que la justice de Dieu se face." (40B) Et "Hélas, que feront-ils alors? Il sera trop tard de leur repentir il sera trop tard de croyre ce qu'ils verront. Il n'y aura plus que mort éternelle qui les attendra voire ung seul mot du juger." (2B) Cette fois-ci, la troisième lieu manque. Ce que le texte insiste est la certitude de la vie. "Mourir corporellement et partir de ce monde est aller spirituellement et en l'esperit au Père." (32B) Et "ne doubtons riens que en nous partant de ce monde nous nous trouvons les haultes pasteurs céléstes." (39B) Le ton n'est pas celui que nous trouvons dans les textes de Farel[11] et de Luther.

Notre texte, ne parlant pas ouvertement du purgatoire, reste très modéré.

Pendant le procès de Pauvant et Saulnier, il était question de culte des saints. Dans notre texte, nous ne trouvons pas le négation littérale du cultes aux saints. Au lieu de la négation, nous trouvons le christocentrisme.

Nous lisons au jour d'Estienne, "le jours-cy est dict de Saint Estienne. Non point que ce ne soit le jour de Jesuchrist et solennite de son nostre seigneur de son advenement." (6A) La raison en est bien montrée. "Pour ce que on honnore aujourd'hui nostre seigneur par la grace et force qu'il donna à ung tel jours à celuy que représente ce jour, à Sainct Estienne son serviteur, premier martyr entre ses chevaliers." Estienne n'est qu'un serviteur de Dieu. Et quand

10. Herminjard, t-1, 167.
11. Farel, G., *Sommaire* [Turin, 1525], "de la messe".

les adversaires lapidoyent Estienne, il invoque non point "les anges ou Moyse ou Abraham, Issac ou Jacob ou aucuns des prophetes mais seulement Jesuchrist." Et nos auteurs continuent "C'est Dieu et nostre Seigneur Jesuchrist que on doibt invoquer et non point ange ou autre creature." Pour nos auteurs, Jesus-Christ est "vie, salut, rédempteur, justice, gloire, esperance, tout, plus que tout." (28A) La négation du culte aux saints est manifestée par un moyen indirect; c'est le christcentrisme qui nie la doctrine humaine.

IV. La position des auteurs de "Epistres et Evangiles"

Il est bien possible que les *Ep. et Ev.* sont écrits pour faire la lecture du N.T. selon l'année ecclésiastique. Pour cette raison, les *Ep. et Ev.* n'ont pas de caractère de pamphlets religieux. Il est vrai dans un sens. Pourtant si nous les mettons dans le contexte historique, un autre aspect nous relève. C'est que les auteurs des *Ep. et Ev.*, étant ai courant de ce qui se passe entre les prédicateurs de Meaux et le Sorbonistes, ne voulaient pas toucher aux sujets délicats comme la messe et le purgatoire. Or, si les auteurs des *Ep. et Ev.* se déclaraient orthodoxe, le texte serait conforme à arrête de 1526.

Il nous paraît que les auteurs des *Ep. et Ev.* ont évité intentionellement d'être appelés "luthériens" et n'ont pas cédé à la pression de la Sorbonne. Pour cette raison, la position historique de *Ep. et Ev.* est difficile. Il faut dire que les auteurs de *Ep. et Ev.* restent fidèles à l'exigence évangélique. Dans la situation que nous venons d'écrire, que d'être fidèle à l'évangile, ce serait quelque chose assez hardi, et radical dans un sens étymologique du mot.

V. La deuxième édition de "Epistres et Evangiles," 1530

Une chose. La deuxième édition des *Ep. et Ev.* est publiée en 1530 à Lyon chez Pierre de Vingle. Cette date est justement la même époque que la publication de la deuxième édition de N.T. français, comme les alphabets qu'on trouve dans les *Ep. et Ev.* à partir du cinquième dimanche après pâques se coïncident avec les alphabets mis à la marge de la traduction du N.T. de Pierre de Vingle (N [c. 1530, win]).

Il nous reste à savoir qui est "gens doctes en la saincte escripture". Il est fort possible qu'il soit Farel, comme il connaît bien ce qui se passe à Meaux. Ou Pierre de Vingle lui-même?

The Marriage Laws Calvin
Drafted for Geneva

Jeffrey R. Watt

I. Introduction

The texts this seminar examined were the marriage laws that John Calvin proposed in 1545 and the ecclesiastical ordinances on marriage that were eventually adopted in Geneva in 1561.[1] The reason I recommended an examination of these texts is that though his importance as a theologian has long been recognized, Calvin's significance in the area of law has to a large extent been neglected. Calvin, however, had more formal training in law than in theology and probably had the best legal background of all magisterial reformers. It is particularly important to examine the laws on marriage that Calvin drafted for Geneva. Marriage and the family are arguably our most fundamental and influential institutions, and Calvin's matrimonial laws would have been among the most immediately felt by Genevans. While most residents of sixteenth-century Geneva knew little about Calvin's doctrines on the eucharist or predestination, they could not have avoided the requirements concerning marriage. In this seminar we tried to discern how Calvin's laws compared with Canon Law, since the Roman Catholic Church had for centuries defined the laws on European marriage. Moreover, since Calvin was not the first Protestant reformer to write on marriage or even to draft laws on marriage, it is equally important to put Calvin's matrimonial laws in the broader Protestant context, comparing his views on marriage with those of other reformers. An examination of the marriage laws Calvin drafted for Geneva and the manner they were put into practice reveals the interplay between church history, legal history, and social history.

1. *Calvini Opera,* vol. 10 / a, 33-44, 105-14.

As the texts reveal, the edicts Calvin composed in 1545 are virtually identical to those actually adopted by the Genevan government in 1561. One may wonder why the City Council waited so long before officially adopting Calvin's proposed marriage laws. The answer most likely is that Calvin's inflexible convictions caused Geneva's magistrates to think twice before agreeing to his proposals. In any event, the content of Calvin's marriage laws was already in effect well before 1561 — magistrates evidently wanted to test the new laws for a few years before actually committing themselves to Calvin's ordinances.[2]

After Calvin's return from Strasbourg in 1541, the control of marriage was overseen by the *Petit Conseil* (Small Council) and the Consistory, a type of morals court composed of the pastors and elders and dominated by Calvin. The Consistory heard all sorts of moral concerns including questions related to marriage, such as divorces, contract disputes, and police actions against domestic unrest and illegal separations. The Consistory often censured delinquents and forbade them to take communion, but it could not impose any secular penalties; any parties who deserved punishment were referred to the Small Council, along with the Consistory's opinion on how to proceed. Moreover, it was the Small Council that would have the final say in divorce cases and marriage contract disputes. Geneva, like all Protestant areas, thus experienced the laicization of the control of marriage. Since Canon Law held that marriage was a sacrament, Roman Catholics argued that the church alone had the authority to control and legislate on marriage. All magisterial reformers denied the church the major role in the control of marriage, primarily because they held that marriage, though sacred, was not a sacrament.[3]

II. The Formation of Marriage

The first part of Calvin's matrimonial ordinances deals with the formation of marriage. Here we see a clear rejection of the so-called clandestine marriage that Canon lawyers had for centuries upheld as valid. Roman Catholic doctrine on how one entered into marriage had been set in the twelfth century when Pope Alexander III (1159-81) decreed that marriage was theoretically indissoluble from the moment of consent, but not perfected until sexual union. In extraordinary circumstances, unions could be dissolved in the absence of consummation. An important ramification of this theory was that there was no

---

2. Cornelia Seeger, *Nullité de mariage, divorce et séparation de corps à Genève, au temps de Calvin* (Lausanne, 1989), 196.
3. *Ibid.*, 24.

need for a public ceremony or for witnesses to an engagement to have a valid marriage. True, it was a sin to marry without the publication of the banns or the benediction of a priest. But though the offenders were subject to "the spiritual penalties of penance," the marriage remained valid.[4] Furthermore, the age at which one could legally contract a marriage was 14 for boys and 12 for girls.[5] Having attained these respective ages, adolescent boys and girls could contract binding marriages without the authorization of their parents.

Calvin and other reformers opposed clandestine marriages for a number of reasons. Protestant reformers held that such marriages violated the commandment to honor one's father and mother. In requiring parental permission to marry until the age of 24 for men and 20 for women (changed to 20 and 18 respectively in the ordinances), Calvin was in line with all other reformers. One nuance, however, is that Calvin was more patriarchal than Luther, Zwingli, and others, stressing paternal more than parental permission. Moreover, to avoid legal complications, Calvin, like other reformers, insisted on the presence of witnesses to engagements to ensure that the parties had actually consented.

As in all Protestant areas, Calvin insisted on the publication of the banns — announcements made in church on three different Sundays in order to ensure that there were no impediments to marry. It was particularly important to know whether either party was already married — magistrates obviously wanted to avoid bigamous unions. The banns could also serve to turn up evidence of whether the man and woman were too closely related to be husband and wife. As the marriage laws indicate, Calvin, like all reformers, reduced impediments for reasons of consanguinity and affinity. The Roman Catholic Church had forbidden marriage as far as the seventh degree of consanguinity and affinity, though the Fourth Lateran Council of 1215 reduced impediments to the fourth degree, thus prohibiting marriages between third cousins.[6] The reformers deemed these rules too strict and followed the standards set in Leviticus 18. Calvin, like Zwingli, interpreted these passages less literally than did Luther, extending impediments to members of the opposite sex and forbidding marriages between first cousins.[7] The impediment that prevented those who com-

---

4. A. Esmein, *Le Mariage en droit canonique*, 2 vols., 2nd ed. (Paris, 1929), 1.100-101; R. H. Helmholz, *Marriage Litigation in Medieval England* (Cambridge, 1974), 26-27.

5. Paul Viollet, *Histoire du droit civil français* (Paris, 1905), 445. This was the age set by Roman Law.

6. James A. Brundage, *Law, Sex, and Christian Society in Medieval Europe* (Chicago, 1987), 356.

7. Seeger, 454. For example, unlike Luther, Calvin and Zwingli held that a man was not to marry his former wife's sister. Though it prohibits a man from having intercourse with his brother's wife, the Bible does not expressly forbid a man from marrying his wife's sister after his wife's death: "Do not take your wife's sister as one of your wives, as long as your wife is living" (Lev. 18:18).

mitted adultery together from later marrying one another was adopted from Canon Law.

Calvin's most important debt to Canon Law was the belief that marriage was already binding from the moment of consent, not simply from the time of the wedding. Like Roman Catholics, Calvin held that there were two stages in the formation of marriage: first consent and then the wedding. Unlike Canon lawyers, he held that marriage was perfected not by consummation, but by the celebration of the wedding in church.[8] Calvin clearly recognized a difference between fiancés and spouses, as witnessed by the fact that fiancés were not to live together. Nevertheless, fiancés could not simply change their minds and not marry. Evidence from court records reveals that barring impediments, couples who had freely consented to marry in the presence of witnesses and with their parents' approval had to marry. Contract disputes, the most common form of matrimonial litigation in Calvin's Geneva and elsewhere in early modern Europe, were usually initiated by plaintiffs who sought to oblige others to honor alleged marriage engagements. Most plaintiffs lost their suits because there were no witnesses to the engagement. Although Calvin warned against making marriage promises frivolously, Protestant courts were known to order couples to marry for simply having shared a drink in the name of marriage. In this ritual of early modern popular culture, the suitor offered a drink — sometimes wine but often simply water — to his prospective fiancée, saying "drink this in the name of marriage." In popular opinion, accepting the drink symbolized the acceptance of the marriage proposal. Members of Reformed consistories took this ritual very seriously. On more than one occasion, Neuchâtel's consistories, for example, ordered women to honor marriage contracts that had been sealed by a drink, even though they had expressed no verbal acceptance of marriage offers.[9]

Couples could be freed from marriage engagements only under very specific circumstances. Rescinding marriage engagements was possible when

8. *Ibid.*, 133.

9. Archives de l'Etat de Neuchâtel, Registres de la Justice matrimoniale de Neuchâtel, 2.67v-68, 69-71; Registres du Consistoire seigneurial de Valangin, vol. 3.213. On the issue of drinking in the name of marriage and other elements of popular lore associated with marriage, see Martin Ingram, *Church Courts, Sex and Marriage in England, 1570-1640* (Cambridge, 1987), 196-98; Lyndal Roper, *The Holy Household: Women and Morals in Reformation Augsburg* (Oxford, 1989), 133; Raymond A. Mentzer, Jr., "*Disciplina nervus ecclesiae:* The Calvinist Reform of Morals at Nîmes," *Sixteenth Century Journal,* 18 (1987), 98; Roderick Phillips, *Putting Asunder: A History of Divorce in Western Society* (Cambridge, 1988), 31; André Burguière, "Le ritual du mariage en France: pratiques ecclésiastiques et pratiques populaires (XVIe-XVIIIe siècle); *Annales. Économies, sociétés, civilisations, S.C.,* 33 (1978), 642; Samuel Pyeatt Menefee, *Wives for Sale: An Ethnographic Study of British Popular Divorce* (New York, 1981), 29.

the man had been deceived into thinking his fiancée was a virgin when she was not, when one of the parties left the country before the wedding, and when one of the fiancés suffered from a contagious disease. With this last provision, Calvin clearly had leprosy in mind; significantly, no other reformer had specifically mentioned illness as a ground for rescinding a contract. Calvin, on the other hand, made it a point to say that the non-payment of the dowry and similar material concerns did not suffice to terminate an engagement. During a period in which property was of overwhelming importance in the choice of spouses, Calvin wanted to ensure the sacred nature of marriage. In spite of his wishes, more than once men appeared before the Consistory not wanting to consecrate marriages because their fiancées had failed to pay the dowry as promised. Three times before 1561, the Consistory and the Small Council ruled that men had to proceed with the weddings even though their fiancees had not provided the promised dowry. In 1562, however, a man convinced the judges that the promises he had made were conditional. Calvin in fact had prescribed that marriage agreements be made directly without conditions — a provision not found in previous marriage laws — and consequently this man was not required to marry the woman.[10] On the other hand, the Consistory was known to recognize the validity of conditional promises if the conditions had been fulfilled. The most common condition cited at the time of engagements was that of parental consent — that is, a person, usually the woman, accepted a marriage proposal provided her parents agreed. If her parents did not approve of the match, then the courts would not recognize the marriage as binding.[11]

III. The Dissolving of Marriage

Litigation involving the termination of marriage was not as common as that concerned with the formation of marriage — a clear indication that the introduction of divorce did not cause revolutionary changes in the institution of marriage in Geneva. In terminating marriages that had already been consecrated in church, Calvin made a distinction between annulments and divorces. As in Canon Law, certain circumstances could suffice for an annulment, implying that a real marriage had never existed because of conditions or events that preceded marriage. Like Canon lawyers before him, Calvin and

10. Seeger, *Nulité de mariage,* 316-17; citing Archives d'Etat de Genève (hereafter AEG), Registres du Consistoire 1.57, 14 September 1542; AEG, Registres du Conseil 36.122, September 1542; Registres du Consistoire 4.42, 5 July 1548; 17.184v, 28 November 1560; 19.110, 30 July 1562; 19.113v, 6 August 1562.
11. Seeger, *Nulité de mariage,* 311-14.

other reformers put much emphasis on the sexual aspect of marriage. Consequently, it is not surprising that sexual dysfunction could serve as a ground for an annulment. In permitting annulments of marriages that could not be consummated, Calvin, in spite of claims to the contrary, was in effect repeating the premise found in Canon Law that marriage was perfected by consummation. It was not easy to get an annulment because of impotence — successful suits for annulments based on impotence usually involved marriages that had not been consummated after several years of cohabitation. Furthermore, once a union was consummated, sexual dysfunction was not a ground for divorce. Luther, by contrast, permitted divorce for impotence and refusal to engage in conjugal sexuality, believing that marriage was a remedy for concupiscence and that men and women should have access to their spouses' bodies, as the Apostle Paul prescribed.[12]

While Canon Law held that a perfected marriage was indissoluble, Calvin and other reformers recognized certain grounds for divorce that, unlike Catholic separations, provided for the possibility of remarriage. In their views on divorce, Calvin and virtually all reformers emphasized matrimonial guilt — there had to be a guilty party and an innocent party, and the person receiving the divorce could in no way contribute to the fault of the other spouse.[13] Adultery was the ground for divorce that all reformers recognized. While for Catholics adultery was one of a number of reasons that warranted separations, Protestants gave greater importance to adultery as a result of their emphasis on the Bible as sole authority. Adultery was the only ground for divorce clearly and unequivocally mentioned in the Bible.[14] Citing the Apostle Paul, Calvin, like Canon lawyers, rejected the notion, found in Roman Law, that adultery was only a female crime, asserting that fidelity was required of both spouses. In practice, however, Calvin and other members of the Consistory passed decisions that suggested that they viewed a woman's infidelity as a greater sin than her husband's. Twice as many men as women filed for divorce on the grounds of adultery, even though it appears that more men than women were excommunicated for illicit sexuality.[15] When women sought to divorce adulterous husbands, the Consistory and Small Council exhorted them to forgive their husbands for their foibles. That was not always the case,

---

12. *Ibid.,* 162.

13. For example, a person could not receive a divorce for adultery if he or she had contributed to the other spouse's infidelity by refusing sexual relations. Phillips, *Putting Asunder,* pp. 56, 59, 85, 90.

14. The reformers cited especially the following words of Jesus: "I tell you, then, that any man who divorces his wife for any cause other than her unfaithfulness, commits adultery if he marries some other woman" (Matt. 18:9). Moreover, the Old Testament had prescribed the death penalty for adulterous women, and Calvin bemoaned the leniency of contemporary magistrates who did not kill those guilty of adultery. *Ibid.,* 53, 85-86.

15. Seeger, *Nulité de mariage,* 404.

however, in divorce suits against unfaithful wives. Calvin's own brother, Antoine, received a divorce in 1557 from his adulterous wife and not a word was said to him in hopes that he would forgive his wife, who was subsequently banished.[16] Moreover, the odds of women receiving a divorce for adultery were much lower than for men: during this period, about twenty men received divorces from adulterous wives, while only six women received divorces on such grounds.[17]

In his commentaries, Calvin wrote that adultery was the only legitimate ground for divorce, while his marriage laws clearly recognized the possibility of divorce for abandonment, be it willful desertion or justified absence. These views are not necessarily irreconcilable. The reasoning behind divorce on the basis of abandonment was that after a certain period of time, one could assume the absent spouse was dead. In such circumstances, divorce has "the appearance of being a substitute death certificate for the missing spouse. . . ."[18] This manner of dissolving a marriage had not been unknown before the Protestant Reformation. Centuries before, Canon lawyers had recognized the possibility of dissolving a marriage after a spouse's extended absence on the presumption of his or her death. Calvin, however, clearly did not limit divorce for desertion to cases in which the absent spouse could be presumed dead. In cases of willful desertion, Calvin also accepted awarding divorces on presumption of adultery, especially in cases of absent wives.[19]

In practice, however, Calvin found himself compelled to go still further.

16. *Ibid.,* 406; citing AEG, Registres du Consistoire 11.95v, 7 January 1557; AEG, Registres du Conseil 42.16v, 16 February 1557.

17. Seeger, *Nulité de mariage,* 414. On the other hand, in Geneva all women who had been divorced, even those who had committed adultery, had the right to have their dowry returned to them. Women who committed adultery elsewhere sometimes forfeited their property. In late medieval Italian towns, for example, adulterous women often had to give all or part of their dowries to their husbands as compensation. Brundage, *Law, Sex, and Christian Society,* 541.

18. Phillips, *Putting Asunder,* 91.

19. *Ibid.,* 54-55; citing V. Norskov Olsen, *The New Testament Logia on Divorce: A Study of Their Interpretation from Erasmus to Milton* (Tübingen, 1971), 101. As the marriage laws reveal, when a woman returned after an unauthorized absence, her husband did not have to take her back if he had reason to suspect that she had committed adultery. If inquiries made in the area in which she had been turned up convincing evidence that she had been unfaithful, her husband could be divorced. No mention was made, however, about making inquiries about men's infidelity during their absences, another indication of a sexual double standard, notwithstanding Calvin's words to the contrary. CO 10 / a.43.112. In the High Middle Ages, most Canon lawyers had felt that it was legitimate under certain circumstances to allow remarriage on the basis of the presumption of death of absent spouses. Pope Alexander III (1159-81) had issued a declaration allowing the dissolution of a marriage for the "protracted absence of a spouse under circumstances in which the absent party's death might reasonably be presumed." Though Alexander set the waiting period at ten years, Celestine III (1191-98) shortened it to seven years, which would remain the most commonly prescribed wait. Brundage, *Law, Sex, and Christian Society,* 334, 374.

The most famous divorce case during his lifetime was that of Galeace Caracciolo, a Neapolitan nobleman and grandnephew of Pope Paul IV, who converted to Protestantism and came to Geneva in 1551. His wife, who remained Catholic, was very much devoted to Caracciolo but refused to come to Geneva to join him. Eventually, at the Consistory's recommendation, the Small Council awarded him a divorce on the grounds of desertion even though she was known to be alive and well and had an impeccable reputation.[20] A woman was expected, within reason, to follow her husband wherever he might go; refusing to do so amounted to abandonment on her part. Notwithstanding this case, absence or desertion was a ground for divorce more often cited by women than men, since men traveled more than women.

It is important to mention a few reasons that were not grounds for divorce. Calvin did not view incompatibility or even cruelty as a valid reason for divorce. There were cases in which women simply left their husbands to avoid their cruel behavior. Calvin and other reformers, however, believed that the introduction of divorce would eliminate the separations permitted under Canon Law. And accordingly, the marriage laws of 1561 made no provisions for separations. During Calvin's lifetime, the Consistory and Small Council did award one judicial separation, involving a woman who suffered from life-threatening mistreatment.[21] The man's behavior must have been extreme, considering that the Consistory had ordered a woman to obey and live peacefully with her husband even though he had beaten her so severely that he put out one of her eyes.[22] Apart from that lone case, if women had no other charges against their husbands — such as infidelity or impotence — they were left with

20. Seeger, *Nulité de mariage,* 302; citing AEG, Registres du Consistoire 15.68v, 20 April 1559; 149, 10 August 1559. AEG, Juridiction pénale et administrative, A 2: 42, 14 August 1559; 60, 17 November 1559.

21. Seeger, *Nulité de mariage,* 441; citing AEG, Registres du Conseil Part 7: 100v, 10 July 1553. This separation was different from those accorded under Canon Law in that it was not intended to be a permanent separation; the separation was to last only until the husband learned to behave himself.

22. AEG, Registres du Consistoire 1.51v-52, 17 August 1542. "ladite Martinaz femme de Claude Soutiez bochier az este interrogue quand elle se fust mal en loye et que la ferme. Respond quil y a bien quatres moys que son mari la battit de sorte quelle en az perdu loye et ny voyt rien que le barbier qui la manda guerir luy coppa ung filet et quelle fust ferme dune rannasse et fit ainsi fayt le cept et donna demande misericorde et ne losoyt dire a cause de son mari que si on luy en faysoyt aulcung semblant il sen iroyt et laysseroit femme et enfans. Et sa mere encore dit quelle en az le tort et quon luy pardonne affin quil ne sen voyse car il layssera grand patie en son mesnage. Le consistoyre est de lavis quon luy face a luy les remonstrances de correction et a la request de sa femme quon ne luy face rien et quon remecte devant messieurs lundy pour se presenter et quil promecte de ne len point corroser ny saz femme avec aulcung corron entre luy et saz femme. Touchant la Martinaz le consistoyre est de lavis et opinion quelle soyt toujour obeysante à son mari et vivent en paix lung avec laultre."

no valid basis for a divorce and were ordered to return to their husbands. That cruelty did not suffice for a divorce in Geneva is no surprise in that the reformers, with the exception of Martin Bucer, generally ignored the question of cruelty in their divorce doctrines. Moreover, Protestant reformers recognized the duty of women to obey their husbands and tolerated the corporal punishment of wives, if used in moderation. Calvin went so far as to say that "even if a Protestant wife were cruelly beaten by her Catholic husband, she should not leave him unless she were convinced that her life was actually in danger."[23] To be sure, as Roderick Phillips observes:

> Discord and violence within marriage were deplored, and attempts were made to correct them, but their presence did not affect the essence of matrimony as it was understood by the Reformers. The existence of adultery and, less unambiguously, desertion, did affect marriage significantly. Hence their status as grounds for divorce in Protestant doctrines.[24]

Consequently, while Protestants throughout the continent permitted divorce for adultery and desertion, rarely did anyone grant divorces for cruelty.[25]

Zwingli went a bit further than either Luther or Calvin on the question of divorce, maintaining that the passage in Matthew simply indicated the least serious offense for which a marriage could be dissolved. Elsewhere in the Bible, other offenses appear worse than adultery — surely they, too, must be grounds for divorce. It is a far greater sin to be an unbeliever than an adulterer, Zwingli argued; therefore someone married to an unbeliever should have the opportunity to terminate the marriage.[26] While Zwingli held that anything

23. Brundage, *Law, Sex, and Christian Society,* 559; Phillips, *Putting Asunder,* 55; citing Charmarie Jenkins Blaisdell, "Calvin's Letters to Women: The Courting of Ladies in High Places," *Sixteenth Century Journal,* 13 (1982), 71.

24. Phillips, *Putting Asunder,* 90.

25. Raymond A. Mentzer, Jr. "Church Discipline and Communal Pressure and the French Protestants," paper delivered at the Sixteenth-Century Studies Conference, St. Louis, Missouri, 29 October 1988, 10; E. William Monter, "Women in Calvinist Geneva (1550-1800)," *Signs,* 6 (1980), 195; Roper, *The Holy Household,* 167; Phillips, *Putting Asunder,* 61. Thomas Max Safley found that in sixteenth-century Basel, physical abuse was cited in 19 divorce cases. Among the examples he provides, however, the *Ehegericht* awarded divorces only when abuse was accompanied by adultery. My guess is that infidelity played a more important role than abuse in such decisions. *Let No Man Put Asunder: The Control of Marriage in the German Southwest: A Comparative Study* (Kirksville, MO, 1984), 137-39, 142.

26. Phillips, *Putting Asunder,* 48, 53-57, 62-63; citing *Selected Works of Huldreich Zwingli (1484-1531), the Reformer of German Switzerland,* ed. Samuel Macauley Jackson (Philadelphia, 1901), 102. That is not to say, however, that divorces were easy to obtain in Zurich. During the period 1525-31, only 80 people filed for divorce, and the *Ehegericht,* or marriage court, granted divorces to only 28 of them. Phillips, *Putting Asunder,* 63, n. 90; citing Jean Rilliet, *Zwingli: Third Man of the Reformation* (London, 1964), 179.

worse than adultery might justify divorce, the reformer with the most radical views on divorce was Martin Bucer. In his work *De Regno Christi* (1557), Bucer expressed libertarian views on marriage, anticipating divorce laws that would not prevail until the twentieth century. Bucer insisted that the purpose of marriage was not primarily procreation and the avoidance of nonmarital sex; rather, companionship was the most fundamental element of Christian marriage, entailing fidelity, mutual love, and cohabitation. Consequently, Bucer not only recognized adultery and desertion as grounds for divorce but also approved of divorce for cruelty and even "by mutual consent and by repudiation" by either spouse.[27] Though of great interest to the modern reader, Bucer's views on marriage and divorce were far ahead of their time.

IV. Conclusion

On the whole, Calvin's marriage laws were in line with the views of other major reformers. One might wonder, then, regarding the possible influence of Luther, Zwingli, or others on Calvin's matrimonial laws. Cornelia Seeger has postulated that during his stay in Strasbourg (1538-41), Calvin probably had the opportunity to read Latin translations of Luther's *Von Ehesachen* and *Vom ehelichen Leben,* two of his most important works that dealt with marriage. Although he almost certainly did not have these works in front of him in 1545, Calvin probably retained their general tenets from a previous reading.[28] The marriage laws of Strasbourg no doubt also had an influence on Calvin, as witnessed by the fact that the grounds for annulment and divorce were identical in these cities.[29] Zwingli authored the marriage laws of Zurich in 1525 that served as the model for other Swiss matrimonial ordinances, such as those of Bern. Through his close contacts with Viret and Farel, Calvin undoubtedly was familiar with Bern's matrimonial laws of 1537, which were put into effect in the neighboring Pays de Vaud. Seeger notes that the similarities between divorce laws in Bern and Geneva were so great that they could not have been by chance.

    Nevertheless, Calvin did make a few original contributions, such as

---

27. According to Bucer, other grounds that merited divorce were witchcraft, "desecration of sepulchers, committing sacrilege, favoring thieves, the wife's feasting with strangers without her husband's knowledge or consent, the husband's frequenting lewd women within his wife's sight, and violence. . . ." According to Bucer, these were all serious offenses that merited death, and there was no need to remain with a partner who committed such heinous acts. Phillips, *Putting Asunder,* 69-71.

28. Seeger, *Nulité de mariage,* 165-66.

29. *Ibid.,* 166-67.

annulling engagements that had been frivolously or conditionally made or that involved someone suffering from a contagious disease.[30] Although Geneva's marriage laws made no significant departures from previous Protestant views and practices on marriage, it was nonetheless Calvin, along with Luther, who wrote the most influential marriage doctrines of the sixteenth century: "legislation based on one or the other of them was widespread throughout Europe, mainly in the Protestant states, but also among Reformed populations within Roman Catholic states, as among the Protestants of France" until the Revocation of the Edict of Nantes in 1685. Throughout Europe, Protestants followed the lead of Luther and Calvin by allowing divorce for reasons of adultery and willful desertion, reducing the impediments to marry and requiring parental permission, the presence of witnesses, and the publication of the banns when forming marriages.[31] These were the major departures from Canon Law.

---

30. *Ibid.,* 453.

31. *Ibid.,* 175-78; Ingram, *Church Courts, Sex, and Marriage,* 147; Phillips, *Putting Asunder,* 50, 60, 62.

Syllogismus practicus bei Calvin

Kwang-Woong Yu

I. Das Problem

Die bekannteste Stelle der Institutio, an der Calvin über den Syllogismus practicus spricht, ist Inst. III.14.18. Drei der dort aufeinanderfolgenden Sätze[1] zeigen die Schwierigkeiten an, die diese Lehre mit sich bringt. Zuerst wird das Verhältnis von Glaube und Werke klar beschrieben:

> Wenn es sich um die Begründung und Aufrichtung des Heils handelt, dann sehen die Heiligen von allen ihren Werken ab und richten ihren Blick allein auf Gottes Güte. Sie wenden sich zu Gottes Güte nicht nur vor allem anderen, gewissermaßen als zum Ursprung ihrer Seligkeit, sondern ruhen auf ihr auch als auf der völligen Erfüllung.

Aber es wirkt irritierend, wenn Calvin den Werken anschließend doch eine Bedeutung zuerkennt.

> Ist das Gewissen auf solche Weise gegründet, aufgerichtet und gestärkt, so dient ihm auch die Betrachtung der Werke zur Stärkung, insofern (quatenus) sie nämlich Zeugnisse dafür sind, daß Gott in uns wohnt und regiert.

Ein Widerspruch scheint zwischen beiden Sätzen zu bestehen, den Calvin allerdings leugnet.

> Diese Zuversicht auf die Werke hat also nur da Raum, wo man zuvor alle Zuversicht auf Gottes Barmherzigkeit geworfen hat; sie kann nicht im Widerspruch zu der Zuversicht erscheinen, von der sie doch tatsächlich abhängt!

---

1. OS IV,236,31–237,1.

Es handelt sich hier um den Fragekomplex von Glaube und Werken, Rechtfertigung und Heiligung. Darüber hinaus ist nach der persönlichen Erwählungsgewißheit gefragt. Beruht sie bei Calvin auf Gottes Güte oder auf den Werken des Glaubenden oder auf beiden?

Heilsgewißheit ist das eigentliche Kleinod und Merkmal des evangelischen Christentums. Der Blick auf die Werke kann sie nicht geben. Und doch sagt auch Karl Barth: "Der höchst nachträglich auftretende, höchst unselbständig redende, höchst beiläufig anzuhörende, aber in dieser Stellung und Funktion nun doch höchst unentbehrliche letzte Zeuge Jesu Christi einem Jeden gegenüber ist nun einmal ein Jeder (in und mit dem, was er im Glauben an Jesus Christus ist) sich selber."[2] Wenn sich dies "nachträgliche" Zeugnis in uns selbst findet, dann muß es ein dringendes und jedenfalls einleuchtendes Anliegen sein, deutlich zu machen, wie denn der Trostcharakter des Evangeliums gewahrt werden kann. Denn ich bleibe doch dem Zweifel ausgesetzt, ob nicht der Vorbehalt, ich könnte doch nicht zu den Erwählten gehören, mir gilt. Auf der Ebene des Gemeindeglaubens wirken sich solche Unruhen dann durch das Erschlaffen des eigenen Glaubens aus. Der Versuch, sich auf die praktische Erfahrung zu verlassen, stürzt leicht in Unsicherheit, weil die Erfahrung eine illegitime Vorwegnahme des Schauens ist, das es erst im Himmel gibt. Wie versteht aber dann Calvin die Aussage, daß der Glaubende in seinen Werken eine zusätzliche und nachträgliche Bestätigung seines Glaubens findet?

Umgekehrt besteht auch die große Gefahr, daß "gute Werke" ihre "Spontaneität" einbüßen, wenn ein Syllogismus practicus gelehrt wird. Walther Köhler schreibt: Calvins Ethik sei "nicht die unbefangene, fröhliche Bewegtheit Luthers eigen". Ein herber, gedrungener Zug sei in die Ethik hineingekommen, Disziplin und Strenge bzw. "innerweltliche Askese."[3] In der Tat betont Calvin die Heiligung:

> Ist nun das Ziel der Erwählung die Heiligkeit unseres Lebens, so muß sie uns dazu erwecken und anspornen, nach solcher Heiligkeit wacker zu trachten, statt uns etwa einen Deckmantel für unsere Faulheit zu bieten![4]

Hat Calvin nun den Syllogismus practicus, das heißt, den Rückschluß aus den Werken auf den Glauben gelehrt? Wenn dies zutrifft: Worin besteht bei ihm die Heilsgewißheit?

2. *Kirchliche Dogmatik* II,2, Zürich 1942, S.369.
3. *Dogmengeschichte. Das Zeitalter der Reformation.* Zürich 1951, S. 415.
4. Inst. III,23,12; OS IV,406,24-28.

II. Die Meinung der Calvinforscher

Wilhelm Niesel[5] bezieht den Syllogismus practicus alleine auf das Problem der Erwählungsgewißheit aus den Werken. Er wendet sich also sofort der zweiten Frage zu und betrachtet von ihr aus das Thema Calvin und der Syllogismus practicus. Er meint, daß Calvins Theologie etwas ganz anderes sei als ein prädestinatianisches Gedankensystem über das Verhältnis Gott und Mensch, in dem der Syllogismus practicus seinen guten Platz habe. Niesel behauptet, daß Calvin strenge Offenbarungstheologie treibe, die kein Raum für den Syllogismus practicus zu haben gestatte, weil er den Blick von Gott, der sich in Christus offenbare, ablenke und ihn zum Menschen hinwende. Grundsätzlich versucht Niesel von Anfang an, den Syllogismus practicus bei Calvin wegzuinterpretieren. Sein Anliegen ist es, "das Zerrbild reformierter Lehre" zu korrigieren.[6] Doch wenn Calvin wirklich keine Erwählungsgewißheit aufgrund der Werke gelehrt hat, so bleibt doch die Frage, was denn der Syllogismus practicus bei Calvin sei.

Otto Ritschl behauptet, herausgefunden zu haben, daß Calvin über die direkten Wirkungen der Rechtfertigung hinaus dem beharrlichen Fortschreiten der Wiedergeborenen in der sittlichen Erneuerung des Lebens die entscheidende Bedeutung für den Gewinn der jenseitigen Seligkeit zuschreiben konnte. Für Ritschl ist es wichtig, daß Calvin das eigentliche Heil doch erst zu erwarten lehre, start zu glauben, daß man es seinem gesamten Gehalt nach bereits besitze. Ritschl kommt zu dem Ergebnis: "Persönlich zwar hat Calvin an der Heilsgewißheit im Sinne Luthers festgehalten und jenes Rückschlußverfahren teils nur im theoretischen Interesse an der systematischen Konsequenz seiner Gedankenbildung, teils aus Rücksicht auf gewisse biblische Instanzen entwikelt. Unter dem Einfluß seiner Lehre aber ist weiterhin in der reformierten Theologie die lutherische Auffassung von der Heilsgewißheit entschieden in den Hintergrund getreten, während der von Calvin angegebene syllogismus practicus durchaus die Vorherrschaft gewonnen hat."[7] Im Blick auf die Heilsgewißheit kommt Ritschl also zu einem ähnlichen Ergebnis wie nach ihm Niesel, bejaht aber die Existenz einer Lehre vom Syllogismus practicus bei Calvin. Zwei Gründe führt er für die Entfaltung dieser Lehre durch Calvin an, "systematische Konsequenz" und die biblischen Aussagen.

Hans Emil Weber meint, daß bei Calvin die Gefahr des Syllogismus

---

5. "Syllogismus practicus?" in Aus *Theologie und Geschichte der reformierten Kirche.* Festgabe für E. F. Karl Müller — Erlangen zu dessen 70. Geburtstag, Neukirchen 1933, S. 158-179.

6. S. 158.

7. *Dogmengeschichte des Protestantismus, Bd. III, Die reformierte Theologie des 16. und 17. Jahrhunderts in ihrer Entstehung und Entwicklung,* Göttingen 1926, S. 208f.

practicus noch nicht brennend gewesen sei. "Er kann eindrücklich machen, wie der Beweis für das Innewohnen des Geistes und die Annahme zur Sohnschaft, der aus den Früchten der Wiedergeburt gewonnen wird, nur für die gilt, die Gottes Güte zuvor in der Verheißung ergriffen haben und so die Gaben Gottes, damit auch die Werke als Zeichen des Wohlwollens zur Stütze und Bestätigung ihres Glaubens werten können."[8] Weber gibt hier eine Erklärung, warum kein Widerspruch zwischen der Heilsgewißheit aus dem Wort und ihrer Bestätigung aus den Werken bei Calvin besteht.

Walter Göhler verwendet den Begriff Syllogismus practicus nicht und zwar deshalb, weil er sich bei Calvin nicht findet. Er hebt bei der Erörterung der "Begründung der Heilsgewißheit" bei Calvin zurecht die Christusgemeinschaft im Glauben hervor, die beide umfaßt, Rechtfertigung und Heiligung. Er stellt den Rückschluß von den Werken auf den Glauben und die Glaubensgewißheit bei Calvin treffend dar. "Bezeichnend für Calvin ist nun, daß die Heiligung ihm ebenso wie die Rechtfertigung ein Erweis der Erwählung sein kann. Diese gleiche Bedeutung der Heiligung für die Begründung der Heilsgewißheit folgt aus dem Grundsatz, daß der Mensch nicht gerechtfertigt werden kann, ohne geheiligt zu werden. Kann also der Mensch an seiner Rechtfertigung seine Erwählung erkennen, dann muß das Gleiche für die Heiligung gelten. . . . Calvin übersieht nicht, daß die Begründung der Heilsgewißheit in der Heiligung ganz anderer Art ist, als ihre Begründung in der Rechtfertigung. Er kann sie deshalb — wie schon die Heiligung und die Rechtfertigung selbst — nicht auf der gleichen Linie sehen. . . . Diese Unterscheidung führt Calvin so streng durch, daß es zunächst so erscheinen mag, als ob er die Werke der Heiligung völlig davon ausschlösse, daß sie den Menschen seines Heiles vergewissern könnten. Die Unvollkommenheit der Werke muß den Menschen gerade in Unsicherheit, Zweifel und Verzweiflung stürtzen, statt ihm Gewißheit geben zu können. Die unvollendete Heiligung des Menschen läßt ihn in diesem Leben niemals zur Ruhe kommen. . . . In scheinbarem Widerspruch zu der Aussage . . . steht nun die andere, daß der Gläubige seines Heils gewiß werden kann, wenn er an die Wirksamkeit des Heiligen Geistes in seinen Werken erkennt, daß er ein Wiedergeborener, ein Gott Geheiligter ist." Dieser Schluß ist ein Rückschluß. "Die Werke der Heiligung treten erst nachträglich hinzu, nachdem der Mensch zuvor im Glauben seines Heils gewiß geworden ist."[9]

8. *Reformation, Orthodoxie und Rationalismus,* Teil I, 1, Gütersloh 1937, S. 226f.
9. *Calvins Lehre von der Heiligung,* München 1934, S. 99f., 103.

III. Das "argumentum a posteriori"

Die Herkunft des Begriffes syllogismus practicus scheint noch nicht erforscht zu sein. O. Ritschl bemerkt, Luther habe darunter die natürliche Gotteserkenntnis nach Römer 1,20 verstanden und Melanchthon das Urteil des Gewissens.[10] Calvin verwendet statt syllogismus practicus den Begriff der antiken Rhetorik: argumentum a posteriori.

Einige Begriffe und ihre Erklärungen seien aufgezählt:

- argumentum a posteriori (i.e.) a signis subsequentibus (Inst. III.4.37)
- argument des choses subsequentes (=) par les signes qui s'en ensuyvent (ebend.)
- innocentia conscientiae a fructibus reputare (=) a posteriori (Inst. III.14.19)
- les fruicts de vocation . . . prend comme enseigne de la vocation de Dieu (ebend.)
- argumentum non a causa sed ab effectu (z.B. a mutuo amore) (i.e.) a fructibus vel posterioribus effectis arguere (Comm. Luc. 7,41) dilectio (mulieris) non est veniae causa, sed posterius signum (Comm. 7,47)
- testimonium fidei ab operibus (i.e.) posterior probatio instar signi accedat (Comm. 1. Ioh. 2,3)
- caritas non est causa salutis, sed caritas est ordine posterior (=) ratiocinatio a signo, non a causa (Comm. 1. Ioh. 3,14)

Calvins hier verwandte Formeln für syllogismus practicus sind also:

- argumentum a posteriori
- argumentum ab effectu
- ratiocinatio a signo

Die von ihm gebrauchten Begriff entstammen fast alle Quintilians Schrift Institutio oratoria. Sie bedeuten:

- Argumentum: Eine bestimmte Beweisführung (probatio), die aus der vorgegebenen causa rational-schlußfolgernd entwickelt wird.[11]
- Probatio: Ein Allgemeinbegriff für eine Beweisführung; sie ist der Ober begriff im argumentum.[12]

10. *Dogmengeschichte des Protestantismus,* III, 209, Anm. 46.
11. H. Lausberg, *Handbuch der literarischen Rhetorik. Eine Grundlegung der Literaturwissenchaft,* Bd. 1, München 1960, S. 197.
12. Lausberg S. 191.

- Ratiocinatio: Der Syllogismus, das heißt, die Feststellung im argumentum und zwar eine Feststellung von unbezweifeltem Sicherheitsgrad. Ein Syllogismus ist:

  > bonum est, quo nemo male uti potest,
  > virtus nemo male uti potest
  > bonum est ergo virtus.[13]

- Causa: Psychologisch das Tatmotiv, physisch und metaphysisch die Ursache für eine Wirkung (effectus). Es besteht eine Ursache-Wirkung-Bindung, die entweder zwingend ist (necessario) und umkehrbar oder nicht zwingend und nicht umkehrbar (non necessario).
  Z.B. Der Körper hat in der Sonne gewiß einen Schatten;
  wo Schatten ist, ist auch ein Körper (necessario).[14]
- Argumentum ex causis und argumentum ab effectu sind die Schlußfolgerungen entweder aus der Ursache auf eine Wirkung oder aus der Wirkung zurück auf die Ursache. Beispiel für ein argumentum ab effectu ist: Auli Hirtii vita populo cara est, quod ei populus applaudit (Cicero).[15]
- Signum: Ein Sachverhalt [!] und als solcher ein sinnlich wahrnehmbares Zeichen.[16] Calvin bezeichnet damit die sichtbare Wirkung (effectus) einer Ursache (causa). Statt signum verwendet er auch symbolum (Comm. 1. Ioh. 3,14).

Ergebnis: Das argumentum a posteriori ist eine Schlußfolgerung ab effectis. Calvin verwendet den Begriff a posteriori, weil ein argumentum (syllogismus) aus dem Obersatz (prior) und dem Untersatz (posterior) besteht. Der Untersatz ist im syllogismus practicus ein sichtbarer Sachverhalt (signum), aus dem auf die Ursache, z.B. Gottes Wirken, zurückgeschlossen werden kann.

Calvin führt im Kommentar zu 1. Joh. 3,14 ("Wit wissen, daß wir vom Tod zum Leben hinübergegangen sind, denn wir lieben die Brüder") die Möglichkeiten der Beweisführung durch Syllogismen einmal konsequent durch. Zuerst lehnt er einen syllogismus a causa ab. Dann formuliert er einen syllogismus ex effectu:

> Wenn die Nächstenliebe uns unseres 'Lebens' versichert,
> dann beruht unser Vertrauen auf das Heil auf den Werken.

---

13. Lausberg S. 197f., 199.
14. Lausberg S. 208f.
15. Lausberg S. 210.
16. Lausberg S. 195ff.

Aus der Ursache des Heils ist die Versicherung des Heils aus den Wirkungen des Glaubens geworden. Aber diese Schlußfolgerung kann ihn ganz und gar noch nicht befriedigen, weil sie das Vertrauen auf die Werke als Ergebnis hat. Er schränkt ein: Die Werke des Glaubens sind Gnadengaben Gottes, sie sind also nur Hilfsmittel, die über sich hinausweisen. Hilfsmittel stärken nur den Glauben, sie begründen ihn nicht. Die Barmherzigkeit Gottes begründet nur den Glauben, nicht die Nächstenliebe.

Es könnte nun so scheinen, als ob in 1. Joh. 2,3 und 3,14 — anders als in Luk 7,41 — auch der Syllogismus ab effectu versage, weil er den Glauben rational nachweist und nicht nur stärkt. Calvin versucht aber dennoch am Beispiel eines allgemeinen Syllogismus die Möglichkeit des theologischen syllogismus practicus nachzuweisen. Er geht von dem Syllogismus aus:

> Da wir das Licht genießen,
> sind wir sicher, daß die Sonne scheint.

Es ist ein syllogismus ab effectu, der wie der obengenannte Syllogismus beweist, daß uns die (Gnaden)Sonne scheint. Soweit will Calvin aber nicht gehen; es wäre ein zwingender Rückschluß von den Werken auf den Glauben. Darum differenziert er als nächstes die Ursache, er unterscheidet zwischen der Sonne und ihren Strahlen. Der syllogismus a causa lautet:

> Wenn die Sonne den Ort, an dem wir sind, mit ihren Strahlen bestrahlt, haben wir eine klarere Sicht.

Aber warum der Komparativ 'klarer', warum nicht eine 'klare Sicht'? Calvin muß dies erklären:

> Da die sichtbaren Strahlen sich nicht auf uns hinerstrecken, so sind wir selbstverständlich zufrieden, daß die Sonne den Nutzen ihres Glanzes auf uns verbreitet.

Sonne — sichtbare Strahlen — Glanz der Sonne. Nur den letzteren erfahren wir. Und nur aus ihm, das heißt, aus seinem Nutzen können wir auf das Scheinen der Sonne zurückschließen. Calvin zieht die theologische Konsequenz:

> So können, nachdem der Glaube in Christus gegründet ist, auch gewisse Dinge geschehen, die dem Glauben helfen. Dennoch ruht der Glaube inzwischen allein auf der Gnade Christi.

IV. Folgerungen

In Inst. III,14,18 unterscheidet er im selben Sachzusammenhang zwischen dem vollkommenen Licht (summa illa bonitatis lux) und den Strahlen des göttlichen Angesichts (radii divini vultus).[17] Ob er aber nun zwischen dem Licht der Güte Gottes und den göttlichen Strahlen oder zwischen Sonne, Strahlen und Glanz der Sonne unterscheidet, immer geht es ihm darum, daß die Werke zwar den Glauben stärken, sie aber nicht Gottes Willen oder die Gnade direkt erkennen lassen. Das Beispiel vom Licht besagt nicht anderes als: das argumentum ab effectu kann noch kein argumentum a causa sein. Oder mit dem komparativ "deutlicher" ausgedrückt: Der Syllogismus practicus gibt nur partielle Gewißheit; volle Gewißheit gibt nur das Gnadenwort.

Damit ist aber deutlich geworden, daß für Calvin wohl der logische Unterschied zwischen dem argumentum a causa und dem argumentum ab effectu theologisch wichtig ist, er das logische Beweisverfahren aber als Ganzes nicht anwenden kann. Wenn es um die Reichweite des syllogismus practicus, das heißt, um seine Abhängigkeit vom argumentum a causa geht, versagt die Logik. Die Zuhilfenahme der Begriffe Zeichen, Hilfsmittel, stärken, helfen usw. sind — von Ersterem abgesehen — theologischer und nicht logischer Art. Der Syllogismus practicus ist auch bei Calvin nur ein Erklärungsmittel, nicht aber ein wirkliches Beweisverfahren.

Niesel betont daher zurecht, daß das Heil nach Calvin "vollkommen" nur in der "gnädigen Verheißung der Gerechtigkeit" zutage tritt, also im Verkündigungswort,[18] und daß die Güte Gottes durch keine andere als durch die Gewißheit des Verheißungswortes versiegelt wird.[19]

Er irrt sich aber, wenn er meint, die Inst. III,24,4 genannten signa posteriora der Erwählung wären das "äußere Wort".[20] Abgelehnt wird dort gerade "der Glaube an das Evangelium" als "Kraft der Erwählung." Calvin will ausdrücklich vom "äußeren Wort" als der Brunnenröhre hinlenken zu dem Brunnquell selbst.[21] Die signa posteriora, "die sichere Zeugnisse der Erwählung sind", sind "die Berufung in die Kindschaft", sind Christus selbst, wie Calvin ausführt. Er denkt also an ein argumentum a causa, das heißt, im Blick auf die Erwählung also an den ewigen Ratschluß Gottes, dessen signa posteriora Gottes Wohltaten und insbesondere Christus, "der Spiegel der Erwählung", sind (Inst. III,23,5). Vom syllogismus practicus ist dort ebensowenig

17. OS IV,237,7f.
18. Inst. III,14,18; OS IV,237,3f.
19. OS IV,237,27f. Niesel S. 236f. Auch die Betonung des verbum externum, Inst. III,24,3; OS 414,3, vgl. Niesel S. 160.
20. OS IV,23,4; Niesel S. 160.
21. Inst. III,23,3; OS IV,414,1ff.

die Rede wie vom Verkündigungswort. Es bestätigt sich Calvins Aussage, daß es keinen Rückschluß auf die Erwählung gibt. Es bleibt bei Calvins ständiger Auskunft, daß die Erwählung den Menschen verborgen ist. Es gibt aber nachfolgende Zeichen, z.B. Christus. Diese Zeichen liegen aber nicht in der Erfahrung des Menschen.

Niesel sollte darum den Syllogismus practicus in Calvins Theologie nicht leugnen. Der Rüchschluß von den Werken auf den Glauben — nicht auf Erwählung — hat bei ihm seinen festen Platz. Er stärkt den Glauben, aber er gibt — darin hat Niesel recht — keine Glaubensgewißheit. Daß auch Luther den Rückschluß von den Werken auf den Glauben lehrt, hat G. W. Locher aufgezeigt.[22]

22. "Wie auch wir . . ." Die Unser–Vater–Bitte um Vergebung (Mt. 6,12) bei Luther, Zwingli und Calvin, in: Théorie et pratique de l'exégèse, Genf 1990, S. 287-301 (Études de Philologie et d'Histoire Nr. 43).

V. Seminartexte:

Institutio III,4,37 (1536) — OS IV,129,16–130,4

Quantum attinet ad locum Lucae [Cap. 7,f36] . . . Respondet Pharisaeus, Is utique cui plus donatum est. Subiicit Dominus, Hinc agnosce remissa esse huic mulieri peccata, quia dilexit multum. Quibus verbis (ut vides) eius dilectionem non facit causam remissionis peccatorum sed probationem. . . . Atque huc eam similitudinem applicari convenit, in hanc formam. Putas mulierem hanc esse peccatricem; atqui talem non esse, agnoscerent debueras, quando ei remissa sint peccata. Remissionis autem peccatorum fidem tibi facere debuerat eius dilectio, qua ob beneficium gratiam refert. *Est autem argumentum a posteriori, quo aliquid demonstratur a signis sequentibus.* Qua autem ratione peccatorum remissionem illa obtinuerit, palam Dominus testatur. Fides, inquit, tua te salvam fecit. Fide igitur remissionem assequimur: charitate gratias agimus, et Domini beneficentiam testamur.

Institution (1562) — CO 4,157

Et est un argument qu'on appelle des choses subsequentes, par lequel nous demonstrons quelque chose par les signes qui s'en ensuyvent.

Was nun aber die (von Gegnern herangezogene) Stelle Lukas 7,36ff. betrifft. . . . Der Pharisäer antwortet: "Ich achte, dem er am meisten geschenkt hat." Darauf sagt der Herr: daß dieser Frau ihre Sünden vergeben sind, das sollst du daraus erkennen, daß sie "viel geliebt hat." Man sieht deutlich, daß der Herr mit diesen Worten ihre Liebe nicht zur Ursache der Sündenvergebung erklärt, sonder zu deren Beweis. . . . Die Anwendung dieses Gleichnisses muß man sich nun folgendermaßen vorstellen: Du, (Pharisäer,) denkst, dieses Weib sei eine Sünderin; sie ist aber keine, und das hättest du wissen sollen, denn ihr sind Sünden vergeben. Daß ihr aber ihre Sünden vergeben sind, das hätte dir ihre Liebe glaubwürdig machen sollen, mit der sie die empfangene Wohltat dankt. *Es handelt sich daher um eine Beweisführung aus dem Nachfolgenden, bei der also etwas aus den Anzeichen bewiesen wird, die (aus der Ursache) folgen.* Wie aber diese Frau die Vergebung der Sünden erlangt hat, das bezeugt der Herr deutlich: "Dein Glaube hat dir geholfen!" Denn wir empfangen die Vergebung der Sünden durch den Glauben, durch die Liebe sagen wir Dank und geben wir Zeugnis von der Wohltat des Herrn!

Institutio III,14,19 (1539) — OS IV,237,11-23

Quum igitur a conscientiae innocentia fidem suam confirmant sancti, et exultandi materiam sumunt, nihil aliud quam a fructibus vocationis se in filiorum locum a Domino cooptatos esse reputant. Quod ergo a Solomone traditur, in timore Domini esse firmam securitatem [Prov. 14.c.26]: quod interdum hanc obtestationem sancti usurpant quo exaudiantur a Domino, se ambulasse coram facie eius in integritate et simplicitate [Gen. 24.e.40; 2. Reg. 20.a.3]: locum in iaciendo firmandae conscientiae fundamento nullum habent: *sed tum demum valent, si a posteriori sumuntur:* quia et nullibi est timor ille qui securitatem plenam offirmare queat: et sancti sibi talis integritatis conscii sunt cui multae carnis reliquiae adhuc sunt permixtae.

Institution (1562) — CO 4,291

mais lors seulement peut valoir, quand on le prend comme enseigne de la vocation de Dieu.

Wenn also die Heiligen ihren Glauben im Blick auf die Unschuld ihres Gewissens stärken und an ihr den Anlaß zu jubelnder Freude nehmen, so ist das nichts anderes, als daß sie an den Früchten ihrer Berufung merken, daß sie von dem Herrn an Kindes Statt angenommen sind. Wenn also Salomo sagt: "Wer den Herrn fürchtet, der hat eine sicher Festung" (Spr. 14,26), oder wenn die Gläubigen, um von dem Herrn erhört zu werden, zu der Beteuerung greifen, sie hätten doch in Lauterkeit und Einfalt vor seinem Angesicht gewandelt (Gen. 24,40; 2. Kön. 20,3) — so hat das keinerlei Bedeutung, wenn es sich darum handelt, das Fundament zu legen, um unser Gewissen zu stärken. *Alles das hat nur Wert, wenn es als Rückschluß behandelt wird.* Denn tatsächlich ist die "Furcht Gottes" (Spr. 14,26) nirgendwo so beschaffen, daß sie eine völlige Sicherheit begründen könnte. Und die Lauterkeit (Gen. 24,40; 2. Kön. 20,3), deren sich die Gläubigen bewußt sind, ist doch noch immer mit mancherlei Überbleibsel des Fleiches vermischt.

Institutio III,24,3,u.4 (1559) — OS IV,413,8–414,10

Duo autem errores hic cavendi sunt: . . . *Alii,* . . . *nescio tamen qua rationem inducti electionem a posteriori suspendunt:* quasi dubia esset atque etiam inefficax, donec fide confirmetur. Equidem confirmari, quoad nos minime obscurum est; elucescere etiam arcanum Dei consilium quot latebat, ante vidimus: modo hoc verbo nihil aliud intelligas quam comprobari quod incognitum erat, et velut sigillo consignari. Sed falso dicitur electionem tunc esse demum efficacem postquam Evangelium amplexi sumus, suumque inde vigorem sumere. . . . Sed ubi eam nobis patefecit Deus, altius conscendere oportet, ne effectus causam obruat. . . . Ergo perperam faciunt qui electionem vim suspendunt a fide Evangelii, qua illam ad nos sentimus pertinere: ita optimum tenebimus ordinem si inquaerenda electionis nostrae certitudine, in iis *signis posterioribus,* quae sunt certae eius testificationes, haereamus.

Institution (1562) — CO 4,508f.

Les autres, ie ne say pas de quelle raison estans induits, suspendent l'election, de la foy.

Hier muß man sich aber vor zwei Irrtümern hüten. . . . *Andere* . . . *machen die Erwählung doch — ich weiß nicht aus was für einem Grunde! — von dem Nachfolgendum abhängig,* als ob sie zweifelhaft oder auch unwirksam wäre, bis sie vom Glauben bekräftigt wird! Allerdings ist es hell und deutlich, daß die Erwählung, was uns betrifft, vom Glauben bekräftigt wird. Auch haben wir ja bereits gesehen, daß Gottes Ratschluß, der verborgen war, (nun) klar zu sehen ist. Nur soll man darunter nichts anderes verstehen, als daß hierdurch das, was unbekannt war, erwiesen und wie mit einem Siegel verbrieft wird. Falsch geredet ist es aber, wenn man meint, die Erwählung sei erst dann wirksam, wenn wir das Evangelium angenommen hätten, und sie nehme eben daraus ihre Kraft! . . . Sobald uns Gott solche Erwählung aber offenbart hat, da müssen wir höher dringen, damit die Wirkung nicht ihre eigene Ursache überennt. . . . So tut man also verkehrt daran, wenn man die Kraft der Erwählung vom Glauben an das Evangelium abhängig macht, durch den wir erfahren, daß solche Erwählung uns zukommt. Dementsprechend werden wir die beste Ordnung innehalten, wenn wir uns beim Suchen nach der Gewißheit unserer Erwählung an jene *nachfolgenden Zeichen* halten, die deren sichere Bezeugung sind.

Kommentar zu Luk. 7,41, u. 47 — CO 45,378ssq

Summa huius parabolae est errare Simonem in muliere damnanda, quam coelestis iudex absolvit. Probat autem iustam esse, non quia satisfecerit Deo, sed quod remissa sint illi peccata: . . . *Nam argumentum, quo utitur Christus, non a causa, sed ab effectu sumptum est:* quia et prius ordine est beneficium accipere, quam habere gratiam, et causa mutui amoris hic notatur gratuita remissio. In summa, Christus mulierem hanc Deo reconciliatam esse, a fructibus vel posterioribus effectis arguit. . . .

[V, 47] *Caeterum hic dilectio non dicitur esse veniae causa, sed posterius signum,* ut prius admonui.

Die Summe dieses Gleichnisses liegt darin, daß Simon geirrt hat, als er die Frau verdammte, der der himmlische Richter die Sünden vergeben hat. Er beweist, daß sie gerecht ist. Doch nicht, weil sie Gott Genüge getan hat, sondern weil ihr die Sünden vergeben worden sind. . . . *Denn der Beweis, den Christus verwendet, wird nicht von der Ursache her geführt, sondern von der Wirkung,* weil in der Reihenfolge früher genannt wird, die Wohltat zu empfangen, als Dank zu sagen. Als Ursache der Gegenliebe wird hier die unentgeltliche Vergebung bezeichnet.

In Summa, Christus beweist hier, aus den Früchten oder nachfolgenden Zeichen, daß dises Frau mit Gott versöhnt worden ist. . . . *Im übrigen wird hier die Liebe nicht als Ursache der Vergebung genannt, sondern als nachfolgendes Zeichen,* wie ich schon sagte.

Kommentar zu 1. Johannes 2,3 — CO 55,311

Atque in hoc cognoscimus, quo cognovimus eum, si praecepta eius servamus. Cognoscere, quod noverimus: Significat enim, Dei obedientiam sic coniunctam esse scientiae, ut tamen haec ordine sit prior, sicuti necesse est causam effectu suo esse superiorem.

Si praecepta eius: . . . Nam quoties de fidelium iustitia scriptura loquitur, adeo peccatorum remissionem non excludit, ut potius ab ea faciat exordium. Nec vero inde colligendum est, fidem in opera recumbere. Tametsi enim suae quisque fidei testimonium habet ab operibus: *non tamen sequitur illic fundatam esse, quum posterior haec probatio instar signi accedat.*

"Aber daran erkennen wir, daß wir ihn erkannt haben, daß wir seine Gebote halten." "Aber daran erkennen wir": Der Apostel zeigt an, daß der Gehorsam gegen Gott so mit der Erkenntnis verbunden ist, daß diese doch der Reihenfolge nach die erste bleibt, wie ja die Ursache der Wirkung vorangehen muß. "Daß wir seine Gebote halten": . . . So oft die Schrift von der Gerechtigkeit der Glaubenden redet, schließt sie die Vergebung der Sünden so wenig aus, daß sie vielmehr mit ihr den Anfang macht. Darum soll man auch nicht schließen, daß der Glaube auf den Werken beruht. Obwohl ein jeder aus den Werken ein Zeugnis seines Glaubens hat, *so folgt daraus doch nicht, daß er auf ihnen beruht, da diese nachfolgende Beweisführung in Gestalt eines Zeichens sich anschließt.*

Kommentar zu 1. Johannes 3,14 — CO 55,339

Neque enim hic de salutis causa disputat: sed quum caritas praecipuus sit fructus spiritus, certum quoque est regenerationis symbolum. *Proinde a signo ratiocinatur apostolus, non autem a causa.* . . .

Sed praepostere inde quispiam inferret, caritate vitam acquiri, quum sit caritas ordine posterior. Plus coloris haberet hoc argumentum:

> si vitae nostrae certiores
> facit nos caritas,
> salutis igitur fiduciam in opera
> recumbere.

Sed eius quoque non difficilis est solutio. Etsi enim omnibus Dei gratiis, tamquam adminiculis, confirmatur fides, non tamen suum in una Dei misericordia fundamentum habere desinit. Exempli gratia:

> quum luce fruimur,
> certi sumus solem lucere;

si locum, in quo sumus, sol irradiat, habemus clariorem quemdam adspectum; sed tamen, ut non pertingant ad nos visibiles radii, hoc ipso contenti sumus, quod sol spendoris sui usum ad nos diffundit. Ita, postquam in Christo fundata est fides, possunt quaedam accidere, quae illam iuvent; in sola tamen Christi gratia interim acquiescit.

"Wir wissen, daß wir aus dem Tod ins Leben gekommen sind, denn wir lieben die Brüder." . . . Er redet hier nich von der Ursache des Heils. Aber da die Liebe die hauptsächlichste Frucht des Geistes ist, so ist sie auch ein gewisses Zeichen der Wiedergeburt. *Daher führt der Apostel das Beweisverfahren vom Zeichen, nicht aber von der Ursache her durch.* . . .

Aber falsch wäre, wenn jemand folgerte, daß durch die Nächstenliebe das (ewige) Leben erworben werde, denn die Liebe stehe in der Reihenfolge an zweiter Stelle. Mehr 'Farbe' hat die folgende Beweisführung:

> Wenn die Nächstenliebe uns
> unseres (ewigen) Lebens
> versichert,
> dann beruht unser Vertrauen auf
> das Heil auf den Werken.

Aber die (richtige) Lösung dieser Beweisführung ist nicht schwierig: Auch wenn nämlich der Glaube durch alle Gnadengaben Gottes, gleichsam durch Hilfsmittel, gestärkt wird, so hört er dennoch nicht auf, sein Fundament in der einen Barmherzigkeit Gottes zu haben. Als Beweis dafür (dient der Syllogismus):

> Da wir das Licht genißen,
> sind wir gewiß, daß die
> Sonne scheint.

Wenn die Sonne den Ort, an dem wir sind, bestrahlt, haben wir eine klarere Sicht. Dennoch gilt aber: Da die sichtbaren Strahlen sich nicht auf uns erstrecken, so sind wir selbstverständlich zufrieden, daß die Sonne den Nutzen ihres Glanzes auf uns verbreitet. Ebenso kann, nachdem der Glaube auf Christus gegründet ist, einiges hinzukommen, was ihn unterstützt. Dennoch beruht er inzwischen allein auf der Gnade Christi.

The Secretary's Report

Wilhelm H. Neuser

1. Suddenly and unexpectedly the following members of the presidency died:

- Prof. Dr. Rodolphe Peter from Strasbourg
- Prof. Dr. Laszlo Makkai from Budapest

Although his actual subject had been Practical Theology, Rodolphe Peter passionately devoted himself to Calvin research. He not only published many articles but also formed several notable Calvin researchers. Prof. B. Roussel (Paris) has published an obituary notice in the volume of reports, "Calvinus Servus Christi," about the congress at Debrecen 1986.

Many of us still remember that in Geneva, in 1982, Lazlo Makkai invited us to come to Debrecen. He took much care that political impediments did not hamper the work of the congress. He had been building bridges between East and West.

2. In 1988, in Vienna, the presidency not only worked out the program for this congress but decided to ask Prof. B. G. Armstrong from Atlanta to enter the presidency from the congress on. Prof. Armstrong accepted.

President De Jong was co-opted to prepare this congress. In the meantime, the participants have been able to get an idea of the work he and his co-workers have done. We owe him a debt of gratitude.

3. A great number of territorial Calvin congresses took place in the last four years. I could participate in most of them. They are listed here:

- Third Colloquium on Calvin Research, Davidson 1986
- First East Asian Calvin Congress, Kobe / Japan 1987
- Sixth Colloquium on Calvin and Calvin Studies, Grand Rapids 1987
- 3. Calvinkongress Mittelosteuropa, Vienna 1988
- Third African Congress for Calvin Research, Stellenbosch 1988

- Fourth Colloquium on Calvin Studies, Seoul 1989
- The Rutherford House Calvin Studies Group, Edinburgh 1989
- Fifth Colloquium on Calvin Studies, Davidson 1990

With these probably only the regularly organized congresses and the like are listed. I suppose that there are even more of these meetings.

4. The new Calvin edition, *Ioannis Calvini Opera Omnia,* is going to be published soon. The editorial commission has passed the Latin and French principles of the edition. The edition will be published in five sections:

Series I Institutio Religionis Christianae
      II Opera exegetica / Commentarii et praelectiones in sacram scripturam
    III Scripta didactica
    IV Epistolae
     V Scripta varia

I had good hopes that the publishing house Droz in Geneva would already give a subscription list to you at this congress, but the first manuscript was not yet ready for the press. To begin with, the following will be published:

- Calvin's Commentary on the Letters to the Galatians, Ephesians, Philippians (Feld)
- Calvin's Commentary on the Letter to Hebrews
- De Scandalis (1550) and Consensus Genevensis (1552), in Latin and French (Fatio, Neuser)
- Calvin's Correspondence, vol. 1 (Augustijn)

Others will follow.

5. Since the congress in Geneva in 1982, plenary sessions with lectures and comprehensive discussions and many seminars in small groups have been offered. This form has proved to be good and shall be maintained. The presidency asks for proposals of themes for the next congress in the business meeting.

Bibliotheca Calviniana (1531-1600)

Jean-François Gilmont

I. Une nouvelle bibliographie calvinienne

Depuis la publication en 1900 de la *Bibliographia calviniana* d'A. Erichson, il n'y a plus eu d'aperçu d'ensemble des éditions anciennes de Calvin. Il existe par contre de bons répertoires des travaux modernes sur Calvin (Niesel, Kempff, Tylenda et, depuis plus de vingt ans, la chronique régulière de Peter De Klerk dans *Calvin Theological Journal*).

Le progrès des recherches impose pourtant une refonte de la bibliographie des éditions anciennes de Calvin. Une meilleure connaissance des textes permet de restituer à cet auteur diverses éditions anonymes. Les études de l'imprimerie ont réussi à identifier nombre de responsables l'éditions calviniennes.

II. Le travail accompli par R. Peter

Le professeur Rodolphe Peter (1916-1987) s'était attaché depuis 1958 à ce travail. Il a tout d'abord mené des enquêtes dans les bibliothèques de France et de l'étranger. Il connaissait ainsi les éditions calviniennes conservées dans la plupart des grandes bibliothèques d'Europe et d'Amérique du Nord.

Profitant des services du prêt inter-bibliothèques, il a décrit une bonne partie des éditions retrouvées. Il s'agit de notices purement techniques, avec de longues transcriptions des titres et relevé des signatures. Parallèlement, il a fait photographier de nombreuses pages de titre.

Mais R. Peter n'a pas seulement rassemblé des notes et des références. Il a acquis quelque 120 éditions calviniennes absentes des autres collections strasbourgeoises (Bibliothèque Nationals et Universitaire et Collegium Wilhelmitanum). Ses héritiers ne voulant pas disperser ce trésor, l'ont donné avec beaucoup de générosité au Collegium Wilhelmitanum. De plus, R. Peter a rassemblé une collection impressionante de plus de 500 microfilms.

Dans l'ensemble, cette documentation est restée à l'état brut. Vers 1966, R. Peter a rédigé une centaine de notices reprenant les éditions de sermons de Calvin. A une date ultérieure, il a ouvert un dossier intitulé *Bibliotheca calviniana, 1531-1564,* mais il n'a mis au point que trois notices seulement.

Si la rédaction définitive de cette bibliographie n'était pas fort avancée, le travail accompli par R. Peter est impressionnant. Il a retrouvé de nombreuses éditions inconnues. Par ailleurs sa connaissance exceptionnelle de l'imprimerie du XVIᵉ siècle lui a permis d'identifier l'origine de beaucoup d'éditions anonymes. Le résultat de ces recherches est dispersé dans de très nombreux articles.

III. La publication de la bibliographie

Après le décès de Rodolphe Peter, survenu à Strasbourg le 4 décembre 1987, ses héritiers m'ont demandé de mener à bien sa recherche bibliographique, en me laissant la disposition totale des notes accumulées par R. Peter. Une mission de deux ans confiée par le Fonds National Suisse de la Recherche Scientifique à l'initiative du prof. O. Fatio, me permet de me livrer entièrement à ce travail depuis octobre 1989. Dans le cadre de cette mission, mon travail actuel se limite aux éditions des œuvres de Calvin parues au XVIᵉ siècle.

En raison de la qualité du travail heuristique déjà accompli, il m'a semblé que ma mission consistait avant tout à classer les informations réunies et à rédiger les notices catalographiques. Contrairement à R. Peter qui rêvait à une "bibliographie définitive", j'estime qu'il est urgent que l'on fasse le point sur nos connaissances actuelles. Le travail que je publierai comportera inévitablement des lacunes; mais il aura l'avantage de révéler que telle ou telle édition est encore inconnue ou méconnue. En conséquence:

- L'enquête sur les éditions calviniennes est considérée comme suffisante; je me limite donc à des vérifications occasionelles.
- Mon premier effort a porté sur le classement des informations rassemblées par R. Peter, et sur le dépouillement des grandes bibliographies parues récemment (*National Union Catalog,* réédition du *Short Title Catalogue* anglais, *Verzeichnis des im deutschen Sprachbereich erschienen Drucke des XVI. Jarhunderts: VD 16,* etc.). Ce travail est pratiquement achevé.
- Il convient désormais de décrire les éditions selon un schema mis au point en collaboration avec O. Fatio et Fr. Higman. La rédaction des

notices est entreprise depuis quelque temps. Elle suppose que je prenne en mains un exemplaire au moins de chaque édition.

La publication de la bibliographie se fera par étapes. Parmi les éditions anciennes que l'on peut attribuer à Calvin, une distinction sera faite entre trois séries:

- ouvrages dont Calvin est l'auteur principal et dont il assume la responsabilité à titre personnel (environ 520 éditions)
- ouvrages dont Calvin n'est qu'un collaborateur, en particulier préfacier (environ 70 éditions)
- ouvrages rédigés en tout ou en partie par Calvin, publiés sous l'autorité de l'Église (manuel liturgique, confession de foi, catéchisme, ordonnances ecclésiastiques, etc.; environ 470 éditions)

Cela représente donc plus de 1000 éditions à décrire, pour lesquelles plus de 9000 exemplaires sont connus, mais certaines éditions n'ont pas encore été retrouvées. Le délai relativement court qui m'est imparti ne me permettra pas de respecter toutes les exigences de l'*Analitical Bibliography,* en consultant tous les exemplaires connus de chaque édition.

Les éléments essentiels de cette documentation sont gérés sur un micro-ordinateur portable.

IV. Présentation de la bibliographie

Il ne me semble pas utile d'expliquer ici tous les détails de la présentation technique. La bibliographie suivra, pour chaque section citée plus haut, l'ordre chronologique de parution. Des tables et des renvois permettront de retrouver toutes les rééditions d'une même œuvre.

La technique de description suit évidemment les modèles des bibliographies détaillées. Le lecteur doit disposer d'informations tant sur le contenu que sur l'aspect extérieur de l'édition. Je donnerai aussi la liste complète des exemplaires qui me sont connus.

Le point d'équilibre le plus délicat à trouver concerne l'annotation. Il n'est pas question de faire chaque fois une monographie sur chaque édition, ni même de dresser une bibliographie complète des travaux suscités par chaque ouvrage de Calvin. Je cherche une solution qui réponde à l'attente des lecteurs sans me demander une nouvelle vie de recherches.

V. En guise de conclusion

Le travail déjà effectué m'a fait mesurer les progrès accomplis en bibliographie depuis 30 ans. Les enquêtes sur les éditions du XVIe siècle se sont multipliées et beaucoup de bonnes bibliographies ont été éditées. Dans le domaine précis des œuvres de Calvin, un travail important a été réalisé en premier lieu par Rodolphe Peter, mais aussi par d'autres chercheurs comme Eugénie Droz, Louis Desgraves, Gabrielle Berthoud, Francis Higman, Paul Chaix, Hans-Joachim Bremme, Pierre Aquilon et Alain Girard. Le monde de l'édition protestante, surtout de langue française, est désormais connu avec plus de précision.

Pour terminer je voudrais rendre hommage à la générosité de Mme Peter et de ses enfants. Ils ont mis le souci du travail vraiment scientifique audessus de toutes les considérations égoïstes. Ils entendent continuer à servir les études sur Calvin avec ce désintéressement qui était la marque de Rodolphe Peter.

Adressen der Referenten und Seminsarleiter

Luke Anderson, O.Cist., St. Mary's Monastery, R.D. 1, Box 206, New Ring-gold, PA 17960, USA

Cornelis Augustijn, Sophialaan 47, NL-1075 BM Amsterdam

Irena D. Backus, Institut d'Histoire de la Réformation, Bibliothèque Publique et Universitaire, CH-1211 Genève 4

Erik A. de Boer, Dunwoodie Laan 1326, Waverley, 0186 Pretoria, Rep. of South Africa

James A. De Jong, Calvin Theological Seminary, 3233 Burton Street, S.E., Grand Rapids, MI 49546, USA

Richard C. Gamble, Calvin Theological Seminary, 3233 Burton Street, S.E., Grand Rapids, MI 49546, USA

I. John Hesselink, Jr., Western Theological Seminary, 86 East Twelfth Street, Holland, MI 49423, USA

Francis M. Higman, Institut d'Histoire de la Réformation, Bibliothèque Pu-blique et Universitaire, CH-1211 Genève 4

Philip C. Holtrop, Calvin College, 3107 Burton Street, S.E., Grand Rapids, MI 49546, USA

Richard Hörcsik, H-3950 Sárospatak, Rákóczi ut 1

John H. Leith, 3401 Brook Road, Richmond, VA 23227, USA

Robert D. Linder, Dept. of History, Eisenhower Hall, Kansas State University, Manhattan, KS 66506, USA

Wilhelm H. Neuser, Lehmbrock 17, D-4412 Ostbevern

Heiko A. Oberman, History Department, University of Arizona, Social Sciences Building, Room 10, Tucson, AZ 85721, USA

Adrianus D. Pont, 461 Wishbone South, 0081 Pretoria, Rep. of South Africa

Paul Rorem, 1100 E. Street, Chicago, IL 60615, USA

Mitsuru Shimura, 3-8-1-205 Shin-Cho, Hino-Shi, Tokyo, Japan

James B. Torrance, 3 Greenbank Crescent, Edinburgh KE10 5TE, Scotland

Nobuo Watanabe, Kita-Karasuyama 1-51-12, Setagaya-ku, Tokyo, Japan

Jeffrey R. Watt, Dept. of History, University of Mississippi, University, MS 38677, USA

Kwang-Woong Yu, Asian Center for Theological Studies and Mission, 187 Choong Jeongro 3-ka, Seodaemoon-Ku, Seoul, Korea